LEW WALLACE
(1893)

LEW WALLACE

AN AUTOBIOGRAPHY

ILLUSTRATED

VOL. I

NEW YORK AND LONDON
HARPER & BROTHERS PUBLISHERS
MCMVI

Published October, 1906.

CONTENTS OF VOL. I

CONTENTS OF VOL. I

CONTENTS OF VOL. I

CONTENTS OF VOL. I

XXI

XXII

XXIII

XXIV

XXV

XXVI

XXVII

CONTENTS OF VOL. I

CONTENTS OF VOL. I

CONTENTS OF VOL. I

CONTENTS OF VOL. I

ILLUSTRATIONS OF VOL. I

LEW WALLACE

AN AUTOBIOGRAPHY

LEW WALLACE

AN AUTOBIOGRAPHY

I

Belief in Christianity—Ancestry—John Paul Jones, uncle of grandmother—Andrew Wallace, grandfather—Letters from Almira—Professor of mathematics at West Point—David Wallace—Morse telegraph and defeat for Congress—Member of Congress—Lieutenant-Governor—Governor—Judge Court of Common Pleas—Died September, 1859.

THE most that can at present be said of the work before me is that it shall be honest and untainted with cynicism. The life itself has been, on the whole, so happy, comfortable, and fortunate, that the world, meaning society and my fellow-men, seems an esteemed associate in a long journey.

In the very beginning, before distractions overtake me, I wish to say that I believe absolutely in the Christian conception of God. As far as it goes, this confession is broad and unqualified, and it ought and would be sufficient were it not that books of mine—*Ben-Hur* and *The Prince of India*—have led many persons to speculate concerning my creed. It seems best, therefore, to recognize that more is demanded of me. In doing so I will speak frankly, begging only that in thus finally disposing of the matter the reader will not judge me careless of the sanctities.

I am not a member of any church or denomination, nor have I ever been. Not that churches are objectionable to me, but simply because my freedom is enjoyable, and I do not think myself good enough to be a communicant. None the less I believe in the Divinity of Jesus Christ; and that there may be no suspicion of haggling over the word "divinity," permission is besought to quote the preface of a little volume of mine, *The Boyhood of Christ:* "Should one ask of another, or wonder in himself, why I, who am neither minister of the Gospel, nor theologian, nor churchman, have presumed to write this book, it pleases me to answer him, respectfully—I wrote it to fix an impression distinctly in my mind. Asks he for the impression thus sought to be fixed in my mind, then I would be twice happy did he content himself with this answer—The Jesus Christ in whom I believe was, in all the stages of his life, a human being. His divinity was the Spirit within him, 'and the Spirit was God.'"

Mine were folk who cared little for ancestry. The grandmother on the paternal side was the exception. A correspondent writes me of hearing her speak often and proudly of her uncle John Paul, he of the famous surname *Jones*. She was wont to take fire, also, when telling of her Virginia birth, and of being trotted on his knees by George Washington. My American readers will forgive her, I am sure, if she never forgave the British for killing one of her brothers at Brandywine.

Andrew Wallace, my grandfather, emigrated from Pennsylvania to Cincinnati, Ohio, when that city was a village in loose assemblage under the guns of a fort. Who his progenitors were, and whence they came, are now beyond my ascertainment. Though active and of a venturesome nature, he never overtook a fortune.

Probably he was of the kind so often likened to a rolling stone. Moving from Cincinnati to Brookville, Franklin County, Indiana, he brought with him his seven boys and one daughter, of whom my father, David Wallace, was the eldest. In this manner my people became identified with Indiana.

My father ran an honorable career, and, having a biography of his own, I may be excused from giving more than an outline of it in these pages.

A fortunate event befell him while a lad. Through General William Henry Harrison he obtained a cadetship at the West Point Military Academy.[1] Graduating in 1821, he was detailed professor of mathematics, a capacity in which he served three years. Concluding then that he had rendered a fair return for the education the government had given him, he resigned from the army.

He had his romance while wearing the gray. Among forgotten packages of letters, I find a tattered one, mailed without envelope, postmarked Norwich, Vermont. It had missed its first address and been forwarded; and to the first postage of eighteen cents was added twenty-five cents, making a heavy charge for so light a missive. The ends of the foolscap sheet are doubled and folded, sealed with a large, red wafer; the cramped handwriting is nearly illegible.

The writer tells of a composition on "Friendship" which she had received from the cadet after it had been weeks on the road. Every one to whom she has shown it wishes to know the genius who could produce anything so beautiful. She wishes she were a man, men

[1] General Harrison had secured the appointment for one of his own sons; but yielding to the entreaty of Andrew Wallace, he generously requested that the warrant be issued in my father's name.

can do so much that women cannot. It appears young David had also written a dream which she thought very wonderful, and she reminds him of a promise to visit her, and offers the harmless inducement of a certain custard, a delicacy she has discovered he is fond of. And if he does not come she will know he is not what she had supposed him "a shining specimen of perfection," but will be forever suspicious of every being with a brilliant exterior.

Later she goes to a lecture on the battle of Waterloo, explained by maps, and after the lecture writes:

"I am alone. I have been gazing upon the mild and peaceful moon gliding with majesty through the deep-blue expanse. It ever inclines me to sadness, more now than formerly. A pleasing contemplation I love to indulge. A feeling well expressed in the verse:

"'Go, you may call it madness, folly,
You shall not chase my gloom away.
There's such a charm in melancholy,
I would not, if I could be gay.'

"Perhaps at this moment one I admire at West Point is gazing on the same lovely orb, perhaps in the same train of thought.

"How delightful the idea!

"Your true friend,

"ALMIRA."

Beyond this tender epistle we have no legend of the pensive Almira. She is with the other dear, dead women, merely a name. It was Rosaline, not Juliet, who dropped a rose from the balcony, and David Wallace might then have been our ideal Romeo. He was a man of noble presence in the slender elegance of youth, straight and tall, with a well-shaped head set squarely on his shoulders. His refined face, correct in outline, was lighted by the brightest and blackest eyes; dark, straight hair shaded a forehead white as a girl's; his smooth-shaven chin was well rounded and lips thin and sensitive.

Add to these graces a pleasant voice and manner more stately and gracious than we meet to-day; the urbane sweetness to which we give the name of high-breeding. There were fewer books then, and they were of the best, and constant familiarity with them gave a stateliness of speech and a certain dignity that comes of keeping good company. They dined with Horace and supped with Plutarch, and were scholars without knowing it.

Almost the earliest of my recollections is the gray uniform of Cadet Wallace. The small tail and shining bullet-buttons of the coat captured my childish fancy. None of the good man's after honors exalted him in my eyes like that scant garment.

He became a lawyer, and opened an office in Brookville, where he married Esther French Test, the third daughter of John Test, at one time a judge and politician of note in Indiana. [1]

Henry Clay was my father's ideal orator and great man; so in 1842 he launched into politics as a Whig. In 1828, 1829, and 1830, he represented Franklin County in the lower house of the Legislature. In 1831 he reached out for the Lieutenant-Governorship of the State and secured it. Re-election followed in 1834. In 1837 his party promoted him Governor. Retired in 1840, he resumed practice of the law, but next year was elected

[1] John Test was twice a member of Congress. Indulging in speculation, he lost much of his property, and to better pursue his profession eventually moved to Mobile, Alabama.

to Congress. In the ensuing race he was beaten.[1] Then, cutting loose from politics, he returned to his profession, and pursued it successfully until, in 1850, he was chosen delegate from Marion County to the Consti-

[1] The cause of the defeat was singular. Professor Morse had perfected his telegraph. All it needed, he said, was a long-distance trial, which he was too poor to make. As a last resort, he applied to Congress, asking an appropriation of thirty thousand dollars, barely enough to wire a connection from Washington to Baltimore. A bill was introduced and referred to a special committee of five. The member from the Indianapolis district was of the committee. A meeting was promptly held, and a vote taken, resulting in a tie, of two for and two against a favorable report. The professor meantime stretched a wire connecting the Senate and the House, and at the critical moment of action by the committee my father was off witnessing a trial of the invention. Morse made an explanation of the working of the apparatus, calling it the Electro-Magnetic-Telegraph. It may be doubted if the explanation was perfectly understood; yet the special committee-man, standing by, saw a message sent over the line, and read the message received in reply. He could not refuse the testimony of his own senses. Hastening to the session, he was barely in time. The vote had been taken by his colleagues. My father's name was called, and he answered "aye." An affirmative report followed. The House passed the bill, and the world presently received the benefit of the most wonderful discovery of the age.

Whatever the honor attached to that decisive vote, there was also a responsibility, as Congressman Wallace was soon aware. His party renominated him. To the average statesman of the present era thirty thousand dollars is a bagatelle; but the gentleman chosen to make the race by the Democrats was a wit and mimic of the first class, and he not only managed to impress his audiences with the enormity of the appropriation; in telling them what it was for, his twisting and distortion of the name "Electro-Magnetic-Telegraph" were vastly humorous and effective. In vain my father tried to explain the marvellous invention; in vain he dwelt upon its results to commerce, individuals, society, and nations; he could get nobody to understand its operation, and on that issue alone he was badly beaten at the polls.

Later, when the ocean cable was laid, Indianapolis held a great night meeting in the Governor's Circle to celebrate the event. My father was selected to make the address of the occasion, and we may believe he did so with peculiar gratification. The honor came late, but apologies are always in order.

tutional Convention. Six years later, having become somewhat easier in circumstances, he allowed his friends to elect him Judge of the Court of Common Pleas, in which, as his biographer naïvely remarks, he "made the best record of his life." He died suddenly September, 1859.

II

Birthplace—Appearance—Removal to Covington—Death of brother John—Covington—Nebeker's ferry—Servant-girl's story of hanging—Fear of ghosts—The Irish school-master—Learns to draw pictures of battles—Little colonel—Black Hawk War—Review of militia by Lieutenant-Governor—Playing Scottish chiefs—Bruce's heart.

I WAS born in Brookville, Indiana, April 10, 1827, the second of four boys, of whom William was the eldest, John the third, and Edward the baby. Black eyes were common to all my mother's children, and all had black hair except me—mine was the color of tow a trifle yellowed by exposure to sun and air. My eyes, moreover, seemed to have an attraction for the hair aside from mere gravitation, insomuch that a hat was a superfluity at all seasons, and, seen through occasional openings in the thick thatch over the forehead, they had a glitter suggestive of jet in constant motion.

My days in Brookville ran through five years. They were what the Arabs would call days of ignorance. A brick house a little removed from the brow of a hill, and enclosed by split palings, is the only recollection I can now extract from the period passed in the old town—old in the New World's habit of thought and speech; and even that recollection is so very faint that, independently of friends, it would be beyond me to affirm anything of its form, dimensions, arrangement, or relative situation. The picture of the house, ventured on another page, is from a drawing kindly sent me by a lady who was often a guest within its doors.

HOUSE IN WHICH GENERAL LEW WALLACE WAS BORN, BROOKVILLE, INDIANA

AN AUTOBIOGRAPHY

In the first summer month of 1832, my father, having become a silent partner with a brother merchandising in Covington, Indiana, removed thither, taking his family and household goods.

The journey was, of course, by horse and carriage. On reaching Indianapolis a stop was made, not so much to rest as to care for two of the party sick with scarlet-fever. My brother John and I were the patients. He, poor boy, died. Of the sickness and death I recall but two things distinctly—horrible draughts of saffron tea, hot almost to scalding, and the large, brown eyes of my mother swimming in tears.

That which was our dwelling in Covington is still standing, though shifted from its original location. It was of wood, one story, with a kitchen, and an apartment at the front that served for sitting-room, bedroom, and parlor. An attic completed the structure. The Lieutenant-Governor of the State was quite content with his new residence.

The site of the town to which we were now come was an elevated plain. A broad strip of lowland—in the vernacular, a bottom—bounded it on the south, while on the sides north, east, and west a primeval forest extended indefinitely, with an undergrowth of hazel and sumac dense as a Rio Grande chaparral.

The thornless thickets were somewhat awesome, owing to one telling me that the dye the sumac took on ripening was the blood of Indian children. Nevertheless, a little girl friend and I used to scour them far and near, gathering apronfuls of the brilliant leaves. What wreaths and chaplets they made when dexterously pinned together with thorns!

The Wabash skirted the low ground mentioned, swishing the limb-tips of the trees on both shores. I do not remember how I made the acquaintance of the river, but as my sixth year was the beginning of a habit of truancy which followed me through my school terms, and has even yet to be struggled against, it may be presumed that I ran away to see it, and that nobody was with me.

Since that time I have seen many of the famous rivers of the earth, among them the Danube, the Rhine, and the Nile; never one of them so impressed me as did the Wabash in that stolen interview. It looked so wide, so deep, so like the passing of a flood going down in its own majestic way to what would be a deluge when it was at last arrived. Yet it had a coaxing power. My fears were soothed, and I went and, as it were, laid my hand on its mane; and thence we were friends. No one better than Dickens knew what conjurers such things are to imaginative children. I became its playmate the summers through.

A man named Nebeker owned and plied a ferry in those days. The employment was lonesome, and he welcomed me for my company. On the farther side, chained to a tree, he kept a long, tin horn. A traveller, coming to the bank and finding us on the townward side, blew to get our attention. I say *us*. The good man swung an oar to the boat suitable to my muscular degree, and in the day, asking only time for breakfast, I was at my post whether it rained or shone. He shared his dinner with me, nor asked where my hat and coat were. Generally I was without either. In the intervals when there was no demand on us I fished for minnows or proudly watched his lines. But most I loved to lean over the low gunwale on the shadow's side and look down into the waters; they seemed so mysterious and moved with such silent power. Whence did they come? And whither were they hastening? They were friendly, and of themselves taught a wholesome dread of what might come of too great familiarity. So it happened that, what with my own caution and the watchfulness of my human friend, I was really in no danger. Then, when the voice of the big horn on the thither side called to us— How it startled me! What music there was in it! What haste I made to unship my oar! How I bent to it, and strove, imagining that but for me we would be pulled down by the current and never reach shore.

And those at home, especially my mother! The days were days of suspense with her. She came to know where I was to be found, and, in my father's absences, followed after me. Finally she made a treaty with the ferryman, and, assured of my safety when with him, left me to my pleasure. And if since then I have been an ardent fisherman, believing with my friend Maurice Thompson that

"Halcyon prophecies come to pass
In the haunts of the bream and bass";

and if the song of Butler, the soldier-poet of Kentucky—

"Oh, boatman, wind that horn again!
For never did the joyous air
Upon its lambent bosom bear
So wild, so soft, so sweet a strain"—

is still a favorite of mine, with power to stir my pulses and return me to a freak of childhood full of joyousness alloyed only with thought of my mother's fears, the shrewd reader will know at once how such tastes inured to me. And as swimming seems to have been one of my natural accomplishments, I must have acquired it during my days at the ferry.

In the description of the site of Covington I should have mentioned the wide hollow on the east, the purpose of which seems to have been the accommodation of a small "branch" wending towards the river. The hollow is worth mention, since it was there I came by another impression of long duration.

A man had been convicted of murder in the Fountain Circuit Court, and hung, and when my father arrived at his new place of abode the four posts of the platform of the scaffold were standing a little to the left of the road descending to the branch. They were pointed out to me, with a full account of the hanging and the crime. The narrator was an ignorant servant-girl who had been present at the scene. She omitted nothing likely to affect me as she had been affected by it. She led me to see the crowd in attendance. She described minutely the handling of the cord, and the tying it under the left ear by a certain cunning knot known only to officiating sheriffs. The cord, she carefully informed me, had been procured in Kentucky for the special purpose. For a long time the idea clung to me that the manufacture of such ropes was one of the chief industries of that state. She described the appearance of the murderer on the scaffold, and how the sheriff had smothered his protestation of innocence by dropping a black cap over his head, buckling it under the chin. She spoke of the awful silence of the multitude at that moment, broken at last by the crash of the trap in its dropping. She led me to imagine the convulsions and the twisting and swaying of the body, and the doctors pulsing the man, watches in hand, and solemnly announcing him dead. Then followed the rush of the crowd to secure pieces of the rope. These circumstances were all bad enough, but the master-stroke of the story-teller did the work on which she was intent. On moonlight nights, she said, particularly of moonlight nights in winter, the season of the hanging, the ghost of the murderer revisited the place of the taking-off, and perched itself on one or other of the posts of the platform, awaking the echoes of the hollow with groans. She said a number of respectable people had seen the spirit and heard the blood-curdling noises. To relieve me of doubt, had I been equal to one, she gave me the names of some of them, adding that they all believed the man innocent. So argumentative had the narrator been that it was impossible for me not to believe in ghosts. The faith continued with me so vividly that in passing graveyards alone even in daytime I took to my heels, and with such advantage that if I did not see any of the sheeted tenantry it was because I outflew the very sight of them.

This year—the sixth—was memorable to me as the commencement of my school life. A small brick house, with two windows to a side, the door to the west, the north side of the room given up to the teacher and his table and a bunch of selected *rods*, the latter hanging from the wall in plain view, such was the academy to which my mother took me.

The master was an Irishman — exactly what that meant I do not know — an Irishman, yellow-haired, freckle-faced, stout, with whom flogging was a fine art which he seemed fearful of losing. Lest such a calamity should overtake him, he kept his hand in on the big boys. Should one think the description too finely drawn for a lad so young and untrained, with a memory so callow as mine was, he is politely reminded of what a terror the man was to me, and that now and then he made a playground for his practice of my back. With him lying and thieving were trifles light as air compared with truancy. Thus early was I made acquainted with the rod.

I pause to say, with blessings on her dear head, that my mother had in some way found time to teach me the alphabet and spelling in double syllables, and to make letters in capitals.

My elder brother and I were delivered over together to the sanguinary professor. Our respective outfits were a Webster's spelling-book, a paper slate, and a bluestone pencil. Before the first day was over a little girl ate my pencil, and I took my first flogging because I could not produce it. Yet it was a day of triumph. I was put into a line with children of my class to spell. We were given the word "ba-ker." I rendered it correctly, and went up head. The honor was short-lived, however, for next day I was overtaken with a lapse of application remarkable for its continuance.

Ere that red-letter day was done I made two discoveries of great interest. The first one was that I could draw a portrait in profile or full-face. Thereafter I was kept busy. My small mates must have their pictures; for which they brought me white paper and pencils of hammered lead. Unfortunately this pursuit, in rivalry with the boy Di Bondone[1]—of course, I knew nothing of him then—was so fascinating that it occupied me, and I grew indifferent alike to the main object of my attendance at school and the bundle of rods on the wall. This first dash of education began in the winter; directly with the outbursting of spring I renewed the copartnership with the more genial Nebeker down at the ferry, and played at it with delighted obstinacy.

The second discovery was of a very different taste. About that time—at least, while my first school engagement lasted—the Black Hawk War was in occurrence, and a company of horsemen formed in Covington to go out after the ferocious chief. The excitement ran high,

[1] A careful consideration gives this reference a smack of vanity. It was not so intended, and I humbly pray pardon. Besides which, Giotto has been dead nearly seven hundred years.

and culminated the day the volunteers packed their saddle-bags with crackers and cheese, swung their fire-arms to their backs, and in files of two rode away amid the tears of wives and mothers. There was no school, to be sure, while that scene was enacting, and I saw it all, and was filled with it. Thereafter my hours in the contracted academy were divided between making pictures and fighting battles on my paper slate. The manner of the latter suggests a reproduction of two of the countless sketches I made—one of the idea in its first crude state, the other of the idea in evolution.

The point in the first instance was to crowd the field with men—the more the better. Every battle was to be a great battle. How could the multitude be given except by straight marks in processions, making the slaughter of thousands in an hour impossible? So, slaughter being the main object, some other method must be practised in actual war. But what? I pothered my brains daily through many sessions of the school over the problem. At last—O happy moment! —at last I saw it. Then, instead of processions, I brought my forces into lines confronting each other; whereupon every battle became truly great and awful. Flags, smoke, hills, hollows, fighters, runaways, dead men, everything of battle, in fact, except artillery and cavalry, for which I had no room, were accessories, allowing infinite variety in the composition. Alexander, Cæsar, Napoleon, Genghis Khan, and Tamerlane the limp-legged, were heroes in reserve, as it were; yet none of them — no, not all of them together — slew half the number of men I wiped from my fields of carnage in course of a week with dashes of the ready sponge.

Just now the reader may not see why I dwell upon the newly discovered taste. Perhaps the word is not exactly descriptive, yet it will suffice if understood as meaning an interest in a pastime which was to grow into a passion. In the next place, by dwelling a trifle more upon the incipient passion I may succeed in entertaining young folk, if not in catering to a faith seldom wanting in adults of a philosophic turn—that the characteristics of the man have their outcropping in the child.

Wherefore I proceed to say that in the spring following my entry at school another affair occurred tending further to deepen the impression graven in my memory by the departure of the volunteers bent on bringing the noble Indian back to duty. Early one morning my attention was challenged by seeing my father's horse brought to the gate bedight in gay trappings, the details of which I cannot now specify. The effect, however, was stunning. After thorough inspection the good steed was led away to be brought back later.

The public square, when I reached it after breakfast, was fast filling with people from the out-towns and country, and I had only to look at their attire to know that something warlike was at hand. It will not do for me to say they were in uniform. Their coats were bedizened with cotton cords and tape in various forms and hues. Such of their hats as were not of straw, homemade and in slouch, were adorned with rosettes and cockades. Now and then a plume of great height, made of white feathers, ruffled, and tipped with the choicest furnishment of red roosters, complemented tall hats of the bell-crown type. A few swords were in place, and yet more rarely an individual strode by sashed and epauletted—that is, he wore one epaulet—and a streak of red wrapped his waist. Sometimes I shuddered to see a musket; though, as a rule, the martial apparitions were armed with umbrellas, corn-stalks, and hickory staves. The sky above them seemed tremulous with the thunder of bass-drums; and, what was most curious to me, these monsters drew to them men with lesser drums and instruments which I came to know as fifes.

After dinner a cavalcade in diverse uniforms, some with immense hats half-moon in form and gorgeously plumed, trotted to our gate. My father went out to them, himself in blue frock-coat, brass buttons, sash, and hat of the same half-moon style, mounted with a white silk cockade. There was an animated consultation, then they all rode down-town together, and I was too overcome with awe to follow them, except at a more than respectful distance.

In the description I make use of the names of things drawn from later experience.

Afar off I saw the crowd form and march away in leading of the big-hatted horsemen and the thunderous drums. They took the road to the river-bottom, and over their heads in the going I saw for the first time the flutter and stream of colors, or, more simply, the flag which was to become better known to me as "Old Glory."

In a razzle-dazzle — as a definition in brief of my mental condition, the term is so apt that I will not apologize for borrowing it from "Pinafore"—I stole down to a secure ambush of ironweeds on the hill-side, and watched the militia of the county in regimental drill, Colonel (Lieutenant-Governor) Wallace commanding. They would wheel into column—again I resort to my after-experience—and ploy and deploy, and change front, and, maugre the canes, corn-stalks, and umbrellas, the ignorance of captains and the deficiencies of guides, I do not hesitate to say that to the dazed reviewer in the ironweeds on the hill-side nothing of military circumstances half so splendid and inspiring had ever taken place.

At last the regiment halted and wheeled into line, and, after placement of the guides and colors, the colonel marched it forward. When next halted it was in easy range below and facing me. The colonel galloped to the rear, and gave commands in a loud voice. The men with muskets and those without muskets obeyed with equal alacrity. Coming to a ready, they aimed up the hill. A word rang out—there was a ragged volley—and the subsequent proceedings interested me no more. In plainer speech, I sprang from my hiding and ran. Up the height and through the town I ran, and not until safely home was I entirely sure that my performance had been in the flesh.

By-and-by I got my little courage back and betook myself to the public square again. The parade was over and the crowd dispersed. Only the drinkers and bass-drums remained. The fighting was on. A spectacle of the kind fell to me. As I passed through the gateway two men took to quarrelling. There was a rush, and I mounted the fence to see the fray. One of the combatants was a small man in uniform. His want of stature was more than compensated by a willing spirit and a tall, bell-crowned hat surcharged by a taller plume of white and red chicken feathers. The enemy, judged by his attire, was an every-day citizen, large, brawny, and unheroic - looking. I wondered at his temerity. *He* fight a soldier—a *soldier* whose business was to kill! Had he no friends to take him away? They made at each other—a moment, and he in uniform went down, and the crowd massed in around the belligerents, one of whom was presently carried out. I followed—and, lo! it was the soldier. The buttons on his braided coat shone dimly through a besmearing of mud—gone were the hat and supereminent plume—gone was my faith in the invincibility of men of war as such. When night came, and my mother tucked me in the little trundle-bed with my elder brother, I had gained such store of wisdom pertaining to war that it passed into my dreams, and from them into my life; so I promised myself, saying many times, "Wait until I am a man." The discomfiture of the soldier was without moral to me; only in my battle pictures thereafter I peppered my lines and columns with horses and riders hatted and plumed like these:

In time I came to great pride in my horses, and would have none not in action. A hero flourishing a sword on a tame steed was too ludicrous.

It should not be supposed that I made no progress in school. The freckled Irishman taught me to read. It was a day never to be forgotten when I could stand before the school and, without pause or break, deliver the thrilling story of the bad boy in the apple-tree. Thence the step to a book was short.

My first book! Ah, how distinctly it comes to me through the years! One of Peter Parley's. A Yankee lad ran away and went to sea, and in the Mediterranean was taken, ship and all, by Algerines. But he escaped. The vessel lay close under the guns of a fort. The prisoners were to be sold for slaves next morning. A shipmate, looking through a port, saw a small boat loose on the water. The squeeze through the port was trying, but they made it and the small boat. By good luck, the oars were there ready. Better still, the pirates kept no watch. The two rowed to sea, and, after suffering hunger and thirst, were picked up by Christians. How it made me shiver, that crisis when the lad, afraid to drop, hung to the edge of the narrow window, thinking of home and mother, and muttering the prayer she had taught him. Then the dark water closing over him—Goodness! Would he rise? Could he swim? I got the tale nearly by heart. The craving it awoke is not yet satisfied.

My mother, meantime, made discovery that to keep me in bounds there was nothing like a book. So she bethought her of a long, good one—*The Scottish Chiefs.* I was a slow reader, and Miss Porter's pages lacked the charming simplicity of Mr. Goodrich's. There was halting and stumbling at first; the broad Scotch proper names refused to be spelled; but at length I reached the current of the story, and when it dawned upon me that it was about a man who was actually named after my brother William—it did not occur to me that my brother could have been named after him—astonishment and delight came to the help of my understanding, and bore it up and on as in the Arabian Nights friendly genii were wont to carry distressed princes through the air. Then my brother read the wondrous tale, and we debated it early and late. We cried over its sorrowful passages, trembled while the battles were in progress, and were genuine Scots whether the victory were for or against us, especially when the sword and directing genius of our mighty kinsman were in the least conspicuous. That he was our kinsman we had no doubt.

Was such pleasure to be bottled up for us alone? We called in our chums, one Robert Evans, and two others, Henderson Rawles and Wesley Harper.[1] The five read the heroic chronicles together; whereupon we turned them into a play. Each took a character. On account of his name my brother's right to the rôle of Sir William was admitted. Evans took Robert Bruce; Rawles and Harper had their parts; and I was given the rôle of the youthful brother of the love-lorn Helen Mar. Then, in

[1] Robert Evans served as a captain in the regiment to which I belonged in the war with Mexico. Rawles died in early childhood. Harper lives in Cincinnati, a most worthy and respected citizen.

deadliest earnest, we went to war with the haughty English. We made helmets of pasteboard and swords of seasoned clapboards. The young hazel-shoots we wove into shields. Our steeds we found ready in the bottom, and that they were of ironweeds did not detract from their fitness. Under us they had the endurance of Arabs and the strength of the big Flemings so affected by knights who ate, drank, and slept in steel. Neither did we see any inconsistency in converting the same weeds into lances. Thus armed and panoplied we ranged the country round. Woe to the elder, the mullen, and the white-crowned lobelias. Woe particularly to the wild sunflower cropping myriadly in the dry hollows under the trees along the river-bank. A vigorous growth of fruiting pokeberries was an enemy to be dealt with in single combat. The sword was then the preferred weapon. Out rode Sir William or the Bruce, and they always came back victorious, their blades dyed to the hilt, their shields dripping with gore.

The campaigns were necessarily fast and furious. Their seasons were short, generally about eight hours; this for a reason that will be keenly appreciated by every fully vitalized boy. If (beginning at nine o'clock morning) we were not at home by five in the evening, our mothers would be looking for us; and I am forced to admit that in instances there were preventive means resorted to by them in large denial of the dignities assumed by the heroes of Bannockburn and the bridge over the Forth. Nor would it be fair to suppose us wholly without tactical sense in our operations. When we came upon the enemy in force—and every weed, it must be remembered, was an Englishman — we held council how best to attack, the object being extermination. Did we resolve upon a charge in mass, we began by discharging our lances from a distance; then, tossing the bridle-reins over head, and advancing shields, we drew swords and rushed in pell-mell. The cries with which we rang the scene were not vulgar yells or even the "Hurrahs" traditional with all Saxons. We dealt in *slogans*—A Bruce! A Wallace! A Douglas!

Probably our most effective play was a rendition of the melancholy story of the heart of Bruce. The monarch was supposed to be recently dead. We took the member which had throbbed for Scotland through so many years of ennobled struggle and put it reverently in a silver case, to be borne to Palestine and laid on the Holy Sepulchre; that is, we secured a tin can of suitable size, and, loading it with sand, put a burnish upon its outside. The mission of the Black Douglas was regarded as so highly honorable that we took turns at its performance, and it never happened that he and his train failed in becomingly simulating sorrow. The first close patch of sunflowers reached in the pilgrimage was the signal that we had arrived in Spain and that the detested Moors were in our front. Then Douglas cried, "Charge!" In the heat of combat, to arouse us to nobler effort, he would snatch the silver case from his neck and fling it far into the ranks of the infidels.

Sad to say, however, we at last lost the heart. This was the way of it: My brother one day essayed the part of Douglas. We found the Moors in the bend above the town under a grove of sturdy water-maples and ghostly sycamores. Nothing daunted by their numbers, our leader flung the sacred relic and called on us to follow him. Our valor quite equalled the havoc we wrought. The sunflowers strewed the ground. We were winning a splendid victory. We sent our slogans to the echoes a mile away. Suddenly a great growl arose before us. Sword arms hung suspended; the steeds stopped their ramping. We had not time to ask what now. Out of the thicket rushed the mother of a litter of half-grown pigs. The bristles on her back were long as the pins on a Georgia conifer, and they all stood erect. Right at us she dashed. And we—well, we forgot our knightly vows, our battle passion, the mission on which we were bent, the silver case intrusted to us by the redeemed people of Scotland; we forgot our swords and shields, and, leaving our trained steeds each to his own care, we ran. Presently the world, had it taste for a bit of genuine fun, might have seen the Black Douglas and all his peerless chivalry of Scone high on the limbs of trees and wondering when the ferocious enemy would raise the siege. We reached home by the directest path, but never returned for the heart of Bruce. Doubtless the next freshet buried it under the shifting silt.[1]

[1] Bruce was under vow to betake himself to the Holy Sepulchre. Finding he could not accomplish the purpose in person, he requested Douglas, his favorite knight, to carry the heart there; but the noble delegate was slain in Spain, fighting the Moors. Another faithful Scot (Sir William Keith) recovered the sacred relic and it was buried at Melrose.

III

A woman teacher — Studies geography — Truancy — Autumn and winter—Advent of stove—The circus—Servant-girl's superstition —Illness of mother—Death and burial—Mrs. John Hawkins.

MEANTIME my education was advancing. The Irishman disappeared; whither, Heaven at least knew, although I cannot persuade myself that it was in that direction. There was jubilation among the lads and lasses of the town. My joy was surpassing; not more from the brute's dismissal than because I could look forward to a breathing-time in which my back would have a chance to resume its normal condition.

When the door of the little red school-house on the brow of the eastern hill next opened, and we of the generation to be instructed filed in to our backless benches, lo! a woman was in the master's chair. Who was she? And whence descended? The installation was new to the biggest boy. A woman! Submission to a woman! Could we bring our manhood to *that?* So the others thought and talked; but I took a look at her to make sure of the fact, and then another look at the wall above her table. *The rods were gone!* Through the cloud of unasked questions which blew over me, like smoke from a discharged gun, vaguely but positively I felt that the change of dynasty meant a change of government. Something was to take the place of the rods. What could it be? And I waited. Time has ships always coming in laden with revelations.

The new teacher put two new books into my hand—

an elementary arithmetic and an Olney's Geography. The first had a dismal look about it. Further investigation satisfied me that it and I could never be friends. I say *never*, and so it has proved. The other book captivated me at once. Turning its leaves, I was arrested by a display of maps and pictures. The horizon, theretofore bounding the village and its vicinity, seemed to undergo a swift and vast extension. I caught glimpses of other countries and peoples. The sea teemed with islands, and actually there were rivers larger than the Wabash. Most marvellous — incredible — impossible— the earth was round, like an apple. To catch a boy and hold him fast one has only to set the delicate machinery of the wonder-box in him at work. The suggestion is respectfully submitted to teachers. Mothers, with better understanding, practise it when lullabies fail. At all events, I became interested in the study, and to such a degree that through the years intervening nothing pertaining to geography has been allowed to escape me. With Columbus and Magellan, La Pérouse, Cook, and Perry I still sail and sail. In more modern times, I volunteer under Franklin and Kane, and ingratiate myself hail-fellow-well-met with Livingstone and Stanley. The increase of knowledge due to their heroism has been practically an enlargement of the world; yet— I go back to the repetition knowingly—none of their discoveries has been so wonderful to me, so hard to reconcile with appearances, so defiant of problematic solution, as that the earth is not flat, like a pancake.

One of the wonders of childhood I have never seen satisfactorily explained is the greater length of the divisions of time in passage. A day then was like a month now, a summer like a lifetime in fulness. And those summers! There was not a minute of them between sunrise and sunset which I did not devote to physical delights of some kind. So eager was I to be doing something with hands and feet—walking, running, swimming, hunting, exploring, playing—that shoes and hat and coat were alike abominations. Breakfast over, I was off for the day. If dinners had grown on the trees like bread-fruit in some of the Pacific islands, and the getting them had required the abandonment of an amusement, though for a time barely enough to pluck and eat them, they might as well not have been. Hunger did not seem to exhaust me, or rather in my mid-going I never thought of food. Malaria, the curse of the beautiful new country, attacked without stopping me. The rigor and the fever often struck me in the woods or water; I took them as matters of course and went on.

It would be unjust to my parents to suppose they made no effort to control me. The rod in my father's hand was terrible for the moment. The punishments resorted to by my mother were annoying. Sometimes she tied me to a bedpost. Dressing me in a woman's frock or petticoat shut me in quite effectively. More potent were her entreaties and tears. The contrition they brought about lasted until the vitality which was the unconquerable part of my nature drove me to going again. It seemed that I must go. The Wandering Jew was not more possessed in that way; only his possession was a curse, and mine the completest happiness. Going was life.

Why this, now that I am in my sixty-ninth year? Certainly not because it appears peculiar or commendable. There are thousands of lads similarly overstocked with vitality; so much so that restraints of self or by others are impossible. I do not mean to say that in such cases the object of solicitude should be allowed to run wild. I simply plead for discrimination, for forbearance, for teaching, for sympathy. Whoso lays his hand heavily on a boy of spirit such as I am describing is himself an offender in far greater degree than his victim. The school-master who cannot discriminate between pupils lacks the first essential to perfection in an honorable calling.

Autumn, it is to be added, was but an extension of summer a little sobered, and different in that things ceased growing that they might ripen—a difference I saw and felt without understanding. I speak altogether of wild things—richnesses with which men had nothing to do. Who better than I knew where to look for the fattest hazel and hickory nuts, chincapins the least acrid, grapes in largest cluster, pawpaws the most melting? And were they not mine? Had I not been first to see them? And in their passing from bloom to form and color, had I not been their most faithful watcher? And, with the birds and chipmunks, had I not counted on gathering them? And when at last they were ready for gathering, and I went out after them, the shimmering of the summer having given place to smoky mists of the melancholy days—went out after them with my mother's big reticule on my shoulder—if, then, the owner of the land had bidden me off, with what a rebellious spirit I had submitted to his larger hand, if I had submitted at all? What did I know of the moral and the law incident to right in property? And not knowing, what did I care? Every boy is originally a red communist.

But alas for me when winter came and the universal green had vanished, and the snow lay over my haunts and even the river yielded itself to bonds hateful and icy! *That* was an end of going. And, in recognition of the distasteful fact, I submitted to hat, shoes, and coat, and became an *habitué* of the red school-house on the hill. There my penmanship improved. I could copy a copy with an identicalness really wonderful considering that we are bound to the use of quills not always clarified. True, the multiplication table continued a rough corduroy over a swamp of bottomless depth; yet my maps were unexcelled. In fact, had the one crowded room of the small building been better furnished, my progress might have been more satisfactory. As it was, in periods extremely cold, a struggle began with us the moment we were rapped to order. The fireplace was ample and wood in plenty, but the floors and windows were open; they and the big boys and girls monopolized the warmth. In the rush for the fire at recess, the small children were shut out unanimously. The wall of writhing bodies that cut them off could not be climbed, while the process of tunnelling under was dangerous. Study requires favorable conditions. It may be questioned if the author of *Vathek* could have finished his marvellous story in the prescribed time if compelled to pause between sentences to blow the blood back in his frosting fingers. It is also beyond belief that *Nuova Vita* could have been conceived while zero was nibbling at Dante's toes.[1]

[1] I remember yet the wonder which fell upon the school and held it when, without notice, a party of men entered the room one bitter cold day and set a large iron box tenderly upon the floor; then fixed legs to it, and, after knocking a hole in the chimney above the fireplace, put up a long line of iron pipes in connection. Of all the urchin eyes watching the operation not one lost a motion while their rough but gentle friends kindled a fire in the box. And then, when the draught began to sing, and presently the warmth intensified and pervaded from the centre to the corners, and we *all alike* felt the summery effect, if the inventor of stoves had been of a nature purely Samaritan and conscious of silent blessings in the air about him that moment, doubloons in showers fresh from the Spanish mints had not been more to his satisfaction. It was my first encounter with a stove.

In the foregoing paragraph, I perceive, upon second reading, room for a suspicion that I was capable of a studious habit. The truth is, a reading was the utmost a lesson had from me in that early day, and for a long time after. To be still, much less buckle seriously to a school-book, was greatly beyond my will. The reader may smile, thinking of the old witticism of sitting on a dictionary to acquire a language; still, there is such a thing as absorption of knowledge, a point on which I offer myself in testimony. If the task were to my taste, or one that called for work with hand, eye, and thought in combination, my patience was inexhaustible. The difference between work with pleasure at the bottom of it and downright mental effort to master the abstruse, difficult, or uninteresting is within the personal experience of everybody.

In either my sixth or seventh year I was introduced to what may be called the amusement department of society. I laughed then, and laugh now, only a trifle more quietly.

The servant-girl who, in connection with the hanging of the murderer on the roadside down in the hollow east of the town, gave me my first chapter on ghosts was permitted to take me and my elder brother to a circus. She was really an accomplished cicerone for such an occasion. All the folk-lore of a settlement hardly to be dignified as provincial was at her tongue's end. She knew the rhymes and songs, the tales and superstitions, the homely words and cabalistic formulas of witchcraft and magic so largely composing the intelligence of the ignorant class to which she belonged. She read fortunes with singular facility, and, being yet unadvanced to palmistry and cards, her bases were most elementary — such as the grounds in a teacup, marks in the ashes, the seeds of an apple. She delighted in death-heraldry. If a dog, abroad by moonlight, stopped before the door or under a window and howled, or if a whippoorwill dropped its mournful note while on the wing above the house at night, she knew some one was doomed, or, in her style, "was agoin' to die for certain." She not only knew the names of the spooks and fairies, but had seen them, and, to hear and believe her, there was a personal devil, and everybody his game. I was her favorite auditor; probably because my imagination was more easily played upon. The times she sent me shivering to bed or to my mother, white and trembling, it were unsafe to tell. The circus referred to gave her an opportunity to manifest her curious knowledge. Through the whole preceding week she had me looking for four-leaf clovers. She would tell me why after the show. I could not find the clover, so she was safe in the divulgement. The riding and tumbling had most profoundly astonished me. "Ah," she said, with an airy toss of her frowsy head, "them wasn't men you seen. You only thought them men. If you'd 'a' had a four-leafed clover in the toe of your shoe, you'd 'a' seen that they was speerits." In this manner, strange to say, I was furnished a lesson in hypnotism long before Robert Houdin advanced the occult principle in explanation of tricks played before his eyes by the fakirs of the East.

My next glimpse at amusements was quite as entertaining. A solitary showman, making a tour of the West, gave a performance in the court-house. The first part of the programme was a dance on a slack wire. In place of dancing, the "talent" confined himself to a slow walk forward and back, and, to reduce the danger to a minimum in case he lost his balance, the floor was at no time more than three inches beneath his chalked slippers. The audience clapped vigorously; while with me the shortcomings in the exhibition, admitting them to have occurred, were offset by the black hose, spangled shirt, and starred crown of the exhibitor. The glory of Solomon, of which I afterwards heard, was shoddy in comparison. The second part of the programme aroused the entertained, myself included, to a white heat of enthusiasm. It was made up entirely of plantation songs and jigs, executed in costume—burned cork, shovel shoes, and all. Two of the songs I yet remember—"Jump, Jim Crow" and "The Blue-tailed Fly." The chorus rang through my head for years; and as I walked home through the night I was unconscious of any special increase of wisdom; at the same time, I felt that the world was full of fun and life worth living, if only for fun. I had an inexpressible joy thinking of what all there was before me.

My mother, the Esther French Test already mentioned, died in her twenty-seventh year, leaving me so young that her sweet motherliness is a clearer impression on my mind than either her qualities or her appearance. Of the latter, all I can now recall are her eyes, large, sparkling, and deeply brown. They follow me yet. Indeed, through my seventy years there has never been a day so bright or a night so dark that, upon recurrence of the thought of them, I have been unable to see them seeing me.

A rejected suitor has helped me to knowledge of her in her young womanhood. Sprightliness, beauty, and graces of person, he said, brought her beaus in numbers. She was an instance, he further observed, in which coquetry added to a character altogether perfect. He spoke of her as the strangest compound he ever met. Though delicate to frailty, she could dance from Sunday to Sunday. A Methodist, charitable as a Sister of Mercy, devout as a Puritan, the enjoyment she found in the party and the ball, in visitation and in society, were irrepressible. I may remark that at the time he was speaking the suitor was old and semi-paralytic; still, he made it clear to me that the subject of his speech was the unforgotten brightest light on the receding hill-top of his youth.

The decline in health was rapid, so rapid as to justify the homely entitlement of the disease, galloping consumption. Yet her eyes grew brighter and dwelt upon her boys with a gaze longer and more intense. Now I know why. She was thinking of the inevitable separation. My father was in New York on business, and dreamless of what was to occur. The sufferer wanted nothing possible to be had. One night I lay asleep before the fire upon a rug which I affected on account of the great Persian lion woven in it. One of the women in attendance shook me, saying, "Wake up—your mother is dying; come and see her." My elder brother was already at the bedside, crying bitterly. He knew the meaning of what was passing; I did not. In dull apprehension I joined him. The alabaster tinge was on her face. In the eyes there was no light. The hands and tongue had lost their affectionate cunning. I called her, using the endearment that had never before failed —"Mother, mother!" She did not answer, and then I understood the silence. The comprehension fell upon me as darkness leaps in on the blowing-out of the last light, and it seemed a strong hand caught my heart and tried to wring the life out of it. And so I made acquaintance with death. I have seen it since in many forms, at times under circumstances hideous because of its accessories—in flood, in pestilence, in battle—but never realized its awful import, due, as I can now perceive, to an intuitive perception of the extent of the bereavement it so remorselessly inflicted on me. She was to be buried. I was never to see her more. Her love, with all its countless illustrations of touch, look, care, sympathy, and word, was to become but a memory. In my defeats, how often I have said to myself, "Ah, if she were here to console me!" in triumphs, "How proud and happy she would be!"

When the final services were over, a neighbor led the three of us to her house and there installed us. Not to mention her name were to prove me an ingrate. She was Mrs. John Hawkins. It often happens that women, themselves indifferent to the world and its applause, come to enviable places in it through their children. Such was her case. The mother of Mrs. General Edward S. Canby and General John Hawkins still has a generous share in the respect universally accorded them by their contemporaries. We became of her family. The government she laid down for her own children was extended to us, and in the largeness of her charity there was never an observable distinction.

IV

Goes to College—" Nuts "—Mother's apparition to William—Empty house — David Wallace — Runs off to Crawfordsville — Wabash College—First appearance as student—The seminary—Reverend H——t—The Kerrs—The farm—The new mother.

My boyhood, as a subject of reflection, furnishes me now with so much quiet amusement that I am tempted to give it a chapter. To do so ingenuously requires a somewhat trying exposure. Indeed, I much doubt if I had been equal to the trial twenty years ago. To be able to laugh at himself is pretty good evidence that one has reached the philosophic stage of life; to invite others to join him in the laugh is a final test conclusive of the fact.

The utter carelessness which was my most marked trait in childhood underwent no change in consequence of the loss of my mother. I possessed an animal enjoyment of existence so pure and deep that it was an absolute governor. Where the faculty of reflection is wanting, advice goes the way of spilled wine, and punishment is cruelty. Two years more went by in Covington, and, though supposedly given to school, the summers were really spent in the woods and along the river, and the winters in sledding and trapping birds. Out on the road one day I was assailed by the cries of a dog in pain. Hurrying to the scene, I found a small, half-starved, flea-bitten sample of the species that had been run over by a wagon and deserted. Examination disclosed a broken leg. I took the sufferer in my arms and carried it home.

My best surgical care could not save the limb from a crook and its owner from a limp which, while seriously affecting its speed, did not in the least diminish its gratitude and devotion. "Nuts"—the new christening—was in good time promoted chief associate in my truancies. In an attempt to defend him against the boys at school I had my first fight. The cause was righteous and I did my best, but they were too many for me, and truth compels the admission that I was whipped. Retreating with a wad of hair wrenched from the head of an enemy, I soothed my hurts by disentangling the trophy and tying it conspicuously to my dog's collar.

Circumstances certainly do alter cases. My elder brother had long played on my fear of ghosts. He did not believe in them. At length I turned the tables on him. Upon my mother's final departure, the house had been closed and left locked up and grewsomely silent, but with everything in place within. One day he wanted something in the front room. Taking the youngest of the Hawkins boys with him, he pried up a back window, and the two crawled into the kitchen, leaving me outside waiting their return. Presently they came rushing back. Both were white with terror. Not standing on order, they swung themselves over the sill to the ground, where they stopped long enough for me to ask the matter. My brother answered: "We saw mother. She was sitting in the rocking-chair." "Did she speak to you?" I asked. "No, she only looked at me. Come away." And they ran off, forgetting in their haste to let the sash down. Somehow I did not scare. A graveyard was too much for me, but not *that* ghost; so I swung myself into the window and ran through the whole house, looking everywhere. Nothing strange was to be seen. Thinking if she had, indeed, returned she might speak to me, I took seat in the rocking-chair, but without reward. Out of the stillness there was not even a word. By-and-by the boys called me to come out. They asked eagerly if I had seen her. Both of them lived to be men, always insisting upon their assertion. The curious part of the incident is that my dread of spirits and all horrors of night and darkness left me then.

My elder brother was in every point my opposite. Handsome, neat, polite, studious, obedient, respectful, he was a universal favorite. Our father had great hope of him, and the promise was excellent. Some good men, genuine missionaries of learning, had recently come out of the East and founded a college over in Crawfordsville, some thirty miles away. Thither my brother was taken and duly entered as of the preparatory department.

The separation nearly broke my heart. The feeling between the new collegiate and myself was more than fraternal. In his chiding he was so gentle, and in the griefs of constant happening to me, generally of hands with rods in them, he was so sympathetic, my love for him was seasoned with much that was secretly worshipful. It is singular, as I view it now, that the frequency with which he was held up to me as an example, far from tiring me, served rather to increase my pride in him. Had he been more like me, perhaps it had been different. In a few days the desire for his companionship got the mastery, and I resolved to go after him.

There had been much preparation for his departure. He had new shirts, shoes, and clothing. His boarding had been carefully prearranged. Of these preliminaries I never thought. Nor did it occur to me as the least needful to have my father's permission to make the change of residence. What was to become of me at Crawfordsville, with whom I was to live, what do, did not bother me; they were points too trifling or too profound for my small modicum of prudence and foresight. There are lads, cleanly, clever, good - looking, who are always welcome with strangers; that I was not of them was a circumstance of which I was blissfully ignorant.

What was a college? The question is a puzzle to wise men even at this day of high-schools. I had a dim perception that it was a big house reared on the side of a road leading into the world which I had such a passionate longing to see, and that in the house there were books in bewilderment, and nice people, young and old, always coming and going, and new experiences in store for me. If I liked the change, very good; if not, very good. I could quit on getting tired. Anyhow, my brother was there.

There was living in Covington an uncle not greatly my senior in years or in wisdom. To my delight I one day heard he was going to Crawfordsville. He would ride over on horseback, and there would be plenty of room behind him for me. The chance was too good to be lost.

I went out early in advance of him two or three miles and lay in ambush for the traveller. He was of course, surprised at seeing me.

"What are you doing here?" he asked.

"Waiting for you."

"What for?"

"I want to go to Crawfordsville with you."

"Have you any business there?"

"Yes, I want to go to college."

"To college!"

He fairly choked with laughter. His good-nature, however, finally overcame his scruples, and, letting me mount behind him, he jogged on. The pony was fat and slow, and of prodigious breadth of beam. My legs cramped, and I suffered in every bone and muscle, but I set my teeth and gave no sign. About the middle of the afternoon we drew up in front of the basement entrance of the college, and, unloading me, my kinsman pushed on to town.

The basement was of the dugout style of architecture, fronting north, and sunk half in a rise of the ground to the south. A low door, flanked with dirty windows of eight-by-ten lights, was the principal feature of that part of the building. I raised my eyes, and swept the unpainted elevation. Was this a college? I remember yet the spasm of disappointment that struck me.[1]

The house was not more a curiosity to me than I presently became to a benevolent-looking old gentleman who issued from the door, followed by a woman, some children, and half a dozen young men whom I came to know afterwards as students.

Small wonder that the party, one and all, viewed me askance. My straw hat, besides being a production of the country, and ragged and rain-stained, hung to the back of my head as if there had been a peg there for its special accommodation, allowing my shocky hair the broadest liberty. My feet were bare and unwashed, and, to make them more conspicuous, one of my great toes was garnished by a rag most unprofessionally applied. My trousers, rolled nearly to my knees, hung to my gaunt torso dependent upon a single suspender of cloth listing. My shirt, guiltless of a button, offered a display of neck and breast red as a Mohave Indian's. Not to leave anything to the imagination of the reader, I append a few of the questions put to me by the benevo-

[1] The building here described should not be confounded with any of the spacious, substantial, and tasteful edifices of the college at present adorning the great campus of Wabash College at Crawfordsville.

lent-looking gentleman, who, by-the-way, was as hatless, coatless, and brown as myself, and like me still further in that his shirt was buttonless and flaring. Somewhat later I came to know him as Uncle John Beard, a member of the legislature and proprietor of a boarding-house located in the basement for impecunious students.

"Where are you from, my son?"

"Covington," I answered.

"What's your name?"

"Lewis Wallace."

"A son of Governor Wallace?"

"Yes."

The spectators nudged each other and smiled, but the old gentleman proved his benevolence. "Run, one of you," he said, "and find the young man's brother."

Then he resumed the examination.

"Where are you going?"

"Nowhere. I've just come."

"Any friends here?"

"Only William."

"Know anybody else?"

"No."

"Does your father know of your coming?"

"No."

"Or your mother?"

"She's dead."

"What do you expect to do?"

"Go to college, if I like it."

The circle hemming me in broke into a laugh that put a stop to the inquisition. It was ill-mannered in them, even rude, especially in the students. Viewing me as a competitor for honors, they could not help demonstration of some kind. What a travesty upon their ideals of oratory and literature they must have thought me! What a satire upon them personally! On high occasions, like commencement, what an ornament to the carpeted platform I would prove! Bare feet, straw hat, uncombed hair, rags, marbles, a most unconventional drapery of neck and breast—I laugh thinking of myself.

In the midst of the fun my brother appeared, himself a model of attire and deportment. I see him now, dumb with astonishment. Yet, to his credit be it said, he did not disown me.

"Why, Lew, when did you come?" he asked, taking my hand.

"Just now."

"How?"

"On a horse with Uncle Milton."

"What for?"

"To be with you and go to college."

There were tears in the good fellow's eyes as he led me out of the circle and off to his boarding-house in town. By the next week he had me dressed decently.

The faculty, out of respect for my father, doubtless, admitted me to the preparatory department, and set me at grammar, arithmetic, and Latin, with weekly compositions and recitations. A man named Barlow was the tutor. He also was of the army of indiscriminates who think they are doing their duty in giving impossible tasks to helpless incapables, and, if they are small, punishing them. I, a boy of nine, was expected to be ready with lessons which tried the grown men of my class. I strove hard, but gave up in a few weeks.

The building was in the woods west of Crawfordsville. North of it, under a hill, there was a stream, half river, half creek. And they, the woods and the little river, invited me, and I accepted and took to them. Returning once, the tutor caught me, and, in full session of the class, stood me on a stove through the afternoon. At the letting-out I escaped for good. There are people who think me a graduate with a diploma to fatten my pride. In fact, I was a "prep" of Wabash College less than two months. Further it is not mine to boast. The faculty did not expel me. Most likely they were glad when I took myself off. Discipline had to be maintained.[1]

From the college I transferred myself to a county seminary in Crawfordsville conducted by an Episcopalian divine of recent emigration from the state of New York. The youth of the village knew him as the Reverend H——t, a person of education, fine clerical appearance, and most immaculate cravats. In his system of government the ferule was close competitor with the gad. His order of business was also somewhat peculiar. The first procedure after prayer in the morning was the infliction of punishment for offences noted the day before, and, as none of us knew whether our names were on the proscribed list, the holy master took a world of grim delight watching while we in fear and trembling stole to our seats. So frequently was I his victim that the régime of the college faculty seemed benign enough to have been borrowed from paradise.

Between this teacher and myself the *casus belli* were not recurrent but continuous, with intermissions during the severer snaps of winter. The river was a siren with a song everlasting in my ears. I could hear it the day long. It seemed specially addressed to me, and was at no time so sweet and irresistible as when I was struggling

[1] [As one enters the beautiful library of Wabash College to-day, above the door of entrance he may see a marble slab with three names chiselled on it — Major-General Edward S. Canby, Major-General Joseph J. Reynolds, and Major-General Lewis Wallace. Thus the loyal gentlemen who composed the faculty in 1865 sought to perpetuate the three students of the institution who in the great War of the Rebellion had risen to the highest rank at the time known to the Union army organization].

with the multiplication table or some abstruse rule of grammar. Trying now to discover the charms of the stream, I think them resolvable into the absolute clarity of the water limping over the brown-glazed rocks or gliding along stretches of sand Pactolian white and yellow, on through masses of transparent shade dropped by the vine-clad trees leaning from the shores—in other words, the mystery and splendor of all-abounding color. A farmer living in a two-story hewn-log house on a hill west of town, close by my friend, the little river, owned an apple orchard and a canoe. He had a heart which in some way I touched. Possibly he pitied the ragged, unwashed, lonesome lad who came to his door of mornings with simple requests; possibly he was a Whig who had voted for my father; in those days politics begot bonds strenuous as in this; anyhow, he gave me the privilege of the orchard and the canoe, and would come himself to the crest of the hill above the stream and blow a horn to call me to dinner. The exactions he put upon me were few and simple—not to get drowned or forget to bring the paddle home. Usually his first salutation was, "Well, did he [H——t] thrash you yesterday?" To which I made return, "Yes, but he didn't make me holler." And I would show him the welts on my legs. His honest face would flush red. "Can't you get him down here? I'd like a chance to give him a dose of his own cholagogue." The name of this excellent man was Beeler. God rest him!

I would like it clearly understood how profound my respect and reverence are for good women. The feeling is owing, perhaps, to my falling so often into the care of so many of them. The days here dwelt upon were passed when at home, a boarder in fact but hardly less a son, with Mrs. Kerr, the mother of the late United States Senator Joseph E. McDonald. A small, black-eyed woman, with a voice wonderfully soft and persuasive, because it was always speaking from her heart, if I had permitted her she would have done for me as for "Joe." That she did not do more was my fault. She lured me occasionally to church with her, and at one time had me well up in "Come thou fount of every blessing." Heaven rest her, also!

My father, it should be said, was by no means indifferent to my habits, especially the indisposition to study, which he fancied due in great part to town associations; so he gave much time casting about for means to get me out of them. The Kerrs were owners of a farm some six miles north of Crawfordsville, and, hearing that they were to move to it, he prevailed upon them to take me to the country. I welcomed the change, and went gladly. Unfortunately, the youngest of the McDonalds was the owner of a rifle. That circumstance, apparently so trifling, brought partial discomfiture to the parental scheme of reform. Instead of falling into bucolic ways, such as churning butter, hoeing corn, milking cows, helping in harvest time, I became a hunter. The solitude lurking under the old oak fastnesses of the vicinity was to my taste, and, game abounding, I passed the days shooting. My proneness to mischief spent itself on squirrels and birds. In brief time I attained singular cleverness as a shot, and, as I managed to keep the table fairly supplied with rarities in the line of game, my indulgent guardians not only winked at my wanderings, they condoned my aversion to work, and actually supplied me with ammunition. At the end of six months I graduated a farmer.

Whether profitable or unprofitable, they were certainly among the very happiest of my early life. Withal, moreover, I persisted in reading, and, returning to town, was richer of a thorough knowledge of *Plu-*

tarch's Lives and *The Life of Daniel Boone*, which, by happy chance, constituted Mr. Kerr's entire library, unless his family Bible be catalogued a part of it. The heroes of the latter, however, were not nearly so engaging to my boyish fancy as those of the immortal Bœotian.

Then there came a long change, and for the better. But for the waywardness, now become chronic, I might have turned tolerable, and, if not more like other lads, at least less savage. Going to my boarding-house one day, my elder brother met me.

"Come," he said, "make haste and wash yourself, and put on some clean clothes."

"Why, what's the matter?" I asked.

"Father's at the tavern, and he has brought us a—" He hesitated.

"A what?" said I.

"A new mother."

All the rebellious sparks in my nature blew together and broke into flame.

"Well, she may be your mother, but she's not mine. I'll not go. Who is she?"

My father had taken to him a second wife. Towards the close of the last year of his last term of lieutenant-governor he made acquaintance with Zerelda G. Sanders, eldest daughter of Dr. John H. Sanders, a Kentucky gentleman of recent removal to Indianapolis. An excellent physician, of high character and considerable means, the young city received the doctor and gave him its confidence and lucrative practice. There was opposition to the match, but the young lady had a mind of her own, and ended negotiation by going to the hotel and there quietly becoming Mrs. David Wallace. This was on December 26, 1836. Of course, I had not been consulted.

After adjournment of the legislature, in session at

the time of the wedding, my father brought his bride to Crawfordsville, where he took residence and engaged in his profession with fresh assiduity. Then the three brothers of us were once more united. I may be pardoned wondering if, when she saw us first, her courage was not severely tried. But she proved herself mistress of tact quite as remarkable as the lovingness of her nature. She won my brother instantly.

I met her first at table in the tavern. She gave me every attention, but I was sulky and stubborn, and, refusing every overture, resumed intimacy with the woods and the creek. The poor woman dead in her youth and lying in her lonely grave at Covington crept back into my thoughts. The others might forget her, but I would not. *She* was my mother, and I would have no other—I would die sooner. But the stranger in the little old public-house up-town seemed oblivious to my obstinacy. She bided the time when I would need her, knowing it would certainly come; and so it did. One evening I returned from a two days of truancy nearly dead of croup. She put me to bed, and nursed me with infinite skill and tenderness. I had sense enough to know she was the savior of my life, and called her mother, and in speech and fact mother she has been to me ever since.[1]

[1] This is a proper place for me to add that the world has been as unable to resist her as I was. In all the states of the Union, in every village and city, there are good people who know and speak of her as Mother Wallace, the sweet-tongued apostle of temperance and reform.

V

Father elected governor—Removal to Indianapolis—The capital—Sketching in church—Jacob Cox—Learns to paint—First picture—State-house library—Books—Professor Hoshour—Lessons in English—*Lorenzo Altisonant*—The turning-point.

DIRECTLY after his election to the governorship, in 1837, my father changed residence from Crawfordsville to Indianapolis, taking his family with him; and presently he was installed first occupant of a convenient though plain dwelling bought by the state for occupancy by its chief magistrates.

This transfer was to me like being set down in a new world. Indianapolis was, in fact, scarcely emerged from the woods. Stumps were frequent in its vacant downtown lots, and wagons stalled on its main streets; nevertheless, the "Capital" had all the effect upon me of a great metropolis. The overwhelming sense with which I beheld the state-house, then recently finished, and gala in its fresh stucco, serves me now as a ready measure of my verdancy and inexperience. What a marvellous achievement it appeared within and without! And when, in fulfilment of years of patient dreaming, I at last stood under the portico of the Acropolis at Athens, its pillars, with all their height and hugeness of diameter, affected me less than did those of the cheap imitation of which I am writing. Where the Soldiers' Monument stands there was then a pretentious quadrangular brick building designed originally as a residence for the governors of the commonwealth, but about as unfit for the purpose as a painted balloon; indeed, there was never wife of a governor so foolish as to wish to try living in it; withal, however, the Versailles of one of the most extravagant of the French kings was not nearly the palace I saw in that red habitation of rats, bats, and twittering swallows. Verily, the creative in the imagination of a man, even though he be a poet, is not a tithe part of that in the eyes of a boy!

My life in Indianapolis, it must be said, became more regular and tame, a result due in part to the authority sternly exercised by my father, but mostly to the gentler, if not wiser, influence of my step-mother, who, by looking after me, keeping me washed, combed, and well-clad, gradually initiated me into the comforts of a home intelligently managed.

She was a member of the Christian Church, and insisted upon my attendance once every Sunday. I fear the services failed to impress me as she desired. My headgear was a flat-topped, black oil-cloth cap, visored before and behind, and, as it allowed pencilling of delicacy on its surface invisible until held at a certain angle against the light, I converted it into a drawing-tablet. Greasy, and always in need of deodorizing, still it was eagerly sought on the return from "meeting." The preacher, his assistant, the *characters* of the congregation, and all who had a peculiarity of face or manner were there pencilled in unmistakable likeness. So the prayer, the sermon, even the communion, observed as it was every Lord's day, might have been tedious to the others in attendance; they were not to me. I carried an occupation into the pew.

Apropos this facility in drawing, Indianapolis was fortunate in the possession of a painter. Mr. Jacob Cox was a tinner by trade, but, having the divine impulse, he broke away from the shop. Old age and death found him at last, a pure, sunny-souled man, *vis-à-vis* with his easel. When I heard that Mr. Cox painted pictures in oil, I nerved myself and boldly invaded his studio. He was painting my father's portrait when I went in. The coincidence excused me. We became good friends, and not a few of my truancies were passed watching him at work. In that day, it will be remembered, colors in tubes had not crossed the mountains, and grinding on a marble slab was preliminary to the make-up of a palette. After a while I offered to do the grinding. What pleasure I had in the reduction of the raw materials! How in especial the richness of the *lakes* appealed to the color-love deep-seated in my eyes! How in fancy I applied them to their several uses, now to flowers, now to fruits, now to the lips of girls, now to the bloom on the cheeks of children! My fingers itched to try them.

At length I yielded to the temptation. Doubtless my friend would have given me of his pigments had I asked him for them, and even set me down before an easel, palette and brushes in hand; but the passion was attended with a peculiar shrinking. A laugh at my awkwardness in the first attempt was dreadful in thought. So I looked up a clean tin plate, and, seeing nothing wrong or criminal in the conversion, loaded it with dabs of paints, hastened home, and, with the coveted plunder, stole up into the garret as the safest place from intrusion.

There I found myself in want of everything else needful, yet my ingenuity was equal to the trial. For brushes, I plucked hairs from the tail of a dog and tied them to a stick. Of the floor of a wooden box I made a panel to receive the picture. There came a loud demand for oil. The servant-girl was sick, and that morning the doctor had left some castor-oil, part of a prescription for her. I stole it; and, fearing the judgment usually attaching to such misdeeds, I pause to say that the patient recovered in despite. Finally, what should I paint? I chose a portrait of Black Hawk, the old chief with one eye, conspicuous in a book of Indians.

Days were given to the picture until finally the colors *livered* on the tin. Meantime my whereabouts became a mystery. Conducting a reconnoissance into the garret, my mother found the portrait, and produced it in a full session of the family. "Lewis," she shrewdly asked, "didn't you take the castor-oil the doctor left for ——?" The smell of the ingredient had betrayed me. My father's gravity was upset. I never knew him to laugh so long and heartily as when, in obedience to his command, I produced the outfit of my studio.

The predilection for art might have become a passion, seeing that it was already strong enough seriously to interfere with my attendance at school. My father at length resolved on repression. Calling me into his study one day, he said: "You must give up drawing. I will not have it. If you are thinking of being an artist, listen to me. In our country art is to have its day, and the day may not come in your time. There is no demand for pictures. Rich men are too few, and the poor cannot afford to indulge a taste of the kind. To give yourself up to the pursuit means starvation. Do you understand me?"

I made a feeble attempt at argument.

"But—Mr. Cox—"

"Oh yes," he replied, "Mr. Cox is a good man; but he has a trade to fall back upon—a shop to help him make the ends meet."

Seeing the impression he was making, he went on:

"I suppose you don't want to be a poor artist—poor in the sense of inability as well as poverty. To be a great painter, two things have always been necessary—a people of cultivated taste and then education for the man himself. You have neither."

And so on for quantity. The talk was too old for me—too old at least for full appreciation—and I persisted in the practice. Not long afterwards an expected coadjutor came to my father's assistance.

I was then supposedly in attendance at the county seminary, conducted by a Mr. K——r, a teacher of ability but more remarkable for his violent temper. He, too, kept a ferule and a bundle of selected rods.

In a recess, one afternoon, when everybody else was out on the playground, I took a piece of chalk and drew a rabbit on the blackboard. The subject was easy and inoffensive; unfortunately, in the finish I substituted the master's head for bunny's, intending to rub it out in good time; but somebody called me and I forgot to apply the green baize extinguisher. Straightway, on resumption of the session, the school broke into a "snigger." The man in authority tried to stay the unseemly demonstration. Presently his wandering eyes fell upon the picture. Then he took the *fasces* from the wall. In the midst of the hush pervading he summoned me to the stand and beat me until the blood ran down my bare legs. His wrath appeased, he allowed me to take my seat, then bade me wipe the offence off the board. I declined. He started for me, fury in his face. Directly in my rear there was an open window. Before he could reach me I jumped out of the window, and, taking the gait of an antelope startled by hunter and hounds, fled, never stopping until under the roof of an old farmer friend three miles in the country.[1]

[1] Farmer Taffe. A Whig of the straitest sect, and well-to-do. He had three boys; the second, about my age, was afterwards delegate to Congress from Nebraska. They, the house, the farm, and

My father's peremptory lecture against the allurements of art had failed its purpose. Now, however, one point in it had landed home. After the affair with Mr. K——r, I could no longer deny the non-existence of the appreciation urged as a prime essential to success in the life. To starvation there was superadded a likelihood of being done to death by sticks and stones. I resolved to give up the dream. Still it haunts me. At this day even, I cannot look at a great picture without envying its creator the delight he must have had the while it was in evolution. And why not make the confession unreservedly? Why not admit that in biographical literature there are no lives so fascinating and zestful to me as those of master-artists? And that while reading them I am always hard put to smother an impulse to renew my youth in so far, at least, as the purest and sweetest of its inclination is concerned? The age is propitious; there are patrons in plenty; schools abound; the great galleries of Europe are scarce a week away; taste prevails, and invention survives despite photography.

The extinguishment of the beautiful dream left me disconsolate, but not for a great while.

The library in the state-house was just across the rotunda from the executive office. Two west windows, though frequently muddled by the festoonery of intrusive spiders, lighted the room of afternoons, but not of mornings. In the latter, it was pervaded with a gloom which, while somewhat troublesome to a visitor anxious to get a volume quickly that he might the sooner be gone, was yet in harmony with the delicious silence of the place. Howbeit others view the matter, I prefer, when entering apartments of the kind, to have

all on it, were at my service. Time was never counted on me there, nor did my welcome, though often tried, ever stale.

the inscriptions on the books develop slowly from modest glow to golden gleam, for then they give depth to the enshadowment and enrich it as starlight enriches the dark-turning violet of evening skies.

On this occasion my entry was in the forenoon early. There was a suggestion of stealth in the stillness of my steps on the carpeted floor. From having been in the British Museum and the Vatican, I now know how small the total of the collection of books was; at that time, however, I had never imagined such a presence of volumes *en masse.* The observation was from a central position. Slowly, very slowly, I swept the four sides, lined with shelving to a height out of reach except with the aid of a ladder. Books everywhere, of all sizes, of all colors! Had any one ever read them all? Of the cumulative labor required for their production, and the *mind* in them, I did not think, any more than I thought of the motive, that deepest abstraction underlying each of them—they were revelations time was to bring me.

Presently an itching of the fingers, like that which caught me when grinding colors for my friend the artist, seized me; only, in this instance, it went not further than an intense desire to handle separately every book in the array, exactly as one boy always wants to feel the pocket-knife and marbles he sees in the hands of another boy. There was a step-ladder, the property of the librarian, and he being out—it would have mattered nothing had he been present—I carried it into a corner and set about prospecting the shelves. Noon came, and I was still at work. Thinking, doubtless, that my father was a colleague of his in the government of the state, and that so much comity might not be unsafe, the keeper let me have my bent. I forgot I was due at school, and that dinner was a due of mine. Closing hour in the evening arrived; then I gave up to return next day—and the next—and next—until the review was done. At the end, I had located every picture-book in the heap, even as a sportsman marks his fallen birds.

The last remark, I perceive, is open to an inference that none but the picture-books interested me. But the incident is not concluded—far from it. In the overhaul I came upon a volume entitled *Astoria*, and another, *The Last of the Mohicans*. Let say to the contrary who will, there is something in names. These attracted me, and in good time I went back to them, with result that I uncovered one of the most continuous, if not the greatest, happinesses which had befallen me. In the most impressionable period of my life I was introduced to Washington Irving and Fenimore Cooper, or, more plainly, to their works; and I revelled in them, especially Cooper's, whose subjects were better adapted to my opening mind. For months and months after that discovery my name figured on the receipt register of the library more frequently than any other. I took the treasures, now a sea story, now a Leatherstocking Tale, and, in the haymow or off alone in the woods, sailed and sailed with the Red Rover, or, from the store of quaint old Natty Bumpo, eked my fill of wisdom. My rating at school was the worst; yet, strange to say, education went on with me, for I was acquiring a habit of reading. Looking back to the thrashings I took stoically and without a whimper, I console myself thinking of the successful lives there have been with not a jot of algebra in them.

It were well, probably, if an hiatus were made of my years from the tenth including the fourteenth. The days throughout were given to fun.

The fun was of the kind elderly people did not relish, and with great unanimity they branded it wickedness, and me a bad boy sure to be hung. For the sake of the *genus* boy—presumably they are all alike—I must interpose a distinction between wickedness and mischief. The latter is always void of malice. It was so at least in my practice. Raids upon gardens and melon-patches were of course, but it was a point religiously observed to spare the trees and the vines; nor can I recall a case of injury to person. I had my *compadres*. Discovering early the advantages there are in organization, we begat the Red Eye and the Hay Press Club, and housed it in the attic of a three-story business house which had two indispensable virtues—a roomy fireplace and access by a movable ladder through a trap-door. There we had banquets not exactly Apicean, yet of marvellous variety, for which the town and country were unknowing but generous contributors. The menu on such occasions can be easily imagined. Thence we made excursions to the river, and, adjourning to the woods, cultivated athletics —running, jumping, tumbling, boxing, the last terminating frequently in bloody noses, blackened eyes, and bruised bodies. Boxing-gloves were a saving grace in reserve. Our Corn Dance is never to be forgotten. It was an annual feast celebrated in the milky time of the ivory ears. With thought and preparation, we turned it into an elaborate symposium spiced with cocking-mains. Adjournment always waited on the evening of the third day.

Fun, fairly distinguished from wickedness, has its wholesome uses. Health is better than learning without health.

My thirteenth year was passed in Centreville, Indiana, where there was a teacher of such repute that my father decided to send me to him. An aunt dwelt there also, and it was thought she would occasionally look after me; that is, see to the buttons on my clothes, keep my hair down, and trifles of the sort. She did not fail expectation. My elder brother was assigned to me as companion, principally, I think, to assist my aunt.

Professor Samuel K. Hoshour—his name is purposely given in full—came more nearly to my ideal school-master than any to whose tender mercies it had been my lot to fall. He wielded the rod and vigorously, but with discrimination and undeniable justice, and really taught me. He even interested me in arithmetic. Getting me to his house of evenings, with infinite patience he would cipher me over the knottier problems, explaining the rules pencil in hand. Better evidence of Christian nature no man can furnish.

Professor Hoshour was the first to observe a glimmer of writing capacity in me. An indifferent teacher would have allowed the discovery to pass without account; but he set about making the most of it, and in his method there was so much wisdom that it were wrong not to give it with particularity, the more so as some modern pedagogue may in that way be helped to an understanding of what I mean by discrimination applied to pupils.

The general principle on which the professor acted is plain to me now. The lack of aptitude for mathematics in my case was too decided not to be apparent to him; instead of beating me for it, he humanely applied himself to cultivating a faculty he thought within my powers and to my taste. Or, in another form, poverty of talent in one line, as he reasoned, might be compensated for by the development of ability in another.

I remember his beginning perfectly; inasmuch as it set me to wondering that one could waste time and effort in plying a lad like me with a subject so serious and seemingly beyond my years. What had he on which to believe that I could even understand what he said to me? But when at length I saw I could understand him, and that he too saw it, how delicious the flattery! And what stimulation there was in it!

The first sitting he gave me was in one of the evening séances at his house without witnesses. By a series of questions, artfully put, he led me to expose the whole field of my reading, and I think it encouraged as well as surprised him, for he presently brought out two volumes of size.

"These," he said, "are lectures on rhetoric by John Quincy Adams. They are given to rules for composition. You must dig them out for yourself sometime, for there can be no good writing if one of them be violated."

I recall also a saying of the professor's own.

"Were you to ask me," he said, "which of the rules is the most important, which comes nearest being the essence of the whole art, here it is: In writing, everything is to be sacrificed to clearness of expression—everything."

By way of illustration, I suppose, he next produced a volume which he called *The Spectator.*

"Here," he said, "are some of the finest examples of clear English ever printed. I will select some of the best. Now listen." He read a paragraph, and declared, "You can't help understanding that."

From the table he then picked a thin pamphlet, premising, "This is a work of my own, *Lorenzo Altisonant* by name." At the end of an example he looked at me quizzically and said, "You don't understand a word of it, do you?"

"Is it English?" I asked.

The professor had a habit of tugging at the lower skin of his cheek, and as a result the skin hung to the jaw like a flabby purse of yellow leather. Giving the purse an extra pull, he chuckled inwardly, making me think of Natty Bumpo, and explained.

"This, you see, is a story in words of five syllables. I wrote it to show the absurdity of big words so striven after by young writers, and, for the matter of that, by many old ones as well."

Taking another book, he selected a passage and had me read it aloud, saying, at the conclusion, "How clear and simple that is! Now try *Altisonant* again."

I tried, but gave it up.

And he commented: "The first was from *The Vicar of Wakefield,* by one Oliver Goldsmith. You must take the book home with you. Washington Irving borrowed his style from Goldsmith. What style is we will come to after a while. Let me speak of language now. Our English is mainly composed of Saxon and Latin. *Altisonant* is very little Saxon. See how preferable the Saxon is. Our conversation is almost altogether Saxon. Let me give you an example of the very purest Saxon."

Taking a New Testament, "There," he said, "read that. It is the story of the birth of Jesus Christ."

This was entirely new to me, and I recall the impression made by the small part given to the three wise men. Little did I dream then what those few verses were to bring me—that out of them *Ben-Hur* was one day to be evoked.

I can see the professor standing in his door, lamp in hand and bareheaded, dismissing me for the night, with exactly the same civilities he would have sped an official the most important in the state. Ah, the kindly cunning of the shrewd old gentleman! He had dropped a light into my understanding and caught me.

So, step by step, the professor led me into and out of depths I had never dreamed of, and through tangles of subtlety and appreciations which proved his mind as thoroughly as they tried mine. Before the year was out he had, as it were, taken my hand in his and introduced me to Byron, Shakespeare, and old Isaiah. The year was the turning-point of my life, and out of my age and across his grave I send him, Gentle master, hail, and all sweet rest! Now I know wherein I am most obliged to you—unconsciously, perhaps, but certainly you taught me how to educate myself up to every practical need.

VI

The literary society—Goldsmith's essay—Historical poem—Smith and Powhatan—*The Man-at-Arms: A Tale of the Tenth Century.*

A LITERARY SOCIETY was a feature of the seminary course to which, on return from Centreville, I was subjected; and if I write of it with some particularity, it is because the society was more interesting and useful to me than the regular instruction of the school. Its membership was not exclusive. The master had nothing to do with it; he merely permitted the use of the schoolroom for its sessions, which were on Friday evenings. The exercises included debates, recitations, compositions, and criticisms. We also studied parliamentary law, with *Jefferson's Manual* for text-book, and practised it in moot legislatures. The chairman arbitrarily assigned a duty to each of us, and if we failed in performance or absented ourselves without good excuse we were fined. I cannot say the treasury was greatly enriched from the penal part of our code, for the reason chiefly that we seldom had wherewith to pay our assessments. Such organizations are usually short of life; this one, however, endured and was faithfully attended through several years.

It would be pleasant to give a list of the men who in that society made their first signs of talent—lawyers, politicians, journalists, useful men generally, some of them of national distinction. Among those still abroad in the land — and even yet they are not a few — there exists a comradeship not unlike that obtaining with old soldiers; and when they chance to meet they grow reminiscent and tell of the haps and mishaps which took place in the old literary club.

Careless and indifferent though I was as a scholar—that was the term then used to denote a pupil—I yet undertook the parts assigned me in the society, whether in debate, recitation, or composition. The competition stimulated me to effort. My successes, I am bound to confess, were due to my father's library; and, while my brother was much better as a speaker, I may, without immodesty, claim that I excelled him as a writer.

Our master-critic was a young Mr. M——k, who was well-read in English literature, of a sarcastic turn, and in the habit of disposing of our essays with a freedom against which we sometimes rebelled. As my productions seemed particularly obnoxious to him, I once thought to get the laugh on him, and, going to Goldsmith for help, copied a paper and read it as my own. The trap worked perfectly. M——k had never been so severe. My language was pedantic; the sentences were stiff and obscurely turned; the ideas puerile. At the conclusion of his critique I arose and made explanation, book in hand. Much I doubt if our reviewer ever forgot the shouts of the audience or the gibes which followed him into the school-room and out on the playground. "Poor Goldsmith" was not to be trifled with. The medallion in Westminster Abbey, and the long Johnsonian epitaph in Latin under it, were certificates of a mastery of good English all too strong for such impeachment.

I must have achieved some popularity as a writer with my mates of the society. Under their encouragement I commenced the fabrication of verses. Lyrics flowed freely from my pen. A newspaper of the city opened its columns to me, and I flourished with considerable promise, especially in the opinion of the young ladies who were my inspiration.[1]

My most ambitious effort was a historical poem in the style and measure of "Marmion" and the "Lay of the Last Minstrel," and with John Smith—Virginia John—for hero. I followed the redoubtable swashbuckler through his affair with Powhatan. The several hundred lines concluded with his dramatic salvation by Pocahontas. All I remember of them is that the catastrophe was to my perfect satisfaction.

Another elaborate performance was an epic entitled the "Travels of a Bed-bug." The subject, according to the veracious story, was born in the office of a lawyer of Indianapolis well known throughout the state for cynicism and ability; thence it passes from office to office, and from hotel to hotel, with adventures by the way, until, like Alexander, it succumbed to overdrink. I had the impudence to publish the scurrilous squib, to the amusement of the town and the just indignation of the gentlemen concerned. Learning that several of them were looking for me, canes in hand, I went hunting, and was gone time enough for the flurry to blow over. Thereupon, finding that, like painting, poetry did not succeed best in the shadow of cudgels, I wisely quit it. I say wisely, for it is my mature judgment that under similar circumstances Homer had not persisted in supplying the world with masterpieces.

The discouragement was great, and I acknowledged it to myself sorrowfully; but thinking, if I could not do better in prose production, it could at least be prosecuted in peace and without danger, I conceived the idea of writing a novel and reading it to the society

[1] A lady of Indianapolis has some of my earliest attempts, and she holds them as a "rod of terror" over my head.

in instalments. This was in my sixteenth year. After a great deal of casting about for a plot, I finally decided on one likely to be agreeable to my auditors. Even then the importance to a writer of first discerning a body of readers possible of capture and then addressing himself to their tastes was a matter of instinct with me. It was high noon, moreover, of the day when G. P. R. James was holding the English world in very respectable rivalry with Walter Scott.[1]

As first efforts, in whatever line, are usually interesting, a synopsis of this one may at least satisfy the curiosity of young readers and writers.

So I remark that the composition of the story, and the reading and study required to veneer it with what is now known as *color*, gave me so much pleasure that the personages who figured in it and the general plot linger clearly in my memory.

I began by naming it *The Man-at-Arms: A Tale of the Tenth Century*, a preliminary so nearly like putting the cart before the horse that I now decline to recommend it to beginners in the story-telling art. My next step, demanded by the first, was to invent incidents and characters to bear out the title and at the same time invest the work with as much interest as possible. To be sure, love was the central idea. For hero I had a page who, besides being of good blood, would have graduated in another year to knighthood. He was an extraordinary youth. In his lord's tilting court he already bore himself like a paladin. He played the lute, sang ballads of knights and fair ladies, excelled in horsemanship, and, withal, was so graceful and had

[1] Mr. James did some good work; and why he has so utterly disappeared cannot be explained except on the theory that he wrote so much as to fall into unpardonable repetition of himself. In novel-writing it will not do for the same "solitary horseman" to ride through one's chapters too frequently.

such a taking turn of speech it was hard to say which adored him more, the men or the women.

The Duke of ——— (I regret having forgotten the rest of the name), to whom this military apprentice was bounden, divided his time between camp and castle. He was also very proud—who ever heard of a humble Spaniard? This one, however, had reason to be proud. His blood was blue as a Biscayan bay; the bearings of his escutcheon filled the kingdom with envy; his duchy was broad as an ordinary state; his castle could have been easily mistaken for a royal palace; his train in the field was an army.

The family of the great man consisted of a duchess, haughty as her lord, and one daughter, Inez by name, young, romantic, and beautiful as a painter's dream of beauty. In the songs of the minstrels she was the Rose of Guadalajara. Though but sixteen—the reader will understand, I am sure, why it was not possible for me to make her older than myself—nobles of high degree, at home and from France and Italy and other far countries, offered her their titles, honors, and estates; it was even said that once a king had come and laid himself and his crown at her feet. But she would none of her suitors, old or young; whereat the women said biting things of her, and the men whom she refused swore oaths all unlicensed by the Church.

But in tales all mysteries come to solution. An early chapter in the book, calling it such by grace, was given to an escapade of the wilful heiress. Down in the crypt of the castle she met Pedro, the page, by appointment. The passage was very affecting, and, lover-like, the two swore eternal fidelity to each other. A hunchback jester of the duke's caught them in the tryst, and, being a lover of the young lady himself, all mindless of his deformity, he hastened to profit by the discovery. The description of the scene when the imp yelled hoarsely at the devoted pair from a hole in the wall which was the terminus of a hidden gallery unknown to them, afforded me much comfort.

The duchess's mother put the maiden to an exacting cross-examination. Alas, then, for the daughter! Alas, also, for Pedro! The course of their true love became a roaring cataract. He was deposed and stripped of his doublet of Flanders wool and his silken hose and morocco slippers with high toes chained to his golden garters. In menial garb he was dismissed the castle. The servants who deposited him on the thither side of the drawbridge, all eyes beholding, were rewarded as for a deed of high emprise. The ambitious Pedro nevertheless haunted the vicinity. He could not tear himself away. Oh, for a minute's interview! That were long enough to assure him if his paragon were faithful. He had a scheme with which to try her.

She, on her side, was subjected to semi-imprisonment. A *dueñaza,* as the Spaniards term a hateful old widow, was given charge of her, with orders not to allow her out of sight. But by-and-by the termagant came to sympathize with her, and was then as accommodating as Juliet's nurse. She took long walks in the vicinity of the castle, and at length stumbled upon Pedro. Thereafter, especially of dark nights, a rope ladder dropped from a balcony helped the new Romeo to interviews all the sweeter because stolen. These, it was noticeable, were incidents entirely to the taste of my audience of the literary society.

It then appeared that from the castle, presently after his drumming-out, my hero had betaken himself to a hermit who, in enjoyment of most odorous reputation for sanctity, dwelt in a cavern of a mountain two or three leagues distant. Nor was it difficult to enlist the good man—everybody loves a lover. He offered advice and help. If Pedro would bring his lady to the cave, he would marry them; then the duke and duchess might go mad—only the Pope could undo the binding.

An elopement ensued—an incident which called out my best description. The gallant Pedro bore his lady-love down the swaying ladder successfully. The night was dark, but he had the assistance of the *dueñaza,* who cast the ladder loose when the descent was accomplished. A horse was ready in a near grove of olive-trees. A stout steed it was, to be sure, and with his paragon on the cantle behind him Pedro rode fast as he could go to the hermitage. The path was rough, and rivulets crossed the broken path. Through the shadowy pine woods cascades roared in ghostly music. At break of day the refuge was reached. The gentle hermit was in waiting for them. His altar was rude; nevertheless, there were lighted candles on it, and a Madonna, crowned and veiled, was in hovering on the wall behind. He knew the need of haste, and married the fugitives.

Hardly was the last word said—the last word of the blessing—when the myrmidons of the duke appeared at the cavern door. The accursed hunchback had seen the flight and alarmed the castle. Six knights, on duty at the time, leaped into their saddles and set out in pursuit.

The scene in the cavern was made duly terrible. The bride fainted and fell as dead in front of the altar. When the retainer laid hands upon her, Pedro snatched a sword from one of them and used it so valiantly that soon three of them were past fighting, dying, if not dead, and their companions fled. Rallying, however, they returned, and at length succeeded in overpowering the plucky husband. As they were about to administer the *coup de grâce,* the hermit rushed forward, crucifix in hand, and saved him, wounded and bleeding, though he could not so much for the ill-starred Inez. She was lifted on a horse and borne back to the castle.

Pedro had made a manful fight; so much the bodies of his assailants laid out on the chapel floor of the lordly fortress attested. Indeed, he might have been even more successful had he been provided with shield and armor. For days and nights he continued delirious and raving for his bride; but the hermit proved himself a skilful leech—true hermits are always skilful leeches—and finally he brought the youth around. This part of the tale was received with heartiest approval. The only criticism offered was that I had not killed more of the myrmidons; and I confess to shame at the shortcoming.

The duke, becomingly stern-minded and unforgiving, refused to recognize the validity of the marriage. To make sure, however, he despatched an agent to Rome, and, after obtaining an annulment of the bonds, such as they were, he contracted the unhappy child to a suitor of princely degree. The day of the wedding arrived. The hidalgos of Guadalajara and noble guests, men and women, were assembled in multitude. The rich altar blazed with tall candles. An archbishop, in canonicals of golden cloth, stood before it ready to celebrate the function at once the most solemn and binding of his office. All the circumstances were in contrast with the shorn and hurried ceremony of the first wedding. At the last moment the mind of the bride gave way, and in view of the assemblage she sank a raving maniac. The archbishop refused to proceed. It is hardly necessary to remark upon my appreciation of this "situation." It furnished me an opportunity of which, everything considered, I made the most.

Pedro at length recovered, and, listening to the counsel of the wise hermit, took a resolve in accordance with the spirit of the time. He became a Soldier of the Cross. Through the anchorite he obtained arms, a suit of armor, and a horse suitable for the emprise. His vows were peculiar. He would live in armor. No man should know his name or history, no one see his face, not even a servant. Alone he would spend his days, and so, God pleased, he would die. His cloak was black, relieved by a red cross on breast and back. His shield, of the same funereal hue, bore a bleeding heart pierced with a stiletto. The morning of his departure the hermit revealed that he was a nobleman, and that he had been a knight; doffing his gown, and arraying himself in layman's garb, he laid a sword thrice across Pedro's shoulders and bade him rise a knight dedicated to the Holy Sepulchre.

Pedro joined the most famous hero of the first crusade, Tancred, and became his favorite man-at-arms. In the great battle of Dorylæum he performed such prodigies of valor that thousands of the devoted besieged him to set up a standard of his own and accept them as followers. But he declined, thinking that as a chief it would be impossible for him to keep his vow of privacy inviolate. In the final assault of Jerusalem he was first on a scaling-ladder, and would have been first on the wall had he not voluntarily stayed and given way to Tancred next below him. Tancred publicly acknowledged the courtesy, and the increase of fame following was tremendous. The great chiefs — Godfrey, Hugh Vermandois, Robert of Flanders, Robert of Normandy, Raymond of Toulouse, Tancred, and others—vied in doing honors to the peerless Knight of the Bleeding Heart. Nor was he unknown to the infidels. At sight of him they gave way. Once, in the press of a great battle with Arslan the Sultan, he came hand-to-hand with that doughty leader of the enemies of God, and would have slain him but for an unlooked-for intervention. As it was, he wrenched the shield of the arch-infidel from his arm and brought it into camp. Fame, however, wrought no change of habit in him. He kept his tent alone, prepared his own frugal meals, and cared for his horse himself; when there was plenty, he attended no banquets; in time of famine —and they were frequent—he was never heard complaining. Plumeless and plain in guise, he was diligent in prayer, and therefore the exemplar always on the tongues of the preaching priests. The King of Jerusalem, Godfrey, offered him office and title; he rejected them, and, as he never took off his helmet, nobody knew him by countenance, or if he were old or young. Unequalled in fight, he was without a rival in the tourney. His vows were known, and they covered and excused his eccentricities and saved him from the gossips.

All this took place, if the story may be believed, in the year of our Lord 1097. Leaving Pedro to his glory in Jerusalem, the scenes shifted back to Guadalajara and the duke. The unfortunate Inez, at death's door, recovered her mind. The titled world justified the father's cruelty, yet was he ill in conscience. One day a priest, with a retinue, stopped at the castle gate and asked audience of him; and, being admitted, he stood and taxed the noble with offence against God in refusing recognition of the sacrament of marriage lawfully celebrated in the cavern of the recluse. To the inquiry what he knew about that affair, the visitor boldly declared himself the celebrant on the occasion. The duke at first wrangled, pleading the annulment by the Pope. He was answered that the release was obtained by misrepresentation and fraud; in proof of which a certificate to that effect by the Holy Father, done in form at the Vatican, was exhibited. The visitor proceeded to denunciation.

"Your agent," he said, "told his Holiness, with blasphemous falsehood, that I, who bound the two in bonds indissoluble by man, was neither monk nor priest, but a fugitive hiding from justice and unauthorized to perform any function of the Church. See—" he continued, with growing intensity—"see what is here written, also under seal."

The duke read the paper delivered him, from which it appeared that at the time the marriage was celebrated the recluse, besides being of ducal rank, was a priest in voluntary retreat preparatory to promotion to a vacant cardinalate.

With that the duke yielded. Already weakened by remorse, he dropped to his knees, offering to do any penance. The visitor attacked him again.

"See and read," he cried, presenting a second paper attested like the other. This the offender read with trembling, and well he might. It bade him don the cross, and with all his retainers betake himself to the Holy Land. So only could he hope forgiveness of Heaven. Arrived there, he was to seek the lost Pedro, and, on finding, restore him to the arms of his wife. A year of military service was also required of the duke. The penalty for refusal was excommunication. What could the man do but obey? In the spring of 1099 he sailed and joined Godfrey in Jerusalem, with three thousand Spanish lances. The faithful Inez accompanied him with a train of noble ladies.

Here was a new "situation," and the possibilities in the way of fine writing can be easily discerned. Pedro was a denizen of the same camp with the beloved mistress of his bleeding heart. Times and times again he met the duke, always without betraying himself. Though aware of the search made for him by the now humbled lord, he sternly held to his vows. There were battles and battles with increase of renown for him; yet he contented himself with an occasional far view of the woman whose every breath was a sigh for him. Her face told him her tale of sorrow and faithfulness. Only he did not know that the duke was there by papal order to find and restore him, and the proverbial pride of his race was a restraint in addition to his vows. These, it should be understood, were points all carefully elaborated.

I remember being worried about the *finale*. There were many ways of bringing the hero and heroine once more together. It seemed best to accomplish that end in a manner which would have the appearance of a heavenly interposition. So a famine was allowed to introduce a plague into the camp and city. The misery became general, and the women, the high-born especially, wishing to serve Christ, resolved themselves into relief corps and went about fearlessly nursing the afflicted soldiery. The lady Inez, by this time fully restored in health and more lovely than ever, did not spare herself in the merciful work.

It passed through the camp one day that the Knight of the Bleeding Heart had not been seen. Observers remarked that his tent remained closed and silent. The lady Inez, in lead of her corps of ministrants, was first to enter it. On a bed of straw she found him lying, to all appearances dying. Not minding his feeble protest, she unlaced his helmet and took it off. The recognition was instantaneous. The scene that ensued was to the author's heart, and he gave it his best power.

The romantic meeting of the two, so faithful under such trying circumstances, spread through the camp, bringing the duke in haste to the tent, and the *dénouement* was happy as could be asked. Brought back to life and health—there is no leech like love—and formally delivered from his vows, Pedro returned to Spain, and in time succeeded to the title and possessions of his repentant father-in-law. All his days thereafter were divided between duty to his family and king.

Such was my first formal attempt at fiction. There were probably fifteen chapters in the story, and quite two hundred and fifty closely written pages of foolscap, the whole done in a bound book. The work lay for several years at home, but was misplaced or destroyed during my absence as a soldier in the war with Mexico. I looked for it on my return from that service without success. Its loss, I freely confess, has been one of my standing regrets, if only for the amusement it would have given me through the succeeding years.

The composition furnished most agreeable employment, and that the plot was carried forward to a finish proves that, with all my proneness to waste of time, I must have been capable even then of some continuity of purpose, if not steady application.

With respect to quality, if further remark upon the subject is pardonable, no doubt the writing was sophomoric; for the sentimentalism which ruled me in those days was of the fervid kind, intolerant of sober expression—the kind to keep a boyish imagination in lurid glow. It is to be added that there was a copy of *Ossian* in my father's library to which I was addicted. I remember keeping it at hand, and appealing to it frequently, especially when engaged in the description of personal encounters; from which it is fair inference, I think, that my battle scenes must have been overfull of thunderous accessories, such as war-cries, Christian and infidel, clangor of shields, crash of swords and battle-axes, ghosts in air, horses in mad career, and the like for quantity. Still, of one thing I am certain—the society always turned out in force such times as my readings came round.

VII

Youth—The trip to Tippecanoe battle-ground—The red petticoat—Attempt to go to Texas—Capture by Dr. S——rs and a constable—School bills—Life at home—Reading Macaulay—English reviews—Leave home.

THE period of life to which I now come, that of youth, was largely given to reading. Occasionally I broke away to indulge the passion for adventure; in course of which I did foolish things too numerous and petty for mention, mixed with things not foolish except as they were thoughtlessly done. An illustration or two may be excused.

In 1840, taking advantage of my father's absence from home, I did myself the honor to represent him as a delegate to the great convention held at the Tippecanoe battle-ground in the interest of General William Henry Harrison. That my delegacy was by self-appointment did not, as I saw it then, interfere with its attractiveness. In plainer terms, I ran away.

The round I knew would take ten or twelve days. My preparations consisted of a ragged straw hat, the shirt on my back, trousers rolled up to my knees. That I had neither coat nor vest, that I was barefooted and without a cent in my pocket or the slightest idea of how I was to subsist, were trifles too light to excite concern. The getting through under such circumstances is worth recital now if only as a revelation of the humor of that celebrated campaign.

In mortal fear lest I should be turned back by some

one of the Indianapolis delegation who knew me, I scouted the forenoon of the first day in advance of the procession of wagons lumbering slowly and with vast labor of horses over the corduroy and through the almost bottomless pits of the so-called Michigan road. I had one companion, a school-mate, also a runaway.[1] The first village was ———, ten miles from the capital. On the right hand going into the village stood a tavern of ancient pattern; opposite it, at the left, was a blacksmith-shop of logs. A crowd filled the space in front of the tavern, and they were Democrats who, in derision, had laid a pole from the shop over the attenuated sidewalk, garnished with a red flannel petticoat. The reference was to one of the scandals which the political enemies of General Harrison had handed down from a former generation.

Now, while trudging through the mud I had been intent upon finding a way to make myself and companion acceptable to the cheering enthusiasts behind us; for soon or late, if the journey were made, it would become necessary to fall back upon them. The detestable ensign drew our attention, and, looking from it to the democracy blatant in front of the tavern, I saw my chance. Up the rough corner of the shop to the roof I went like a squirrel. There was a storm of threats and curses, of course. Nothing daunted, I tore the pole from its fastenings, and followed it to the sidewalk; then down the road we ran with our prize.

The first wagon of the train belonged, as luck would have it, to an old gentleman, a Whig of the intensest color from Noblesville, named Cole.

"What have you there?" he asked, stopping.

We held the petticoat up.

[1] Afterwards I had him appointed assistant commissary-general of my division—Major Joseph P. Pope.

"Where did you get it?"

We told him.

"Who are you?" he next asked.

That we answered also.

"Where are you going?"

"To the convention—if you'll take us."

"Get right in," he shouted.

I made haste to obey him. My comrade's heart failed, and he went home.

After that the trip was easy. The wagon, bedding, mess-chest—everything the old gentleman had with him, including a barrel of hard cider—was at my service. At Lafayette he even bought me a suit of clothes new from head to foot. I candidly believe that no one of the multitude attending the convention saw or heard more of it than I did; for, once on the ground, I took no rest, neither did I sleep.

Another of my enterprises was vastly wilder, but, fortunately for me, less successful.

It was in 1842 or '43. The Texas war of independence was at its height. All sympathy, especially in the West and South, was with the Texans. They were Americans, and the names of Crockett, Travis, and Bowie were on every tongue. The fever caught me. To my desk-mate, Aquilla C——k, my senior by a couple of years, and bright, I said one morning:

"Let's go and join Commodore Moore." [1]

"I'll do it," he returned, and the reply bespeaks the elements in his composition.

"He'll make us midshipmen," I argued.

We got a skiff, laid in a supply of provisions and an armament consisting of a rifle and shot-gun and big butcher-knives strapped sailor-fashion to our manly

[1] Commodore Moore was at the head of the Texan navy.

hips. A few days prior a flat-boat had sailed from the port of Indianapolis bound for New Orleans. To overtake it was our first point. White River was in friendly boom, and all would have gone well but for our overzeal in the sacred cause. To make Commodore Moore and all his co-laborers willing to die for liberty completely happy, we decided to do a bit of recruiting among the big boys of the school. We failed, of course, which was bad, yet not so bad as the publication of our enterprise, as will presently appear.

The day of departure arrived. C——k and I went to our boat separately. What was our astonishment to find the whole male faction of the seminary on the bank above the landing. It seemed half the town was out. They cheered us, and we jumped in, unshipped our oars, waved our hats in farewell, and shot heroically into the friendly current.

In wise forethought of supper in some lonesome jungle of the river at night, my comrade landed on an island to kill a goose with a stick. We flung the bird aboard, thinking it dead; but just as we swung past a field lively with harvesters the goose revived and uttered a "honk" so loud, so long, made doubly embarrassing by a fight for life with its great wings, that I have ever since been able to understand how its possible ancestors on the Capitoline Hill could have saved Rome. The harvesters heard the outcry, grasped the situation, and, unmooring a canoe below the bank, set out in pursuit. They were swift; so were we. For miles they kept the chase. Once we cleared for action—that is, we loaded our guns. We were awfully strung up, and I fear it would have made little difference to us then where the war we were seeking began, whether in Indiana or Texas. Fortunately they quit.

Below Indianapolis ten miles are the Bluffs, noteworthy because of a dam across the river to supply the canal finished to that point. The fall over the dam was too high for shooting, making it necessary to land in the canal for portage. We reconnoitred as we drew near, but saw nobody. C——k stayed with the boat, while I went ashore for some kindling. He saw a couple of men whom he recognized come out of a saw-mill where they had been hiding—Dr. S——rs, my mother's father, and a constable. A panic seized him; he yelled to me, but gave the skiff a shove, and when I reached the place he had put the canal between us. While I was imploring him to come back for me the constable made me his prisoner.

Dr. S——rs was a wise man. Without a lecture on my wickedness, or so much as a reference to my elopement, he landed me in Indianapolis after night. He also effected a treaty with the bloody-minded schoolteacher, by the terms of which the man of the rod agreed to let me go unflogged. Certainly I was greatly indebted to the good doctor; but, wishing to be strictly just, my obligation to the constable was of an equal measure. The one saved me from humiliation, the other saved my prestige in the juvenile world of my being. To have been arrested and brought back by a constable was altogether different from meekly losing heart and voluntarily abandoning my comrade.

I come now to an incident so grave in its effect upon my life that it cannot be omitted. The reader is to think of me in my sixteenth year, unusually tall, thin, olive-hued, and of an all-abiding confidence in myself hard to distinguish from vanity, due mostly to a physical condition wholly without an ailment. The incident referred to could not have found a more able-bodied subject.

My father's eyes were black and intensely penetrative, and latterly I had observed them unusually observant of me. Calling me into the library one morning after breakfast, he told me he had something to say. From the drawer of a table supporting the bookcase he drew a package of papers neatly folded and tied with red tape. Seldom have I seen him so deliberate and serious.

"I want you to look at the papers in this package," he said.

I returned the parcel.

"What are they?" he asked.

"Receipts."

"Receipts for what?"

"I take them to be receipted school-bills."

"Were I to die to-night," he continued, "your portion of my estate would not keep you a month. I have struggled to give you and your brothers what, in my opinion, is better than money—education. Since your sixth year I have paid school-bills for you; but—one day you will regret the opportunities you have wilfully thrown away. I am sorry, disappointed, mortified; so, without shutting the door upon you, I am resolved that from to-day you must go out and earn your own livelihood. I shall watch your course hopefully. That is all I have to say."

He waited to hear from me, and, as he was standing, I brought him a chair.

The announcement did not surprise me. Indeed, it had frequently occurred to me to ask him for permission to do the thing he now laid upon me. What I could resort to had been considered. As it was, he had not cast me off, but simply left me to myself—that saved my self-love. I admitted the justice of his course. I admitted also the duty he owed the younger children, my half-brother and his sister, and ended by thanking him for all his kindness to me in the past. That I could take care of myself was not to be doubted.

At the close of the interview he said, "Had you not better keep the receipts?"

"Why should I keep them?"

"Some time," he returned, "you may be disposed to think I have not done a whole part by you; should that happen, you have only to turn to this package and count the years it covers."

I assured him I needed no reminder.

Only a skeleton of the conversation is given. There was no argument, no reproach, no entreaty. The affair was merely as if one party were making the other a present; and such in fact it was—he had given me my freedom. His affection stood demonstrated. He had punished me often and severely, but never undeservedly. He was a good man and patient; I had been a bad boy—that was all. Life was before me in which to make him amends. Had I been less confident of earning my bread respectably, my feelings might have worn a different color. He offered me his hand. I took it, and passed out of the house and into the street rather lightsomely.

At the gate in going I remember stopping to look back at the house; and I see it yet made more lasting in recollection by my father standing in the open door under the low portico. It will not be hard to understand what brought and held him there while I remained in sight.

A one-story, weather-boarded log building, squat on the ground, small windows, the glass of minimum panes; a narrow hall cutting it in the centre; at the west end, a parlor; at the east, a sitting-room; back of the parlor, the library; the hall terminating in a dining-room; behind the main building, separated from it by a porch-like covered way, the kitchen; the whole fronting southwardly—such was the residence.

The lot thus occupied was one of the right-angle triangles on Massachusetts Avenue, and a large part garden, a larger part orchard. The yard in front was interspersed with cherry-trees and rose-bushes. In the extreme southwest corner stood the gate out of which, the memorable day of which I am speaking, I passed into the world. The avenue formed the hypothenuse of the spacious triangle.

What made that humble home so dear to me that when I think of it now I feel a softening of the tear-ducts and a hardening in the throat?

Father, mother — the time had long gone since I refused the word to her who had so wisely replaced my mother in fact—brothers of the old family and brother and sister of the new had dwelt there with me. Still, that is not wholly satisfying. To find the perfect answer, I have to go deep. Here it is, nothing simpler when at last reached—it was the life of daily passage under that roof.

The housekeeping had been exquisite, the hours easy and natural, and without hectoring or scolding. We had known but one despotic law—that we should be present and ready for meals. Often as it pleased us, we had attended church. Every nook and cranny had been free to us.

Of the manual labor to be done the sufficiency had been scant. My brother and I had taken care of the garden, planted the trees, fed the cows, sawed the wood, and brought it in.

A nobler soul than that elder brother never was. His affection for me had in it something sisterly—it was so tender, patient, and invariably forgiving. I believe my punishments hurt him more than me.

But of all that went to make pleasant life there nothing returns to me so delightfully as my father's part. I have spoken of his love for literature. It was little short of a passion, and he stinted himself in many ways to gratify it. He was a subscriber to all the great British quarterly magazines, and bought the best editions of the best books. The efforts he made to impart his feelings for them to us were untiring. Of contemporary writers, Macaulay commanded his highest admiration. The *Essays,* he declared, were the perfection of English. The impatience with which he awaited the arrival of the *Edinburgh Review* was undisguised; and if the number, at last to hand, contained a paper of Macaulay's, he plunged into it as a hungry child falls to over a bowl of bread-and-milk. Finished, then came one of what we called his readings.

In the summer those readings were given irregularly. They were rather sovereign graces reserved for winter evenings, and then he was accustomed to favor us two or three times a week. We prepared for them. One of us brought in the wood and piled it against the foot of the mantel in the sitting-room. The fireplace was broad and high, and the hearth a real old-fashioned, pioneer hearth. Except as it has been perpetuated in verse and story, its like is vanishing, if not entirely lost. Beginning with the laying of the back-log, the making the fire was an art calling for skill; then, in its initial state of smoke and crackle, the table was rolled forward, the lamp adjusted, and the easy-chair put in place. What matter if outside the snow grizzled the world or the wind blew distempered down to zero? Presently the blaze broke out, the hearth reddened, a new light leaped along the low ceiling and over the curtains of the bed in the corner, and summer shut the doors against the uninvited winter at its back. We were ready; so was the reader.

My father had a face complementary of a beautiful head. A more serviceable voice for the carriage of delicate feeling I never heard. It was of all the middle tones, and remarkably sensitive to the touch of the thought to be rendered. Rather weak for denunciation, in pathetic passages it was like a master ballad-singer's. The featuring and eye-rolling, the mouthing and falsetto tricks of the professional recitationist he abhorred, saying they were unnatural and distractive. I have heard three men whose faces in animated speech suffused with glow suggestive of transfiguration—S. S. Prentiss, Edward A. Hannegan, and David Wallace.

It should not be inferred that in his readings my father confined himself to Macaulay; he gave us the choicest of everything, though, as with all who find pleasure in general literature, he had his favorites. He delighted, for example, in the *Essays of Elia;* Shakespeare and Milton he regarded with a kind of awe. It was from him I first had the full effects of "The Lay of the Last Minstrel" and "Childe Harold." He fixed my standard of pulpit eloquence by the sermons of Dr. Chalmers, Robert Hall, Bossuet, and Bourdaloue. Once he gave an evening to Thucydides, and so powerful was his rendition of the retreat of the Athenians from Syracuse that it has since been one of my exemplars in historical writing. Nor have I yet lost the impression he made on me by Bancroft's exquisite story of the Jesuits in New France. In a word, by his reading he relieved every masterly production to which he addressed himself of heaviness, or, rather, he brought it down to my perfect comprehension.

These readings, it should be further said, did not always occupy the whole of the evenings. My brother and I were frequently required to take the floor and conclude them with declamations. The method pursued at such times permitted us to go through our respective exercises once without interruption and as best we could; after which we were subjected to criticisms covering every part of each performance from the first to the last bow. Of the parts, in our father's opinion, particularly objectionable, repetitions were had until they often ran into laborious drilling. His most peremptory requirement was that we should speak every word distinctly. A man might be awkward in manner, he argued, careless in dress, homely in feature, false in premise, illogical, even ungrammatical, yet a good speaker, if he only enunciated clearly, and was in earnest.

The paternal law allowed us to select the pieces in which we were to appear. If they were unfamiliar to the grave president, he called for the book and held it on us; if we halted in the delivery, he turned us down summarily. On such occasions the audience was privileged to laugh at our discomfiture. Ere long we got beyond "Hohenlinden" and "Marco Bozzaris," and, growing ambitious, advanced to longer themes; such as, in prose, extracts from Webster, Emmet's "Vindication," Phillips's "Washington"; in poetry, Collins's "Ode to the Passions," Byron's "Corsair," Scott's "Marmion" and the "Battle of Beal-un-duine."

I dwell on these things to make it easy to see what life was in the old homestead, and that it was not merely well-regulated and comfortable in the creature point of view, but had an educational side as well. So, too, a stranger will better understand how much I was losing now that I was to cut loose and take care of myself; that, besides the loss of home in the purest sense of the term, I was abandoning the oversight and care of a preceptor whose capacity to instruct was quickened marvellously by his natural affection. What were the new associations awaiting me? Out of the gate into the street, never to return except as guest! I very much fear there was lacking in me the proper appreciation of the solemnity and uncertainties of the crises.

VIII

Enter office of Robert S. Duncan—Buy a gun—Preparation for authorship—Study of grammar—Prescott's *Conquest of Mexico*—Begin *The Fair God*—Dancing-lessons.

THE first thing I betook myself to the office of the clerk of the county, then occupied—and most worthily—by the late Robert S. Duncan, still a familiar name in Indianapolis. After telling that gentleman what had happened, I applied for employment. He gave me a quizzical look and asked:

"You want to settle down, do you?"

I replied, "Yes—if I can."

"You can. Come with me."

He took me into an arched vault constructed for the security of books and papers.

"I'll set you to making complete records."

"I know nothing about the work, Mr. Duncan."

"Of course you don't. I'll show you."

Then, with a patience impossible to forget, he stood by me at a table and initiated me into the mysteries of captions, pleadings, orders, judgments, dates of filing, saying at the end of the lesson, "Now, I'll give you ten cents for every hundred words you write; so that how much you'll make will depend upon yourself."

With that he left me, and presently I earned my first dollar; after which I knew myself secure of bread, and that if, as many believe, the tailor makes the man, it was in my power to be renewed every quarter in the year. The feeling was most comfortable.

Mrs. Elizabeth Knowland, a motherly old lady with whom I had long been a favorite, kept a half-hotel on Washington Street. Miss Jane, her daughter, was music-loving and socially very popular. Besides playing the piano with grace, she always commanded an audience as a singer. It was at one of her "sociables" I first met Lovell H. Rousseau, then a state senator, afterwards captain in the Second Indiana Volunteers, in which capacity he greatly distinguished himself at Buena Vista; still later, in the War of the Rebellion.

One cannot reform himself in a day or week. The old habits persisted in following me into the vault, and pulling at me. I was watchful against dropping back. After the first settlement with my employer, I paid my landlady and had eleven dollars over. The money made me restless and uneasy, and burned in my pocket. I could not keep it, but bought a rifle. Mr. Duncan was the best squirrel and turkey shot in the county. To my great happiness, he approved the purchase and invited me to the woods with him. We returned with good strings of game. My shooting seemed to give me a lift in his estimation. On parting, he asked me:

"What are you going to do with your squirrels?"

"Take them home," I replied.

"That's right"; then he added, quickly: "A gun is a great thing to run away with its owner. Suppose you always come to me when you want to take it out. It may be I can go with you."

I saw in an instant that he understood the struggle upon me and was seeking to be helpful on my side. The management was cunning. In a time surprisingly short the rifle had lapsed into a thing purely ornamental.

Several months passed, and, becoming expert at record-making, I found that beginning nine o'clock in the morning and quitting at five in the evening, with a break-off for dinner, I could write easily three thousand words; or, in direct phrase, that it was in my power to make eighteen dollars a week, and more by night-work. This appeared good, but there was a result even better. I began to be capable of continuous daily labor and of being stern with myself. Nevertheless, a curious discontent crept in on me. Theretofore books had been sedative in their effect; while reading, I had always been able to curl up like a caterpillar asleep or flatten out like a lizard in the sun; now the sight of an old favorite or the title-page of a new publication made me restless. Was I losing my taste? That would have been a calamity; and the very fear of it moved me to a closer study of the matter. I noticed, among other things, the act of composition produced the quieting effect formerly the result of reading. At last the real cause of the malady uncovered itself. In connection with impulses to try something as a writer, I was not doing anything in preparation for the work. There were hours—whole evenings — possible of devotion to the self-education which was now all I could promise myself—time separable without filching from the forenoons and afternoons demanded for actual bread-getting. And I was sharp enough to see the opportunities held in the lock-up of those precious hours. What should I do with them? The question followed me, obtruded itself incongruously, now at the point of the pen on the page of a record, now in the street, now while Miss Jane's skilful fingers drew melodious volumes from the depths of the music behind the ivories of her piano; in the end it lodged itself in my conscience, a prickle keeping it in a state of incessant irritation. To lay the unrest thus occasioned I reached a resolution, though with misgivings of will-power enough to keep it, in the first instance, and of ability to realize what I hoped from the effort, in the next. This was nothing more than a reversion to Professor Hoshour's idea of one teaching himself.

The veteran professor's insistence that all scholars are self-made, school and college courses being but preparatories for the great, final accomplishment lying beyond, was too broad for perfect appreciation, certainly too unqualified for adoption by a young person so unadvanced as I knew myself. Yet the idea seemed to admit of a limited application to my case. It were worth the while, at all events, to seize some of the hours vanishing so unprofitably and give them to an attempt at making myself sufficiently acquainted with the English language to write it grammatically. Then out of the bone-yard of old school-books in the homestead I resurrected a Lindley Murray, and, with the aid of a lamp, in the hush and must of the vault which was the scene of my daily work, I took off my coat, so to speak, and gave an evening to an honest trial of study. It surprised me to find that I could really penetrate to the meaning of rules heretofore opaque as millstones. To be sure, this was one of the results of the whole mind given to a task; nevertheless, I shut the book encouraged and quieted in conscience. The next evening went the same way—and the next; then, ere long, came the habitude; and I made headway—no pun intended—leaving nothing behind not worked out to a fair understanding.

Further on it occurred to me, why not write? All that I worked out of the grammar would then have the reinforcement of practical application. Instead of parsing somebody else, I could parse myself.

By happy chance, one of the latest acquisitions to my father's library had been Prescott's *Conquest of Mexico*, a book of such wonderful brilliance that I devoured it, preface, text, notes, and appendix. As a history, how delightful it was! as a tale, how rich in attractive elements!—adventure, exploration, combat, heroisms, oppositions of fate and fortune, characters for sympathy, characters for detestation, civilization and religion in mortal issue. Who, intent upon it, could relax his inthralment long enough to splatter the narrative with doubts respecting its truthfulness? Small invention was required to develop the possibilities of the theme—tears for Montezuma, and for Cortés admiration overriding maledictions. The progression, in my hand necessarily slow, would require years and years. What matter? The subject could not tire me, neither would it leaden with monotony. Besides, and most conclusive, nobody, to my knowledge, had attempted to dress its history in any of the liveries of fiction. It could not be handled except originally.

These were some of the considerations which determined me—I would write, and the Conquest of Mexico should be my theme.

The conclusion may be thought a trifle by the tyro, since it would seem that I had only to find an easy-chair, and sit, and propel a pen. But with me *The Man-at-Arms* was an experience. It taught me that there was a deal to be done preliminarily. There was a plot to be invented and arranged; that is, taking Prescott's narrative for skeleton, a mass of successive incidents had to be devised and applied as flesh to the skeleton. Then there were characters to be chosen. Of the Aztecs, whom should I use? Of the Spaniards, whom? Next, how can one depict a dead people with so much as an approach to realism unless he first make himself thoroughly acquainted with them — their customs, costumes, sociology, and their political and religious systems? Of the races to figure in the plot he must have all the knowledge obtainable; so of the geography, topography, and vegetation of their country. Here, an especial need, I had to familiarize myself with a great capital city, its palaces and temples, its thoroughfares, all *à la* Venitia; otherwise how could I take a stranger in and out? In such points lie the colors, without which a historical story shall be lifeless as a cosmograph. At that time, perhaps, I could not have stated these things as they are given here; yet I saw them and felt their significance.

Prescott is generous in the citation of his authorities. From his notes, one and another, a student can make a list of all the books upon the conquest, with the names and, in instances, biographies of their authors.[1] I made such a list very early, and was particularly drawn to an account purporting to have been by Bernal Diaz del Castillo, one of the *conquistadores;* and it struck me that what he had to say must have a sanction by virtue of his opportunities as an eye-witness. To get his book took time; at last I had it; and then the two, Prescott and Diaz, were always within touch when needed. Later on, during sojourns in Washington, I annotated the authorities in the Congressional Library, Hervara, Sahagún, and Torquemada.

Such was the inception of *The Fair God.*

It was begun,[2] I well remember, in the vault of the clerk's office in Indianapolis one winter night when

"The owl, for all his feathers, was a-cold."

[1] Of the three volumes of Prescott, I have now but two. The hardest usage fell upon the first. Many of its fly-leaves, margins, and vacant spaces were chock-full of my notes in narrow compression, not a few of them in Spanish; for eventually the spur of necessity drove me to acquire the language. Very naturally I set store by the volume; yet it is missing, and search and inquiry for it have been in vain. By this time, doubtless, the unscrupulous relic-hunter who purloined it feels secure in its possession.

[2] The blank-book, very long and almost as broad, in which the first writing was done is still one of the curios of our study.

There was no thought of publication in the beginning, and during the years until its completion the work continued what it was at first—my reserve pastime. While it was in hand there was always something for me to turn to. It was like the attendant of the Aztec king, in service to amuse and entertain his master. In the cars, at way-stations, of evenings here and there, in breaks of business, I had only to take paper and pencil and my entertainment was ready. In anticipation of such opportunities, it grew a habit with me after a while to carry scraps of paper in my pocket to receive such jottings as appeared worthy a place in the manuscript; or, wanting them, I utilized envelopes and blank spaces in letters for the purpose. A singular facility was the outgrowth. The last writing might have ended in the middle of a sentence, yet weeks after, whether on the street or in an assemblage, I could begin where the stop occurred and go on exactly as if the manuscript were before me.

References to *The Fair God* will be met hereafter; for the present, it may be useful to others who, in the routine of daily tasks, dream dreams and open and shut the windows of imagination to remark that the story and the work upon it went, as it were, hand in hand with the grammar until the latter could be safely laid aside.

To leave here an impression that I sank into a recluse and gave myself entirely to study would be deceptive. In confessing a love of amusement, it is only saying truth that I hunted it diligently and in all its lawful diversities.

In the winter of '43 a wandering dancing-master opened school in Indianapolis, greatly to the delight of the young society. Together with the usual Terpsichorean accomplishments, he taught a new science—the

Science of Manners. The worthy professor was his own object-lesson. He clung to the old fashions, wore frilled shirt-bosoms, silk stockings, and pumps ablaze with silver buckles. He also made his own music. "The Fisher's Hornpipe" with which he sped a quadrille was tearing enough to have quickened the bones of the unknown in a catacomb. He enrolled me a pupil of his academy; and, simple as the topic looks, I am bound to say there was never such a tempest of fun as when he called us out one by one to practise bowing, hat salutes, and posturing seated and standing. Since the day of his advent, I have read and heard much of Colonial society, Colonial dames, Colonial beaus, and of their stately mannerisms. No one, I yet think, ever reproduced them to the life like our old Do-ci-do. In a minuet he always made me think of France and the king in a ballroom imposing form upon his courtiers—so solemn and grandiose was his deportment.

IX

The military companies—"Marion Rifles"—Sham battle—Henry Clay—Reporter for legislature, 1844-5—Studies law with his father.

A MILITARY company known as the "City Greys" had been organized in Indianapolis under the captaincy of Thomas A. Morris,[1] then a recent graduate of the academy at West Point. Its success led to another company, of which I had the honor to be elected second sergeant. When mounted upon my sleeve, the chevron was to me significant of a dignity to excite the jealousy of the great Caius Julius. Nor did any of us think of unfitness attaching to our captain because to don his uniform on parade-days he must needs step down from a tailor's bench. We adopted the name "Marion Rifles."

The differences between the companies were not of a kind to foster what the French call *camaraderie*. The Greys were solid men, verging many of them upon middle life; the enlisted of the Rifles were mostly incapable of mustaches. The uniform of the Greys was of rich cloth; that of the Rifles consisted of a cap, a cotton hunting-shirt, blue and yellow fringed, and fashioned after the style bequeathed to the American people by General Daniel Morgan of Revolutionary renown. The Greys carried muskets with bayonets; the Rifles, Hall's patent breech-loaders. The Greys timed

[1] In the Civil War, Major-General Thomas A. Morris, to whom all the credit of the early successes in West Virginia was really due.

their steps to the sonorous music of a brass-band; the Rifles were contented with the fife and drum. The Rifles despised the aristocratic airs of the Greys; the Greys laughed at the Rifles, and the good-natured contempt could have been endured had they stopped with it. Their last insult was the nickname "Arabs."

We waited a long time for a chance to punish the Greys. At last a sham battle between the companies was hippodromed in celebration of January 8th, with Washington Street for scene of action. We were posted at the intersection of Meridian Street, facing eastward; while, turning from Delaware up by the court-house, the enemy moved to the attack in column of sections, their band playing vociferously. Their appearance was beautiful; and it was then I first knew what inspiration there is in white handkerchiefs shaken out by fair hands from overlooking windows. The Greys opened with volleys; we replied, lying down and firing at will. All went well until in the crisis of the engagement our captain forgot to order the retreat provided for in the schedule of manœuvres. The mêlée that ensued was tremendous. Wads flew like bullets. We shot one man, took several prisoners, and were left masters of the field. At sight of the haughty foe in flight I yelled my throat into tatters. The incident is, of course, trivial; yet it was of consequence to me. It put a final finish upon the taste for military life by turning it into a genuine passion. It was my initiation into the Ancient and Honorable Order of Soldiers.

About that time a first volume of Scott's *Infantry Tactics,* published by order of Lewis Cass, Secretary of War, fell into my hands. The find of a diamond in the mud had not made me happier. Everything—work, visitation, rest, sleep — was put aside; so that soon I saw myself taking on the graces of a drill-master.

Those were proud moments when the captain condescended to advise with me about points determinable in the school of the soldier.

Of the things of this period to make a lasting impression upon me, not the least by any means was the coming of Henry Clay to Indianapolis. To realize the gravity of this event, the generations risen since 1844, when it took place, must be reminded of the greatness of the man, and that of all living at the time none had the same hold upon his contemporaries—none was so utterly detested on the one hand, none so nearly adored on the other.

Mr. Clay was "swinging around the circle," a candidate for the presidency. When it went abroad that he would come to Indianapolis, there were no bounds to the expectations excited. The high grounds at the east end were selected for the function. That the thousands might see and hear him an open platform of unusual elevation was built. His entry was along the national road of which he had been projector and congressional godfather. A barbecue was celebrated in his honor; that is, a herd of fat cattle was slaughtered and roasted over fires in superheated pits. Both the military companies escorted the distinguished guest to the mansion of Governor Noble.

The crowd was up to the most sanguine hope; and when at length there was not in all the multitude a hungry man, woman, or child, the speaking began.

Mr. Clay was of a personality once seen never to be forgotten. Tall, slender, graceful, he had, besides, the air majestic which kings affect, imagining it exclusive property. Yet he was not a handsome man. The largeness of his lower features was a serious detraction. His forehead was retreating; the skull narrowed in its rise to the crown; his ears were loby, his eyes heavily overshaded, his cheek-bones of almost aboriginal prominence.

Throughout Mr. Clay's performance my eyes scarcely left his countenance, which, as he proceeded, sank from sight until, by the familiar optical illusion, nothing of it remained but the mouth, and that kept enlarging and widening until it seemed an elastic link holding the ears together. Indeed, at this late writing, my one distinct recollection of the man and his speech is the mouth and its capacity for infinite distention.

The visitation is historically known as a failure. Mr. Clay arrived in bad humor, spoke in bad humor, and departed in bad humor. It was only natural that his auditors should catch his mood.

The legislature (1844–5) brought me an interesting experience. Some work of mine descriptive of social events in the city having drawn the favorable attention of Mr. John D. Defrees, editor and proprietor of the Indianapolis *Daily Journal*, the recognized organ of the Whig Party in Indiana, he proposed that I should report the House proceedings for his paper. The employment was novel and the pay to my satisfaction, so I gladly accepted the offer, Mr. Duncan kindly agreeing to reserve my place in his office.

At the end of the session I had been initiated into legislative methods, besides being wiser in parliamentary law. If not an expert in the subtleties of the manual, such as the previous question, the amendments, and the precedencies, I have congratulated myself often at finding how easy it is to brush up on the law in anticipation of an immediate need.

I have many pleasant recollections of that reporting, not the least of which was the somewhat lucrative business I drove doing small literary jobs for members of the House. They had resolutions to be drawn, committee reports wanting revision, bills to be formulated. In every such body there are the incapables and the capables and the capables weak or lazy. My patrons were of the first and third classes, and, as a rule, I found them liberal paymasters.

My eighteenth year seemed a long term, given, as it was, the days to work and the nights to study. I could, in likelihood, have found some relief against the tedium in society, but its charms passed me by. To be perfectly candid, I had doubts of the welcome in wait for me. My reputation for outlawry had not been lived down. Of the prophets who had appointed me to the gallows there were too many still in the flesh loaded with reminiscences.

Days off were infrequent, but still given to the old haunts along the creek and river, for there I could be alone. Even then, however, the rod or the gun was counterbalanced by a book in pocket. If the squirrels were shy or the bass out of humor, they were not allowed to spoil the outing—Byron and Scott were just as good in the greenwood as in a furnished library.

Meantime *The Fair God* grew in interest as well as bulk. Montezuma, Guatamozin, Mualox, Hualpa, and Tecetl had admitted me to intimacy; and on the sea, much more than were clairvoyant spectres, Cortés and his *cidelantados* passed the time not devoted to their steeds watching the Tabascan coast and speculating upon the mines and *haciendos* awaiting them in the vast perspective of the unknown called Mexico.

Now, too, more distinctly than ever, I felt the impulses of manhood in near approach. The ego in me began its wrestle with the question, probably the most serious of life to every one not in condition to exist without labor—what am I to do with myself? A fine speech, a bit of good writing, something brave read of in the world of action, had often a disturbing effect; and then, were I in the vault, work upon the record under hand turned into a process like nothing I could think of so much as pouring precious wine into a rat-hole. In the years to come, who would ask for the book or for the clerk whose days it had converted? Was I to be always a copyist?

It happened that my elder brother had already entered himself with my father a student of law. Why should I not do likewise?

With what may be called the economy of the law office I had been familiar from childhood, and its routine had always appeared to me the champion horror of horrors. That, however, was but one side of the practice—its ugly side—and I shrank from it. On the other hand, often as I held the opposite at angles for study the routine vanished. Appearances in court, for instance, with their accessories—judge, jury, the public, and the commonwealth behind them—was there an occupation so fascinating to a soul confident in itself to the superlative of vanity? Then, dropping the mere personal consideration, was there a progressive movement in organized society or a useful scheme involving co-operative energy, from a town ordinance to a continental railway, that had not its fashioning and finish from a lawyer? And as to the stepping-stones in politics—well, ideas of the sort caught me, and I determined to take to the law.

Now my father was a methodical instructor. With him it was not enough to acquaint one's self with general principles; the law, he held, had a language of its own, and to be an advocate, especially in argument to a judge, ability to speak that language fluently and with correctness was indispensable; so, by his requirement, the student must begin by reducing Blackstone to questions and answers, then, by memorizing, with recitations to him on Saturdays. In comparison with such tasks, how trifling the tax upon the memorative powers of an actor! Yet the system attracted me. There were flattering possibilities in it, and I joined my brother in the study.

Thereafter, for a year or more, the flow of life became regular, each day in incident like its predecessor: breakfast; then the dissection of Blackstone or *Chitty's Pleading*, in the method mentioned, continuing through the day; dinner and supper; and night and *The Fair God,* with book diversities. Not seldom day, stealing softly through the windows of the office, found me asleep in a chair. When a bill fell due, or there was need of clothes, I presented myself to Mr. Duncan, and always, with unfailing good-nature, he pointed to the vault and bade me help myself.

In the spring following my entry as a student I commenced *practice*—so, by grace, I call appearances before justices of the peace, pettifogging being a term obnoxious to all *lawyers.*

X

First law practice — War with Mexico — Interest in war news — Examined for attorney's license—First conflicts with the Mexicans—Captain Charles Mav—Governor Whitcomb—Judge Isaac Blackford.

To practise in a justice's court with so little preparation, assurance in large measure was more needful than a formal license; and, looking coolly back from my present stand-point, it must be confessed that I came to my full share of the quality early. The business brought me was of the misdemeanor class in criminal law, and now and then a civil cause with bad feeling between the parties for motive. Of defences in proceedings for violation of city ordinances I made a specialty. Sometimes I went into the country. Sometimes, also, I confronted old lawyers whose very justifiable contempt for my presumption I offset with an audacity they did not always know how to meet. It is creditable to the average judgment that their sympathy, where it has room for play, is generally with young fellows offering front to professional seniors. Most frequently, however, my antagonist was a John Quarles, about my age. He was a great lawyer in promise. I doubt if he could talk as fast and loud, yet he had from nature a managing knack that kept me in wholesome awe of him. Usually we had good audiences. Indeed, we agreed that there were instances in which our clients resorted to the law quite as much to hear the enemy abused as for the profit discernible in the proceeding. Quarles's early death was a poignant sorrow to all who knew him.

So, in the spring of '46, the summons of need which required me at the clerk's office was of lessening frequency. A pettifogger of some local renown, I was actually making money; yet, withal, I pounded away at the text-books and *The Fair God,* and was feeling the ease of mind which is a first cousin of contentment, when an unexpected interruption came along.

A history of the war with Mexico would be a departure from the purpose of this work. While full of honor to our arms, it now excites no interest, not even in military circles. My connection with it, moreover, was very humble, insomuch that I view the term of service it had from me as a mere passing adventure, and prefer to so treat it. The most I dare with the general occurrence is, as I go along, a daub here and a scumble there, much as impressionists paint pictures.

That our government would be eventually drawn into the Texan revolution was in the air, a perceptible haze along the horizon south; and if, through the haze, statesmen of the South saw political advantages—the extension of slavery, for instance, and additional votes in the United States Senate—and reached out to realize them, *that* was not treasonable. At length, following the lead of France, Congress, in 1839, recognized the independence of Texas.

For ten years, then, annexation vexed the country. Should the new republic be taken into the Union? Just as the decade was expiring the gate was opened to her. There had been plenty of time for the American public to inform itself upon the question.

It is my opinion now that the war with Mexico, the first consequence of the admission of Texas as a state, was justifiable; this because of a fact lost sight of in the wrangling of the period. Certain European powers coveted the new republic. France went so far in her intrigue as to make recognition dependent upon an engagement that the latter should not join the United States,[1] and the proposal was energetically supported by an influential party of Texans. Which was preferable—Texas a state of the Union, or Texas a subject of a French protectorate? [2]

If our government was forcing war with Mexico, as is charged, it was certainly easy-going. It tried negotiation, but the Mexicans were violent. In August, four months after annexation, General Zachary Taylor, sailing from New Orleans, established a camp at Corpus Christi. His "Army of Occupation," as he facetiously called his command, consisted of part of a regiment of infantry. Shortly after he reported a Mexican army, under General Arista, moving from Monterey to Matamoras. This was menacing; so, in October, Taylor was reinforced with five regiments of regular infantry and some cavalry and artillery, most of the latter without guns. Early in February he set out for the Rio Grande, instructed carefully to avoid a first act of hostility. In March, he was at Point Isabel. On March 28th, his army pitched its tents on the Rio Grande opposite Matamoras. That is to say, from March 1, 1845, when annexation was resolved on by

[1] President Polk's first annual message.

[2] "But Texas had passed definitely and finally beyond the control of Mexico; and the practical issue was, whether we should incorporate her in the Union or leave her to drift in uncertain currents—possibly to form European alliances, which we should afterwards be compelled in self-defence to destroy. An astute statesman of that period summed up the whole case when he declared that it was wiser policy to annex Texas, and accept the issue of immediate war with Mexico, than to leave Texas in nominal independence to involve us probably in ultimate war with England. The entire history of subsequent events has vindicated the wisdom, the courage, and the statesmanship with which the Democratic party dealt with this question in 1844."—*James G. Blaine.*

Congress, it took more than one year to push a small column of troops to the farther edge of the land in debate. And it was not a far cry, either.

Returning now to myself, it will be difficult, I think, for persons not themselves filled ardently with a spirit of adventure to understand the passionate interest I took in the Texan business from the time of General Taylor's departure from New Orleans. His destination was unknown to the public further than that it was some point on the coast of Texas.

But where? The coast was long, and the stopping-places few—Galveston, Corpus Christi, Brazos de Santiago, and the mouth of the Rio Grande. If he disembarked at any point west of Corpus Christi, it was understood that the Mexicans must fight or surrender their opposition. The uncertainty was more than interesting—it plunged me into a fever of excitement. I wanted the war, thinking of little else, and I went about hunting news and debating the probabilities. I haunted the *Journal* office, squeezing its exchanges for all they had to say upon the subject. My pockets were plethoric with newspapers, especially those of New Orleans and New York. Every bit of discussion, every scrap of intelligence was eagerly devoured. Where would the expedition land? Denial and qualification aside, I was hungry for war. Had I not been reading about it all my life? And had not all I had read about it wrought in me that battle was the climax of the sublime and terrible, and that without at least one experience of the kind no life could be perfect?

At length General Taylor was heard from; he had landed at Corpus Christi, on the western shore of the Nueces Bay. Descriptions of the camp established there were suggestive of live-oak groves in festoons of flying mosses, and of gardens gay with tropical enrichments—

all well enough but for the air of permanency that pervaded everything. When people once get settled in paradise it takes wrenching to get them away. This, together with the other circumstances, that the camp was pitched on the very edge of the territory in dispute, left the main question absolutely void of favorable probabilities. It seemed that the event most within my wish depended upon the Mexicans, and I despaired —so small was my faith in their hardihood. With the wane of faith in a belligerent outcome, I returned to study.

To become a recognized lawyer every student in that day was required to procure a license, issuable or not after an examination for which he was free to apply to the Supreme Court or to the judge of a Circuit Court. A license from the former was preferable, partly because of the greater honor attaching to it, but chiefly from the fact that the privileges conferred were more extensive. Enrolment in the Supreme Court entitled an attorney to rights of appearance in all the subordinate courts of the state. I determined to try for admission there.

The making ready comprehended a thorough review of the text-books and a degree of familiarity with the revised statutes. Who could tell through what lanes and byways, not to speak of travelled roads, the learned examining judge would lead me? I addressed a note of application to the court, and received notice that a hearing would be allowed applicants on a given day. A room in the state-house was designated for the purpose.

My confidence in the result was not overweening. I was strong in Kent and Blackstone, and fairly so in Starkie, but weak in Chitty and Equity Pleading. A consciousness of this sapped my confidence, and as the day of trial drew near I grew nervous and cowardly. It was one thing to beard a justice of the peace in his den, and quite another to confront a chief-justice of the Supreme Court. Still, I believe the venture would have gone well but for an intervention which, if it did not actually rob me of much I really knew, plunged me into a state of indifference as to the outcome. The effect of the incident may be likened to that of a sudden squall upon a small boat under too much sail.

Word came up from Texas that General Taylor had razed his beautiful camp on the Nueces Bay, and, with a force enlarged to the proportions of a respectable army, was in full march for the Rio Grande River. This was the occurrence so malefic upon me.

That there would be war was no longer doubtful. The Mexicans were in force waiting—so much was already known. I was to have my wish. There would be a battle, then other battles. Hurrah! Of what consequence was a license to practise law? How petty the soul which could be screwed down to prefer a court to a camp! A light went out that night in my father's office. The books which had occupied me became offensive. I shut them, and laid them away—perhaps forever.

The order for the movement of the army westward had proceeded from the War Department in the beginning of February. On the map the space to be traversed seemed trifling; yet the month went out, and nothing determinate. Then the middle of March. Why the delay? I was hot with impatience. It looked as if a snail could have made the distance in the time. I knew nothing then of the desert nature of the country through which the columns toiled—desert in everything but the tufted gray grasses which at that season lent character and complexion to the land.

At last news—this time positive. Taylor had reached Point Isabel. Then—in a day or two, I think—his army was in camp on the Rio Grande opposite Matamoras.

In what followed I lost not a point—not the most trivial incident. The insolent protest of the mayor of Matamoras—the fire at Point Isabel, and its extinguishment by our cavalry—the blockade of the mouth of the river by our vessels—the hasty erection of Fort Brown—the correspondence with the Mexican general Ampudia, so bombastic on his side, so dignified on ours—the arrival of reinforcements at Matamoras — then Arista's assumption of command of the Mexican army—these, and more like them, I stuffed into my budget of evidence of a collision inevitable and close at hand. Presently General Taylor, leaving a garrison in Fort Brown, marched his army down to Point Isabel. Simultaneously Arista crossed the Rio Grande and cut communication with the fort. Then I knew Taylor was bound to make an effort to save the garrison, and that on his return for that purpose the opposing armies must meet.

I read of the murder of Colonel Cross, and of the mysterious disappearance of Lieutenant Porter and his twelve infantrymen out on a reconnoissance. Then came the story of Captain Thornton, told with sad but curious details—how he set out with a squadron of dragoons looking for the enemy—how while working through a close chaparral he found himself penned in with lariats tied to trees in front and rear—how, after a gallant fight, he and another captain surrendered. The country, all unused to war, stood aghast, and vented its spleen on the Mexicans by denouncing them for treachery. As if ambuscades were new things in war!

These preliminaries, so wholly unrelieved on our side,

were of good consequence, notwithstanding. They induced the government to lend a willing ear to General Taylor's call for reinforcements.

News travelled slower in that day than in this. There was an interval without intelligence from the army. That something of importance had happened everybody knew. Taylor was not a man to let an opportunity slip him. There had been a battle, but the uncertainty deepened the intensity of feeling. All the United States may be imagined on tiptoe, holding breath to hear.

Then came the report of Palo Alto, clouded by the death of Major Ringgold. The States breathed long enough to shout victory without relaxing their anxiety. The enemy had simply retired to another position.

Resaca de la Palma occurred next day, and it was decisive. The Mexicans never stopped flight until securely behind the yellow flood of the Rio Grande. Then all the land between that river and the Nueces ceased to be debatable. It was reduced to possession, and there is no title so perfect as that of conquest.

Gallantries! Why, that battle of Resaca was illuminated with them. I thrill yet thinking of young Churchill lugging his eighteen-pounders from position to position with oxen, geeing and whoa-hawing them along the smoky, grape-swept prairie merrily as a Wisconsin logger. And there was May's heroism. Some one has pronounced it a myth; if so, it is one of the myths that do men good, and ought for that reason to be perpetuated. An infantry officer was forming his company to charge a battery, when down came May at the head of his dragoons, crying, "Hold!—hold on there! Let me draw their fire!" Next moment he was amid the gunners, with La Vega a prisoner. Prior to that he had been Captain May, but the people drew him from the mass and promoted him to Charley—Charley May.

At breakfast a few days after the battle of Resaca some one said there was a rumor in town of a call for troops by the government. This was what I had been hoping and expecting. I could scarcely wait the hour when the adjutant-general of the state might be encountered in his office. Then, promptly, I interviewed the gentleman.

Prior to that day the adjutant-generalcy had been bare of importance, because without patronage or a decent salary the title was its only attraction. The office had its habitat in the state-house. I call it "office" in lack of another word more exactly descriptive. There being no organized militia, why an office, or, for that matter, an adjutant-general?

David Reynolds, the incumbent, was a good-looking person, stout, rubicund, affable, who had not yet appeared in uniform. He knew nothing military, and, to his credit, he made no pretension to such knowledge. His appreciation of the title even needed cultivation. He was intelligent and willing to learn. I found him in a flustered state not unlike that of a mother hen unexpectedly visited by a marauding hawk. There were a hundred things to do—blanks to be prepared, books to be opened—everything, indeed, that ought to have been done long before, and that would have been done but for lack of the needful appropriation. A corresponding inexperience on the part of the governor heightened the confusion of the staff-officers.

A statue in bronze of James Whitcomb, governor of Indiana in 1846, is a conspicuous object in connection with the soldiers' monument at Indianapolis. As a tribute to a citizen who happened to be chief magistrate at the outbreak of the war with Mexico, it is well deserved. I had the good-fortune to know him, though at a distance. His position was too exalted for familiar acquaintance with so young a man. He was a lover of books. His fine library was useful as well as ornamental. It was a certificate that his reputation for learning and scholarly attainments was deserved.

There were certain peculiarities of taste and habit which impressed the governor upon me. He was a musician who, like Thomas Jefferson, did not disdain when in privacy to ease himself of care by the exorcism there is in a violin masterfully dominated. He knew how to pass from a melody of Tom Moore's to a plantation jig, and to bring out the differences between them. He was also a smoker. With him there was no obscuration to thought in the ring blown dexterously from his lighted cigar. Smoking was his only dissipation. He excelled in exhausting a cigar to its least possible dimensions; sometimes he thrust a knife-blade into the abbreviated remainder. It was even said he sometimes resorted to a pin.

His picture in the state library is a better likeness of the first war governor than the statue under the monument. If in speaking of him one confines remarks to his abilities as a statesman, the choicest terms of eulogy may be used with propriety; but he was not a soldier.

I found Adjutant-General Reynolds in a mood communicative. The mail of the day preceding had brought the governor an official notice that Congress, besides formally declaring war against Mexico, had appropriated ten million dollars to carry it on, and authorized the president to call out fifty thousand volunteers.

This was great news, and I made haste to ask:

"Will any of the troops be from Indiana?"

"Yes, that's what's bothering me," the general replied. "We are asked to furnish three regiments—and the business is entirely new—no forms, no precedents—nothing for our guidance."

I was shaking with excitement.

"Well," I asked, "can any one raise a company? Or must authority be first had from the governor?"

"I suppose any one can go about it; only when raised it must, of course, be tendered to the governor for regimental assignment and muster-in."

I went out resolved to raise a company, if no one older and better known did not set about it.

By a singular chance, as it appeared to me then, this very satisfactory turn in the Mexican business happened about the time appointed for my ordeal before the Supreme Court. The thought of the latter now set me to shivering. The weeks which should have been devoted, day and night, to persistent review had been taken up with Scott's *Infantry Tactics*. The precious contents of the law-books, when I tried to look back over them, refused to rise at call. What I really knew had become gelatinous pulp in the cells of my brain. To be sure, the reserved right of withdrawal from the examination was still mine; yet I resolved to make the trial. The license, if I won it, would not spoil.

Accordingly, on the day stated, I attended at the state-house. Court was in session, and the bench full. I looked at the array with creeping of the spirit. One of the judges was well known to me, and I to him. Our acquaintance came about in a way to make it lasting.

Some years before, this particular judge had taken lodgings and an office in the mansion-house already spoken of as obstructing the Governor's Circle. Thither his brethren of the ermine, by invitation, were in the habit of flocking for consultation; and a very quiet place it was, except on occasions. The basement of the house was a vast, unlighted cellar, filled with boxes, barrels, and a débris of such varied ins and outs as to be dangerous, if not quite impassable, to the unfamiliar.

It had the reputation, moreover, of being haunted. A workman was said to have been buried in it. Yet a few of us—boys, of course—used it as a rendezvous to amuse ourselves with the judges. When they were assembled, and buried in study or loud in debate, we would raise thunder by punching the floor beneath their feet with scantling and long poles. Their yells but stimulated the charivari. In point of sensitiveness, what is the nerve of an eye worth, and in delicacy what is a Sèvres cup, in comparison with the superfine thing called judicial dignity? With the rush of the tortured, easily heard overhead, we sought our hiding-places and in spasms of delight bided their fierce pursuit. Shall I speak of profanity? And from *them?* But they turned the joke. The sheriff of the court, with a support of bailiffs, lay in wait for us one day. At the first thump of our staves on the floor they seized the doors and, with lanterns, fished us one by one out of the débris. With an inconceivable hardness of heart, the myrmidons took us up-stairs and before the judges. There I made the acquaintance of Isaac Blackford and Charles Dewey, in the annals of Indiana the first, last, and greatest of her old-school judiciary. From that day the reciprocity of recollection between them and myself continued without a break.

I made myself easy as possible until the adjournment of court. The lawyers hustled out of the chamber, and then the judges departed, all but one. An officer remained with him. Looking round, I beheld my fellows of the ordeal, twelve or fifteen in number. We advanced and stood in a body outside the railing. As we did so, I observed the clear, gray eyes of his honor, Isaac Blackford, rest on me with a look so sharp and cold it shot me full of rigors. He had waited a long time for what the baseballists would call his *innings.*

At last it was come. Would he make a worm of me and thread me on his hook? Was he so mean? Had I believed it, I should not have stayed.

The judge did not make a speech. From his seat he told us to follow an officer.

The room into which we were then taken had been prepared. There were tables and chairs, and in front of each chair writing materials in complement. As we passed in, the bailiff, standing by the door, took our names and gave each of us a package sealed and addressed.

"You will take seats," he said, adding, "I am instructed by the judge to see that you do not communicate with one another. When you finish your answers, put them in envelopes, and seal and direct them and give them to me. You have till court meets in the morning."

The worthy thereupon coolly lit a pipe and took a chair near the door.

I presume the questions furnished the several members of the class were the same in number and purport. We read them, and then began our replies. The silence was broken only by the scratching of pens. At supper-time we were allowed out. About two o'clock in the morning I delivered my contribution to the drowsy detective at the door, and sallied forth, leaving a number of my fellow-sufferers still wrestling with the conundrums.

I was not at all satisfied with my work, and at the foot of the last page appended a note, the flippancy of which makes my face burn as I now write:

"*Hon. Isaac Blackford, Examining Judge:*

"DEAR SIR,—I hope the foregoing answers will be to your satisfaction more than they are to mine; whether they are or not, I shall go to Mexico.

"Respectfully, LEW WALLACE."

If the judge were wanting an excuse to punish me, I had furnished it. Two or three days afterwards I received a notice through the post-office:

"Supreme Court-Room, INDIANAPOLIS.

"*Mr. Lew Wallace:*

"DEAR SIR,—The Court interposes no objection to your going to Mexico. Respectfully,

"ISAAC BLACKFORD."

The communication was *un*accompanied with a license.

XI

Opens recruiting-office in Indianapolis for volunteers for war with Mexico—The company leaves for New Albany *via* Edinburg in wagons—Three Indiana regiments encamped at Camp Clark—Colonel Drake—Henry S. Lane—Landing in New Orleans—General Jackson—Voyage to Brazos—The turtle—Ship.

THERE was much talk in Indianapolis about volunteering. Other parts of the state were showing activity. I bustled about, interviewing members of the "Greys" and "Arabs." To my argument that the term of service was short, only one year, some of them, with an earnestness implying personal experience, replied that a year was ample time in which to die. Finally, in fear of the passing of the opportunity, I resolved to open a recruiting-office myself. The town could not more than laugh at me.

So I took a room on Washington Street and hired a drummer and fifer. Out of the one front window of the building I projected a flag, then a transparency inscribed on its four faces, "FOR MEXICO. FALL IN." I attacked the astonished public in the street. The first round was productive. A dozen or more young men fell into the procession. Within three days the company was full.

In the election of officers, James P. Drake was chosen captain and John McDougal first lieutenant. The second lieutenancy was given to me. Upon acceptation by the governor, we were ordered to the general rendezvous at New Albany, on the Ohio River.

In addition to the townfolk, the population of the entire country seemed present at our departure from Indianapolis. Lawyer John H. Bradley made an affecting farewell address. Mexico was a long way off, and the journey thither beset by dangers of sea and land. There were thousands who shook hands with us as with men never to return.

We were taken in wagons to Edinburg, up to which a railroad had slowly crawled from Madison. The railroad is only so called. In reality it was a tramway.

The solemnities of the public farewell scarcely moved me. That which excited sorrow in others did but stir my imagination. Nevertheless, a circumstance broke me down. We went afoot to the wagons. My father marched with me. He was in the prime of manhood; a soldier by education, he should have been at the head of the whole Indiana contingent. At my side, keeping step with me, he trudged along through the dust. The moment came for me to climb into the wagon. Up to that he had kept silent, which was well enough, seeing I had only to look into his face to know he was proud of me and approved my going; then he took my hand and said:

"Good-bye. Come back a man."

Suddenly I gave him a shower of tears.

On the northern shore of the Ohio, midway between the present cities of Jeffersonville and New Albany, there is a ground famous in history. A wooded island at the foot of the falls used to be its *vis-à-vis*. There General George Rogers Clark held high revelry after his style, master of all he beheld—a brave, ambitious, profane, drunken, baronial Virginian. There the three Indiana regiments were assembled, organized, equipped, and mustered into the national service, my company being assigned to the First Indiana Infantry, letter

H. The rendezvous was appropriately named Camp Clark.

In the election of field-officers for my regiment there was but one ticket: for colonel, James P. Drake; for lieutenant-colonel, Christian C. Nave; for major, Henry S. Lane; and there was no scratching. I remember being puzzled by the absence of contest. My experience was then too limited to help me comprehend the bit of furniture called a *slate.* Here is the slate of that day: Brigadier-General, Joseph Lane, *Democrat;* Colonel, First Regiment, James P. Drake, *Democrat;* Colonel, Second Regiment, William H. Bowles, *Democrat;* Colonel, Third Regiment, James H. Lane, *Whig.* Certainly the able Democratic governor knew how to provide for himself and his party.

Sergeant Charles C. Smith, a school-mate, fine-looking and clever, was by my nomination promoted to the vacant first lieutenancy, McDougal becoming captain. As a rule, jealousies among men come with years and competition.

The three field-officers are now in their graves. Neither of them selected could have carried his company through the manual of arms.

Colonel Drake was rich in good-nature—possibly too much so. He had a presence, however, to excite respect, especially on horseback, and an uncommon aptitude for tactics. In three months he had mastered the "School of the Battalion," according to Scott, whose system was then in force, and brought his command into excellent drill and discipline. In the rush to the color-line under alarm, his face would redden and shine like a harvest moon; and then, in the wake-up by the long roll at dead of night, his voice was wonderfully cheering. Ultimately he emigrated to Georgia and ended his days there an honored and useful citizen.

The command and its responsibilities never devolved on Major Henry S. Lane. Successful at the bar and in politics,[1] he was singularly careless as a soldier. On parade he often appeared with his sword and sword-belt in hand. He hated a horse; so that on the march his saddle was always pre-emptible by the sick and foot-sore. For a shirk he had the eyes of a detective. In his kindness, even, he was reserved and dignified. No one knew better than he that with volunteers, at least, respect for an officer is more essential than fear. He was the soul of honor and brave to a fault; and so was he esteemed by the regiment that his indifference to formalities, though sometimes laughed at, was always forgiven.

The company officers were far above the average. Some of them were remarkable men. Captain Robert Milroy, in the Civil War a major-general, dubbed by his division "Gray Eagle," must be mentioned with particularity. A graduate of the Partridge Military School, then next to West Point in reputation, he was one of the very few whom I have met actually lovers of combat. Eager, impetuous, fierce in anger, he was a genuine colonel of cavalry. In fence with sabres his wrist was like flexible steel; besides which he had a reach to make another swordsman, though ever so skilful, chary of engaging him. This I know, having been one of a class under his instruction.

I have dealt somewhat elaborately with the few officers named in order that the *verve* of the regiment may be understood. At the end of six months it could have been depended upon for heroic action under the most adverse circumstances—and, as will be seen, the remark is not made conjecturally. Few commands

[1] Henry S. Lane was afterwards governor of Indiana and United States senator.

have been subjected to trials so bitter; yet it did not weaken or falter in discipline.

On July 5th rations were issued and the arms and accoutrements stowed in the hold; then, with colors flying and "Yankee Doodle" from fife and drum, we marched aboard the steamboat chartered to take us to New Orleans. There were many of the regiments with sombre countenances; probably they had a better appreciation of the hazards to which we were going; but for my part the situation was full of joyances. Now, indeed, I was a soldier. My name was on the roster and the national uniform on my back; the surroundings, all martial, kept me reminded of the life at last certainly arrived.

I have made voyages since, some of them on the seas to far countries, when every hour was charged with novelties and delights unspeakable; yet they were as views by moonlight pale in comparison with this one, so full of the zest of youth that even the Mississippi River was beautiful and its low-lying ugliness of flood and forest successions of miraculous mirage. Mexico, the land of Montezuma and Cortés, and its people, and the campaign through palmetto lands and wide *pasturas,* and battles and the taking of cities — I was to see them—all else faded into the commonplace.

At New Orleans we were landed below the city to wait for ships. There we had our introduction to soldier life, mask off. Of dry ground there was not enough for a bed. We had not a wisp of straw. Our blankets turned into blubbery slime. The officers were responsible. They should have held on to the steamers.

Along with the rest, I was wretched until an old negro peddling eggs and chickens visited us. He told me casually that we were occupying a portion of the field Andrew Jackson turned into a garden of glory in 1815.

Then I hired him as a guide. The battle-ground was more interesting to me than the city. Where was the breastwork of cotton? Where did Jackson's line begin on the right? In what direction did it stretch? That line fixed, I had the key to the fight; standing on it, I faced the British assaults, and in the patriotic indulgence of fancy cared not a whit whether I was on a slippery tussock or knee-deep in water. Four killed here; two red-coated thousands yonder! Sir Edward could have afforded a month of manœuvring for some other point of attack than this one. His haughtiness was a piece with Braddock's; so was the penalty.

Three ships were at last warped to the bank of the river; then, getting our mouldy regimental properties stowed, we thanked God for a blessed deliverance and sailed for Brazos Santiago, on the other side of the gulf.

A Baltimore clipper-built brig, new, sweet-smelling, clean, and fast, was assigned to Company H and two others, Lieutenant-Colonel Nave in command. The sea has always been kind to me. Throughout the transit I kept the deck without a qualm of the terrible *mal de mer;* and when, in the second night out, the lights of Brazos rose to view, I saw them with downright regret.

Of that outing—there may be too much familiarity in the word—there remain to me two distinct recollections. One of an enormous turtle on its back on the deck under a tarpaulin. To my landsman's eye the creature was a curiosity of itself; what stamped it on my memory, however, was the use and treatment to which it was put. Twice each day of the voyage the cook resorted to it to supply the officers' table—in the morning for steak, in the afternoon for soup—and when we landed the animal was alive.

The moonlight of the nights was of a whiteness to shut out the stars. Once I was roused from sleep and brought to my feet thrilled through and through. A strange object within pistol-shot was moving swiftly in a direction the opposite of ours. It seemed indefinitely large and high. The silence of its going deepened the mystery. It acted as if self-controlled. Then I realized that it was permitted me to see a spectacle fast disappearing, and the most imposing and majestic of the apparitions of the sea—a three-mast merchantman, full-rigged, every sail set, and laden so deep that the light waves gave it no lateral motion. On it went, glacial white, mountain high, deathly still, a spectral, gliding glory of moonlit space. Whence was it? Whither bound? Whom did it serve? It passed, vanished, and made no sign. When now and then the curious ask me of the beautiful things I have seen, even the most beautiful, I astonish them by honoring that ship. My standards of the sublime are few—it is one of them.

XII

Brazos—Death of Reck—The camp at the mouth of the Rio Grande —Sickness—Suffering—Burials—Major Lane appeals to General Taylor for relief.

THE brig laid off shore during the night. Next morning, early, I went on deck to take a look at Brazos. An inlet scarce wider than a canal let into a bay three or four miles wide. On the farther shore of the bay a snow-white tower of fair elevation arose apparently out of the water. The tower I came to know as a light-house on Point Isabel, General Taylor's base of operations against Matamoras. A chain of low dunes or shifting sand-hills ran parallel with the beach, hiding the landscape behind it; and the dunes were naked, except that here and there a vine sprawled itself out too verdureless to cast a shadow. One hut, with a chimney of barrels, half buried in a sea of driftage, and curtained roundabout by hides drying in the wind and sun, was all that spoke of human habitation. There, they told me, Padre Island terminated, while all south of the inlet constituted Brazos de Santiago. No town, no grass, not a tree. Heavens, what an awakening!

Now, I did not keep a diary, and it is too late to invent one—this in relief of all who follow me through these pages. But my memory serves me respecting two orders—the first one from Brigadier-General Lane, and it sent us to Camp Belknap, ten miles above the mouth of the Rio Grande.

There I went one day to the river. With me were

Luther Reck and John Anderson, who had been for years my closest companions. Indeed, they enlisted to be with me as much as anything else. At home we had been given to the "dare" habit; and the deeper the water, the thinner the ice, the longer the run, the hotter the blaze, the more certain the challenge, which had with us an unlikeness to the ordinary practice in that the challenger was bound to go first.

The Rio Grande nearing the gulf is always angry-looking. That day it was in flood. We stood idling awhile on the bank. The sun was at noon, and hot. Then Anderson, "What do you say to a swim?"

"No," I answered, "this is not White River."

Then he, old-time-like, "I dare you to follow me."

Our clothes were off in an instant. Anderson plunged in first. I called to them to go with the current diagonally. The pull was long and trying. At last we drew to the opposite shore, Reck behind, but striking out vigorously. All at once he screamed. We looked back in time to see him rise half out of the water, then sink. I marked the spot, and, with Anderson, made for it. The drowning generally rise twice; so we swam round and back and forth—uselessly, we never saw our friend again. He had gone down cramp-struck—down like a stone never to rise. We reported his loss in camp and to his mother, and it was many weeks before we, the survivors, recovered spirits enough to talk of the death. I doubt if Anderson ever forgot that he was the challenger.

The second order—from General Taylor, then in headquarters at Matamoras—sent the regiment into garrison at the mouth of the Rio Grande.

It is not amiss for me to say here that I accept the wisdom of the dispensations generally accredited to God as among the highest proofs of His being and goodness. Had we known in advance—I speak illustratively—what all of misery and humiliation there was awaiting us in that camp to which we now marched, I think it not unlikely that despair would have unloosed every bond of discipline and sunk our eight hundred good men into an ungovernable mob. In all my reading of American wars, the colonial included, I cannot recall another instance of a command so wantonly neglected and so brutally mislocated. A description may be useful. If it prove unpleasant reading, I make no apology. They to take arms hereafter should have a standard by which to measure the worst conditions possible to their service.

The camp, it is to be said, was not of our choosing. We inherited it from the First Mississippi Volunteers, Colonel Jefferson Davis commanding. As we marched in, they took to steamboats going up the river. I remember yet the sense of desolateness that shocked me viewing the place for the first time.

On the right of the camp, defending it from the sea, were sand-dunes like those at Brazos; its left was a few hundred yards in remove from the river; on the north it faced a reach of land level as a floor, treeless, apparently interminable, and subject to overflow by the tides. Across the river a ragged Mexican hamlet nicknamed "Bagdad" harbored a band of smugglers. The landing, calling it such, afforded mooring for vessels, mostly lighters. Occasionally a steamboat came down from Matamoras, staying long enough to take on supplies. From Brazos the mails were sent to Point Isabel, thence to headquarters, wherever that might be, leaving delivery to us a thing of chance. McGahan, I think it is, describes the Kirghiz out of the world, as were we—only they were nomads.

All the drinking-water to be had was from the river,

a tepid mixture about thirty per cent. sand and the rest half yellow mud. Against the purgative effect of a full draught there was nothing available except a pill of opium.

The ration, of tri-weekly issue, consisted of beans, coffee, sugar, pickled pork, and flour or biscuit; no vegetables — not even onions. The biscuits, disk-shaped and alive with brown bugs, were often subjects of sarcastic play—the men on inspection frequently substituted pieces of them for gun-flints. Occasionally parties went hunting, returning sometimes with a maverick over-ripened in the portage home; our main reliance for fresh meat was shrimps taken in the river.

A monotony descended upon the camp—a monotony unrelieved as an arctic night, as telling on the spirit as the blue mist of the plague Weyman tells of in his *Gentleman of France.* Now and then we heard of operations by General Taylor. A steamboat-man would stray in among us with the news. General Taylor had set out from Matamoras for the up-country; then had taken Camargo, the enemy having abandoned it; and thereafter, with a regiment in garrison at Matamoras, there was not the slightest need of us where we were—none earthly. A post-guard of twenty men would have been ample to hold the mouth of the Rio Grande, admitting it an indispensable depot of supplies. Occasionally, too, an inspector came down and took a snap-look at our tents from the guard of his steamer. So, directly, there was not a soul among us so simple as not to see that we were practically in limbo; then, to complete the wretchedness of the situation, a disease planted itself in our midst.

A vulgar name and anticlimacteric, I grant; yet he who has seen a man sicken and die of chronic diarrhœa shall always shudder at the name, though he live a hundred years. How the scourge got into our camp, whether by the river, or by the spoiled pork we ate, calling it meat, or by the bad cookery which was the rule with the messes, or by all these causes in combination, which I think the most likely, were idle conjecturing. Not less idle would it be saying this one or that was responsible for its introduction. Let me rather tell how it wrought upon us.

The soldier may have been in perfect health the day we went into the camp, which, singularly, was never named; at roll-call, three weeks having passed, I notice a change in his appearance. His cheeks have the tinge of old gunny-sacks; under the jaws the skin is ween and flabby; his eyes are filmy and sinking; he moves listlessly; the voice answering the sergeant is flat; instead of supporting the gun at order arms, the gun is supporting him. Observing the signs, I know without asking that he has been to the surgeon, and that the surgeon gave him an opium pill—I know it from knowing that in the meagre schedule of medicines at command there is no other corrective for diarrhœa. Another week and his place in the ranks is vacant. A messmate answers for him. No need of looking for him in the hospital. The post is a fixed one, yet there is no hospital of any kind. It will go hard with him, one of six in a close tent, nine feet by nine, for the night will not bring him enough of blessed coolness to soothe the fever made burning through the day. His comrades not themselves sick are his nurses. They do their best, but their best is wanting, not least in the touch which every man once mortally ailing recollects as the divine belonging of mother or wife. A delicacy of any sort would be a relief; he prays for it pitifully, and they bring him the very food which laid him on his back in the first instance — bean-soup, unleavened slapjacks, and bacon. Another week and he is giving his remnant of strength to decency. At last he has no vigor left; mind and will are down together; the final stage is come, and—the pen refuses to go on.

As to the loss of life, I cannot give the number. There were days when a dress parade with two hundred present was encouraging—weeks when funerals were so multiplied upon us that the hours between sunup and sundown were too few—that is, for the customary honors. Then night was drawn upon. There is no forgetting, try as I will, the effect of the dead-march rendered on fife and muffled drum at night, heard first faintly and scarcely distinguishable from the distant monotone of breakers. And if, as sometimes happened, the corporal led his squad just outside my tent, the hour and the hush and darkness turned the music into a stunning tremolo of thunder.

Nor did our trials end always with the end of the sick man's life. The supply of lumber for coffins was soon exhausted; so were the gunboxes and staves of cracker barrels to which we next resorted; a little later we were driven to the use of blankets for shrouds. And even then the poor men were not always allowed their natural rest in the sands of the dunes where we laid them, for the winds, blowing fitfully, now a "norther," now from the gulf, thought nothing, it seemed, of uncovering a corpse and exposing it naked.

Skill in pathology is not required to divine the effect of such conditions upon the men. Probably there were not ten of them in the regiment who had seen the ocean or any part of it before taking ship at New Orleans. For a while to walk along the beach, to chase the crabs and be in turn chased by the breakers, to gather shells and dissect the stranded nautili was jolly fun, being all so strange. But the fun was short-lived, and when it wore out there was nothing left to do except speculate upon what was to become of them.

Once in a while some other regiment would come from Brazos. The sight of them marching by, flags flying, drums beating, and hurrying aboard boats as if they smelled the contagion in our camp or feared an order for them to stop and take our place, was maddening, and presently led to a general belief that we were victims of an unfriendly discrimination at headquarters of the army or that there were traitors among us. Still—and I write it with becoming loyalty—there was never a round-robin or a refusal of duty, never so much as a military propriety disregarded.

As to responsibility for all this suffering and death, I only know it was wrong to blame Colonel Drake. All in his power to do towards saving the well from falling sick and the sick from dying he did. One day—it was when General Taylor was at Matamoras—the colonel sent for Major Lane. I heard the conversation between them.

The colonel said: "Surgeon J——s has just been here to report that the supply of medicines with which he started from New Orleans is almost gone, and that his repeated requisitions for more have received no attention. If kept here much longer, he says the sick will all die. The condition is too bad. I am ready to try an unsoldierly thing."

"What is that?" the major asked.

"To go to Matamoras and see General Taylor."

"Without leave?"

"Yes."

The major shook his head doubtfully.

"What will you say to him?"

"That there is no reason in keeping the regiment here, now that Matamoras is ours. I think he should know, too, exactly what its condition is. There certainly can be no harm, then, in asking General Taylor to let us go up the river with the column of advance, or, at least, change to a more healthful camp."

The major answered, promptly: "Very well. I will go with you, if you say so."

They went next day. The major's plea, it was said, was unusually fervid. Unfortunately, the general was not used to such eloquence; either that, or to his perceptions, dulled by long service, the solicitation was as much a military offence as outright protest. Anyhow, we were left to our misery.

XIII

The march to Monterey—Attempt to go with the army—Paris C. Dunning—An instructor in tactics—The episode with Stipp.

General Taylor, as I now remember, set out from Matamoras against Monterey in September. Up to the last minute I persisted in believing he would take the First Indiana along with him. At length a man of the commissariat gave the *coup de grâce* to my hope. He told me in an interview that the army already under orders to move was greater than could be well supplied beyond Camargo. To Colonel Drake he showed memoranda of an estimate of rations for the expedition pared down to the narrowest limit. A little figuring on the basis of the estimate was conclusive. *We had been left out.*

It is hard for me now to understand the state of mind into which I then fell. The operations of the army filled my thought. My imagination painted them in the most exaggerated colors. The route would lead hundreds of miles into the interior of the country, by rivers, along fertile plains, over mountains, through villages and towns, ending at the City of Mexico, said to be the most beautiful capital in the world. There would, of course, be opposition and occasionally a battle. By report the people inland were superior to such as we were meeting on the frontier, and the superiority kept increasing in steady ratio. If my fancy disdained the soberness of fact, if it permitted no suggestion of danger or defeat, if it wilfully converted deserts into gardens, and adobe towns into fair Sevilles, it should be remembered apologetically that my story of *The Man-at-Arms* had been of Spain and Spaniards, and that in the manuscript of my new work I had left Cortés on the causeway about to make his first entrance into Tenochtitlan.

To this mood, of the intensity of which I was not at all conscious, I lay one of the most serious of the follies marking my beginning.

There are young fellows who should be kept apart, a continent between them; unfortunately, the reasons for keeping them apart are generally reasons for their coming together. Such were Charley ——— and I. He was a second lieutenant, like myself, though a trifle older. He, too, had an almost insane desire to see a battle; our conferences upon the subject had been latterly of daily occurrence. I went to him now with the intelligence that our regiment was to be left out, and said that to be in at the taking of Monterey we must cut loose and do for ourselves. He agreed with me. Then, to raise money for the venture, we decided to sell our pay accounts to date. The sutler, we thought, would be happy to discount them. If we could not get passage on a boat, we could buy horses and overtake the cavalry who were to march overland.

Now nothing could have been more certain than that our appearance with troops anywhere would have led to inquiry and to our instant arrest as deserters. We considered that possibility — so much is due to our common-sense—but agreed that it was one of the risks of the scheme. We argued, also, that we were going with the army, not away from it.

The sutler upon whom we waited offering to sell our pay accounts was Paris C. Dunning, whose portrait may be seen in the gallery of governors, part of the state library at Indianapolis, a rare presentment of intelligence and amiability. He heard us in his private tent; and when we were through he gave way to a violent fit of laughter, as he well might; becoming serious presently, he refused peremptorily to buy our accounts; then, after lecturing us upon the enormity of the military offence we were contemplating, the results of which would be disgrace to our families and friends, he concluded: "Now, young gentlemen, if you pledge me your words of honor to drop this project, your coming to me shall never be known; if you refuse, I will at once notify Colonel Drake. I give you three minutes for decision."

We looked at each other a moment. Each saw that without money the journey was impossible, and that there was no person else in camp of whom we could safely ask it. We tried to laugh; he was serious; and directly we gave him the parole. He kept the faith with us, and I still hold him in grateful recollection.

The snubbing Colonel Drake and Major Lane had from General Taylor must have been a severe trial to those worthy officers. Nevertheless, thinking the regiment would be better of employment as a diversion from its hard conditions, the colonel had published hours of service, requiring squad and company drills in the forenoon and battalion drills in the afternoon. Then, curiously, I dropped into disfavor with the men of my company—in plainer speech, I became desperately unpopular.

Our arm, it will be recalled, was a heavy muzzle-loading musket of Revolutionary pattern, and the tactics (*Scott's Infantry*) smothered by details. Only a student with positive aptitude could master the latter. Loading, for instance, other than at will, was by twelve commands. If, on this account, there was need of patience on the part of an instructor, how much greater the need on the part of the soldier, out in the sun, his person swathed in a closely buttoned woollen coat overlaid with three broad belts—one at the waist, the others crossing his breast and back! Imagine the man listening with attention, his blood at boiling-pitch! It turned out, in short, that my superior company officers had neither taste nor inclination to attempt the tactics, and they threw the duty of instructing the company upon me.

The progress made won me compliments. Had I been older, my intentions would have been credited to me; but men do not like being taught by boys, so it befell as said—I became generally odious, and there were threats of shooting me. The circumstance was the more regretful because I was then too inexperienced to know that the anger which caused my fall is a malady peculiar to recruits—a malady less serious because it eventually cures itself.

This, to my great relief, did not last. The incident which restored me to favor is stranger even than the circumstance that caused its loss.

The up-country ten or fifteen miles from our camp was all a saline plain broken here and there by what we called islands. These, rising abruptly from the dead level twenty or thirty feet, and a mile or two across, were covered with a rank growth of vines, shrubs, and pretentious trees, the verdure of which furnished cropping for wild cattle the year round. They were also good haunts for Mexican guerillas, who, sneaking across the river, were occasionally seen on our side.

Now, I was of those who when off duty killed time hunting—it was such a relief to get away from the horrors which locked the regiment in so terribly.

An account having reached me of an island unusually large, with vegetation more than semi-tropical and a spring of cool, white water at one side, I thought it too distant for the easy-going forager, and that possibly it might be stocked with game enough to pay. So, with four men and the necessary leave, I set out one day to try it. We provided ourselves with guns and cartridges, a frying-pan, a coffee-pot, haversacks well filled, and three canteens of water to the man. Just as we passed the line of sentinels private Perry Stipp came up and asked to go with us.

Stipp, it is for the saying now, was physically and morally a bogie who ought not to have passed muster. He was humped before and behind, had arms like a gorilla, eyes limpidly blue, a fighter unwhipped, the bulldozer of the regiment. More particularly, he was ringleader in the war on me; and in threatening to kill me he had not thought it needful to speak privately. The colonel had been advised to discharge him as a lunatic who might some day take it into his head to run amuck. In fairness, however, the advice was not mine.

I looked Stipp in the eyes, thinking of his threats, and told him to provide himself as we were and overtake us. Whatever his motive in asking to go with me, it seemed a good time to have it out with him, only I should be careful.

The men, glad like myself to get away from camp, talked freely while we were going—all except Stipp, and him I kept in front, always in eye. About four o'clock the island we were seeking rose in sight. A profusion of palmettos, both cabbage-head and of the fan variety, gave it character. It was also bolder in elevation and of broader spread.

"Hello!"

This was from Stipp—his first word. We all stopped.

"What is it?" I asked.

"There—don't you see?"

Some men came out of the thicket on the edge of the bluff. There were sombreros among them, and parti-colored ponchos, and guns glistened distinctly.

"Mexicans," Stipp said next, bringing his gun to the ground. I caught his eyes, bright and steady as candles burning in a well, and knew, instinct interpreting, that he thought he had me in a corner. It was for me to say forward or back; if back, my standing was gone. I resolved to turn the table and try him.

"Are they Mexicans?" I asked.

"I should say so," Kise answered, speaking for the party.

"And there are twenty of them, at least," Edwards added.

"Well," I said, "if there are so many armed Mexicans near camp as this, the colonel should know it. Now you four stay here, ready to make for camp—Stipp, you and I will go on."

A queerish expression which I took for doubt or surprise appeared on his face; but he raised his gun and we started.

"Look!" he said, as if I were not looking.

The party on the bluff disappeared; after which they were to be imagined in ambush.

Two hundred yards from where the unknown were last seen—and not a shot. Were they making sure of us?

One hundred yards. My flesh began to crawl. Stipp's teeth were clinched.

Now we were at the foot of the bluff, and it was time for the *finale*. Then Stipp stopped.

"Not here, Stipp," I said, knowing his nerve going. "We are dead men if we stop here."

He fell in behind me.

The ascent was difficult, and on the top—nobody. With my cap I waved come on to the four still where they had been left.

They joined us and we all set out to find the Mexicans. The sun was going down when we reached the brink of the island on the opposite side to that by which we had come. Then we noticed a smoke rising. Creeping on, and looking down from the height, we saw a party from our own regiment out hunting like ourselves. We had magnified their number nearly a third. Some of them wore sombreros and blankets Mexican in style. They had found the spring, and were making coffee and roasting veal for supper. We joined them, of course.

In camp a few days afterwards there was a row and an arrest. I inquired about them. Some one had opened on me in Stipp's presence, and he thrashed the man so he had to be carried off. Stripp also gave notice to everybody who didn't like Wallace that he was for him.

That was enough. The wind veered and blew my way again.

XIV

The march to Walnut Springs—The church robbery at Cervalvo—The inquiry—The doctor's confession on the return.

AT last General Robert Patterson set foot in the camp at the mouth of the Rio Grande, and, after an informal review of the regiment, gave Colonel Drake an order in writing to proceed to Walnut Springs near Monterey, where General Taylor had headquarters.

To Camargo by river about two hundred and ten miles. From Camargo by land to Walnut Springs one hundred and eighty miles. The sick to be left in hospital at Matamoras. It may be believed when that programme was published there was celebration, every man according to his bent—the religiously disposed thanking God, while those of another tendency hastened to the sutlers for flowing bowls. It may be believed, also, that there was not an hour lost in getting away from the scourged post. As we had relieved the First Mississippi, the Second Mississippi relieved us—but not to stay.

When my father bade me, in the farewell at Indianapolis, to come home a man, I am sure he did not leave the injunction with me thinking I could so far forget him or myself as to become a party to the robbery of a church. That, however, was exactly what happened at the town of Cervalvo on the road from Camargo to Monterey. The story will be admirably illustrative of two phases of life—one, how a man can involuntarily aid and abet in the commission of a crime shocking to none more than to himself; the other, the degree to which enthusiasm in the practice of an honorable profession can pervert one's moral nature.

Cervalvo, on account of its fame for beauty, was one of the inspiring promises of the country between Camargo and Monterey; and on reaching it the promise was so generously realized that a day of rest was taken there. I still recollect how, being unused to mountains, those about that site seemed to glorify the earth. Nor did I wonder less at the inhabitants showing no alarm at sight of us. Indeed, I could not understand them until it was explained that there was a padre up in the cathedral, a really holy man, who exercised a kind of paternal government over the members of his diocese, and had such influence that they only knew of the war by standing in their doors and seeing the armies go by.

We had with us a contract surgeon from Georgia—Macon, I believe—educated, agreeable, unusually gifted in smothering his "r's"—a veritable Knight of the Dissecting Table. His references had been excellent.

Shortly after it was given out that the regiment would remain at Cervalvo for the day, the doctor came and proposed to me that we go and see the cathedral, an overture to which I was the more willing because the padre had already called on the colonel with an interpreter, and, while paying his respects, considerately said he would be pleased if the officers would do him the honor to walk through the house. It was quite old, and he was confident the pictures would interest them.

The air that morning being of the mountain variety, I put on an overcoat, while the doctor wrapped himself in a cloak of dark cloth.

At the door we were met by a Mexican, bareheaded, clothed from head to foot in a gown tied at the waist.

He could not speak English nor we Spanish. I was afterwards told he was not a priest, but a custodian called sacristan. The first thing he would have us see was a room on the right of the door of entrance. We found it spacious, well lighted, scrupulously clean, cold, and unfurnished except with a table on which, under a glass cover globular at the top, there was a human skull. I noticed on being taken to the table that the guide twice crossed himself, from which it was a fair inference that the relic was of special sanctity. Why it was so he could not tell us, though he tried to with earnestness. The glass cover was free of dust, the skull itself white, perfect, and a remarkably attractive specimen. Its owner must have been of high endowments, mentally and morally—that is, if there be verity in phrenology.

We passed from the chamber of the skull, the sacristan leading the way. As I went out the doctor whispered to me: "Follow him. I will join you directly."

The pictures were not all equally good. A few were of masterly production. While we were examining the altar, the candlesticks of silver, the spangled effigies of the Virgin and Child, the guide doing his best in explanation, talking volubly, his soul intent, the doctor joined us. Finally we took leave, the sacristan going to the door with us.

On the way to camp the doctor seemed in high spirits. He criticised the pictures; they were daubs, he said, some of them vilely irreligious in treatment. He laughed at the custodian, and denounced priests generally as frauds and hypocrites—preachers of ideas libellous of God. Within the lines we separated, each going to his quarters.

In an hour or thereabouts the padre reappeared in camp accompanied by the sacristan and the interpreter.

Seeing them go to the colonel's tent, I went there, too. Besides the colonel, the major and the adjutant were present. The visitors were excited. The sacristan at sight of me whispered to his superior, who thenceforward kept me in observation.

This is the substance of what the padre said to the colonel evolved slowly through the interpreter. In Mexico and other Roman Catholic countries, he said, it was customary to render honors to the memory of deceased founders of churches and cathedrals. Their bodies were laid away with impressive ceremonies. In time the skulls were taken up, and kept in the edifices of their building for the veneration of communicants through generations. The exalted father to whom the world was indebted for the cathedral of Cervalvo had received such honors. Only that morning his skull had been in its usual place on exhibition under glass in the first room at the right-hand after-entrance of the holy house. But now, the padre proceeded, the relic was not to be found, though the most diligent search had been made for it. Immediately that the disappearance had been reported to him, he hurried to make it known to the colonel, not doubting that he would exercise his authority in effecting discovery of the robbers and return of the relic. The prayers at the old altar were of value, and they should be for his excellency the colonel as for a second founder.

The colonel asked the padre gravely if he wished to be understood as accusing any of his officers or men. The padre replied diplomatically that he had not knowledge to justify a direct accusation; his object was merely recovery of the skull, and he could see no offence in desiring inquiry to be made of such officers as had been to the cathedral that morning. He was confident they would all reply honorably to questions. He begged to add that the keeper of the house had shown him two young gentlemen who had been through it within an hour and a half, of whom one had worn an overcoat, the other a cloak, and it was directly after their departure that the loss had been noticed.

"Could the keeper recognize them?" the colonel asked.

The padre looked at me, and returned, "The sacristan here who guided them through the interior tells me the officer at your excellency's side is one of them."

This was bluntly done; but repressing every show of feeling as well as I could, all eyes being upon me, I requested the interpreter to ask the padre if he meant to charge me with the offence. The padre made haste to say no. Thanking him, I then admitted having been conducted by the guide present. I admitted having worn an overcoat, and requested permission to go and get it. Returning with it on, I asked the guide if this was the coat. He said it was at least of a like kind.

"Were you not with me from my entrance to my going out?"

"Yes."

"Did you not attend me and my companion to the door?"

"Yes, sir."

"Look at me now with the coat on," I said, stepping and turning before him—"look, and explain how it was possible for me to have walked with you, stopping at the altar and the pictures, and come away with a bulky thing like the skull under my coat, which was without cape, as you now see it."

His replies were accepted as conclusive of my innocence, and the affair was in the way of a happy ending when Major Lane ventured a question of me.

"You had company to the cathedral, I think you said?"

"Yes."

"Who?"

"Dr. ———."

I have seen the expression, half a smile, that came over the major's face then, on the faces of lawyers when in cross-examination they thought they had struck a promising pointer.

"What kind of a coat did the doctor wear?"

"He wore a cloak," I returned.

The major and the colonel exchanged glances. Both of them saw a motive in the doctor which I could not have had, since it was professional; they also saw how an object like a skull, which was of size, if not weight, could have been concealed under the loose folds of a cloak. The colonel sent his orderly to request Dr. ——— to come to him immediately.

There was an explanation when the doctor came, during which his countenance was a study. He confessed having gone to the cathedral with me wearing a cloak, and that he had seen the skull under the glass cover. He even admitted thinking, while looking at it, how ornamental it would be under such a case in his office at home, and how useful to students and others interested in craniology. Then, with becoming vehemence, he denied the taking, and requested the colonel to have his tent and effects searched. That the padre might be satisfied, he invited him to be one of the examiners. In short, the impression left by the new suspect was favorable to him. I was confident of his innocence.

Nevertheless, the colonel sent for the officer of the day, and presently that gentleman, with the sacristan as witness, overhauled the doctor's quarters, discovering nothing like the relic in question; after which the visitors left, the padre profuse in thanks and apologies.

Some days afterwards, while descending the Rio Grande going back to Matamoras, as will be narrated, Dr. ——— was detailed for duty on the same boat with myself. From the hour his quarters had been searched, he had not alluded to the affair of the skull; but as I was passing the door of his state-room once, he called to me, and I went in.

"See here," he said to me. "Something to interest you."

Lifting the lid of a box doing duty as a trunk, he took out a parcel of bulk with wrappings of heavy brown paper and a stout hempen cord. A little work at the tie of the cord, and he produced the skull and gave it into my hands.

"Good God, Dr. ———! And you did do it?" I said, shocked clear through.

He laughed heartily, then explained:

"It's a beauty, isn't it? I had it under my cloak all the time that Mexican idiot was showing us round. I knew pursuit would follow; and quick as I got into camp I made a package of the find, dropped it into a mess-kettle, and gave a teamster half a dollar to hide it in his feed-box. Not wishing to compromise you, I didn't let you into the secret sooner. A lovely piece of furniture for my office. What good was it doing there? Think of it in my hands! Practical science is of more worth than sentiment. You'll say nothing, of course."

I kept his secret.

XV

Order to return to former camp—General Taylor's act—Lieutenant-Colonel Nave resigns—Major Lane elected to his place—The killing of Captain Thornton—Carvajal—The attack on Old Reynosa—The town spared—Gratitude of the women—The serenade.

THE last afternoon of the long march under General Patterson's order came. The world and the sky had turned to dust since we left Cervalvo, so there was but one hue to be seen, look where we might—that of dirty ochre. And now it was three o'clock in the afternoon, and only six miles to Walnut Springs, where we were to become in reality a part of an army, a consummation long devoutly wished.

Our feet were sore, but that was nothing; our hearts were light. Suddenly the column jammed into the advance-guard, and there was a halt. Then a courier rode to the colonel and delivered a despatch to him, and he read it—read it twice. The second time he kept his saddle unsteadily, his face much redder than usual. Something had hit him hard, yet he managed to give commands; and when we were faced front, aligned, and brought arms ordered, he began to read the despatch just received, but choked, and called the adjutant, a young man, who took the paper and finished it; and when he was through we all stood dazed. Some demonstration would have ensued, I am sure, but the colonel recovering made haste to put us in motion by the left flank, whereas we had been marching right in front. In plainer words, easy for people not soldiers,

Walnut Springs, to which we had been sending our thoughts bright with high hopes, was now behind us, and we were to double upon our tracks back, clear back, to the accursed camp at the mouth of the Rio Grande, eating, as it were, the three hundred and ninety miles we had come.

The order had proceeded, of course, from General Taylor. In all the files thus turned back there was not a man so dull as not to know that he and his regiment were being punished; on the other hand, had the brightest of the lot been asked what the punishment was for, he could not have replied with a suggestion, though his life depended upon it. My own opinion now, with experience to help me, is that General Taylor was governed by one of two motives: either he was reminding Colonel Drake of the unofficer-like request he and his major had made of him at Matamoras, or he intended a reprimand of General Patterson for his assumption of authority in giving the order of march.[1]

Whichever surmise is correct, one thing is not less true—the general who could serve innocent soldiers of his command so scurvily, allowing them under such circumstances to get within two hours of his camp, after a movement of such length and labor, must have been of a soul which no successes could have made great.

The proof of discipline is obedience, not cheerful obedience. After a while I suppose the regiment came to my way of thinking—that we had an outing anyhow.

[1] Years afterwards, when under command of the same General Robert Patterson, ascertaining that he remembered giving Colonel Drake the order to march to Walnut Springs, I asked if he had General Taylor's authority to give it. He answered no; that he acted from pity, having never seen men in the service in such a state of neglect and suffering. He doubted if General Taylor actually knew of the condition of the regiment, and upon that assumption he had acted.

Lieutenant-Colonel Nave, in deep resentment, resigned, whereupon the four hundred and odd survivors hastened to elect Major Lane to the vacancy.

On the way to Camargo we were overtaken by another order from General Taylor materially modifying the first one. Colonel Drake was to send two companies of the regiment to the mouth of the Rio Grande; with the rest he was to take command of Matamoras. This put us all in better spirits.

The descent of the San Juan and the Rio Grande rivers being now before us, Company H, with three other companies, embarked on the steamboat *Enterprise,* Captain Milroy in command of the detachment. Four days were thought time enough to make Matamoras, and on that supposition rations were issued. At the close of the fifth day, we were scarcely half-way to our destination, and hanging with our boat's nose over a low bank. A famine struck us, and it became necessary to forage. Five men went out in search of cattle. Two of them came back soon to tell how the party had been ambushed, and that they had barely escaped, having left three of their comrades dead.

The captain of the boat was taken into consultation. He knew the river and the region, and from him it was learned that Old Reynosa, a town of bad repute, lay off the river three or four miles, and that it was the haunt of General Jesus Maria Carvajal, whom everybody recollected as the famous guerilla who lured Captain Thornton into the fatal lariat-trap down by Fort Brown in the beginning of the war. The inference was safe, we thought, that Carvajal and his band had murdered our foragers and were then in the town.

Captain Milroy now showed himself to advantage; only instead of ordering us, he buckled on his sword, jumped ashore, and called for volunteers, declaring he would recover the bodies of our men first, and then burn the town, and if we could catch Carvajal, the natives should be treated to a hanging in imitation of Haman's. The four companies responded to a man. Even the boatmen begged for guns that they too might go. One company was left to keep the steamer.

The dead men were found horribly mutilated. Tearing through the brush, then, we reached the town, where, as a glance disclosed, the advantages were all against us. First, a stretch of meadow-land; then a bluff fifteen or twenty feet high, its face gullied by rains; at the edge of the bluff on top a palisade of tree-trunks set side and side, and taller than our heads; behind the palisade the enemy—how many we could not see. I could see their guns glistening in the sunlight. So, by the signs, I had stumbled on my first fight, though at the moment too much excited to recognize the fact.

There was a brief halt while Milroy arranged the attack. Then, in double files, and with a yell, we rushed across the meadow. I was in command of Company H. Heavens! What furnace heat there was in that go! We reached the foot of the bluff, and not a shot had been fired at us. How I got up the face of the bluff I do not know; how over the tall palisading I would never have known had not some of the men afterwards spoken of the boosting they gave me. And then the disappointment! The Mexicans ran out of the town into the chaparral on the other side faster than we could get into it.

The barking of dogs, the only creatures that offered fight, and the screaming of women and children running in and out of the doorways, were stunning, but not enough to keep us from following the *ladrones* and pelting them with fire and yells. At the edge of the chaparral they stopped once and gave us a ragged round that spent itself over our heads. That stop was of better avail to our quick-sighted ready squirrel-hunters.

Now the sight of men lying in their blood on the ground, one killed and four wounded, was new to me; and when we got to them and the wretches began praying to us in their unknown tongue for life, my feelings, I confess, underwent a sudden revulsion, and out of pity I would have interfered for them had there been any need of interference. The change, which was general on our side, may have been accelerated by the women who ran to the scene from all parts, and on their knees, and with tears and the most piteous moans and cries, joined in the supplications of the wounded. Then, when Captain Milroy ordered the men to be carried into the houses, and it was done instantly and tenderly, the women ran to their kitchens and got us dinners of baked beans, corn-cakes, and *carne seca* (dried beef). Nor was that all. When we paid them for what they gave us, I thought they would have been glad to have us stay longer.

Carvajal escaped,[1] and the town was not burned. Regaining our boat without molestation, we buried our dead on the bank of the river. Experience had hardened us not a little against death and burial; but thinking of it now I can see all the grewsomeness of that sepulture. Poor boys! They had their mourners at home, if not there.

We were lucky enough while returning to secure four beeves, fat for that part of the world; and the current of the river having kindly washed the sand and loam

[1] Further on it will appear that at one time later I had much to do with General Carvajal. I asked once why he did not fire on us while we were crossing the meadow. His answer was a good one. "I saw you had men enough to take the town, and thought it best not to fight on account of the women and children."

from under the keel of the steamboat, it was soon in motion. In the evening of the tenth day of the voyage, the four companies disembarked at Matamoras none the worse of the wear.

There was little to except to in our new quarters. We needed a rest, and had it; even drilling in the plaza in the heart of the city, treated as work, had its social counterbalances. *Bailes* were of nightly occurrence. The ultra-fashionable of New York and Boston might have smiled at the Mexican belles who were the bright lights on such occasions; nevertheless, in waltzing only a belle of Madrid could have excelled them. To natural grace and perfected sense of time, they added matchless endurance.

Those days in Matamoras, enlivened as they were by incidents illustrative of the life led there, were not without pleasantness.

To me, at least, one of the most delightful and touching occurrences was a serenade. The city lay in the hush of midnight, deeper for the military occupation it was undergoing. Much I fear even the sentinels slept on their posts. Suddenly a burst of music rose clear and high through the silence. The harmony rushing wavelike into the quarters of my company—the legislative hall of the state of Tamalipas—startled us from sleep, and we hurried to the balcony overlooking the plaza and listened. The air was "Hail Columbia," in magnificent rendition by a brass-band. We peered through the moonlight, straining to make the musicians out, but they were under the towers of the church opposite draped impenetrably in shadow. What band was it? We had none. How came it there? I heard with tears in my eyes and an unwonted commotion in my heart. I was transported home, and stung to the quick by a reminder of how rapidly it was wearing out in my recollection. The players gave but the one number, and at its conclusion disappeared mysteriously as they had come. Morning brought an explanation. A steamboat with the band of the Second United States Cavalry aboard had touched for supplies at the city, landing in the night, and, having an hour at disposal, the men had mounted their horses and stolen into the plaza. That there were such depth and touch in the old air had never before entered my thought.

There are few things that amuse me more than the freshness of youth, a quality which I now suspect must have been mine in large share: for what else was this?

Urvea, a Mexican general, appeared between Matamoras and Victoria with four thousand lancers, sent down by President Santa Anna to raid General Taylor's long line of supplies. It was reported, also, that Urvea was watching to strike us. This put Colonel Drake on his mettle. Among other precautions taken, he ditched the corner of the plaza, and had us practice with the six-pounder field-pieces, the target being two cracker barrels set one on the other. I was out with the guns one day and it came my turn to shoot. A flock of sheep happened to be moving across the flat about three hundred yards away, grazing as they went. Calling for a spherical case-shot, while it was being rammed home I made a hasty guess at the distance and the elevation required to reach the flock; then, all being ready, I suddenly swung the gun round, took a glance over it, and fired. There was mutton next day in nearly every mess-kettle, and compliments poured in on me in a shower. The third day, however, the colonel sent me his compliments. Would I please come to him? A matter of business. I complied, of course, and he put a bill in my hand from the owner of the slaughtered sheep. I protested, but without avail. The shot cost me more than half a month's pay; and thenceforth I knew a regimental laugh peculiar in that it takes such a time to cool and quit.

XVI

The First Indiana at Walnut Springs—General Taylor—The camp at Walnut Springs—A visit to Monterey—An adventure in the chaparral—A test of courage—The first panic.

AGAIN the First Indiana drew near Walnut Springs, still the site of General Taylor's headquarters. The exact date I do not remember; yet it must have been in February, the first week, I think. This time the order bore the sign-manual of Bliss, adjutant-general.

Over a thousand miles of marching—three times by the same route—and now, as in the first up-country movement, we had the same incentive to keep us in heart—a hope of battle. The whole region was rife with news of Santa Anna at San Luis Potosi assembling an army to come down and put an end to the audacious Gringos.

With the exception of Colonel Drake and Lieutenant-Colonel Lane, none of the regiment had seen General Taylor. What has been from the beginning will go on, I suppose, to the end; a hero will always be more than a man; so, although the general had, as we thought, dealt us great unkindness, and needlessly stored the dunes at the mouth of the Rio Grande with our dead, we had a craving to see him; and despite the nickname, "Rough and Ready," it was impossible for us to think of him entirely divested of pomp and circumstance. His tent must be out of the usual, a central hall, as it were, of a town of tents. Horsemen and horses must be at his door signifying martial authority at home. In a word, the feeling was general that even before approaching his quarters there would be something to advise us, without the asking, that we were near the WILL which was law unto us — something though but a sword-belt or a mien to bid us, "Here—look here—this is HE!"

Moving forward with lengthening steps, and drawing nearer and nearer, we strained our eyes to catch every point in the surroundings of the hero. A tall white flag-staff was the first thing observable. A flag floated from it high up, but the flag was dingy and worn. That was a disappointment. Next, back of the staff, fifteen or twenty steps, perhaps, we noticed two marquees one in rear of the other, a fly before the first answering for a porch; and they, too, were dingy and discolored. Under the fly there were a few camp-stools, a small table, also dirty, and a deal bench, long and straight-backed. No orderlies in trim dress uniforms; not even a sentinel stiffly stalking a beat suggested state thereabout. These HIS quarters?

Presently, without halting, we broke into column of companies—quickly and without a break we did it, and then advanced intervals and alignment perfected. Where was HE?

Now the head of the column was passing the dingy flag on the tall pole. One by one in quick succession the companies reached the prescribed saluting distance. Officers glanced to the right. *Their swords remained at carry*. So, also, the color-bearer swept by, his nose, like his flag, mutinously in the air. And all there asked themselves, anxiously, Where is HE?

It came my turn to salute from my place behind the rear rank. I readjusted the sword-grip in my hand, and looked for the reviewing officer out of the corner of my eye first, then broadly. Leaning lazily against the butt of the white pole, I saw a man of low stature, dressed in a blouse unbuttoned and so faded it could not be said to have been of any color, a limp-bosomed shirt certainly not white,[1] a hang-down collar without a tie of any kind, trousers once light blue now stripeless, rough marching shoes, foxy from long wear—such the dress of the man. He also wore a slouch wool hat drawn down low over a face unshaven, and dull and expressionless as the wooden Indian's habitually on duty in front of tobacco-shops. I did not salute him, but, like all who had preceded me, and all who came after me, passed on wondering, Where can HE be?

Looking backward once, I noticed Colonel Drake riding to the man with the slouch hat. There is reason to think he stopped with him and dismounted. Still I plodded on grumbling to myself, "HE is treating us shabbily, as usual."

That evening, when the good colonel's tent was pitched, I went to see him, unable to contain my indignation.

"Colonel," I said, "did General Taylor tell you that he would review us as we marched past his quarters?"

"Yes. I sent the adjutant to notify him of our coming. Didn't you see him?"

"No, sir, or I would have saluted."

The colonel's face sobered as he said, "Nobody saluted."

"Why, there was nobody to salute."

[1] This is to give the impression made upon me *at the time*. Since then I came to know that general officers are not entirely exempt from the effects of field life in actual campaigning. Their uniforms fade, the buttons dim, and sometimes their shirts get soiled. Though, if the latter happen when the *gentlemen* is at a fixed post where change of linen is at command, as in the instance given, one must look for the reason in the personal preference of the individual.

"Yes there was."

"Who?"

"*The man leaning against the flag-staff.*"

"That General Taylor? I took him to be a teamster."

We cleared first a spacious parade-ground; then our encampment became beautiful. A stream of spring-water ran through a grove of pecan-trees hardly distinguishable from oaks majestic, as we fancy Druidical temples. A range of mountains, nearly always cloud-capped, in the southeast, Monterey nestling beneath it, lifted the horizon in that direction. Nearer by rose Saddle Mountain, a solitary pyramidal peak accessible to climbers with muscles of steel. The purer the air the bluer the sky—with Walnut Springs hard-by Monterey one has not to go to Italy to test the saying. And yet camp life went on as usual. We did little day after day but buckle the disciplinary harness tighter about us. For now it was an assured thing—everybody said it—we were to be in the coming battle, the greatest of the war.

I have been often asked if I were ever scared. It seems now that an answer may be found in an incident of occurrence to me while the regiment lay at Walnut Springs.

A paymaster arrived in Monterey, and a number of the lieutenants requested to be allowed to go to the city and interview him. Unfortunately, the time set covered my turn to be officer of the guard; but by much importunity, and the most solemn promises to be in camp at the "turning off," I was permitted to be one of the party.

The quartermaster put a wagon at our disposal, and we piled into it, accommodating ourselves to the loose board seats as best we could. There must have been a dozen of us; and a merrier, wilder, more reckless mob, one readier to laugh at broken bones and peril to necks, was not in all the army. Where are they now?

It is not my purpose to describe the ride. Every man reading who can remember the happy-go-lucky of his own lusty youth can imagine it. Providentially, the harness was sound and all the material under us good American stuff. The road, too, was in our favor, having been cut through the chaparral for the passage of gun-carriages during the siege; while narrow, it was level and unencumbered. Tired and winded, the six mules at last slowed down and rolled us safely into the city.

After dinner at the hotel, we betook ourselves in a body to the paymaster's, where our several accounts were squared in United States silver dollars newly minted. And then—well, I take the liberty of making a long hiatus of "the subsequent proceedings," except to say that near one o'clock in the night, as the one sober Indianian, I succeeded in getting the last man to bed, and left the party in care of the hostelry.

It is only just to say that I had not thought of violating my promise to the colonel to be in camp next morning, so, the teamster not to be found, I set out alone and on foot to do the six miles.

I remember a stone bridge in the city limits garnished midway with a statue of some holy personage. The image had been set up for the convenience of people piously inclined; but, as if in travesty, the district beyond the bridge was admittedly the most dangerous of the town. There, on that bridge and in front of the statue, I thought for the first time of the risks before me. Nevertheless, I went on. If the reflection left an impression on my nerves, I did not at the time notice it.

I passed the ugly precinct safely. Once some dogs in front of an adobe house assailed me, and I picked up a couple of stones, one for each hand. From the main road—to Marin, I think—I turned into the narrow passageway cut, as mentioned, by the pioneers. Occasionally it ran across openings in the chaparral. Occasionally a clump of brush projected into the passage, and there were loose stones; otherwise the way was clear, and I had not to stop and deliberate about the direction. Moreover, the stars were all out twinkling the brighter because of the absolute lethargy in the air. The hush was soothing, the coolness delicious.

Three miles had been put behind me certainly, and I was bowling swiftly and lightly along, when all at once it struck me that I had nothing with which to defend myself—not even a penknife. I stopped, my ears wide open. There was only the universal silence, and I moved on again, but not with a free step. I was aware, too, of cold shivers, now on my cheeks, now along my scalp; and I fancied noises, the breaking of twigs in the brush, whirrings overhead, beetles a-wing, birds restless and shifting on their roosts. The truth is, my nerve was going, and my will.

A clump had been left at a certain point in the wall of brush hemming the road large enough to have furnished hiding for a horse behind it. I noticed the clump when about twenty feet from it looking unusually black, and came to a dead stop. Then something like a lapse of sensation took me. My feet would not stir; they seemed to have taken root in the ground. I could neither think nor resolve. From the ends of my fingers and toes the blood in icy drops ran to my heart, so that it stood still, refusing to beat. In a word, I stood overwhelmed by all the phenomena to terror.

The very strange part of the affair was that I fell

into this state, so almost identical with nightmare, before anything in the least likely to cause it had really happened. Premonition suggests itself here; anyhow, the clutch upon me was hard—harder possibly of a recollection, at the moment too faint to be spoken of as an idea, that near where I was standing the servant of an officer had been waylaid only the week before, and murdered. And if, in this faint of will and nerve —such was the condition—anything in the least unusual were to happen, a general collapse was sure to overtake me.

And exactly that happened. I heard a sharp metallic *click, click,* as of the hammer of a gunlock raised first to half, then to full cock, slowly, and with care lest the game should startle and run. Then a hiss flew out—the familiar hiss of powder burning in a pan—and all the chaparral behind the clump flashed red; and quick as the flash my senses left me.

Upon "coming to," I found myself hugging the ground like a snake. How long the lapse had lasted I cannot begin to tell, whether five minutes or an hour; neither have I an idea how I came to do what I did; none the less it was the best thing. Springing to the side of the road—the left, as I soon made out—I dropped down, and dragged myself into the chaparral, striking, by happy chance, one of the many paths tunnelled through the fastness by wandering goats and hogs.

It is doubtful if any man could have got closer to the ground than I had without digging into it. I lay still awhile listening. My heart beat, I fancied, like a bass drum, and a cold sweat covered me. Then, suddenly, I thought, "Good Heavens! what if some of the fellows in camp who knew I was to return are in the waylaying?" A thrill of shame splattered me as with hot water, and completed my recovery. I crawled on farther through the tunnel. The movement was slow and sore, for every leaf I came in contact with had its thorns keen as needles. At last I gained an opening, and stood up never more myself. There was a light in the sky signifying morning, and, taking direction from it, I walked around the place of ambush. Fortune favored me. Standing in the road, I listened again. There was nothing. Strangely enough, however, in that instant the panic caught me in full force again, and I started and ran. I ran with all my might, and so blind and headlong that if a regiment of Urvea's lancers had risen in front of me and blocked the narrow passage, I believe I should have dashed into them. The tents of the camp at length appeared, and I knew myself safe.

For a time I went about chary lest some one should blister me with the story, but no, the incident was never mentioned.

The sight of a child in fear always stops me now with quick appeal—or, with greater emphasis perhaps, since that night I have seen masses of soldiers in flight, and let them go by, partly out of sympathy, partly because no one knows better than I how blind and unreasoning panic is.

XVII

The battle of Buena Vista—February, 1847—Permission to go to the front—Saltillo—La Rinconada—Biscuits and onions—The Kentucky lieutenant—The adobe house—The three days' siege.

About the middle of the month (February) General Taylor astonished the command at Walnut Springs by disappearing, leaving nothing of headquarters except the white flag-staff. Presently we heard he had been seen going in the direction of Saltillo, with an escort of cavalry, and fast, as if the business were urgent. Had Santa Anna emerged from the desert?

A few days later, Captain S——n, of the Third Indiana, rode into camp en route to join his company wherever it might be. He was straining every nerve to reach it before the fight, and wanted somebody to go with him. Colonel Drake consented to my going. Here was another chance for me. Borrowing a mustang and riding-gear, I was on the road with the captain within thirty minutes. A double-barrelled shotgun of caliber to carry a service cartridge lay across my lap. The captain was custodian of a lunch contributed by Colonel Drake.

After leaving San Katrina we neither met nor were overtaken by a human being; this though the road was a broad highway connecting two capital cities. To such distance hostile armies approaching each other can interrupt the every-day courses of life!

Saltillo and Monterey lie separate sixty miles, with La Rinconada, a hacienda, half-way. Tired, hungry, sore, we were glad when near nightfall a picket from the hacienda halted us. At the house in use as barracks we made ourselves known to a lieutenant, who proved himself a brave and hospitable gentleman. He was a Kentuckian. His reply to our request for entertainment was merely this:

"Certainly, gentlemen. You shall be made, man and beast, comfortable as possible. Sorry I can't do better by you. To-day we were to have received an instalment of rations. We draw from Saltillo. For some reason our teamster is not on time. Lancers probably on the road. Anyhow, we are reduced to hardtack, with onions from a garden back of the house for dessert. Still, I can promise you salt of good quality, American made, with choice water from a ditch near by. If your stomachs work well, all right. Come in, and make yourselves at home."

A man set the table. The biscuits were of the cracker variety and the onions artistically sliced. The tin cups were not immaculately bright. There was no coffee. While we ate, the lieutenant generously opened his budget of news. La Rinconada, he said, had been occupied—I speak from memory—by Brigadier-General Marshall, his command consisting of a battalion of Kentucky horse, with two or three twenty-four-pounder guns and as many eight-inch howitzers. Only that morning the general had set out for Saltillo under fast-marching orders received during the night, leaving a half company in garrison. Extending his news beyond La Rinconada, our host further apprised us that Taylor and Wool, were doing business together. The army was out at Encantados waiting for Santa Anna advancing by forced marches. When last heard from the Mexican was at a village called Encornacion. There had been some skirmishing, and the armies would come together soon—exactly when or where no one could say. "The Old Man" (Taylor) had a mouth for secrets.

In the midst of the discourse—not more, in fact, than thirty minutes after our dismount—a soldier appeared and said, with suppressed excitement, "The pickets are firing, sir."

"From what direction?"

"From the direction of Saltillo."

The lieutenant buckled on his sword with gravity.

"Excuse me, gentlemen, if I leave you awhile," he said. "I think there is business in this interruption. I have been expecting it, and see now why my teamster isn't on time. If you want any more dessert, call for it."

He was gone fifteen or twenty minutes. Meantime the sound of a dropping fire penetrated to where we sat. We quit munching crackers. Pretty soon we distinguished the tramp of men in files. The door flew open under the impulse of an energetic kick outside, and the garrison, or a part of it, marched in arms at trail. The light was dim—from a candle or two stuck in red onions—but there was enough to help to a glance at the soldiers who passed through the room steadily; after which the door admitting them was banged to and securely barred.

The lieutenant stopped to explain.

"It's business, gentlemen. The house is being surrounded."

"What kind of a house is it?" S——n asked.

"It's adobe, sir, and pretty solid. There is a fence of the same material enclosing it on all sides, except here in front. If the Greasers have no artillery, we can stand them off."

He looked over us, for we were then on our feet, and went on. "I suppose you prefer to take a hand with us; so, if you are through supper"—he smiled grimly—"and will come with me, I'll see you have front seats."

S——n was accommodated with a musket and cartridges. I caught up my shot-gun; whereupon we followed the lieutenant.

"There's the back door," he said. "It's open to let the rest of the men in, if there's a rush. I'm taking you to the roof. Here's the ladder."

On the roof the night air seemed chilly—or the situation may have had an effect on me—and I could not help thinking it strange that my chronic longing to get into a fight should be gratified at such an out-of-the-way place. Sure enough the house was surrounded. Then S——n and I lay down behind the adobe wall rising above the roof like a parapet, and helped the garrison within and the leaguerers without to fill the night with intermittent musketry. Nobody of ours was hurt. At dawn the enemy retired out of range, and in that way as good as said we were not in their mind's eye—that they were holding the road merely to prevent communication until the crises up-country had passed.

We remained thus in leaguer until morning of the 25th, ample time to test thoroughly the theory of the vegetarians, and satisfy ourselves that crackers and onions, reinforced though they were with salt, American made, and choice water from a ditch, were susceptible of improvement as a ration. That day the Mexicans suddenly disappeared in the direction of Monterey, and S——n and I took to the road and its chances. In the afternoon we met the overdue teamster hurrying, under escort of four cavalrymen, to the relief of the lieutenant at La Rinconada.

AN AUTOBIOGRAPHY

XVIII

Saltillo—February 25th—General Wool—Major Cravens—The field of Buena Vista after the battle—The Indiana regiments—The disposition of troops—Description of the battle—Mexican forces and generals (names)—The first day's fight—Colonel Gell—Colonels Hadden and Davis—Marshall—The fight in the ravine—Violation of flag of truce—Bragg—" A little more grape, Bragg "—The day is saved.

We, the captain and I, reached Saltillo in the evening of the 25th without further interruption. Thence we rode to Buena Vista, five miles out.

Tired as I was, I spent most of the night listening to accounts of the battle. When, finally, my blanket unrolled to receive my aching bones, I was stuffed with talk and gossip, and the mass lay in my mind indigestible, like a late supper on a provincial stomach.

First thing next day were calls on the Lanes, General "Joe" and Colonel "Jim." To the former I reported, explaining my presence.

Then followed my respects to General Wool, whom my father admired extravagantly. With volunteers General Wool's reputation was that of a martinet, prim, formal, and stern to an offensive degree. They said he would not allow himself the compliment of a serenade; that he was always in uniform, with a leather stock about his neck and epaulets on his shoulders; that he received visitors capped, booted, and spurred; that he began business at daybreak, and ate with his sword on; some believed he even slept with his sword. In short, there was no limit to the general's unpopularity. I found him an agreeable gentleman, kind and sympathetic, and left him a subscriber to my father's opinion.

From General Wool, in company with friends who had been in the battle, notably Major Cravens, of the Second Indiana, I passed to the field. There the wrecks still lay in awful significance—dead men and horses, bayonets, accoutrements, broken muskets, hats, caps, cartridge-paper, fragments of clothing. The earth and rocks were in places black with blood, here a splotch, there a little rill. Details were still digging pits for the sepulture of Americans; other parties were hauling the unfortunates in and depositing them in ghastly rows by the pits. The civil authorities of Saltillo had been ordered to bury the Mexican dead; they were having the bodies dragged to the nearest ravines, pitched pitilessly down into the depths, and half covered with stones. Groups of swarthy peons, women and men, went about clipping the manes and tails of the dead horses.[1]

Though too late to make the battle of Buena Vista a part of my life, there is a reason, and I think it a good one, why I should deal with it somewhat in detail.

In his official report, General Taylor condemned a portion of the troops from Indiana, and in a manner so sweeping that the reputation of the state suffered from it through a long series of years—down, in fact, to the War of the Rebellion. And believing myself in possession of evidence to show the judgment unjust, and in material points officially false, it would seem a duty required of me to correct the wrong. That I will do in the next chapter. First the main features of the field should be considered.

It was crossed by a road its whole length from north

[1] To make lariats and saddle-girths.

to south. Blocking that road brought Santa Anna to a stand-still and compelled him to give battle.

In selecting the field, General Wool had been governed by its defensive advantages, exactly as General Taylor was governed when he approved the selection.

Going south from Saltillo, say to San Luis, one comes, after passing the height above the city, to a sheep-ranch called San Juan de la Buena Vista, from which the name of the battle was taken. Aside from a few clay-roofed habitations more nearly *jocales* than houses, the hacienda is unmarked save by a corral probably one hundred and fifty feet square. Indeed, everything about the place is in keeping with the plateau extending thence far to the south, a valley of desolation bounded by mountains on the east and west. Cacti and Spanish-bayonets are the only green things to vary the dun-gray color of the spacious stretch.

Beyond the hacienda there is a spread of the plateau, crossing which the traveller comes next to the Pass of Angostura.

The road there descends into a squeeze between ridged heights on the left and gullies on the right, the latter shapeless and of such width and depths as to be passable by nothing living but birds. A spur of the mountain dropping down to the gullies secured the position against attempts at turning. A simple earthwork for the accommodation of a battery across the road up where the descent into the squeeze begins would hold the pass against direct attacks along the road. General Wool, quick to see these advantages and accept them as kindnesses of nature, caused a breastwork to be thrown up at the point mentioned, and intrusted it to Captain J. M. Washington, of the Fourth United States Artillery. Two companies of the First Illinois Infantry behind the breastwork, and six other companies constituting the body of the regiment under Colonel Hardin on the hill above it, supported Washington and his five guns. And still not content, knowing the pass to be the key to the whole field of battle, he posted Colonel Lane's Third Indiana in reserve on a summit a little to Washington's rear.

Thus La Angostura and the road through it, together with a safe position on which to rest the right of the little army, were happily secured, leaving Santa Anna but one other point of attack.

Ravines, eight or ten in number, break the plateau east of the pass into ridges. Trending a little south of east, they all bear down towards the pass and become gorges sixty or seventy feet in depth, immense natural ditches absolutely deterrent except by going around them up by the foot-hills where there was a passage-way, rough yet practicable for infantry and horsemen, which once gained necessarily operated the turning of the pass. Knowing that to succeed Santa Anna must secure that way, no other being left him, General Wool applied himself to fencing it in.

A table of the commands other than those we have seen posted in support of Washington available for the upper defence may now be submitted. And we are startled here, they are so few:

REGULARS

Third Artillery, Sherman and Bragg.
First Dragoons, Captain Steene.
Second Dragoons, Lieutenant-Colonel May.

VOLUNTEERS

CAVALRY

Arkansas, Colonel Gell.
Kentucky, Colonel Marshall.
Texas Volunteers, Major McCullough.

INFANTRY

First Illinois, Colonel Hardin.
Second Illinois, Colonel Bissell.
Second Kentucky, Colonel McKee.
First Mississippi, Colonel Davis.
Second Indiana, Colonel Bowles.

Meagre to the eye, meagre in fact. But worse, the commands were all fractional. Thus, the First Illinois was less four companies garrisoning Saltillo. Two companies of the First Mississippi were guarding headquarters and the train in park near the hacienda. So, as will be presently seen, the Second and Third Indiana each lost two companies by detachment. All this aside from the reductions wrought by disease, on which account few, if any, of the regiments could boast four hundred effectives all told.

To post this inadequate force to the best advantage over a ground so spacious and peculiar was indeed a most difficult problem.

Let us see how it was done.

Three ravines in the south all lead from the road through the pass up to the now all-important passageway along the base of the mountains. These were, in fact, what in military phrase may be termed covered ways, every one of them possible of use for the ascent of infantry to the plateau, all of which had to be defended.

The extreme southern situation had a salience certain to attract Santa Anna, and General Wool thought best to establish his left at the head of that ravine; so he began the posting by placing Colonel Bowles's Second Indiana there, in support of Lieutenant O'Brien with three guns. General Lane had charge of the regiment and battery, and all the dispositions else had relation to that most advanced position.

At the left of the Second Indiana, but some distance to its rear, and directly across the passageway, Colonel Humphrey Marshall's Kentucky cavalry and a squadron of the Second United States Dragoons were placed.

Then in *echelon*—the word is somewhat strained—at the right rear of the Second Indiana, but nearly a quarter of a mile removed, Bissell's Second Illinois and a section of Bragg's battery were established fronting south to lend Bowles a helping hand, if need should be, and at the same time look after the heads of the second and third ravines.

Left of Bissell, at a wide interval, there were two guns and a squadron of dragoons.

Next, at another interval, Colonel McKee's Second Kentucky infantry was posted.

Then behind a ravine in rear of all these — the mother ravine, so to speak, having its head far up in the mountains, and christened La Bosca de la Bestarros — Colonel Gell's Arkansas cavalry was in reserve.

Finally, to keep the position of the Second Indiana from being turned by infantry scaling the mountain at its left, a provisional battalion was formed of two companies from the Second and Third Indiana respectively, and extended along a convenient ridge overlooking the plateau.[1]

Then dispositions made—they are given as of mid-afternoon, February 22d — General Wool rested. He had done the best with his scant force; and, following his example, it is for us now to look at the enemy.

[1] Davis's First Mississippi is omitted from mention, it having been called off, together with a squadron of dragoons under Lieutenant-Colonel May, as escort for General Taylor returning to Saltillo.

Heavy clouds of dust seen in the morning of the 22d in the direction of Angostura notified General Taylor of the approach of the Mexicans.

At eleven o'clock a summons to surrender at discretion was politely rejected.

The summons had ample backing. Twenty-eight battalions of infantry; thirty-nine squadrons of cavalry; artillery: three twenty-four pounders, three sixteen-pounders, five twelve-pounders, five eight-pounders, one seven-inch howitzer, with four hundred and thirteen artillerists to serve them. That is to say, eighteen thousand one hundred and thirty-three men were closing in behind the last ridge out on the waterless land in front of Buena Vista.[1]

These were commanded by the ablest generals of the Mexican Republic, eager, each of them, to share with his chief magistrate the harvest of glory which they doubted not was ready for his reaping: José Miñon, Michel Torena, Pedro Ampudia, Manuel Andrade, Ignacio de Mora y Villamil, Manuel Lombardini, Francisco Pacheco, Julien Juvera, José Maria Ortega, Angel Guzman, Antonio Corona, Francisco Perez.[2]

Santa Anna began the battle directly after the rejection of the demand for surrender by feigning an attack along the road through the Pass of Angostura. Then, amid a flourish of batteries in position here and there, Ampudia's light brigade commenced swarming up a ridge facing the American riflemen at General Lane's left. All eyes on the plateau below turned to follow the crackling which ensued. Ere long night hid the combatants. Said Major Cravens, standing with me

[1] This statement of numbers from Santa Anna's official report. Commands not mentioned by him, however, brought his army to over twenty thousand men actually engaged.

[2] The reader is requested to give each of these names the honorable prefix *General Don*.

where his regiment lay trying to sleep: "I sat on my blanket for hours watching the affair on the ridge yonder. I couldn't hear the rifles, but the sparkles reminded me of June in Indiana and of fire-flies gleaming across a meadow."

That Santa Anna designed turning the American left by gaining the passageway at the base of the mountains was now obvious.

To that end, under cover of night, he shifted Ballarta to the right where, by a laborious pull up an eminence, the shrewd artilleryman planted his five eight-pounders in range to enfilade Bowles and O'Brien. Juvera, chief of cavalry, together with Torrejon and Andrade, was next posted in support of Ballarta. Then, to gain the advantage of a surprise, the infantry divisions of Lombardini and Pacheco, seven thousand strong, were drawn noiselessly into a broad ravine where they bivouacked.

On the morning of the 23d a furious outbreak of Mexican artillery announced dawn over the mountains and seemed a chosen signal of action. Ampudia at the sound rushed the riflemen in his front; but reinforced they held their own. Juvera gained ground, while Villamil and Blanco down in the pass lost heavily repeating the feint of the day before.

The desolate valley was yet ringing with the unwonted thunder, when suddenly Lombardini's division burst out of the broad ravine; gaining space on the plateau, it faced by the left flank, and in column of brigades confronted O'Brien and the Second Indiana.[1]

While the issue of fire waxed hot, another stream of pomponed-shakos poured out of the same ravine, and

[1] The execution of this manœuvre was so beautiful that it was a subject of general commendation while I was in General Taylor's camp.

Pacheco, repeating Lombardini's simple manœuvre, took post on his colleague's right and joined in the battle.

With all their weight, the Mexicans wavered. Then to get closer, and partly to avoid the enfilading of Ballarta, General Lane ordered an advance. O'Brien obeyed; but in the midst of the movement Colonel Bowles ordered, "Cease firing, and retreat." Twice he gave the order; whereupon his regiment began breaking at its right, company after company, until, presently, the greater part dissolved into a mob flying aimlessly to the rear. O'Brien, left without support, withdrew two of his guns, the horses and men of the Third having been killed or disabled.

Results followed rapidly.

Juvera advanced trotting.

The American riflemen in the mountain, about to be cut off, made haste down, and ran, most of them, to the hacienda, stopping in the corral. Of those who tried to rejoin their standards, many were slain.

The Kentuckians at the left of the Second Indiana—Marshall having reached them safely—faced to the rear, and plying their spurs joined Colonel Gell on the thitherside of La Bosca.

Most serious, however, between Lombardini and Washington in the pass there now stood but three regiments all seriously reduced—Bissell's Second Illinois, McKee's Second Kentucky, and Hardin's First Illinois. The gallant Mexican half-wheeled his battle front to the left, and it seemed that the three regiments, beaten in detail, must go the way of the Second Indiana; but General Wool kept a clear head. At his orders, Bissell fell back, while Hardin and McKee advanced running to him; and meeting, the three formed a line into which Bragg and Sherman thrust their batteries. Then Lombardini and Pacheco were upon them with a roar of "vivas"; the ravines as they approached reducing the opposing fronts to an equality, it became a question with the combatants which could longest endure the killing.

Juvera allowed Marshall and Gell no pause. Crossing La Bosca, he fell upon them, and pushed them back—back almost to the corral of the hacienda. Gell, refusing to yield an inch, died sword in hand.

Then in the nick of time—eight o'clock—General Taylor appeared returning from Saltillo with the First Mississippi and May's dragoons. By every rule of scientific war he was beaten;[1] rising in his stirrups and looking back he could see Miñon's pennons fluttering between the hacienda and the city; his left was turned; his cavalry was beating back overwhelmed; one thin line—thinner for the smoke enveloping it—was hardly staying Lombardini's masses seeking clutch of the Pass of Angostura. If then he had a sinking of the heart, no one of those about him saw it in his stolid countenance. Lane, of the Third Indiana, had been in reserve chafing; him he ordered to join Davis; the two to cross La Bosca and crush Pacheco's flank. One gun—Kilburn's—would go with them.

Lane started on the run. Davis halted once to repel an attack of lancers. Then about two hundred of the Second Indiana under their own colors, and led by their Lieutenant-Colonel (Hadden), met Davis, and, without halting, formed on his left. It was a long run, but finally the three regiments together reached La Bosca, and crossing it, and deploying with cheers, poured a plunging fire into Pacheco's column at a time when his at-

[1] The story that General Wool rode to General Taylor upon the latter's appearance on the field, and said to him, "We are beaten," is apocryphal. At that moment the two were separate from each other by a ravine too deep for passage by horsemen.

tention was wholly absorbed by Hardin, McKee, and Bissell. In a time incredibly short the portion of the plateau down which Lombardini and Pacheco had descended so triumphantly was clear of the living. Lombardini himself rode off wounded.

General Taylor had leisure now to give attention to the fight which had been going on strenuously between Marshall and Juvera, begun, as has been seen, directly that Colonel Bowles ordered his regiment to retreat.

Following and crowding Marshall, Juvera was drawn down close to the hacienda. Suddenly the coping-stones on three sides of the corral seemed to burst into flame. The cheer that followed was as stunning as the volley. Strangely, then, the Mexicans divided; one part of them sped past the corral, and, crossing the valley, disappeared in a defile of the mountain in the west; the others turned, and in great disorder rode just as madly back over the bloody track by which they had come, intending to rejoin the main body of their army. Bragg was sent to intercept them, with Davis, Lane, and Hadden in support. The broken, panic-stricken horsemen tried to find refuge in the foot-hills, where they would have been forced to surrender had not Santa Anna despatched a messenger to General Taylor asking what he wanted. It is not often the sanctity of a flag of truce is so infamously abused. While it was coming and going the enemy escaped.

At two o'clock the plateau was in possession of the Americans, all save a corner in the southeast where the enemy was in apparent confusion but busy about something. Occasionally the sullen report of a heavy gun and the scream of a shell in flight over the ridges broke an hour of inaction. The weary soldiers availed themselves of the calm to rest, lying in semi-order about their colors.

But Santa Anna was not beaten. The hour so welcome to his enemies, because of its quiet, was on his part an hour of intrepid action.

Assembling the remains of the divisions of Lombardini and Pacheco, he united them with Ampudia's light brigade and Ortega's third division which was intact, having been in reserve. He also moved to the right a column of Villamil's that had been making feints against Washington, and mobilized a battery of twenty-four-pounders. Ballarta he brought down to the plain. Corona had already posted the four twelve-pounders in what he judged the best place.

By this thrifty management the president-general was able to make his final attack with twelve thousand men, General Don Francisco Perez in command. The strategy was Napoleonic.

Colonels Hardin and McKee, it appears, had undertaken a reconnoissance to expose the enemy in his corner of the plateau. Supporting O'Brien and his two pieces, they reached the ground which the Second Indiana had held in the morning; just then, Santa Anna's preparation completed, Perez advanced. In the words of General Taylor, both regiments were "entirely routed"; and this time O'Brien lost all his guns. Hardin and McKee and his lieutenant-colonel, young Henry Clay, refusing to retreat or to order retreat, died with their faces to the foe.[1]

The two regiments, carrying their heroic dead tenderly, retreated down a ravine opening into the pass under Washington's breastwork. There were pursuers who shot at them from the sides of the ravine; though a greater multitude entered the ravine after them, and in

[1] One cannot avoid contrasting the conduct of Hardin and McKee and Clay with the behavior of Colonel Bowles; yet it was to the latter the commanding general applied the term *gallant*.

their eagerness kept on until in the area spreading and rockbound at the exit. There, looking up, they beheld the mouths of Washington's five guns staring upon them with unwinking blackness. They turned to get back, but the crowd behind pushed them forward. Washington withheld his fire; when the last fugitive was safe, he opened upon the shrieking mass packed in the area, his guns all double-shotted with grape and canister.[1]

Perez, depending upon weight of attack and impetus, delivered it in column.

Still General Taylor was undismayed. He ordered Bragg and his supports — Davis and Lane — to fall upon the enemy's left flank, for which they had to recross La Bosca; and they did it on the run, Hadden with them. Then they were attacked; whereupon, Davis directing, they formed a "V," the angle resting on the edge of the ravine, and by the cross-fire they were thus enabled to give ground swept the assailants from their front; then they hurried after Bragg.

Bragg, meantime, pushed on with all the speed the ground permitted, and without waiting for support. When he wheeled his guns into battery, the enemy was within a few yards of their muzzles, and at first he gave

[1] That area, I do not hesitate saying, all my subsequent experience in mind, was the most horrible after-battle scene I ever saw. The dead lay in the pent space body on body, a blending and interlacement of parts of men as defiant of the imagination as of the pen.

In 1867 I spent a day on the field of Buena Vista renewing my recollections of 1847. I remember seeing a man coming slowly towards me. In the distance his actions were so strange that I waited for him. Hoe in hand, he was leading a rill of water somewhere, and it ran gently after him. Finally, and to my surprise, he led it down to the area described in the text, then a patch of wheat in luxurious growth. Could it have been, I asked myself, that the crop he was fostering derived its emerald richness from the blood spilled there the terrible day so long gone?

ground as the pieces recoiled. Then it was that General Taylor sent the famous order, "A little more grape, Captain Bragg." And speaking of results, General Taylor adds in his report, "The first discharge of canister caused the enemy to hesitate; the second and third drove him back in disorder, *and the day was saved.*"[1]

Six o'clock and the repulse was complete. Night fell cold, and in the morning Santa Anna and all his host, save the wounded and those never to rise again, were back at Agua Nueva.

[1] The italics are mine; the expression is General Taylor's.

XIX

General Taylor's report of the battle of Buena Vista—Report of court of inquiry exonerating Indiana regiments charged with cowardice—Colonel Bowles—A physician and botanist—Brigadier-General Lane—The battle.

IN General Taylor's official report of the battle of Buena Vista there is this sentence:

"The Second Indiana, which had fallen back as stated, could not be rallied, and took no further part in the action, except a handful of men who, under its gallant Colonel Bowles, joined the Mississippi regiment and did good service."

I say now that in all American history there is not another sentence which, taken as a judgment of men in mass, equals that one for cruelty and injustice—none so wanton in misstatement, none of malice so obstinately adhered to by its author, none so comprehensive in its damage, since it dishonored a whole state, and, though half a century has passed, still holds the state subject to stigma.

Let me now make my words good. It is necessary in the very beginning to get the charges covered by the extract quoted distinctly in mind.

General Taylor says the regiment fell back. That is true; but as the statement is wholly unqualified, the inference is left that the falling back was from cowardice, and to that I except.

General Taylor says, next, that the regiment could not be rallied. That I say is untrue.

General Taylor says, in the third place, that the regiment after it fell back took no further part in the action. To this he makes an exception in favor of a "handful of men who, under its gallant Colonel Bowles, joined the Mississippi regiment and did good service." That, I say, is one of those cunning partial truths which, by forcing a contrast between the meritorious conduct of a few and the supposed infamous conduct of the many, but intensifies a wrong.

The question now presents itself, How am I to make my exceptions good against General Taylor? By putting my dictum against his? The American people are discriminative, and to none are they so generous as to the dead; wherefore no one appreciates more keenly the need upon me, which is that the testimony offered must be of sanctity superior to his word. And that it shall be.

Colonel Jefferson Davis, learning, after the battle, that Colonel Bowles, of the Second Indiana, had fallen into the ranks of his Mississippi regiment as a private, and behaved well, conceived the idea of specially recognizing the conduct. So he ceremoniously presented to Colonel Bowles the Mississippi rifle used by him. The publicity of the affair affronted the survivors of the Second Indiana, who held that acceptance of the present was an admission to their dishonor. Then General Lane, thinking to get the facts of the retreat of record, sought a court of inquiry, the regiment having been part of his command in the battle.

I now submit extracts from the records of that court, premising that they are in Washington.

"(Orders No. 279.)

"Headquarters Camp at Buena Vista, *April* 26, 1847.

"1. By a court of inquiry which convened at this camp in pursuance of Order No. 233, current series, and of which

Brigadier-General Marshall is president, . . . the following have been announced as the facts of the case. . . .

"Facts— . . . That through the exertions of General Lane and other officers, from one hundred and fifty to two hundred men of the Second Regiment of Indiana Volunteers were rallied, and attached to the Mississippi regiment and the Third Indiana, and remained with them on the field of battle during the remainder of the day.

. . . .

"By command of Brigadier-General Wool.

"IRVIN MCDOWELL, A. A.-General."

General Taylor said the regiment could not be rallied, and after the retreat it took no further part in the action. Attention is directed to the squareness of denial with which the court meets the two assertions.

General Lane then determined to put the blame for the retreat where it belonged; and with that in view he preferred charges against Colonel Bowles. These General Taylor ignored by declining to order a court. In a short time, however, public opinion—the term is as justly applicable to a camp as to a city—drove Colonel Bowles in turn to ask a court of inquiry upon his conduct; and General Wool, who had succeeded to the command at Buena Vista, ordered a court with Colonel Bissell, of the Second Illinois Volunteers, for president, and from its report I submit extracts, not doubting that their pertinency will be instantly admitted.

"(Orders No. 281.)

"HEADQUARTERS CAMP AT BUENA VISTA, *April* 27, 1847.

"1. A court of inquiry, of which Colonel Bissell, Second Illinois Volunteers, is president, convened at this camp on the 12th instant, pursuant to Orders No. 267, current series, being instituted at the request of Colonel W. A. Bowles. . . .

"The court, after diligently and faithfully inquiring into the matter before it, report, from the evidence given, the following as the facts of the case, and its opinion thereon:

"Statement of facts:—In reference to the first charge, it appears from the evidence that Colonel Bowles is ignorant of the company, battalion, and brigade drills. . . .

"In relation to the second charge, it appears from the evidence . . . that Colonel Bowles gave the order, 'Cease firing, and retreat'; that General Lane was present, and that he had no authority from General Lane to give such an order.

. . . .

"The court finds that the fact of Colonel Bowles having given the order above mentioned did induce the regiment to retreat in disorder, and that Colonel Bowles gave the order with the intention of making the regiment leave its position.

. . . .

"The court is of the opinion that at the time Colonel Bowles gave the order, 'retreat,' he was under the impression that the artillery had retreated, when, in fact, the battery at that time had gone to an advanced position under the order of General Lane, which order had not been communicated to Colonel Bowles.

"And in conclusion, the court finds that throughout the engagement, and throughout the whole day, Colonel Bowles evinced no want of personal courage or bravery, but that he did manifest a want of capacity and judgment as a commander.

. . . .

"By command of Brigadier-General Wool.

"Irvin McDowell, A. A.-General."

The reader now has the evidence upon which I rely—viz., the findings and opinions of two military courts; not one, but two courts. To reach the full effect of the clash in simple truth, I will resort to the deadly parallel, the statement of General Taylor, on the one hand, and the findings of the courts, on the other.

GENERAL TAYLOR	THE COURTS
General Taylor imputes the falling back to cowardice.	Colonel Bissell's court found that the regiment was ordered by its colonel to retreat; that the order, "Cease firing, and retreat," was given by its colonel to induce the regiment to retreat, and that the colonel did induce it to leave its position.
General Taylor says the regiment could not be rallied.	General Marshall's court found that from one hundred and fifty to two hundred men of the regiment were rallied by General Lane and other officers.
General Taylor says that with exception of a handful of men who, under its gallant Colonel Bowles, joined the Mississippi regiment, the regiment took no further part in the action.	General Marshall's court found that the one hundred and fifty or two hundred men who were rallied remained on the field of battle during the rest of the day.
General Taylor says that the exceptional handful of men under Colonel Bowles joined the Mississippi regiment.	General Marshall's court found that the one hundred and fifty or two hundred men who were rallied attached themselves to the Mississippi regiment *and the Third Indiana regiment.*

These differences are material; and, being cast into high relief, which is to be believed, the general or the courts? Admitting out of regard for certain susceptibilities that, man to man, the volunteer is not as effective in war as the regular, may not something in this instance be allowed to preponderance, since all military courts are composed of officers acting under the solemnity of an oath?

But here some one may suggest that General Taylor never saw the findings of either of the courts. It is true his report of the battle was forwarded before the trials were had; nevertheless, the facts remain as found, and are not to be lost sight of; indeed, that they were of subsequent discovery but intensifies the obstinacy of the man. The records of the courts engrossed and signed required his indorsement; so he *must* have seen them. If that were not so, however, there is evidence in plenty showing he was besought over and over, importuned, begged, for the credit of the brave men involved, the dead as well as the living, for the honor of a state and for the truth of history, to modify his report and make it conform to the findings of the courts. But without avail. Why? The reason must remain forever in theory. All I know is that commanders are charged with keeping the honor of their men, the honor of the humblest as well as that of those higher in rank, and that they always hail opportunities to change premature reports harsh in terms or mistaken in fact. To the rule Zachary Taylor is the only exception within my reading or personal experience.

Taking the finding of the court to be the truth, the small number found to have been rallied after the retreat —one hundred and fifty or two hundred men—may cause a smile, for *prima facie* it is a weakness in the argument. *That* I will now notice, and in the connection consider the propriety of the special compliment to Colonel Bowles by General Taylor—a compliment the more remarkable in view of the opinion of the Bissell court touching the colonel's general ignorance and incapacity as a commander.

If in what I have now to say any statement should have the tone and color of an eye-witness, it is because, having reached the field so shortly after the battle—only two days—I think my opportunities for information fit me to speak of the things then in controversy there.

Colonel Bowles was a physician of scientific attainments, brave, ambitious, pleasant-mannered, easy-going; but withal it was presently demonstrated that he could not master the elementaries of the tactics in vogue at the time of his enlistment. To make the situation worse for him an extreme attachment had arisen between the regiment and its late colonel, Lane. That officer continued to tent with it after his promotion, and carried it with him as often as he changed location. The relation was precisely that which sprang up between General Taylor and the First Mississippi. Practically, General Lane remained colonel to the suppression of Colonel Bowles. He looked after the discipline and personal welfare of the men. He drilled them, and they were beautifully drilled. To this Colonel Bowles made no objection. His tastes ran in other lines. I myself have seen him while the regiment was on the parade-ground under General Lane ride into camp bringing botanical specimens of the flora of the adjacent country. He seemed incapable of jealousy. Certainly he had no sense of the awful responsibility of command in battle. The men treated him good-naturedly. None of them dreamed that under his order the ultimate martial issue to which they looked forward so ardently would turn out a life-long provocation of tears and shame.

The statement to which I now come will be a surprise to those who have of late been used to hearing of regiments twelve hundred strong. At roll-call in the morning of February 23d, the total of muskets in the stacks of the Second Indiana did not exceed three hundred and sixty. Two companies (Walker's and Osborne's) had been drawn off the day before to help form a provisional battalion of rifles under Major Gorman, of the Third Indiana, leaving with the colors eight companies averaging forty-five men in the ranks.

Nor may it be overlooked that the Third Indiana having been placed in reserve by General Wool, all of actual command possessed by Brigadier-General Lane was the Second Indiana and O'Brien's battery of three guns. We have then the anomaly, brought about by the relation Lane bore to the Second Indiana, of a regiment going into battle with practically two colonels. One cannot help asking, what if in the turmoil and noise the orders of the two *colonels* should happen to conflict? Or, to illustrate, what if one of them should order "Forward," and the other, moved by a different inspiration, should order "Retreat?"

The air had been uncomfortably cold through the night of the 23d, so, what time they were not trying to sleep, the men walked behind their arms in stack, and sang and joked and amused themselves watching the flitting flashes of the combatant rifles on the overlooking heights.

By three o'clock everybody was on the alert. Then, dawn being yet in half-transparency, the deadly business of the day was begun by the Mexicans, of whom a swarm sprang out and spread darkly up and over the low foot-hills next the plateau, going to the assistance of their balking skirmishers. Then on an elevation, advanced well towards the Second Indiana, masses of men appeared dragging guns into position, five in all. General Lane, on his horse and watchful, knew that it would never do for the fire of that battery (Ballarta's) to catch his companies unformed, and he ordered the regiment, "Fall in"—he, be it observed, not Colonel Bowles. Just then the quick report of artillery rolled over the plateau far and near. A few minutes later Colonel Churchill, of General Wool's staff, rode to tell Lane that the enemy was showing down in the road in feint, while the real attack was coming against him up the first ravine in his front. Without a word to Colonel Bowles, who was in rear of the extreme right company, Lane galloped round the left flank of the regiment to a position in front of the colors. He made there as if to deliver a speech; but, observing the alignment merely, he ordered, "Forward—guide centre—march," after which the double colonelcy was an established fact. Well, now, if the real colonel does not awake from his suppression and do some contrary thing which strikes him as the best! Promptly, as if on parade, the regiment stepped out, and O'Brien advanced his three guns.

Then out of the ravine, number one, towards which Lane was heading, a military band richly uniformed appeared and began playing the national air of Mexico. The regiment, observing it, cheered, and took step from the inspiring music. Only for a moment, however, for the band, which did not halt, was succeeded by an array seemingly interminable of infantry in double columns, flag after flag. Suddenly, space being cleared for the manœuvre, the enemy faced by the left flank, and became a line of battle masking another line. Up, too, from the same ravine in rapid succession other shakoed bodies poured and repeated the manœuvre of the first until two full divisions (Lombardini's and Pacheco's) moved forward, a splendid but terrible spectacle.

General Lane's object in advancing had been partly

to reach a point from which to control the ravine before the enemy gained the plateau. Seeing that it was too late, he halted the regiment and sent his aide to order O'Brien into battery; then, clearing the line of fire, he galloped to the rear by the left flank. Had he gone by the right flank, he could have spoken to the other colonel there and told him his wishes; as it was, he did all the commanding directly; at his word the men went to their knees; at his word they began firing.

Then O'Brien opening, Ballarta quickened all his guns, so that now, indeed, the battle for the plateau was joined.

Of the generalship I have nothing to say. My purpose is to help to an intelligent judgment of the conduct of the regiment in question.

There are but three hundred and sixty men in the ranks. Enfilading them from left to right, and within easy range, is a battery of five eight-pounder guns. Advancing upon them in brigade front, thus overlapping their own front, are infantry columns of two divisions variously estimated, the most recent authority putting their strength at seven thousand—eighteen to one!

The regiment is nearly a quarter of a mile in advance of the regiment (Bissell's Second Illinois) next it in the *echelon* of formation—literally on the plateau alone, and unsupported, except we reverse the order of things and call O'Brien's three guns a support.

Lastly, this is the regiment's first battle, and I see no need of stopping to tell what all that means. Set upon by everything that makes battle terrible—overwhelming numbers in front, bullets *swishing* about them, shells bursting, comrades falling—if General Taylor was right, and that a band of cowards, it will certainly break now.

Did they break?

In the box of every man of them there are forty cartridges, each with a bullet and three buckshot, and loading by rammer was a slow process; yet the Mexicans are brought to a halt, and their shooting grows wilder. The distance is about a hundred yards. Some of ours, to be sure, are white of face. A breeze blows fitfully lifting the smoke, so that now and then the very cool among them take deliberate aim, and that means death, for at home they are woodsmen and hunters. The first chill goes quickly—then they are all steady.

Dante, in his *Inferno*, speaks of all horrible sounds, but nowhere of music; so in battle the noises are mostly explosive discordances; still one can become so intent upon his individual performance, whether with sword, musket, or great gun, that action becomes automatic. That was what now happened. The men loaded and fired, and heard nothing, neither whistle of bullet nor shriek of shell or stricken comrade. How full the air was of missiles may be judged. In the first position of the regiment twenty-one of the forty cartridges were fired. Of the three hundred and sixty combatants in the ranks ninety dropped dead or disabled by wounds. The color-sergeant fell. Seeing the flag go down, Paymaster Dix, a volunteer aide with General Lane, being near, ran and picked it up, and kept it flying until Lieutenant Kunkel demanded it of him. Kunkel, brave fellow, bore it the rest of the day, a mark for the enemy, a brave sight for countrymen, if only they chose to see it. My poor friend and school-mate, Captain Kinder, was hit though not mortally wounded. The lancers overtook and killed him in an ambulance. General Lane, in the act of cheering, was shot in the right arm; a hot canister cauterized his cheek; his horse's lower jaw was broken. And now, on account of Ballarta's gunners, it was needful to shift the regiment. Forward or back? Just then General Lane saw the Mexicans in his front faltering, and he resolved to get closer to them. O'Brien must advance. Robinson, Lane's adjutant-general, delivered the order, and it was instantly obeyed. From his place behind McRae's company, the last one on the left, Lane called out, "Forward"—when horror of horrors! The right was going to pieces, and streaming to the rear fast as man could run.

The point of sovereign interest in this most dismal episode at Buena Vista is reached. In certain books, favorites of mine, the catastrophes cause me the keenest anguish. Such is the effect of the fall of Harold in Bulwer's novel of that name. Such, also, is the death of Uncas in Cooper's *Last of the Mohicans*. So always, thinking of the break and flight of the Second Indiana in the midst of its well-doing, I have return of the same pang sharper of a conviction that had the brave fellows been held to the work three or five minutes longer, single-handed they would have routed the divisions before them. And then what glory would have been theirs! And how the state would have shone in the reflected light!

Thanks now to the courts, there is no mystery about the cause of the break. We know it was by order. We know, too, by whose order. Wherefore the question—as the court says Colonel Bowles was not a coward, as General Taylor pronounces him *gallant*, how could he upon his own volition have done a thing so shameful?

The circumstance is one about which everybody can have a theory. I will give mine. The moment General Lane, at the left of the regiment, conceived the idea of shifting it nearer the enemy, Colonel Bowles, over on the right, dismounted, and, too far off for instant communication with his chief, was in a confusion of senses begotten, doubtless, of a consciousness of incapacity, not to speak of the sounds that assailed him, discordant, furious, cyclonic. Old soldiers who have been in the heat of battles know how those sounds do actually buffet one as with blows, and how they are attended with stupefying sensations. Anyhow, holding his horse, if not behind it, he chanced to look through a rift in the smoke, and, not seeing O'Brien or his battery, was seized with an inspiration the opposite of General Lane's. He heard no voice of glory calling. If he saw an advantage, it was in getting the men and himself out of the tremendous broil; and not knowing how to do that by manœuvre, though there are a number of methods prescribed in the books; without thinking to send the flag back to indicate a place of rally; too much dazed, indeed, to remember that he himself was subject to order; too confused to consider anything but escape in the quickest possible time, he called out, "Cease firing, and—retreat," and in those words, doubtless, exhausting his slender store of tactical knowledge. Only the company nearest heard what he said, and they turned and gazed at him in wonder. A second time he raised his voice—"Cease firing, and—retreat."

Now no man shall say this was not an order. It was an order, and by one in authority. And at once all the shame of the flight that followed attaches to him who gave the order—the *gallant Colonel Bowles.*

In the next place there was a rally; and while in camp I myself heard the details of it, and am not permitted to doubt what I heard—else there is not honor among men.

General Lane, looking ahead, saw La Bosca, in the ravine, laying a broad trench across the line of flight, and rode to it full speed, taking Lieutenant-Colonel

Hadden and Major Cravens with him. Wheeling his horse on the thither side, he confronted the men. Fifteen of them in panic ran by him to the sheep-ranch nearly a mile away. There, with others from different commands, mostly riflemen dislodged, as we shall presently see, they did good service later in the forenoon. Quite one hundred and ninety of the regiment heard him and hastened to reform; and when presently Lieutenant Kunkel overtook the body with the colors, an accounting for the absent was easy. This was the table generally agreed upon in the leisure following the fight:

Killed and wounded	90
Absent in care of the wounded	40
Rallied by Colonel Bowles	25
Rallied at the sheep-ranch	15
Rallied by General Lee and other officers . . .	190
	360

Is it reasonable, now, asking more proof of me? Out of a total of three hundred and sixty men, two hundred and fifteen back under their own colors, ought, I insist, to be fact enough of itself, the question being whether there was a rally. Then, as to courage, ninety killed and wounded before the order to retreat—ninety out of three hundred and sixty—one-fourth of the entire firing-line! How often has battle anywhere such a record of proportional loss?

We come next to the compliment to Colonel Bowles paid, as has been seen, by General Taylor. The colonel ordered the retreat; he rallied what his eulogist calls a handful of the men; then, rifle in hand, he spent the rest of the day a private soldier, loading and firing in the front or rear rank of a strange regiment. What is gallantry in a private may be unqualified shame in an officer. This bit of military philosophy was never so pointedly illustrated as by Colonel Bowles when he stepped into the ranks of the Mississippians. The situation at the moment is worth an effort at appreciation. It is after the rally on the farther side of La Bosca. The one hundred and ninety of the Second Indiana are about to attach themselves to Colonel Davis's command. They are under their own colors. Lieutenant-Colonel Hadden is in command. The crisis is terrible. Where is Colonel Bowles? I know nothing in war so strange as his conduct in that thrilling instant. With his rallied "handful" he approaches the Mississippians. First securing a rifle and cartridges—let us suppose from a wounded man or one dead—he takes place in the ranks unobserved by the strangers. Near by is his own regiment. Their colors are his colors. He is entitled to command them. They are the men who voted him colonel, with whom he has tented and marched and lived the whole of his soldier life. He must have seen them—he must have seen the flag. Why did he turn away and abandon them to become for the time a Mississippian? Why prefer the strangers? Why? The question has a depth beyond me. But—and this is the application—what of *gallantry* is there in the behavior?[1]

Finally, on the point of cowardice. I am a dissenter

[1] General O. O. Howard is the most recent author of a biography of General Taylor. In the book he adopts his subject's view of the conduct of the Second Indiana, thinking it not worth while to look behind that officer's report of the battle of Buena Vista.

Here is a sample of his dealing. Summarizing—page 271—he says: "Arkansas, Kentucky, Illinois, Mississippi, Texas, and some Indiana men had fought hard all this dreadful day." By the table on page 192, General Howard is right. There were *some* Indiana men who fought hard; indeed, there were some wounded, others actually killed. As he has the reputation of a Christian gentleman, not to speak of him as a brave soldier, the table quoted is especially recommended to him.

to the opinion often urged that the sovereign test of the conduct of a corps in battle is the list of casualties; still, to apply that test in this instance, here is a table of losses by commands at Buena Vista compiled from official returns:

Corps	Killed	Wounded	Missing	Aggregate	Corps	Killed	Wounded	Missing	Aggregate
					Brought over.........	74	148	4	223
General staff..........	1	3		4	Arkansas Cavalry.....	17	32	4	53
1st Dragoons..........		7		7	2d Kentucky Cavalry..	44	57	1	102
2d Dragoons..........		2		2	1st Illinois regiment...	29	18		47
3d Artillery...........	1	22	2	25	2d Illinois regiment...	48	75	3	116
4th Artillery..........	5	21		26	2d Indiana regiment...	32	71	4	107
Mississippi Rifles......	40	56	2	98	3d Indiana regiment...	9	56		65
Kentucky Cavalry.....	27	37		61	Texas Volunteers......	14	2	7	23
	74	148	4	223		267	459	23	746

When the intelligent reader, far removed from the petty jealousies of the men who fought at Buena Vista, reads that table, and sees, as he certainly will, that there was but one regiment with more casualties than the Second Indiana, he will wonder greatly, but at nothing so much as the general commanding. There may even come to him reading a realization of the lamentable fact that a man may have been a successful general and popular president of the United States, yet lack the elements without which no one can be truly great—justice and truth.

AN AUTOBIOGRAPHY

XX

Departure from Walnut Springs, May 24, 1847—Mustered out—Reception at New Orleans—Sergeant S. Prentiss—Robbed of savings—Return to Indianapolis—Resume law—*The Fair God*—Apply for license again from the Supreme Court.

On May 24, 1847, the First Indiana left Walnut Springs going to "the States" for muster out.

At the mouth of the Rio Grande, while waiting for transports, I strolled out to the dunes so thickly peopled with our dead. The revelations were shocking. Reporting what I had seen, the good colonel ordered me to take a working party and rebury all exposed remains. The sorrowful duty done, I lingered to take a farewell look at the shifting cemetery, wondering if the government would ever set about bringing the bones of the brave back to Indiana. Fifty years are a long time out of one's life to wait for anything; and now I know *that* accomplishment will never be. The poor fellows are abandoned. Even the home folk last to love them are themselves departed. Only the Great Gulf lifts a voice for them—an inarticulate, everlasting moan.

At New Orleans, a number of regiments having arrived with terms of service expiring, the city received us. A poor affair, indeed, cheap, and unworthy mention were it not that Sergeant S. Prentiss was the chosen orator. I went to hear him.

The absence of decorations along the streets struck me dismally while passing to the square selected for the ceremony. Cut off for such a time from newspapers, I had failed to appreciate that the war had been discussed with such bitterness that at least half the people viewed it as an unholy invasion. Of course all holding that opinion were unwilling to jubilate. They kept their flags hid and stuck to their shops.

The preparations in the square were meagre and disappointing. There was the usual out-door platform of boards, raised three or four feet from the ground, railed off on three sides, and decorated with a flag tied to a corner post. Scarcely two thousand people stood about the platform, which was crowded with field-officers and black-coated civilians of aldermanic proportions. Failing to get a seat among the dignitaries, I elbowed myself back of the stand, where, with my toes in a crack of the base-boards, and half swinging by the fingers from the railing, I made out to see the speaker when he arose.

Mr. Prentiss was at his height of fame. I remember his appearance distinctly. He was rather low in stature, full-chested, clean-shaven, and faultlessly dressed. His head was ample, round, superbly set. The brows arched high, allowing the large eyes to fill with light — eyes that would have made an ugly face beautiful. Eyes, countenance, head, mouth permissive of every variety of expression, profile, attitude, the whole man, in fact, brought me to think of pictures of Lord Byron. Like Byron, moreover, he was clubbed in one foot. I had intended taking a glance at him, hear his opening, then go away. To my astonishment, when he sat down more than an hour had passed. I had heard every word in rapt unconsciousness of my discomforts. In moments when his face was turned fully to me I caught the seeming transfiguration elsewhere alluded to. No other orator ever held me so completely. Of the singers whom I have been permitted to hear, not even the divine

Patti ruled me half so tyrannically. Bearded and bronzed as were the soldiers of his audience, they cried till the tears left glistening paths down their cheeks. I alighted from my perch sore and cramped; but from that day to this I have never regretted the year left behind me as a soldier in Mexico; neither have I at any time since been troubled with a qualm about the propriety even to righteousness of the war. Saying nothing about the glory won, our country has been in every respect greater and better of its consequences.

The voyage up the Mississippi from New Orleans gave me some spare hours to resolve upon a course of life now that life was to be begun again. There were two hundred and eighty dollars of savings in my trunk. Doubtless the store could be increased at home. After much reflection, the first I can now recall as in the least tinged with anxiety, I decided to give myself six months to college work somewhere. Latin and mathematics were especially in my mind, the latter because it was a branch in which I was particularly weak.

But here, too, the unexpected happened. While I was debating where I should go, and what institution of learning should be favored with my patronage, somebody relieved me of my money. Fortunately there remained enough in my pocket to take me to Indianapolis. The loss was serious; at the same time the sharpest sting in the mishap was in knowing with a certainty, not admitting of doubt, that a brother officer, Captain ———, for whom my affection had been very positive, was the thief. To prove the crime upon him was beyond me; wherefore I held my peace.

A week in Indianapolis, given chiefly to renewals of acquaintanceship, served me for rest, and I then settled down again in my father's office, mixing study with pettifogging. For society my inclinations were still of the faintest kind; indeed, I had but one object all alive —to capture the license formerly denied me by the Supreme Court.

Where one's wants are few and simple as mine, it ought not in our country to be difficult to earn enough to meet them. It was so at least in my case. Opportunities to turn the traditional honest penny came frequently. Among them I remember offers of agencies of this and that. These were always declined.

Shortly after settling down, when the resolution was beginning to be strong with me, one night I unearthed the manuscript of *The Fair God,* or rather the commonplace book, sixteen inches long and twelve in width, closely ruled, containing the work far as finished. I had been to Mexico now, and knew somewhat of the country, having breathed its air and looked into its sky by night and day, and seen those of its people the descendants of the Aztecs. Should I go on with the work? I turned the covers, and read here and there, and the characters passed before me, all of whom I had written—the brave natives, king, princes, priests, people, and the Spaniards, even Cortés, the boldest where all were bold. Then I set in and read to the last word of the last paragraph. I read the night out. Pastimes are undertakers who bury the hours for nothing. What of it? The writing had been a habit, and a good one, and I resolved to stick to it.

I applied at length for admission to the bar of the Circuit Court, and license to practise was granted me. Still, I did not feel myself a lawyer. That result awaited a formal certificate signed by Isaac Blackford.

This sketch will expose the jumble of employment with which the remainder of the year 1847 was filled. A break then ensued.

AN AUTOBIOGRAPHY

[Fragments of an old journal give an idea of what was passing in the young man's heart. To it, he made confession.—S. E. W.]

INDIANAPOLIS, *July*, 1847.
Half-past eleven P.M.

. . . .

This evening I picked up a copy of Tupper and read his effusion on "Marriage." This sentence seems familiar to my thoughts, "If thou art to have a wife of thy youth, she is now living on the earth; therefore think of her and pray for weal; yea, though thou hast not seen her."

A thousand times have I had the same idea! Even in childhood we have pleasant vagaries of love. They come to us as views of a clear-blue sky through narrow rifts of dark clouds. We hail them with delight and imagine them heaven. Even in my half-wild boyhood there lived a haunting yearning in my heart to see, hear, and live in presence of her whom Fate was to give me as the wife of my youth.

Many a time have I stood beneath the stars, and gazing up at their bright shinings, mumbled over every form of charm and incantation my fancy conceived, hoping all the time I might accidentally hit upon one which the Chaldees used to subdue by their mysterious power and learn from them the locked-up secrets of the future. Had I been successful the first picture I would have had them paint me would have been the miniature of my unbeheld but somewhere living wife whose name the Destiny of mine had written among "the poetry of Heaven." Not only have I asked it of the stars, but my curiosity has carried me to more unpoetic lengths. I never meet a good, pretty girl, but I've asked of my soul, expecting its immortality of nature to endow it with at least that much miraculous knowledge, "Is it she?" When will the radiance of that other life fall over mine?

. . . .

I am a believer in Destiny, and no sceptic to the beautiful theory that the incomplete heart will recognize its perfection instantly it beholds it. I would have made a fiery, energetic follower of Cromwell, or, had I been a Frenchman, would have worshipped the great "N" of "*Le petit Corporal*" with as deep devotion as the Crusader worshipped the holy symbol of his cause. I have always found the enthusiasm of love the wildest, while that of ambition is the steadiest in men's hearts. My noblest dream of life has been one of fame, but my holiest of her whom Fate shall give me for a wife. She must have high qualities to command me. In my aspirations her spirit must follow mine in my war for the world's bubbles, not as a squaw her savage husband, but by my side, a woman's yet an equal spirit. Then I shall tread the *steppes* of a new existence with her. When will my dream come true?

. . . .

What a place for dreaming was Old Mexico! There in the introspection of idleness my ideals almost took shape.

Many a time have I lain on the soft sand, and while the ocean poured its eternal hymn in my scarce conscious sense, watched the cold, round moon as she looked down on the shadows of night and the seething foam of the waters, and tortured imagination to give me a picture of the beloved, the unbeheld. I have somewhere read a wild legend of a German hunter, who, in some of his wanderings amid the Hartz mountains, came across a romantic cascade. Tired, wearied out, he lay down on its banks and went to sleep. In his slumber a form (a woman's) appeared to his vision. And the form was lovely, transparent as a moonbeam, and bright as a star-halo. It addressed him in terms of love, and seemed to watch over him while he slept. After his slumber passed away he returned home. But the vision of the cascade haunted his memory, and in vain he sought to shake it off. Under its influence he revisited the fountain. Again the wild, beautiful spirit greeted him with its low voice. Then a frantic love assumed the mastery of the hunter's heart. Day after day, night after night, his wasting form was laid on the green bank of the singing waterfall. Ever he sighed, murmured, dreamed. The strength forsook his limbs—the blood melted away in his heart. He loved the water-spirit to madness, but she was of the race of souls and as such could not interwed a mortal. To possess her, therefore, he must die. So, one day when the earth was all bright but his heart all dark, while the fairy sang him a song of unimaginable melody, he stretched his arms to grasp the shadowy enchantress, and plunged over into the roaring caldron of the cascade.

My Egeria is of the race of mortals. I shall go to her for wisdom, as Numa did to his, and to win her I need not die. She is waiting for me somewhere in the cool shadows of to-night, and I wait for her.

She will love me, and I shall make her famous by my pen and glorious by my sword.

[Our friend, Mary Clemmer, has written a description of the dreamer beset with aerial fancies living in the golden age of twenty-one. A portion of her letter may be copied without treachery to her memory.]

"Lewis Wallace, of Indiana, is in outward seeming our hero of Provence wearing the bright spurs won on the field of Fornovo. The youthful chevalier *sans peur et sans reproche*, valiant, wise, and loyal.

"He is fashioned of the refined clay of which nature is most sparing, nearly six feet high, perfectly straight, with a fine fibred frame all nerve and muscle, and so thin he cannot weigh more than a hundred and thirty pounds. He has profuse black hair, a dark, beautiful face, correct in every line, keen, black eyes deeply set, with a glance that on occasion may cut like fine steel. Black beard and mustache conceal the firm mouth and chin. His modest, quiet manner is the only *amende* that can be made for being so handsome. In a crowd anywhere you would single him out as a king of men.

LEW WALLACE

"Marked for action rather than words, he is habitually reticent, yet when the time comes for speech is ready with eloquent words, given with a voice at once sweet and strong. A man of convictions, earnest in every nerve of his being, intensely earnest."

XXI

June, 1848—The Whig national convention—Nomination and election of Taylor — Edit a campaign paper opposing Taylor—Indiana refuses to vote for Taylor—A deficit of six hundred dollars—Left in the lurch—Become a Democrat of the straitest sect.

In June, 1848, the Whig national convention met at Philadelphia, and on the fourth ballot nominated Zachary Taylor for the presidency over Henry Clay, Daniel Webster, and Winfield Scott.

This result had been in the air since the victories of Palo Alto and Resaca de la Palma, an anticipation of immense trouble to the politicians, none of whom knew if General Taylor were Whig or Democrat, or if he had any politics. After the fall of Monterey both parties had claimed him; in local meetings both nominated him; while on his side, with a naïveté suspiciously childlike and bland, he was prodigal of thanks and mailed acceptances indiscriminately. Yet it was said he was not dishonest; he wanted to be president, but dreamed of the great honor of a spontaneous offering from the whole people. Finally, Buena Vista came along, and it was decisive. That he was chosen over General Scott was not strange; nevertheless, one does marvel that the Whig party turned its thumbs down on Henry Clay and Daniel Webster, its makers, for a soldier who, when at last driven to definition, reluctantly admitted himself a Whig, and could not see why a formal acceptance of nomination by the Whig national convention should estop him from a like formal acceptance of a later nomination by the Democratic convention of the state of New Jersey.

The nomination of General Taylor found me in the most sophomoric period of my life. It will provoke a smile, I know; yet I actually believed my opposition could seriously shake the old hero's popularity and chances of election.

Though Whig by birth and raising—intensely Whig—it was impossible for me to forget the repeated punishments the First Indiana regiment had suffered from the nominee; nor more could I acquit him of responsibility for the crowded state of the Potter's field at the mouth of the Rio Grande. I remembered, also, his helping hand in dishonoring the Second Indiana at Buena Vista, and the dogged refusal to modify his report in accordance with the facts and opinions of the two courts which investigated the conduct of that unfortunate regiment. I remembered the effect of it all upon the credit of the state with an intensity of resentment which I confess has outlived my youth.

The interest with which I followed the march of events through 1847, down to the convention of June, 1848, may be imagined. I availed myself of every opportunity to declaim against General Taylor. When opportunities were wanting, I sometimes made them. Then, at the meeting of the convention, with what passionate anxiety its action was awaited! Could it be that the delegation from Indiana would support him? At last the report: Taylor, 7; Clay, 1; Scott, 4.

I had not demolished General Taylor—that was plain. After wrestling awhile with the pangs of defeat, I rallied, and resolved to go on with the fight. He should not have the vote of Indiana in the electoral college, if I could help it.

My first idea was to take the stump, in furtherance

of which I wrote a speech aimed at such pride as belonged to the state. The speech dealt with General Taylor and Indiana in the war. It was brimful of invective. *The Philippics of Demosthenes* served me as models. The trial of a case before a justice of the peace took me to the country about the time the screed was well memorized. There were seventy-five or a hundred people present. Before the dispersal began I suggested to his honor, if he would call the assemblage to order I would speak on politics. He did so; and, in observing the effect upon the audience, I noticed the Democrats cheered in season and out, while the Whigs looked glum and made no sign. One old man, I remember, came up to me and asked, significantly, "Your father is living, isn't he?" The experiment was not to my satisfaction, but fortune helped me.

The year will doubtless be recollected as fruitful in presidential candidates. Three parties put tickets in the field—the Whigs with Zachary Taylor, the Democrats with Lewis Cass, the Free-Soilers with Martin Van Buren. The latter were known as "Barnburners"—exactly why, I do not know. They had often been, moreover, the subject of my best denunciation as a conglomeration with but one idea—the abolition of slavery. But now it was to be taken seriously, having the airs of organization. It had even held a convention at Indianapolis, well attended and zealous.

The day after that convention I was surprised by a call from three gentlemen, two of them of Indianapolis, and among the wealthiest residents of the city. Why I do not name them will presently appear. They said they were a committee appointed to provide for a weekly campaign paper to be the organ of the Free-Soil party in Indiana. They had fixed upon a Mr. G——r and myself to conduct the organ. Mr. G——r had consented; would I consent? They kindly agreed to give me a day for consideration.

Now, my war upon candidate Taylor was limited to Indiana. He could hope nothing from Democrats. Good strategy, on the other hand, pointed to weakening the Whigs, for whom, as a rule, abolition had the fewest terrors. Taylor would be a slave-holder's president. His election would mean the extension of slavery. That, as anybody could see, was the string to pull with Whigs. I cared nothing for Lewis Cass or for Martin Van Buren. My only thought was to keep Indiana out of Taylor's column of states. Dignity, honor, self-respect demanded that much of the state.

In the succeeding interview with the committee I inquired if they were to be understood as offering me compensation. They replied with candor that I must take chances with the paper; if, at the end of the campaign, there was a sum in excess of the outlay, Mr. G——r and I might divide it between us. But, I said, suppose there is a deficit; and I ventured to suggest having heard that newspapers were notoriously expensive and dangerous enterprises. Then they broadly assured me if, in the outcome, there was a loss, they would see to it that we were made whole; all we had to do on that score was to be as economical and careful as the interests involved would allow.

Then ensued quite six months of hard work. My associate shared the labor with me fairly. He took the business management. We had no assistants. Week after week, month after month—at last the election! General Taylor became president, but not—and I devoutly thanked God for it—*not with the electoral vote of Indiana.* Having grown to think and feel the fight mine personally, and accounting the result in Indiana a victory, I was happy, and ranted and cheered, and made myself a burden, especially to my father, whose Whig friends insisted on holding him responsible for my treason.

Ere long our printer came to me for a settlement. I referred him to Mr. G——r, who had the books. He said Mr. G——r was not in the city. Where was he? Several days on the road to California. To find the books was of importance. They had been, I found, well and honestly kept, and were balanced showing an indebtedness of over six hundred dollars. With the accounts in hand, it took me a short time to find Messrs. ——— and ———, to remind them of their pledge to make me whole. First one declined, then the other. I pleaded with them. So many months of labor gone, so much time. I had trusted them because they were rich, and professed Christians, known to me all my life. They could at least help me in part. No, not a cent, and they gave no reason. I folded up the statement and left them. What had I to show? Wisdom in the shape of distrust of my fellow-men, counterbalanced, in part, at least, by having worked at the case as a printer. I knew how to punctuate, an acquisition that abides with me. Did the worst come, I had the rudiments of a trade.

The two Christian gentlemen lived long, and passed me often on the street without ever thinking it worth their while to stop and ask me how I was getting on. The debt dragged with me. At the end of the sixth year I lifted the last note. They died in the fulness of their time, and have gone to their reward.

The outcome of the affair may prove curious. The Whigs had elected General Taylor; my connection with the "Barnburners" had been purely instructive; and seeing no middle ground politically for me, I became a Democrat—one of the straitest of the sect.

LEW WALLACE

XXII

Major Isaac C. Elston—His home—Susan Elston—College commencement, July, 1848—Courtship—Receive license from Supreme Court.

In the day of my college career there lived in Crawfordsville a merchant named Elston. His full name on a visiting-card, title and all, would have read—Major Isaac C. Elston.

Major Elston had settled in the town when it was a belonging of the wilderness. Out of a dry-goods store he builded a fair fortune. Then, widening his operations, he bought the site of Michigan City, platted it, sold lots, and became a rich man. His dwelling-house, in the midst of a primeval woods, was the best in the county, and it was furnished to correspond, and the fame thereof went abroad. People visited it just to see things. I heard some of them talking one day of a sofa in the lower hall. What was a sofa? It was altogether unlikely that Major Elston would ever invite me to his house; but was I for that to grow up without sight of a sofa?—a mahogany sofa covered with hair-cloth, so the description ran. I took the liberty of inviting myself to see the wonder, and had my wish, though not without peril; for if caught in the trespass my appearance, so defiant of common requirement, would have justified any suspicion. In the same way it came to my knowledge that Major Elston had recently imported a piano. What was a piano? Those of whom I asked, hardly better informed than myself, told me it was a big musical machine. The description excited my curiosity the more. And again I invited myself into the major's house, and saw the sight without discovery; whereupon I was beset with a greater wonder. How was the playing done? I laid in wait for the solution. One evening the double parlor was a wonder of brilliance. A party was in progress. I worked my way, Indian-like, to a window through which the whole interior was in view. In a little while, sure enough, a young lady went to the machine, opened it, and began a song with an accompaniment. I remember the song:

> "One little, two little, three little Indians,
> Four little, five little, six little Indians."

And so on for quantity.

In 1848 a college commencement drew me back to Crawfordsville. As usual on that day, the town was flung open to visitors. Among those to entertain was Mrs. Henry S. Lane, wife of the lieutenant-colonel of the First Indiana regiment, and second daughter of Major Elston. I had the pleasure of attending. In the midst of the gayety, Major Elston's third daughter appeared. Susan, then eighteen, recently from her graduation at a Quaker school for girls in Poughkeepsie, New York, bearing herself modestly as a veiled nun.

Fifty years and more! I can blow the time aside lightly as smoke from a cigar, and have a return of that evening with Miss Elston, and her blue eyes, wavy hair, fair face, girlish manner, delicate person, and witty flashes to vivify it.

There are young people who think a man past seventy may not be moved by the love of his youth, if he has recollection of it at all. The opinion, I assure them, is an attack upon themselves—they who are in turn to grow old. There was never one, albeit beyond the sage's limit of life, to forget the days he went wooing. Some there are, doubtless, the unsuccessful for instance, who would like to forget them. Be the truth told simply. Far from so much as dimming the recollection, the years but make it holier, until after-while the old man, nothing loath to expose his whole life else, keeps that dear property to himself. So much I extract from my own experience.

Yet, having undertaken to write my life, would the life be complete without the story of how it became subject to its most benign influence? Let me not falter in confession here. What of success has come to me, all that I am, in fact, is owing to her, the girl of whom I am speaking. The admission is broad, yet it leaves justice but half done.

She was beautiful in my eyes when I first saw her; and the word is not used in its common sense; dolls are pretty; so are faces in wax, if only they are fresh and clean. The beauty she gave me to see that evening in the social blaze was after Wordsworth's ideal:

> "A countenance in which did meet
> Sweet records, promises as sweet;
> A creature not too bright and good
> For human nature's daily food,
> For transient sorrows, simple wiles,
> Praise, blame, love, kisses, tears, and smiles."

The promises were in her face when next I saw her in plain daylight; and after all the trials of years come and gone—now—the same promises are as bank-notes redeemed, and there is no need of them more.

When May 6, 1902 comes round, and repeats itself in budding roses, it will be golden-wedding day with us. The advent may freshen recollection of the glad

LEW WALLACE,
Age 21

time, and I bid it welcome in advance, but I will not for that delay the record I have for her as my wife. I have been subject to her; and her gentle soul has controlled me, and bent me to her wishes, but unselfishly, and always for my good, and always so deftly that I was as one blind to the domination. My temper has never been so hot she could not lay it. She has decided me in doubt, defended me against interruptions, saved me my time at the sacrifice of her own, cheered me when down at heart, lured me back to my tasks when the tempter would have whisked me away, held my hand in defeat, and rejoiced with me in my triumphs. In my work she has helped me to the word, and been my one honest critic. Often in the long journey when, at the parting of the ways, I have stopped bewildered, afraid to go on, unwilling to go back, she has set me in the right way, and even gone before to assure me. Her faith in me began with the beginning, when I was unknown and uncertain of myself, and the world all too ready to laugh at my attempts. Hers is a high nature, a composite of genius, common-sense, and all best womanly qualities. The marvel, her memory, has always been at my service. Most fortunately for me, the books she loves are the best, and she knows them by heart. With her in call, I have no use for dictionaries of quotation.

Nor less is she a musician. Not as the divas are, to fill vast interiors and astonish audiences in multitude, but a minnesinger loving to soothe vexed children with lullabies, and set old people to living their lives over again with ballads redolent of things noble and good. Now, grievous to say, a tone has gone out of her voice, and I miss it, and so does she. Sometimes she speaks of it as one of the robberies of old time, but I say no, and insist that she does not practise enough. Still, of long evenings, when the house is quiet and the fire burns, she will bring out the guitar, and with fingers loyal to her feeling as ever, give me the song I have all along most loved, and which, should she be near when I come to die, I would have her sing for the help there will be in it to the spirit crossing the bar. There may be a reader curious to see the lines; and I give them:

"THREE DREAMS

"I dreamed a dream of boyhood's days,
Of high and wild and careless glee.
Around my path ten thousand rays
Sparkling and dancing seemed to be.

"Dream of my boyhood, stay, O stay!
Let me thus sport my life away.
Dream of my boyhood, stay, O stay!—
Alas, alas! It fades away.

"I dreamed a dream of early youth,
A wilderness of sweetest dreams.
I scarce know what of love and truth
Bathing my soul in heavenly beams.

"Dream of my youth, sweet dream, O stay!
Let me thus love my life away.
Dream of my youth, sweet dream, O stay!—
Alas, alas! It fades away!

"I dreamed a dream of Manhood's prime,
Mixed dream of triumph and of strife;
But she at morn and evening's chime
Was there to bless and cheer my life.

"Dream of my prime, stay, O stay!
Thy features court the opening day.
Dream of my prime, stay, O stay!—
Alas! thou too must fade away."

It must not be imagined that I won Miss Elston without trouble. She had many admirers, of whom four were pronouncedly competitors. I believe I may venture to speak of them without mentioning their names; though as a further security against harm, they are all dead. One was a lawyer—a great one, too. He might have given me more vexation had he been younger and less subject to wine. The second was a middle-aged gentleman, who rested his cause on two arguments—he was very rich, and would build his love a splendid house. A strong plea, it must be admitted. The third was a business man. Fortunately for me, he was unaware of the importance of affecting a little sentiment. The last of the list was a preacher, who rested his case on an appeal to the religious inclinations of his idol. In the moment of supreme confidence, when he may be supposed to have been on his knees, Grandison style, telling of his passion and his future, he let it be known that he was to be a missionary, and went so far even as to expose an arrangement by which he was to be sent to the Gaboon — wherever that might be. One suitor failed lacking sentiment, this one failed lacking common-sense.

I have admitted trouble. In telling whence it came I know there will be demur. *She* will say I am too free in disclosure; and I am not sure but she is right. There was opposition. It was insisted there was no promise of good in me—nothing to rest a hope upon in the wayward youth. This meant simply that the outlawry of my boyhood was in the judgment, and I never blamed the parents. Only they did not understand me.

I carried my pleading to the very principal in the controversy — the real party in interest. And this blood in me of the old man now quickens like a lad's, often as I revert to the discovery that the faith of my love was not of the fainting kind. A better day would come, and she agreed to wait for it. The years were ours—three years we waited, and then I led her home, she trusting me when no one else did.

Long, long afterwards she wrote me "A Song of Songs." Here is one verse:

> "Our morning dreams are broken,
> And castles day by day
> With far and floating banners
> In distance fade away.
> Dim arcade and airy tower
> I never more may see,
> But all my lost ideals
> Are found again in thee."

It has always been a wonder to me how old people lose their heads dealing with the love-affairs of the young; that is why they cannot see that opposition is bread and wine to the infatuation they deplore—I call it infatuation out of respect for them. Let us consider. Nonsense, nonsense! you say. Yes, I know; yet—if in their passing, men stop to wring all the nonsense out of their lives, what threadbare rags they would be left holding.

In the first place, the romance of the situation began with the first word of protest. In the next place, I had been willing to work in the hope of making something of myself for self's sake; now here was a new incentive to move me, and its objects of attainment were immediate. I hate repetitions, and therefore advance, summarizing. At the fall term of the Supreme Court, 1849, I again applied for license. Three or four days after the examination I received a carefully sealed official envelope addressed, "Lewis Wallace, Esquire, Attorney-at-Law." It contained two enclosures: one the coveted license, signed "Isaac Blackford, Judge"; the other, a brief explanatory note over the same signature with a postscript—"Permit me to congratulate you upon your safe return from Mexico." So, so! If Blackstone could unbend and indulge in poetry, was it strange that Isaac Blackford could be humorous? I thought of the flippancy of which I had been guilty, and reddened to the tips of my ears. There was but one thing to be done, I went straight to the judge and apologized. He laughed, and said he understood it; boys would be boys. He also invited me to attend court next morning. In calling the roll of attorneys for motions, he was sure it would be pleasant to me to hear my name. Who would have thought the veteran lawyer could have been so delicate in attention?

LEW WALLACE

XXIII

Return to Covington—Senator Hannegan—A wager—D. W. Voorhees—The violin—Judge Ristine—The political meeting at Chambersburg—Mr. M——y—Justice Glasscock—To Danville, Illinois, with Voorhees—Abraham Lincoln.

I HAD now, it will be observed, three incentives to action—bread, ambition, and the obligations inseparable from the dear soul then mine in solemn covenant.

The first thing in order was to choose a location in which to open a law office. I turned from Indianapolis, for the reason that few things are more trying to a young man than to bring the elders who have known him from childhood to admit the possibility of his knowing more than they even in a specialty. This is certainly true of the elders who may have predestined him to the gallows.

The influences that determine men halting, and which finally give them direction, are sometimes amusing, sometimes trifling, but they are always curious. I did not go to New York or to Cincinnati—Chicago was then only a great city in promise—but Covington, the village on the Wabash already familiar to the reader as my playground in childhood. When I remind him of its distance from Crawfordsville—scant thirty miles—he will at once perceive the influence that drew me there.

It was not merely to be within easy ride of the fair partner of my fortunes; to deny it the chiefest inducement would be a poor return for the devotion she was showing; still there was another motive. Of my eventual success at the bar I had no doubt; so in secret I cherished a wish to make my emergement from obscurity under the eyes, as it were, of the distrustful authority in Elston castle; the naturalness of the prompting must relieve every suspicion of pettiness.

The office I opened in Covington corresponded in furnishment with my means. A table, a stove, the revised statutes of the state, the ordinary text-books, Barbour's *Justice of the Peace*, the Supreme Court *Reports* to date, Blackford's inclusive, constituted my law library. To complete the inventory, I must not forget a violin, to which I was addicted, though not offensively, since my practice in that line was limited to hours when the town was asleep. If Thomas Jefferson and Governor Whitcomb did not disdain the seductions of the bow, why should I?

My "shingle" was in plain black and white—"Lew Wallace, Attorney-at-Law." The day I nailed it to the cheek of my office door, I sat down and marshalled my assets in cash. The total was one dollar and seventy-five cents, the dollar being in paper money. That same day came the announcement of the failure of the bank issuing that note. Nothing daunted, I continued boarding at the hotel.

Edward A. Hannegan was the great man of the town, and he ruled it baronially. As United States senator of democratic persuasion, he had distinguished himself in the debate on the boundary-line between our possessions on the Pacific coast and those of the British. The famous utterance, "54—40, or fight," had been his. Could his policy have been resolutely carried out, the tremendous fortification on the northern shore of Vancouver's Island known as the Esquimalt would not now be dominating the inlet to Puget Sound. More recently he had returned from a residence in Berlin as minister.

I have spoken of him as orator. It may be added that he was a man of courtly grace, passionate in his friendships and his hates. To a faculty of attraction, he had the opposite faculty of repulsion, both in larger degree than I have ever seen them in the same person. He and my father had been warm friends in despite of politics. I was much surprised one morning by a visit from him at my office. Besides giving me encouragement, he invited me to make myself free at his house and study. Returning the call, I was astonished at his library, so completely did it cover the world of miscellaneous literature. The privilege of that study was much more than a sounding compliment.

I recall Senator Hannegan as attorney defending a man indicted for murder. In the examination of a witness an objection was offered to one of his questions. The case turned upon the point involved. If the objection were sustained, the conviction of his client was inevitable. He met the opposition with an eloquence so passionate that for years after the speech continued one of the legends of the court. The ruling was in his favor, followed by a verdict of acquittal. His reputation was that of an impromptu speaker. In this instance, however, the argument was so perfect, the sentence so finished, that I smelled the oil of the lamp in it, and to decide a wager he was consulted in his study.

"Mr. Hannegan," my opponent said, "we have come to have you settle a bet. The dispute is whether the speech you made in course of the examination of (giving the name of the witness) was prepared or delivered on the spur of the moment. My friend here says it was carefully prepared; I say it was off-hand. If not offensive, what do you say?"

Hannegan, smiling, went to a drawer and took out a manuscript.

"Here," he said; "if you remember the speech, young gentlemen, this will dispose of the issue between you better than my dixit."

We took the script, and it was the speech word for word without an interlineation or an erasure.

The young gentleman—slightly to modify Senator Hannegan's polite address—thus party of the second part to the wager has since become one of the familiars of the republic. There is little need of more than the mention of his name, so universally known are he and his career. Daniel W. Voorhees opened a law office in Covington about the time of my appearance for the same purpose. Three or four years before his death a trifling cloud arose between us, which, while enough to break our intimacy, failed to weaken the respect we had for each other. A great political party is a mourner at his tomb; yet, of the multitude, few outside his children miss him more than I do, or send sincerer regrets after him. Our bouts, usually in some justice's court, were frequent. They were rough-and-tumble, or, in wrestling parlance, catch-as-catch-can; sometimes almost to the fighting-point. But it was not in his nature to bear malice. I can yet hear the creak of the door of my office as, without a knock, he threw it open and walked in—generally the night of the day of an encounter—a tall man of genuine gladiatorial port. I can hear the greeting with which he threw himself on a chair: "Well, Lew, I got you to-day," or "you got me," according to the fact. "Come, now, put your work up and let's have the fiddle." And with a word out the fiddle came; whereupon there was truce and presently a perfected peace. The "Cracovienne" and "Arkansas Traveller" were his favorites. But as the night wore away he would call for "Annie Laurie," and keep me at it. He was in love then, and engaged, and

—the reader knows my story. "Dan" was the first to marry. At his house-opening nothing would do but that I should help at the first dinner. Mrs. Voorhees prepared it herself. She was a novice, and there were accidents of course. How we did laugh at them!—she the merriest of the company.

Business was shy in the beginning. Nobody knew me. Occasionally there came one wanting a conveyance or a contract written; the fees, however, were not enough to help me meet accruing bills. My host of the hotel was lenient; unfortunately there were necessities more intolerant. The rust on my shoes would shine through the veneer of blacking; a sere struck my coat; and, by no means least, the time arrived when I flinched, seeing a *vis-à-vis* of this or that sex studying a little too closely the visible parts of my shirt. Nevertheless, I held on. At length I reached the turn—none too soon.

The county clerk stopped me one day on the street. It may be doubted if a gentleman more generous than Judge Joseph Ristine abided in all those parts. With what pleasure I write his name in full.

"I understand you have served in the Marion county clerk's office," he said.

"Yes, sir."

"Deputy?"

"No, employé."

"Can you make up entries?"

"Perfectly."

"Well, court is in session. Come over to-morrow."

"Thank you. I'll come."

At the end of the session I paid off all bills against me, bought a new suit of clothes out and in, and had a firm friend besides.

Still the law proper hung fire, and I worried. After a deal of reflection I concluded that want of notoriety was the matter, and I must do something to set the people talking about me. But how—what? There was the rub. Opportunities were not to order. I could only wait for them; and at last one presented itself.

The constitutional convention was held in 1850, with Fountain County entitled to two delegates. Both the political parties put candidates in nomination. Judge Ristine and Mr. M——y, a lawyer, were opposing candidates. As a partisan of the former, I anonymously carded the Democratic paper in his behalf. Mr. M——y answered over his own name. Shrewdly guessing the author of the attack upon him, his denunciation was bitterly personal. Here was the opportunity.

Speaking generally, the people of the county were the original settlers, primitive in habits, large-hearted, Western in spirit. Instead of taking their quarrels into court, they settled them on the spot, resorting to their fists. Giving the lie and getting ready for instant resentment were simultaneous acts; while, if the party affronted hung back, or quailed, no allowances were made for him; he must fight. Especially was this true of lawyers. They might be slow in speech; they might be dishonest; they might lie, in fact, and rob, and still have a clientele; the one thing their respectability could not survive was a reputation for cowardice.

The day the paper appeared with Mr. M——y's reply to my card, there was to be speaking at a little town of the county called Chambersburg. The candidates were to be there and submit their views.

I had a good friend in the sheriff, and, on search, found him in his buggy about to set out for the meeting.

"Tom," I said, "you saw the paper this morning, and what M——y said of me?"

"Yes, what of it?"

"Well, I want that vacant seat. I am going to thrash M——y."

"Jump right in."

The sheriff was a blacksmith and of the fighting set.

"How are you going to manage it?" he asked, on the road. "It will not do for you to disturb the meeting."

"I know that, and you must help me."

"How? I am a conservator, you know."

"Easy enough. What I want you to do is to see a number of the right sort and have M——y put down for the last speech; then, when he quits, have them yell for me. You understand?"

It suited him exactly.

The meeting was in a grove at the edge of the town, with probably three hundred and fifty voters present, county folk almost entirely. One after another the candidates spoke, M——y last in order. As he concluded, a cry went up: "Wallace! Wallace!"

Going forward among the speakers, I responded promptly, beginning with an expression of surprise at being so highly distinguished—I but lately come into the county—a stranger. My next point was a eulogy of Judge Ristine. Hardly had I entered upon it when M——y advanced and protested that I was not a candidate. In his eagerness he laid a hand on my arm. That was justification enough, and I struck him. He staggered back, as luck would have it, into the arms of a justice of the peace, Dempsey Glasscock, a patriarch of Chambersburg, and an eccentric known from the source of the Wabash to its exit into the Ohio.

The meeting went to pieces, of course.

I found myself next on trial before Squire Glasscock, charged with assault and battery.

"Guilty or not guilty," he demanded, sternly.

"Guilty," I answered.

The crowd was great, but silence prevailed while the justice made an entry in his docket. Then he stood up and spoke. "Fellow-citizens, I fine the defendant five dollars and cost him."

There was loud protestation.

"But—"

Silence returned.

"But I remit the costs; and here you, Tom"—meaning the sheriff—"take this hat and raise the fine. If any galoot you speak to refuses to 'ante,' he'd better get out of Fountain County."

The fine was paid; then Justice Glasscock again: "Now, you by the door there, roll a buggy up in front of the shop. I'm goin' to have Wallace finish his speech; and you're all invited out to hear him. Come along."

The part of the speech devoted to M——y gave great satisfaction. And from that day I had business. Soon the lawyer with the best docket in the county offered me a partnership.

This may be regarded the experimental period of my life, and I cannot pass it by without recital of a circumstance which derived an interest from subsequent events greatly out of the ordinary. In fact, it is one of my cherished recollections.

Mr. Voorhees came to my office one day.

"What are you doing?" he asked.

"Nothing."

"Well, it is the same with me; so I propose we chip in and hire a horse and buggy and go to Danville."

The reference was Danville, Illinois.

"What's going on there?"

"Court is in session—that's all."

We reached the town about dusk and stopped at the

tavern. The bar-room, when we entered it after supper, was all a-squeeze with residents, spiced with parties to suits pending, witnesses, and jurors. The ceiling was low, and we had time to admire the depth and richness of the universal smoke-stain of the wooden walls. To edge in we had to bide our time. Every little while there would be bursts of laughter, and now and then a yell of delight. At last, within the zone of sight, this was what we saw: In front of us a spacious pioneer fireplace all aglow with a fire scientifically built. On the right of the fireplace sat three of the best story-tellers of Indiana, Edward A. Hannegan, Dan Mace, and John Pettit. Opposite them, a broad brick hearth intervening, were two strangers to me whom inquiry presently identified as famous lawyers and yarn-spinners of Illinois.

One may travel now from the Kennebec to Puget Sound and never see such a tournament as the five men were holding; only instead of splintering lances they were swapping anecdotes. As to the kind and color of the jokes submitted to the audience, while not always chaste, they never failed to hit home.

The criss-crossing went on till midnight, and for a long time it might not be said whether Illinois or Indiana was ahead. There was one of the contestants, however, who arrested my attention early, partly by his stories, partly by his appearance. Out of the mist of years he comes to me now exactly as he appeared then. His hair was thick, coarse, and defiant; it stood out in every direction. His features were massive, nose long, eyebrows protrusive, mouth large, cheeks hollow, eyes gray and always responsive to the humor. He smiled all the time, but never once did he laugh outright. His hands were large, his arms slender and disproportionately long. His legs were a wonder, particularly when he was in narration; he kept crossing and uncrossing them; sometimes it actually seemed he was trying to tie them into a bow-knot. His dress was more than plain; no part of it fit him. His shirt collar had come from the home laundry innocent of starch. The black cravat about his neck persisted in an ungovernable affinity with his left ear. Altogether I thought him the gauntest, quaintest, and most positively ugly man who had ever attracted me enough to call for study. Still, when he was in speech, my eyes did not quit his face. He held me in unconsciousness. About midnight his competitors were disposed to give in; either their stores were exhausted, or they were tacitly conceding him the crown. From answering them story for story, he gave two or three to their one. At last he took the floor and held it. And looking back, I am now convinced that he frequently invented his replications; which is saying he possessed a marvellous gift of improvisation. Such was Abraham Lincoln. And to be perfectly candid, had one stood at my elbow that night in the old tavern and whispered: "Look at him closely. He will one day be president and the savior of his country," I had laughed at the idea but a little less heartily than I laughed at the man. Afterwards I came to know him better, and then I did not laugh.

XXIV

Made prosecuting attorney—James Wilson—Rival orators—David Brier and Dan Mace—The violin and the interrupted meeting—Removal to Crawfordsville, 1853—*The Fair God*—Scribners' "agent."

NOT wishing to weary one disposed to honor me with an interest in the recital of my life, I shall not linger over the part of it given to the practise of law. Along with many things not admirable, I did some things that were thought smart. I had my triumphs; and it is not a little surprising to me now how readily I bring myself to shove them into the same pigeon-hole devoted to my defeats.

In 1850 the office of prosecuting attorney was of importance, and, being elective, candidates for it were chosen by the political parties at the biennial conventions held for the nomination of congressmen. When well administered it brought the incumbent profit, experience, and extended acquaintance. So, seeking the nomination, I was lucky enough to secure it and be elected—successes which lost nothing of flavor when promptly reported at the castle in Crawfordsville.

On the trial of cases, the main difficulty, as I speedily discovered, was the memory of witnesses. Many of them had a habit of conveniently forgetting in the interval between sessions of the court what they had sworn before the grand jury. The lapses were both fatal and provoking until I hit upon a remedy. It consisted in carefully entering in a journal the testimony as given, reading it to the witness in presence of the jury, and then requiring him to affix his signature to the statement. When, next court, the case was called for trial, I took him apart, read to him from the journal, and confronted him with his signature. If he faltered, a gentle reminder of the pains of perjury always sufficed to bring him round to the side of justice.

The work was heavy, but that mattered nothing. It was profitable, and more—it was love's labor not lost. On May 6, 1852, I was able to go to Crawfordsville and be married. If my great happiness over the event so long in expectancy was tinctured ever so slightly with exultation, I plead the weakness of human nature in extenuation. The wedding was without objection.

I took my wife to my father's house in Indianapolis, and introduced her there. She delighted my people—none more than the old gentleman himself. I returned then to Covington, the birthplace of our only child, Henry Lane Wallace.

In 1852, my term as prosecuting attorney expiring, I was renominated and again elected.

The competitor given me by the opposition made the race warm and in every way worth the while. Mr. James Wilson lived in Crawfordsville. A graduate of Wabash College, by virtue of great speaking qualities, quick wit, a fine presence and a magnetic nature, he rose rapidly, and repeatedly represented the district in Congress. He was a trifle my senior in age. Professional and political rivalry were not enough ever to disturb our good relations.

In the contest alluded to, the candidates for Congress were, on Wilson's side, Mr. David Brier, of Covington, and on mine, Mr. Dan Mace, of Lafayette. The active canvass was scarcely begun when cholera made its appearance in the district, to the terror of Messrs. Brier and Mace, and both of them withdrew from the stump, leaving Wilson and myself deputed to finish the campaign for them. Entering heartily into the spirit of the thing, we turned the contention into a joint discussion. By that time we knew the speeches of our principals by heart. The same horse and buggy served us going from appointment to appointment.

Mr. Brier, I can truthfully say, lost nothing through his representative. Large meetings received us, drawn partly by the novelty of the arrangement and partly by the zeal with which the cases were respectively presented. By-and-by, as might have been expected, we grew over-zealous. At Pleasant Hill, a little town in Montgomery County, the good offices of the sheriff were required to keep us from fighting.

Our next appointment was at Alamo, eight miles distant from Pleasant Hill. The ill-feeling had by no means cooled when in the morning we stepped into our one-seated buggy. We rode the entire journey without speaking.

At Alamo the opening of the discussion fell to me. The platform was just across the road in front of a tavern from which, while getting off my speech, I heard the notes of a violin wretchedly played. My competitor began his reply, and was yet in the introduction when I interviewed the fiddler.

"Give me that violin," I said.

He passed it to me.

"Now, throw the door and windows open—there at the front."

Forthwith I struck up the "Arkansas Traveller." The effect was instantaneous. The silver tongue of my antagonist lost its cunning. His hearers, partisans and enemies alike, were smitten with restlessness. Presently they came streaming across to my side of the road, and when, a little further on, he was driven to an untimely conclusion, I reached a conviction, held ever since, that the power of music is superior to that of eloquence—that the "Arkansas Traveller" in the right key and time, and with the right expression, could have silenced Pericles, or Mirabeau, or any of those accounted of the divine in oratory.

Next day Wilson and I resumed our journey. For four or five miles we said nothing. At last, unable longer to contain himself, he turned to me.

"That was a mean trick you served me yesterday."

"Do you think so? I am glad it was not lost on you."

"I ought to knock you out of the buggy, and I've a mind to do it."

"No, don't. That would breed a tussle and scare our horse. I'll save the trouble."

Turning into a fence corner—I was driving at the time—I got out and threw off my coat. Wilson was not less prompt, and we would have been engaged in a moment, but that a rare piece of luck befell us. In our eagerness we had forgotten to hitch the horse, and he, startled, doubtless, by a coat flung upon the ground, shied, and made a break for liberty. Sight of the vehicle vanishing down the road in a cloud of dust, and a hasty thought of our appearance at the next appointment after walking and with countenances in need of repairs, recalled us to our senses, and with the same impulse we set out side by side in full pursuit.

We captured the runaway finally; then, standing on one side of the dashboard, Wilson on the other, both out of breath, I said:

"See here, Jim. You didn't do the clean thing day before yesterday at Pleasant Hill, and I had a right to get even. I think I am even; so I propose we call the account square, and that we climb in and finish this business like gentlemen. Brier wouldn't fight for you, nor Mace for me."

"I'm agreed."

We drove back, and recovered our coats, then pushed on to the next appointment.

It is proper, I think, to add that my principal was elected.

For good reasons we moved to Crawfordsville in 1853.

Next year I put the finishing touches on *The Fair God*, and laid it away with downright regret. To what should I turn for pastime next? Where could I look in hopes of finding new friends to take the places of my own creations gone now with my farewells? Still the idea of publication was far from me. In fact, it may be doubted if the suggestion of such a step had entered my mind but for a circumstance which must be given despite the laugh against me.

There came to Crawfordsville a well-dressed, smooth-spoken, literary-looking stranger to whom I could but rise immediately upon his entering my office. His card of introduction—a general one—read, "Mr. —— ——, New York." The name is out of mind. Down in the left-hand corner of the card was a reference—"For the Scribners."

Scribners' was then one of the comparatively few publishing houses of note in the republic.

The stranger took a seat, and proceeded to speak of the literature of the day, captivating me with his knowledge of books and his acquaintance with the reigning authors. He was on more than mere speaking terms with Bancroft. The stars of Cambridge he had long since ceased to view at a distance through telescopes. He took tea with Longfellow always on going to Boston. Hawthorne's retreat on the housetop at Concord he knew as a canary-bird knows its cage.

And in England the evenings he had passed listening while Dickens read to him from a book then in writing —could he ever forget them? Coming to the point, he said, in the blandest manner, that on account of the sharpness of competition with the other great houses, the Scribners had sent him out in search of new authors. That the country had writers with works of merit not yet offered for publication was well known, and to nobody better than his employers. He had heard that I had a novel in hand; hence his coming to me. He also understood that Mrs. Wallace amused herself with a pen. Possibly she had something, if only a short story or a lyric, which she would be pleased to submit. And as it was part of his duty to read manuscripts, and report upon them, he hoped we would waive scruples and favor him with an inspection of our work.

The flattery was irresistible.

How the gentleman came by his knowledge stirred my wonder; but as my wife did have a book in her desk, I gained her consent, and delivered to him her manuscript and mine, *The Fair God*, with permission to take them to his hotel. Three or four days afterwards he returned, saying, his face aglow, that he had read every word of them; and that I might know his opinion of their merits he was delighted to show me the report he was about to mail to the Scribners.

I read the paper, and nothing could have been more favorable.

"Now," he said, "the house permits me to receive a small compensation for my recommendation, which you of course understand is equivalent to acceptance of the books. The principle is that of a fee for a written opinion in your noble profession. I have given the manuscripts several days and most of my nights. Do you think fifteen dollars an overcharge?"

I paid the money, and he departed. By-and-by, not hearing from the Scribners, I awoke to the fact of having entertained a confidence man; still I could not help laughing. No neater operation has fallen under my observation—none so insidiously cunning. The fellow might have had a larger fee from me. To have asked more, however, would have been dangerous. His moderation proved him a master in the craft; though he may have addressed himself to others in Crawfordsville, which has always been notoriously literary. As it is, I never see a desk nowadays, whether at home or abroad, without eying it askance — of such are the tombs of dead books.

AN AUTOBIOGRAPHY

XXV

The Republican and other parties in Indiana—Party leaders Lane, Colfax, Allen, Defrees — Contest over slavery — Compromise measures — Stephen A. Douglas and "Squatter Sovereignty"— Thomas A. Hendricks—Joseph E. McDonald—Freedom or slavery—Three specifications.

Politics is always in order with fledglings at the bar; and as I plunged into it with the assiduity of an apprentice just out of bond, giving it time and consideration which might have been better bestowed, perhaps I may be forgiven for lingering through a chapter over the questions at that time in fervid agitation, and glancing at the men who in Indiana led the fighting.

Between 1850 and 1854 the Republican party was in a nebulous condition. That is to say, the whole North was alive with *isms*, some purely sentimental, some sounding in morals, each one, however, an army of zealots. Such, to my inexperienced eyes, were the Abolitionists, the Prohibitionists, and the American or Know-nothing party. These, it is to be added, all had in their organizations men of far sight, scheming and struggling to bring about a general coalition without which there could be no effective opposition to the Democratic party.

The first of them in Indiana was Colonel Henry S. Lane. Discerning that the Whig party must give place to a new organization, if, indeed, it were not already dead, he lent himself and all his power of speech and popularity to the coalition. Master of the stops of eloquence—argument, sarcasm, ridicule, anecdote, pathos—he knew how to attach the willing to a cause, to shame the hesitant, to raise the laugh when it served, and to set men swearing when that was best; withal, however, the great project could not have been successful but for the assistance of John D. Defrees, Schuyler Colfax, and Cyrus Allen.

Mr. Defrees owned and edited the Indianapolis *Journal,* the organ of the Whig party in Indiana. A wiser, shrewder politician there was not in the state.

Mr. Colfax, though very young, was well known throughout Indiana, but more particularly in the northern counties. Of great ability as a writer, he was scarcely inferior to Colonel Lane as a speaker. His newspaper, the South Bend *Free Press,* had a wide circulation.

Mr. Allen's talent lay in party management. The political control south of the national road belonged to him. Though less conspicuous than his associates, his services were indispensable.

There may, possibly, be some of opinion that George W. Julian should be classed with the four; but I do not think so. He eventually swung into line with them; yet, like Garrison and Wendell Phillips, he was from first to last more an enemy of slavery than a Republican. Lane and his colleagues partook of the compromising spirit of Henry Clay. Mr. Julian helped bring his following into the coalition, but while accepting nominations from it after it was a thing accomplished, he was still an abolitionist pure and simple.[1]

[1] Through the whole formative period of the Republican party Oliver P. Morton was a Democrat of the straitest sect. The county in which he resided was an original home of the *isms*—a hot-house in which they all flourished in rankest exuberance. It was impossible to be a Democrat there without being an extreme Democrat, and so extreme was Mr. Morton that he opposed the Wilmot Proviso

The junto—Lane, Defrees, Colfax, and Allen—weighed the several *isms* carefully, and saw that but one of them had groundwork in principle of breadth for their purpose; whereupon they directed their efforts to the projection of one point—that the extension of slavery must be resisted.

For a while their progress was slow. They had history on their side to begin with; then developments in Congress came to their help, and they made the most of them. The student of the time under consideration cannot afford to overlook those developments; and if only because they were seed generative of the war of 1861, they are worth restatement.

By the Missouri Compromise of 1820 all the territory north of 36° 30′ had been *forever* dedicated to freedom. In 1850 the quarrel between the Slave States and the Free States broke out again, the question being upon the admission of California. A second Compromise resulted, one feature of which, supposed to be satisfactory to the South, was an act for the more effectual recovery of fugitive slaves, while by another act, supposedly satisfactory to the North, California became a state with slavery excluded. In 1853 this second Compromise was indorsed as a final settlement of the whole slavery dispute by national conventions of both Whig and Democratic parties.

So in 1852 the status of the great quarrel may be summarized—Congress had exhausted its powers in settlement; the people in conventions had agreed to quit

because it revived the agitation of slavery. The passage of the Kansas-Nebraska bill opened his eyes. In May, 1854, he served as delegate to a Democratic state convention, from which, as it indorsed that act, he voluntarily withdrew. Objecting to the know-nothing plank of the People's party, he took part in the canvass as a Free Democrat, and not until the People's party carried the state in the October election did he openly affiliate with it.

agitating the subject; the sections had shaken hands; leaving the schemers for coalition nothing to stand upon in argument but the talk of Honorables Tom, Dick, and Harry apparently unrepresentative of anybody other than themselves.

But observe now. In that same year (1852) the controversy broke out a third time over a proposition offered in Congress to establish the Territory of Nebraska, and it waxed hotter than ever. Still the advocates of the new party in Indiana derived small comfort from the outburst, for nothing was done with the bill. Still the *isms* clung to their organizations. And thus two years longer. Suddenly the situation changed. In 1854 a bill to organize the Territory of Nebraska being under consideration, a senator, Southern, Democratic, and avowedly pro-slavery, gave notice of a motion that citizens of the several states should be free to take and hold their slaves in any territory. Stephen A. Douglas happened to be chairman of the Senate Committee on Territories. The motion in notice, based as it was on the argument that the Compromise of 1820 was in conflict with the Compromise of 1850, gave Mr. Douglas the opportunity of his life. Already a candidate for presidential honors, and thinking to hush the excitement in prevalence North and South, he advanced a new compromise idea—"to create the Territories of Kansas and Nebraska, coupled with a declaration that the Compromise of 1820 was inoperative and void, because inconsistent with the principle of non-intervention by Congress with slavery in the states and territories as recognized by the Compromise measures of 1850." Then, that there might be no misunderstanding, it was further expressly declared that the true intent and meaning of the bill "was not to legislate slavery into any territory or state, and not to exclude it therefrom, but to leave the people perfectly free to regulate their domestic institutions in their own way."

This was Mr. Douglas's famous "Squatter Sovereignty."

The effect was like the long roll upon a sleeping regiment; it brought the whole North to its feet. In Indiana the divided elements of opposition made haste to get together and organize. In July, 1854, they assembled in state convention, and launched the "People's Party." Temperance, Prohibition, Know-nothingism, Abolition were all kindly remembered in the platform; at the same time *the* flag around which they rallied was that of opposition to the Kansas-Nebraska bill, or, in plainer terms, resistance to the extension of slavery. The Missouri Compromise — all the compromises, in fact — were sponged out. At last the South had shown its hand, and the coalition was accomplished.

The foregoing will be familiar to the gray-beards who took part in the struggle which ensued, and ended ten years afterwards in a battle-field down in old Virginia. I concede it natural that such of them as give the recital attention may shrug their shoulders with impatience; nevertheless, it is to be hoped they will permit me to remind them of the vast majority grown up since, some of whom I am aiming to interest not merely in the struggle itself, but in a picture of the situation confronting me at that time in my youth when I was about to make my first essay in politics. These will see, I am sure, that the drawing now needs a few touches to help them to an understanding of the other party to the fight. I confine myself still to Indiana, for as yet I did not presume to think of affecting by my personal effort anything beyond its limits—hardly, in fact, beyond my county.

The state had been reliably Democratic—that I think may be safely said. It also had a junto composed of four gentlemen not a whit less able than the four serving the opposition.

Jesse D. Bright was United States Senator, a position vastly more dazzling then than now. He was neither orator nor writer; yet he had qualities which amply compensated for those deficiences, for under his management the party was never so nearly reduced to individual possession. As Adam was the first man, Mr. Bright was the first political "boss." The loaves and crumbs of national patronage due Indiana all came to his basket, and he distributed them, and in the matter of candidacies his was the controlling voice.

Next in influence was Thomas A. Hendricks. In point of popularity, indeed, he even surpassed Mr. Bright, to whom he wisely left the bestowal of patronage. He knew the mantle of control must fall to him sooner or later, since to political shrewdness, purity of character, and high social qualities, he added a profound knowledge of the general make-up of the party, and an extraordinary power of speech, the peculiarity of which was a faculty of putting things to the satisfaction of his audiences without actually committing himself.

Next to Mr. Hendricks stood Joseph E. McDonald, who, while not an orator, was often successful as any orator. His hearers had never to look at one another in doubt of his views or of his conscientiousness.

Last of the four, Ashbel P. Willard was a dashing Prince Rupert sort of leader who could speak the Democratic mind more to the approval of his party than either Mr. Bright, Mr. Hendricks, or Mr. McDonald.

To these gentlemen politics seemed a subject of copartnership. They never quarrelled with one another.

If at times they failed appearance in state conventions, they were always apparent in the platform. Did one put his face close to the lines, and look sharply between them, they could all be seen as in the haze of a background. They legislated for the Democracy as Mahomet legislated for his Faithful, and, like him, they had their Alis, Omars, and Khalids.

Now, in that day such as were or hoped to be entities of note in politics—all the great leaders, in fact, whether of this party or that—were specialists of the stump; so, having decided on a trial of my fortune in the uncertain game, I thought to follow the usage, and, in accordance with a habit acquired at the bar, set to preparing a brief covering the main questions at issue in the campaign.

I remember the surprise with which a conviction struck me that the Democratic party was on the defensive. What! The Democracy, rock-ribbed, all-conquering, the mighty Micromégas [1] of American politics, reduced to defence! Our leaders had promised us an easy time of long duration, now that its old Whig enemy had been at last done to death. Nevertheless, I shivered, not being able to hide it from myself while at my brief that the turn of every point in it had to be a dodge, a denial, a deprecation, or a begging the question.

In truth the *isms*, despised and unassimilated though they were, had fighting force in quantity much greater than we were willing to allow them, and in their midst the old party was like a whale assailed at the same time by many boats harpooning it from every direction; the best it could do was to fluke the water and blow.

[1] Voltaire has a satirical story of an inhabitant of Sirius, a Mr. Micromégas, who, to be in ratio proportionate to the bulk of his native planet, was one hundred and twenty thousand feet high.

The weapon the multiplied enemy all used in common, and with the greatest effect was that the Democracy had passed from defending the accursed institution of slavery, and now meant, as a final wickedness, to carry and plant it in the territories. For *that* they had treacherously repealed the Compromises of 1820 and 1850. For *that* they had invented Mr. Douglas's latest villany, "Squatter Sovereignty," and inaugurated a civil war in Kansas.

This, to say the least, had the flash, if not the cutting edge of a ground sword, and called for skilful trimming and dancing down the wind by the others; even our oldest and longest in the business, Oliver P. Morton, fled before it, and as a Free Democrat went over to the help of the People's Party; and we denounced him as a traitor, and pursued him so rancorously that we actually hastened the development of his greatness.

The issue thus forced by the opposition was, in grave distinctness, Freedom or Slavery; so when I sat pondering my brief, I found myself compelled to consider three specifications summarized somewhat as follows:

1. The South claims the right of a master to go with his slaves into a territory, and hold them there. Should the claim be conceded, every new state must necessarily become a slave state.
2. The South having at last a fugitive-slave law operative throughout the North, every man in the North is liable to be turned into a slave-hunter.
3. In the nature of things Freedom and Slavery cannot be coexistent, and if Freedom is lost the Democratic party is responsible.

These were serious counts in the most serious indictment that had ever been returned against the Democracy, and if I persisted in the canvass proposed, they had to be studied to a conclusion. They made a full basket of hard nuts for cracking, and I in the time of my first teeth as a politician. I had visions of Colonel Lane and Mr. Colfax and the old party under their hands a groaning clinic. I saw the colonel in mid-speech, his arms flying like the sails of a windmill in Holland. Not even Wendell Phillips could turn the theme to greater advantage, the point of skill being to keep its dark sides in constant view.

Should I back out? It was not too late. No, that looked cowardly. Then I thought of going slow and waiting to hear the leaders, Hendricks, McDonald, and Willard. To borrow their ideas was usual and always safe. I flattered myself, too, unctuously for that, and my vanity rebelled at playing second fiddle to their key-note. What then?

I would go through the specifications alone. I would go through them, and let my conscience have a hearing in the matter. No man could speak well if not in earnest, and no man could be in earnest without believing in the righteousness of his cause.

First, then, were the presentments true?

After long reflection I concluded they were true. The manly thing for me, then, was to do as Morton had done. By that time I had unearthed the blocks over which he had stumbled. And frankly, but for the prejudice I had formed against the abolitionists, I would have sided with Mr. Julian. To despise half-way houses was a habit with me.

As to the first of the specifications, I could not bring myself to defend the institution of slavery.

With respect to the second, my sympathies would side with the fugitive against his master. In all nature there was nothing more natural than the yearning for freedom. I saw him, look where I pleased, a hunted creature groping blindly along seeking the betterments he had heard of as in store for him up somewhere under the north star.

These were powerful influences, but scarcely less powerful was the help they had from the other side. That is to say, I had grown restive under the dominion of the Southern leaders. They were arrogant, selfish, and inconsiderate of the feelings as well as interests of the party North. I resented the epithet "Mudsills," not to mention the boast of the Georgian bully about calling the roll of his slaves on Bunker Hill. In these considerations there were quick appeals to my manhood and my pride of section; heavy as they were, however, they failed to outweigh the prejudice against the abolitionists. *They* were fanatics and wild men; and, worse, while enemies of slavery, they were also conspirators against the Union. The indecency of Toombs, the swashbuckler, was more than palliated by Garrison, to whom the Constitution was "a covenant with hell." Garrison was a disunionist; Toombs a slaveholder made mad by threats against his property. Garrison was a fanatic and Toombs a fool, and it was hard saying which was the more dangerous, though in my feeling African slavery was more tolerable than treason. I give all this to show the worry I underwent, and in excuse of the pottering and compass-boxing that filled the days and nights during which I strove hard and honestly to find a position in ease of my conscience.

While trying one day to get through the shell to the kernel of the third specification, the idea presented itself interrogatively, Was the South responsible for slavery? And after the rereading of Bancroft, I answered the question—Not more than an unborn child is responsible for the sin of its parent. I pursued the inquiry, and it brought me presently to the clause in the national Constitution providing for the return of fugitives, meaning fugitive slaves, which, interpreted at length, was a recognition of slavery and indirectly its nationalization as an institution.

A light broke in upon me, and I saw what seemed the true position to be taken by the Democracy; which was, not to preach maintenance of the law favoring slavery, for that would be favoring the institution, but simply a loyal observance of the law while the law continued in force.[1] Then the Democracy would be defending itself upon the ground of legal right in the owner of a slave, while the opposition would be assailing the Democracy upon the less tangible ground of natural right in the slave. In other words, if the abolitionists hated slavery more than they loved the Union, there were myriads of people open to appeal who loved the Union more than they hated slavery.

The brief when finished committed me to insistence upon observance of the laws as a first duty. Their propriety might be questioned—their impropriety might be agitated—they were always subject to repeal—but while they endured, social good and the life of the republic required every citizen to submit to them. A little later Chief-Justice Taney handed down the famous opinion in the Dred Scott case, stating what the law was—the decision went no further—then the correctness of my position had the approval of my conscience, leaving me free to deprecate slavery everywhere as earnestly as any abolitionist in the land.

Finally, as I could not see why slavery being a domestic institution might not be left to the decision of the people of a territory as well as to the people of a state, I became a Douglas Democrat.

[1] It is remarkable that the abolitionists never proposed to amend the Constitution by striking out the obnoxious fugitive-slave clause.

XXVI

The prospect of civil war—Preparations—Study of tactics—Organization of Montgomery Guards—Zouaves—Disapproved by "solid citizens"—Record of company—All commissioned officers.

THAT Mr. Douglas's compromise in substitution of that of 1850 was a failure grew clearer as the days advanced. If I looked at the Republican party, it seemed completely abolitionized; if at the Democratic party, it showed two factions embittered to the fighting-point, and headed, respectively, by Mr. Buchanan and Mr. Douglas; if at the sections, it became all too palpable that the line of separation between them had turned into a ditch growing deeper every day, with multitudes organizing on either side wanting only arms to be armies. In short, it was impossible for me not to see that the great quarrel had been aggravated far beyond peaceable settlement—that compromises were worn-out expedients—that war was inevitable. And this conviction was supplemented by another—I made sure that the abolitionists would in some way precipitate the war, possibly by striking the first blow. At length the only uncertainty I had was as to when the overt act would be committed.

Up to this conclusion all my thoughts about war had been of hostilities with some foreign power—England or France—most likely France, for Louis Napoleon was being hard put in those days to keep the French people amused. Such a clash would have had a welcome from me; but this one now in promise, section against section, state against state, Indiana against Kentucky, filled me with unaffected horror. The more so because when it came everybody would have to take a side. Which in that dark day should I choose? The grip of the grim necessity would be upon me, along with all the rest. And thereupon I grouped all the interests together —Freedom, Slavery, Individual Rights, Popular Government—and tried to weigh them dispassionately.

There was immense worry to me while the subject was in the scales; but at last it became sunlight clear that the one thing in the involvement worth all the rest, because it was the one thing upon which all the rest depended, was the union of states. The idea separated itself from everything else, especially from everything in the nature of mere political appeal. It alone had the air of a genuine principle of action. My troubles disappeared with its coming. I might be nothing in the struggle, nevertheless, I resolved to hold myself in readiness to go with the side proposing to uphold the integrity of the Union—this without regard for section or party.

The reader is besought not to think from what is here set down that I am pluming myself upon any superior foresight, much less the possession of prophetic powers. The conclusions reached were reached through application of a very old process—that, namely, by which we say four when two is added to two. There were thousands and thousands of people much more amply minded than I who were studying for their soul's worth along the same lines. It is true they did not separate the same principle of action, and resolve to stay with it; they could not all see alike, and the differences of motive were many and mighty; still they did reflect far enough forward to make sure of the occurrence of war, and if, knowing the characteristics of those bound to be parties to it, they were of opinion, and so said, that the war would be long and great, the coincidences as I see them, were not all remarkable, or at least not more so than the agreement of a jury.

At the same time the opinion had effects upon me somewhat personal. I not only thought the conflict would be long and great, but that it would also be crowded with opportunities for distinction not in the least inconsistent with patriotism. In other words, I could see no prohibition against my attaining respectable rank—a captaincy, at least. The want of officers would be pressing, and at no time more pressing than in the beginning, because of the amazing dearth of men in civil life possessed of practical military experience. I had only to demonstrate a fitness for the employment. And straightway the love of military life, never wholly dead in me, revived with the force of a passion; so the resolve upon a principle led to a resolve to get ready to be a useful servant to it while yet the need was on the road coming.

Then my term in Mexico, though unmarked by a battle, showed itself of advantage to me. The arms of service were the same as in the former war—infantry, cavalry, artillery, and engineering — and I saw that while acquainting myself with all of them theoretically, it would be best for me to choose one for a specialty, and try to excel in it. Of course, being shut out of West Point, there was nothing for me but resort to the self-educating process to which, fortunately, I had been so accustomed.

As a first step, I made a list of the text-books in use at the academy. Some of them are yet on a shelf in my library, a few having escaped — larcenously, or as presents. Thus provided, I began giving my nights to the study, and it proved another delightful pastime.

Presently it appeared that the arm of most reliance in battle, if not in field operations generally, was the infantry. It was also plain that, being the most numerous, promotions from it must be most frequent. The prevailing argument in favor of its adoption, however, was the possibility of my practising the instructions in the books without going away from home.

I proceeded next to organize a military company.

Crawfordsville had its full share of young men, just the material wanted. Sixty-five of them entered into the spirit of the project, organized, and became the Montgomery Guards. The state furnished us arms and equipments; armory, tents, uniforms, and band were all of our own provision. This was in the summer of 1856. We addressed ourselves to Hardee's *Infantry Tactics* for instruction. The proficiency reached was extraordinary, and it brought us notoriety more than we had dreamed of. Wabash College contributed a quota of enthusiasts. A magazine containing an article descriptive of the Algerian Zouaves of France fell into my hands about that time, and I reduced what was there reported to a system, including the bayonet exercises. The book, subsequently enlarged to two volumes and copiously illustrated with diagrams of manœuvres, is still in my possession. The company were so pleased with the drill they bought a Zouave outfit; whereupon emulation was excited until afterwhile there were companies enough for state encampments, which were in every instance preceded by my formal challenge to competitive drill, but always without takers.

The Zouaves—by that description my company became known abroad—received, I am sorry to say, little sympathy and no material support from our fellow-townsmen. Our parades brought the population to the streets without recommending us to the "solid citizens," who, when the gay spectacles disappeared, denounced them as foolishness, and a wicked waste of time and money. Some of them did their utmost to effect a disruption; but I managed to keep the enthusiasm alive. "The old fellows don't know what they are talking about. Stick to this, boys; master all its details. A big war is making ready, and when it comes these carpers will be ashamed of themselves and proud of you. Only stick to the colors, and in that day you will have at command positions to satisfy you for all you are now doing. Commissions will then come hunting you." Such was my argument.

This practice, one may be sure, was expensive; still it was what I wanted, being practical education. It is to be said, however, that I made the mistake usual with amateur officers, the mistake of thinking a knowledge of company and battalion drills, and of sentinel duty, and the ordinary ceremonies, such as guard-mounting, dress-parades, reviews, and inspections the whole of needful attainment. It had been different probably had my vanity permitted me to think of a rank above a captaincy. In other words, I myself failed fully to comprehend the opportunities which I had been so freely promising the bright young fellows of my company.

Nevertheless, the employment more than kept me agreeably employed; it made me watchful of events, then of almost daily occurrence, and helped me to a sharper interpretation of them. The troubles in Kansas, for instance, were generally regarded by those around me as signifying little more than politics unusually lurid on account of a resort to bludgeons, pistols, and long-range rifles; in my view they were the first meeting of opposing forces bent on war. In Atchison and his "Border Ruffians," I saw the South; in Greeley and Beecher, and their hymn-book contributors,

I saw the North. "It is a bad business," I went on saying to my young soldiers, "a very bad business, but also a warning to us to stick to our work."

This employment was not a thing of times and seasons; the practice and study were carried on persistently through the years down to 1861. The *personnel* of my company changed, of course—our young men are, as a rule, birds of passage—howbeit the ranks recruited and stayed full without any perceptible flagging of interest. Nor did I regard the hours thus devoted as lost. They were snatched mostly from night. And as to days of parade, visitation, and encampment, my conscience disposed of them much as the venerable hunter, Rip Van Winkle, disposed of his drinks—they were not counted.[1]

[1] At the breaking out of the Rebellion in the spring of 1861, there were sixty-four members of the Montgomery Guards, of whom all entered the Union army but two, and they wanted to enlist, but as they had dependent families I advised against it. Nearly all of them became officers, their commissions ranging from major-general to second lieutenant.

XXVII

The state Democratic convention—Stephen A. Douglas—Pledges Indiana to support Buchanan and the South — I protest — Elected State Senator—Bill for restraining divorce—Bill for choosing United States Senators by General Assembly — The Douglas and Lincoln debate—First doubts as to Democracy.

THE convention of January 8, 1856, was probably the largest that had ever been held by the Democracy of Indiana. I had the honor to represent my county as a delegate to it. As an introduction to the prevailing modes of party, those of relation to nominations and the construction of platforms—or, more simply, as a political experience—I should regret to be asked to pass that convention.

It was positively clear to me that Mr. Douglas had the support of a majority of the party in Indiana; yet in caucusing, the evening before the meeting, the old leaders to a man were discovered working for Mr. Buchanan. And this time they were all there—Senator Bright, Judge Pettit, United States Marshal Robinson, Judge Hughes, Governor Willard, Mr. McDonald, Mr. Hendricks—the whole array, in fact. They were the sages of the party, heroes of many a fight—victorious Moses who held the wands which, smiting the rock of patronage, set the offices to flowing. And sure enough, in the morning of the meeting, with characteristic calmness and self-possession, coolly as the owner of a carriage would jump into the seat and grasp the reins to move on whip in hand, they assumed the control.

Judge Pettit, as permanent chairman, "fixed" the committee on resolutions solidly for Mr. Buchanan.

The ignorement of the Douglas element was indecent. Was there no one brave enough to resist the usurpation? What if Mr. Douglas's friends were a minority? There was moral advantage in a vigorous fight. From man to man of notoriety I ran begging them to prepare a resolution in behalf of our leader, and have it ready for introduction instantly that the committee reported. None would undertake the business; it was too like insurgency. Then, as the last resort, I myself wrote an amendment, and at a caucus of the Douglas delegates held during the noon adjournment it was adopted. Mr. Holman, afterwards the Great Objector, agreed to present the plank if the committee reported as we all believed it would.

The convention reassembled, a denser jam on the floor than in the morning. In good time the committee on resolutions were ready. While the chairman was reading their report, the silence might have been heard. Mr. Buchanan was indorsed and the state pledged to him. The crisis was come. Where was Mr. Holman? A hundred voices called him. No answer. His courage had failed. Judge Pettit was putting the question upon adoption, and with us it was then or never. Climbing a desk, I succeeded in getting recognition, and, moving an amendment, sent up a copy of my resolution for reading by the secretary. Pettit was declaring it out of order, when such a tempest broke loose as I had never heard in a deliberative body. The yelling seemed to shake the solid pillars of the chamber. It shore the chairman's words from his lips squarely as if cut by scissors. He tried to be heard; so did I. In vain. The roar continued. Suddenly I was seized, passed bodily overhead, and planted on the secretary's desk face to face with the presiding officer. His arms were rising and falling like a wood-chopper's. His countenance was purple with rage. My fear was that apoplexy would strike him. The tumult swept on and on. Occasionally, "Question," "Question," could be distinguished. At last, from sheer exhaustion, the chairman gave in, and permitted me to speak in support of my amendment, and, when put to vote, it was carried.

I scarcely remember ever being so happy. The exultation went to bed with me at night. The perfected sweetness of the victory was that I had beaten the old stagers of the party. In the morning I would wake up famous.

But, alas! Or, as the Spaniards would say, "*Ay de mi!*" I carried the matutinal paper to simmer over at breakfast. The proceedings of the convention claimed attention first. I looked for my resolution. What!—no—yes, somebody had tinkered with it. That which had been a committal to Mr. Douglas, emphatic enough to have made the "Little Giant" blithesome as a bridegroom, was now a song of praise for Mr. Buchanan. My flesh crawled. Good Heavens! What would my *confrères* of the convention say of me? Who was he that had not scrupled at the forgery? I ran over the list of the demi-gods whom I knew to have been present during the great conference, and settled on one really the brightest, boldest, most unscrupulous of them all. He is dead now, and it were wrong to disturb his ghost. Yet I have been wiser ever since, and always look at old manipulators in conventions watchfully. They have a dangerous habit of carrying sleevefuls of trump-cards in wait for the last play.

However, the fight I had made was not entirely unrewarded. An extended notoriety had been gained, and the Democracy of my county gave earnest of their appreciation by nominating me for state senator, and then electing me.

At the organization of the senate in the winter of 1857 I took seat as of that body. There was a special session the year following, and a regular biennial session in 1859, through all which my services extended.

An old man *can* sit in judgment upon his youth. He has only to drop his egoism, and regard the young man to be passed upon as a stranger. Speaking in that philosophic spirit, I cannot be proud of my career as a law-maker. The great error was in fancying myself elected, not to engage seriously in legislative business, but to look after and take care of the Democratic party. An election of a successor to United States Senator Jesse D. Bright fell to us with a Democratic majority in the Lower House and a Republican majority in the Senate. Here, as every reader remembering the status of feeling between the North and South at that time can understand, was ample occasion for bitterness and sharp practices. I pass the details, calling to mind reproachfully the number of hours I spent with my colleagues of the Jacksonian faith warming my heels in the lobby. Bolting is a thing to be ashamed of—as I see it now. Better accept defeat. Appeal to the people is the only real remedy under the American system of government.

There were times, however, in which I tried my hand at serious legislation. Two instances in especial come to mind.

The first had to do with divorces. Some of the causes recited in the existing law were trivial, unchristian, and socially detrimental. The shameful features were the provision for notice of the commencement of the suit, than which nothing could have been more in aid of fraud, and the brevity of residence required for a party plaintiff. As a consequence of the abuses practised the state was odious throughout the Union. My bill for reform unfortunately proved too radical for the committee to which it was referred, and they reported it back with modifications which I could not accept. The worst of the affair, however, was that I and others working for the change became convinced that Congress alone could accomplish what we sought. State lines are sometimes deplorably inconvenient.

The second instance can be given by quoting the title of a bill introduced by me in the session of 1859. "Senate Bill, No. 2. An Act to regulate the choosing of United States Senators by the General Assembly, specifying the time, place, and mode of the choosing, providing for the designation of such Senators by the people, and prescribing the duties of certain officers in connection with such designation and choosing." In other words, far back as 1859 I proposed giving the people the right to choose their United States Senators. The difficulty was I was too far ahead of public opinion.

The idea of such a reference was brought to me rather singularly. It was in the summer of 1858. The contest for the national Senatorship in Illinois was in progress. Upon the challenge of Abraham Lincoln a joint debate had been arranged between that gentleman and Stephen A. Douglas. Three of the seven meetings agreed upon had taken place; and it is not saying too much, I think, that the people North and South were, in a sense, listening, so intense was the feeling excited. The personality of the party challenged had much to do with that feeling; yet there was a deeper cause—the subject of discussion.

To me Mr. Douglas was the first of living orators. What a magnificent spectacle he had presented standing day after day alone in the Senate, flinging answers, now to the abolitionists, now to the slave-holders, now to Mr. Seward, now to the arch-conspirator, Jefferson Davis! At such times he was in my eyes a lion baited by foxes and jackals. That Mr. Lincoln—gaunt, awkward, comic Lincoln whom I had seen in the bar-room of the old tavern at Danville—could get the better of him in debate was ludicrous as a mot of the uncouth clown himself. Yet if he could not get the better of my "Little Giant," he could at least draw him fully out upon all the phases of the mighty clash about Slavery and the Extension of Slavery.

In the afternoon of the day of the fourth meeting of the disputants, I found myself in Charleston, Illinois, lost in a crowd assembled in a grove near that interesting little city. The platform for the speakers reminded me of an island barely visible in a restless sea—so great was the gathering. By good management I succeeded in getting standing-room close up in front of the platform.

Mr. Douglas was first to appear. It had not been my good-fortune to have had sight of him before; now I recognized him by his pictures, a short man with a deep chest, Websterian head, and a countenance somewhat lowering. He seemed worried, and took seat with the air of one too closely occupied with thoughts to notice or care for surroundings. It struck me, also, that he was niggardly in his recognition of friends.

Presently there was a commotion in the crowd and a general looking that way, and Mr. Lincoln mounted the steps. He paused on the platform, and took a look over the crowd and into the countenances near by, and there was a smile on his lips and a whole world of kindness in his eyes. The thin neck craned out over his sweat-wilted shirt collar while he bowed to acquaintances. Mr. Douglas's outer suit had come from an accomplished tailor; Mr. Lincoln's spoke of a slop-shop. The multitude impressed me as the most undemonstrative of all I had ever seen on a political occasion. Every man of them, however, was palpitating with an anxiety too great for noise. So, I fancy, men must behave when they are spectators of a duel to the death.

At Ottawa, Mr. Douglas had presented a number of questions to Mr. Lincoln, which that gentleman answered at the Freeport meeting and countered by interrogatories on his side. It resulted that when the two came to Charleston the issues between them were all joined.

When time was called—if I may use the expression—Mr. Lincoln arose, straightening himself as well as he could. But for the benignant eyes, a more unattractive man I had never seen thus the centre of regard by so many people. His voice was clear without being strong. He was easy and perfectly self-possessed. The great audience received him in utter silence, and the July sun beat mercilessly upon his bare head.

Now, not having been blessed with a vision of the events to come, which were to set this uncouth person in a niche high up alongside Washington, leaving it debatable which of the two is greatest, I confess I inwardly laughed at him; only the laugh was quite as much at the political manager who had led him out against Mr. Douglas. Nevertheless, I gave him attention. Ten minutes—I quit laughing. He was getting hold of me. The pleasantry, the sincerity, the confidence, the amazingly original way of putting things, and the simple, unrestrained manner withal, were doing their perfect work; and then and there I dropped an old theory, that to be a speaker one must needs be graceful and handsome. Twenty minutes—I was listening breathlessly, and with a scarcely defined fear.

I turned from him to Mr. Douglas frequently, wondering if the latter could indeed be so superior to this enemy as to answer and overcome him. Thirty minutes—the house divided against itself was looming up more than a figure of speech. My God, could it be prophetic! An hour—the limit of the speech. Mr. Lincoln took his seat. How many souls sat down with him —that is, how many of the unbelieving like myself were converted to his thinking—I could not know; yet of one thing I was assured—it was in somebody's intention to do the old government to death, and slavery was to be the excuse for the crime. Nor could I get from under a conviction that Mr. Lincoln's speech was a defence of Freedom.

Then Mr. Douglas arose. As his stumpy figure appeared, provoking comparison with his tall rival, I was amused thinking, what if in an alignment of company they should be required to dress right or left upon each other? He had an hour and a half for reply. Despite my predilections, I was driven shortly to acknowledge that the prepossession did not belong to him. His face was darkened by a deepening scowl, and he was angry; and in a situation like his anger is always an admission in the other party's favor. He spoke so gutturally, also, that it was difficult to understand him. Still he was my Gamaliel. From him I had my politics. He failed to draw me like his competitor; he had no magnetism; he was a mind all logic; at the same time, be it said in truth, Stephen A. Douglas could not make a poor speech. I listened almost prayerfully. Whereas Mr. Lincoln had been the fine flower of courtesy, Mr. Douglas made no return in kind. What could be the matter? Afterwards I knew. He was handicapped by a continuous terror lest he should say something that would lose him the support of the South in the vastly more important convention then shortly to be held at Charleston, South Carolina. I did not stay to hear him through, but left carrying with me a damaging contrast—while Mr. Lincoln had been the advocate of Freedom, Mr. Douglas, with all his genius for discussion, had not been able to smother the fact that he was indirectly and speciously acknowledging all the South claimed for slavery.

So Lincoln came into my view a second time.

And so, that day in Charleston, I discerned what all of opportunity the voting masses of the country could have to see and hear the men chosen by their respective parties for United States Senators, and choose between them. Accordingly, my scheme of legislation was to give conventions authority to nominate without disturbing the right of the legislature to elect. For this no change of Constitution was required; neither had I a doubt that the legislature would be governed by the action of the convention. The invariable loyalty of electoral colleges, invested as they are with the utmost freedom, appeared to me precisely in point.

XXVIII

The political situation—Kansas—Democratic secret conference in Indianapolis—Sympathy with the South—I leave the meeting—The reconciliation with Morton—Offer services if needed—Sumter fired on — Telegram from Morton — April 13, 1861—In court at Frankfort—Ride to Colfax on horseback—Thence to Indianapolis by train.

THE political situation in the country kept steadily going from bad to worse. Aside from the war in Kansas, there were mysterious commercial conventions in the South ably manipulated by well-known fire-eaters; Brooks invaded the Senate chamber and assaulted Sumner; arms were going South from the national armories continually and without interruption; the navigation of the lower Mississippi was forcibly shut against Northern traffic—all incidents to me more than mere portents of coming hostilities. Yet, with singular perversity, I persisted in the belief that the abolitionists would precipitate the conflict. What other interpretation could be given old John Brown's attempt upon Virginia? If his backers, the Beechers and Garrisons, imagined that, with eighteen men all told, he could wipe the American soil clean of slavery, they and he were crazy; but they were not crazy—I speak particularly of the backers—and hence could only mean the quick inauguration of war.

The time came, however, when it was given me to see better.

One day, in the winter of 1860, I received a note inviting me to a meeting of Democrats of Indiana to be held at room fourteen of the Palmer House in Indianapolis.

My train was late, and on arrival I hurried to the hotel and room, the latter famous in Democratic history as the place in which party policies had been decided and slates made up. It was full to crowding. The chairman was stating the object of the meeting when I looked in. Many of the elders of the party were there balancing their chins on heavy canes. With them was a shoal of ambitious younger men of whom I might have sat for a type. Edging modestly along a wall, I presently commanded a view of the assemblage. The importance of the subject under consideration was of easy discernment. For a while I listened to the gentleman speaking incredulously, scarcely believing my ears. He was asking quietly, but in so many words, what the Democracy of Indiana should do in the event of war between the sections North and South. And he argued cautiously, saying the state was Democratic and ought to be in sympathy with the brethren South to whom the recent election of Abe Lincoln had been an insult justifying speedy resentment. Then followed a statement that startled me. If Lincoln's inauguration took place in March, there was not power anywhere, he said, to save the Union. He did not say directly that the South would secede or that it would begin hostilities —for that he was too careful—but spoke of such contingencies as so certain that it were wisdom if the party in Indiana took action upon them as upon foregone facts.

The speakers who followed the venerable chairman were some of them much more outspoken. They boldly avowed that war was determined upon, and that there was but one consistent course for the Democracy of Indiana—namely, to go with the South. Doubtless, there were men present to whom the idea of seconding the proposed treason was shocking; nevertheless, not a mouth opened in protest or denial. Then I as good as knew that off somewhere, probably in Charleston, South Carolina, there was a headquarters of secession at that moment, and that those leading in the meeting in progress were in communication with the traitors acting in their behalf. If so, my apologies were due the abolitionists.

I did not stay the conference through. While standing on the curb by the sign-post of the hotel thinking of the revelation so suddenly imparted, and with much certainty, some one tapped me on the shoulder. It was Judge W——k, the chairman, whom I had known since boyhood. I do not pretend to do more than give the substance of the exchange that ensued:

"I saw you leave the room," the judge said; "I suppose it was because you had not a seat. Come back, and I will see to that."

"Why do you want me there?" I asked.

He hesitated, seeing, likely, that he might be pushed to a plainer *exposé.*

"Well," he said, "you know that war is imminent. Plagued and provoked beyond endurance, the South is driven to fight!"

"That's tolerably plain."

And he went on: "Because the South is right, and its cause just, Indiana ought to stand with it."

My reply was with some irritation.

"Let us, for the argument, admit what you say—that the South has just cause; of what has Indiana to complain?"

"But we are Democrats and they are Democrats," he said, and then smirched me with a mess of flattery. "We want you particularly—you are the only Democrat in the state with any military practice."

He was offering me leadership.

"Judge," I said, "I have known you a long time, and will respect your age. This is my native state. I will not leave it to serve the South. Down the street yonder is the old cemetery, and my father lies there going to dust. If I fight, I tell you, it shall be for his bones. In so much I am an Indian. I will not go back to the room with you."

We separated.

It was upon me then—and I saw it ever so plainly—not merely to choose a side in the war the South was ushering in, but to go further, and intrust somebody else with knowledge of the choice. In crossing the street I thought of Governor Morton, and felt that now I owed him an apology. He had forsaken the Democratic party early, and for two years he and I had not spoken.

The governor, when I went into his office, was sitting at the farther end under a window writing. He came forward at sight of me, and took my hand cordially. Doubtless he remembered, as did I, that we had been school-boys together. Declining his invitation to sit, I began at once.

"Governor, I owe you an apology for what I have been saying of you politically. You were right in quitting the Democratic party. Now I, too, will quit it."

He called me familiarly: "Well, Lew, this does not astonish me. Never mind what you have been saying about me. Tell me what has happened—something serious, I know."

"Yes, I now know that war is certain, and soon, and that the South will make it."

"How do you know it?"

Carefully withholding the names of any of the men I had seen at the meeting in room fourteen, I told the governor then what had taken place and been said; after which I concluded, saying: "If these leaders are right, governor, and the South does attempt forcible secession, I tender you my services in advance. You may command me absolutely."

He took my hand again, his eyes humid.

"You could not go with the South," he said, "or with any treasonable organization here at home. That is not in your blood. I tell you, also in advance, if the South goes to the extreme of war, or threatens it by any overt act, I will send for you first man."

Thereupon I thanked him, and took my leave.

Somewhat late in the afternoon of April 13th I was addressing a jury in the Clinton County Circuit Court when the telegraph operator of the town [1] came into the court-room, and told the judge he had a telegram for me. The judge spoke to me, and the sheriff put into my hand a message in words very nearly these:

"Sumter has been fired on. Come immediately.
"OLIVER P. MORTON."

I gave the telegram to the judge to read, and, with his permission, excused myself to the jury, leaving the case to my law partner.

Now, April 13th was Saturday, and to get to Indianapolis that night—there being no Sunday train—it was necessary for me to take a horse, and ride on the run to a station called Colfax, ten miles away. As I went plunging through the mud, there was time to think of what was ahead of the country as well as myself. Not of the right or wrong of the great duel; reflection upon that subject had been closed with me

[1] Frankfort, Clinton County, Indiana.

times and times since the secret meeting of Democrats in Indianapolis. But there were other points scarcely less interesting. The combination of pride, courage, and endurance had always made wars long and bloody, and it was far from me to deny those qualities to men of the South. So, as it appeared to me, the struggle would at least last until the wayward section was utterly exhausted. When that would be, who could say? Then as to proportions—it was easy seeing how they depended upon the success of the conspirators in uniting their states. In the general obscurity there was one thing plain to me, and it was that the Union would be a cause on one side, and secession a cause on the other—secession for the sake of slavery. In other words, I was not going to Indianapolis to engage in old arguments; my mind was made up—I was going simply to become a soldier of the Union. It will be admitted, I think, that the occasion was one to excuse excitement.

AN AUTOBIOGRAPHY

XXIX

Interview with Morton at state-house—Appointed adjutant-general—President's call for seventy-five thousand men—State co-operates—Raises quota—Arrival in Indianapolis—Camp Morton —Eleventh regiment—Zouaves—Barracks.

About seven o'clock Sunday morning I called at the governor's residence in Indianapolis, intending to excuse myself for disturbing him so early. A servant told me he had breakfasted and gone to his office. Knowing the office to be in the state-house—my father had occupied it during his incumbency—I hurried thither.

There was preliminary conversation, after which I told the governor of my readiness for any duty he might think me fit. The colloquy that ensued is still fresh in my memory.

"The firing on Sumter," the governor said, "is the overt act I have been expecting for some days. Mr. Lincoln has now no resort except to suppress the treason by force. He must call for troops. In fact, he has notified me of such an intention, and to answer for Indiana I sent for you. I want you to become adjutant-general."

"But you have an adjutant-general," I returned.

"You mean M——n? He is on the other side—a sympathizer with the enemy."

"Where is the adjutant-general's office?"

"There is none."

"And the books?"

The governor answered, impatiently, "You know there have been none since Whitcomb's day."

"And the law defining the duties of adjutant-general?"

"It provides for little — almost nothing. We will have to cut loose and get on as best as we can."

Then he took from the table a telegram, and read it to me. I can only give the substance of it:

"The president will call immediately for seventy-five thousand men, and the quota of Indiana will be six regiments."

"Those regiments," the governor resumed, "I want raised without the loss of an hour. What do you say?"

I had then an inspiration.

"Governor, I would like to command one of them."

We were looking into each other's faces. His brows contracted and his eyes—they were large, full, and in the shade very black—were sober.

"Is it a condition?" he asked.

"No, I have already told you I am at your command."

The shade disappeared, and he smiled, probably at a suspicion of his own.

"Yes, any one of them you choose."

"That settles it," I said. "I am now sure you have confidence in me, and I am ready to begin work at once. Only one thing more."

"What is that?"

"I must have an assistant—maybe several."

"Have you anybody in mind?"

"Yes—Fred Kneffler, now in the county clerk's office."

"I know him."

"Right off, governor. We can get him, I think."

The governor then led the way to a room communicating with his own on the north.

"This will be your office," he said. "The telegraphing is sure to be heavy. Get a messenger; he must be strictly reliable; and if you discover a need of anything else, ask for it. I will have much to do aside from this business, so I leave it to you. When you are in doubt, come and consult me. Keep me posted all the time, and drive the duty. I want the credit of reporting Indiana's quota full, first of the states."

There was tremendous excitement in the city. There was quiet in my office, however, and, making a good ready, I stocked it with stationery and blank telegrams. Kneffler reported early. On the wall a map of the state was unrolled, showing towns, railroads, and railroad connections. Each of the city papers sent me a reporter. Messages were prepared for forwarding to the county seats. For the names of influential men to be addressed I consulted the governor, and from memory he made me a list rapidly as I could write at his dictation. What struck me at the moment as remarkable, he did not discriminate against Democrats. In giving the name of a person, he simply added "Democrat or Republican." So perfectly did he know, so profoundly had he studied the commonwealth he was governing.

This, I must subjoin, with other things quite as demonstrative, possessed me for the first time with an insight of the governor's political accomplishments. I had heard it said that he was a great man commencing a career; now the truth forced itself upon me. Viewing it, doubtless, as a profession, he had studied politics methodically, and come to know the state as a farmer knows his farm. With a clearer head I had never to do. Seemingly above surprise, he remembered exactly what he himself had said or had me do. He faced each problem as it arose with a confidence mixed equally, I should say, of courage and judgment derived from the logic of the situation, for he had no guides, no precedents, no favoring statutes. The burden of responsibility being his, not mine, he had the right to be consulted, and I did it freely and loyally, and he gave his directions, or orders, if that term is more agreeable, always without hesitation, and positively. For that matter, he gave me lessons which, had I been a politician, selfishly watchful of my own advancement, would have been profitable in the highest degree. To use an old expression, Governor Morton was a born politician, and association with him was a pleasure.

Productive work began in my office Monday morning. Messages in reply poured in. By noon the state was seething. In every county companies were forming or consolidating. All railroad officials were instructed to bring them to the city as fast as they were organized, keeping accounts for future settlement. The wires in Indiana were never hotter than during Monday and Tuesday of that memorable week.

The governor, meantime, appointed a commissary and a quartermaster. Then there was a Camp Morton, which in two days grew into a city of sheds, booths, and tents.

A programme of reception for the incoming soldiers was left to me. It was possible, I thought, to manage the ceremony in such manner that the public looking on from the sidewalks might communicate a deal of patriotism to each arrival in its march along the street, and, at the same time, take back from it even more of the precious virtue. It happened that there were two independent companies of the city elegantly uniformed and already in offer of service. They were employed, and I hired a brass band, with the complement of a fife and drum corps. One or the other of these was always in waiting at the central station. Immediately that an organization disembarked from a train, a column formed; then up Meridian to Washington Street it marched, the frantic cheers of the new soldiers answered by the thousands of men, women, and children lining the sidewalks. Down Washington Street westward the medley of music, men, and flags swept, ending at the state-house. There the governor appeared, and, standing on the great stone at the southeast corner, madė a speech which no volunteer heard without a yet greater assurance of the holiness of his cause. At the end of the glorification, the arrived, officers and men, were conducted by one of my assistants to Camp Morton, where they were provided with bread, coffee, meat, and some kind of a roof under which to sleep in comfort. Until the gate of the camp was passed every attention possible was paid all who came for enlistment. Then and there began that interest on the part of Governor Morton which, instead of waning through the succeeding years of war, kept growing and intensifying; so that of his volunteers none ever got so far away in the spreading fields of conflict as to be beyond his care.

At midnight Friday I waited on the governor and reported one hundred and thirty companies in camp—that is, sixty, the number required by the president's call, and seventy over. He telegraphed the situation instantly, urging the retention of the overplus. I never heard which state was first with its quota; it is my impression, however, that the honor belongs to Indiana.

The governor then said, "I would like to have you stay with me."

I thanked him heartily, and replied, "If you do not positively object, I would rather go to the field."

There was no turning angles in his answer.

"Well, which regiment do you choose?"

"That depends upon where you begin the count."

"I do not understand you."

And I explained. "You remember the five regiments Indiana contributed in the war with Mexico."

"I see."

"Well, I would begin with six."

"Yes," he said, thinking, "that would be a proper complement, and prevent historical confusion."

"And not only that, governor; it would be an easy way of keeping tally of contributions of the kind."

"You are right," he said. "Begin with the Sixth."

"Then I will take the last number."

"You mean the *Eleventh?* Be it so; and when you get fixed in camp I will come and see you."

With the governor's consent, I had already contracted for a thousand Zouave uniforms and for converting an old freight depot into barracks, with a spacious kitchen at one end and bunks in frame against the walls. And now—it was considerably after midnight when I left the executive office to ride to Camp Morton—now I, so lately content with the thought of a captaincy, was a *colonel* going to my command! That the night was over me and the town asleep were gentle things much in my favor; without them I fear my very good-feeling must have made an exhibit of me to passers by. There is no flattery sweeter than that with which one gives himself, and I was not mean with the sweetness, one may be sure. And yet the enjoyment was now and then disturbed by intrusive recollections of the responsibilities that were inseparable from the higher rank. If I failed—how far the fall would be! And I thought of Lucifer and his descent a week in depth, but went on. May a man tell what he can do until he tries? That, I take it, is the soul of the *Americanism* which has made us a peculiar people, almost separatists.

So, with my courage screwed to the sticking-point, having already selected ten companies out of the one hundred and thirty, I marched the Eleventh regiment of Indiana Volunteers out of Camp Morton into barracks. This was done quickly and without notice in the early dawn. In the afternoon of the same day the public was given to see the first dress-parade by a full regiment ever held in the limits of the state.

XXX

Uniform of the Eleventh Regiment Gray Zouaves—Mrs. Cady—"Remember Buena Vista"—Sent to Evansville—Drill—The passing steamer—Winfield Scott—Ordered to Cumberland, Maryland.

There was nothing of the flashy, Algerian colors in the uniform of the Eleventh Indiana; no red fez, a head-gear exclusively Mohammedan, and therefore to be religiously avcided by Christians; no red breeches, no red or yellow sash with tassels big as early cabbages. Our outfit was of the tamest gray twilled goods, not unlike home-made jeans—a visor cap, French in pattern, its top of red cloth not larger than the palm of one's hand; a blue flannel shirt with open neck; a jacket Greekish in form, edged with narrow binding, the red scarcely noticeable; breeches baggy, but not petticoated; button gaiters connecting below the knees with the breeches, and strapped over the shoe. The effect was to magnify the men, though in line two thousand yards off they looked like a smoky ribbon long-drawn out.

The day soon came around, when, after muster in, the Eleventh marched to the state-house to receive its colors from the patriotic ladies of the city. The march down was one continuous ovation. Ployed into column of divisions closed in mass in front of the stone platform at the famous southeast corner, an immense multitude of people crowding the space clear to the street, we heard Mrs. Cady's beautiful speech of presentation, the reply to which, of course, belonged to me. I cannot remember when I so wanted to be an orator. Fortunately, everybody, citizen and soldier, was in the state of feverish excitement that makes the feelings most susceptible; and yet the by-standers were less in mind than the regiment. I wished to impress it memorably, and to that object bent my best endeavor.

After the thanks and promises in reply usual at such times with speakers, I turned, the colors in my hand, to the regiment, then, like myself, all wrought up.

"My men," I said, "you all know of the battle of Buena Vista—twenty thousand Mexican soldiers against four thousand Americans; yet the victory was with our flags. You know, also, that Indiana was represented there by two regiments, the Second and Third. The Third did not yield an inch of ground. The Second was less fortunate. While fighting single-handed two divisions of the enemy, full seven thousand strong—eighteen to one—in the midst of their well-doing their colonel's heart failed him, and he ordered a retreat. He sent no flag back to be rallied on—he took no step whatever looking to a rally. 'Cease firing, and retreat,' he called out; and as they stopped fighting and looked at him in wonder, again he called out, 'Cease firing, and retreat.' There had been but three hundred and sixty of them in line in the beginning, and of that total ninety were upon the ground dead or wounded. Now, all, who could, obeyed the order of their colonel, and broke to the rear—in flight, if you please. Still the greater body of them rallied, and under their own flag and officers kept the field fighting the remainder of the day, their colonel having abandoned them and joined a Mississippi regiment as a private.

"Now, the regiment the colonel joined was commanded by Jefferson Davis, whom you all know as a leader of the unrighteous rebellion we are going to help quell. That day he assisted in proclaiming the Second Indiana cowards, if, indeed, he did not originate the accusation. He was the son-in-law of the general commanding our army, and he induced that officer to repeat the slander in his official report. The sorry tale I have now to tell you clings to the brave men of the Second regiment, the living and the dead. It sticks to the state no less. The stain is upon you and me. It attaches to these flags just received, because they are now our property, and we of Indiana. So what have we to do, my men? What but to recognize that the war we are summoned to is twice holy—for the Union first, then to wipe the blot from our state and infamize our slanderer?

"And that we may not forget our duty, that it may be always present, and never more so than in battle, soldiers of the Eleventh Indiana, I give you a regimental motto levelled at the man who, from having been vilifier, has become the archtraitor of his country. Kneel every one of you."

They went down like one.

"Hold up your right hands."

Every hand raised.

"Repeat after me, and swear now—'God helping us, we will remember Buena Vista.' There, you have a motto, 'Remember Buena Vista.'"

They took the oath and accepted the motto. The witnesses of the scene shouted, their eyes full of tears. We all went back to our quarters better soldiers than when we left them.[1] That was my proudest day. Distinction won in youth is very pleasant, and I was then but thirty-four years old.

[1] I have been asked so often for this speech that there is a justification for its reproduction. It is given nearly as I can now remember. As a motto, "Remember Buena Vista" became of general acceptance by the Indiana regiments.

The term of service — but three months — allowed scant time in which to get the regiment in condition to meet an enemy; and I am free to say that but for the assistance of Lieutenant-Colonel McGinnis and Major Wood, both of whom were well up in the tactics ordinarily practised, the task with all the willingness of the men would have been impossible. Then we realized how fortunate it was that in choosing companies I had taken all at the time of the call organized in the state—three from Indianapolis, two from Terre Haute, and my own of Crawfordsville. The great trouble was that nobody outside the latter knew the first lesson of the Zouave system.

A stout argument in favor of Zouave methods can be given. None other so well cultivates capacity in the soldier to render a good account of himself individually under every battle condition. No veteran will now sneer at being able to fight on his belly as well as on his feet. And what can be said against the double time habitual to the Zouave? Or of the exchange of husky voices of command for exhilarating bugles, making it easy for a colonel to order his regiment stretched though it may be out of sight over a mountain or in the depths of a tangled wood. The tactics of the Boer in action is genuine Zouave; and having come to the system partially, why should not the United States army be trained to it in its purity? All armies, in short, must come to it; so say the repeating-rifle and the breech-loaders, Gatling, Maxim, and field.

Luckily, in my days of waiting for what was upon me, I had written a full course of instruction; and now I had only to call my officers into school and initiate them. Soon the regiment was working at the novelty; and then the rush and tear of a thousand men advancing, retreating, taking and closing intervals, changing front on the centre, firing in all positions, and doing anything of manœuvre on the run or the double-quick, and ordered by the bugle, begot the liveliest interest on the part of participants, while to spectators the practice was a downright show.

The first order that came to me was from Lorenzo Thomas, adjutant-general. It directed that I proceed with my regiment to Evansville in the southwestern corner of Indiana. Kentucky was about to commit herself to neutrality. As if her domain could continue respected by the belligerents! Already there was a suspicion in Washington that military supplies were being shipped through her borders to the South in view of which I was to establish a search of boats passing down the Ohio River. The delicacy of the task can be understood by recalling that the war in prospect merely had not yet broken up any of the established usages of peace.

Moreover, a report had gone to headquarters that Evansville was a hot-bed of secession. Great was the surprise of the city when at daybreak the regiment disembarked from the train and took its way in silence through the streets to a camp-site on the river below the town. The moral effect was wonderful. Though largely in the majority, the Union people had been cowed by influence on the Kentucky side; now, before noon, Evansville looked a-bloom with flowers, such radiant flaunting was there of the stars and stripes on the house-tops and cupolas.

The search of vessels was odious work, especially to the boatmen. Sometimes, doubtless, the details performing the duty were too zealous; still I had no difficulty except with one captain.

I had procured, it should be said, the services of an artillery company of the state in the city. The captain and his men were Germans, and loyal as the best of us. His two six-pounders were in battery night and day on a bluff commanding the river up and down. To bring boats to, the orders were to use blank-cartridges, keeping a shotted gun for emergencies.

The exceptional boat came down one day crowded with passengers. The captain was summoned as usual by a gun. He kept on. A second gun; still no attention. Now he was opposite the battery driving swiftly by. Captain K——s, thinking an emergency had come, began training the shotted piece on the recusant steamer. His German blood was boiling and he certainly would have fired had I not reached him in the nick of time, drawn by the second shot.

The guards of the boat and the hurricane-deck, when I looked at them, were covered with women and children in gay attire, some of whom waved their handkerchiefs, while, dreamless of danger, all stood gazing with innocent wonder at the white tents of our camp shimmering through the trees on the hill-side. Shoot at them? What an unspeakable crime! Though the vessel had been heaped from keel to pilot-house with contraband of war, there could have been no extenuation. Doubtless the captain of the boat counted on their presence. On my cot that night I had visions of a round shot crashing through the flimsy panelling of the steamer, leaving a wake of blood in its track. A long time between then and now; yet my gratitude for that escape is fervid as ever.

In the stay at Evansville I pushed the drill of the regiment. Four hours for company, four for battalion —such the schooling. The grumbling was loud, sometimes angry; but it was met with a spell of stone-deafness. The exercises drew great notice from the townspeople as well as the gentry over the river. Three weeks thus, and the progress was wonderful, not in drill merely, but also in endurance.

Then a change came, and not any too soon. A telegram was put in my hand.

Washington, June 1861.

Colonel Lewis Wallace:

You will proceed, by rail, to Cumberland, Maryland & report to Major General Patterson

Winfield Scott

The foregoing is a copy from memory.

Winfield Scott

One not himself an old soldier may have difficulty imagining in what ways that telegram delighted me. It was not that it relieved me of the unpleasant duty at Evansville; many acquaintances happily made had by that time converted my stay there into pleasantness. Neither was it that my wish for more active service was at length granted. It was—shall I say it?—the name at the foot of the order—*Winfield Scott.* Coming direct from him, instead of through the adjutant-general's office, the order conferred a rare distinction. To be known to Winfield Scott, to be addressed by him—what an appeal to my vanity! What encouragement! I thought of Lundy's Lane, and the battles to which the Mexican capital had succumbed, and the long time, beginning in my childhood, during which he had been my ideal soldier; and now—I read and reread the telegram. The "Winfield Scott" at the bottom made the paper actually shine as with a splendor.

I gave a hurried thought to the general situation. The army at Washington had been reported ready to move against Richmond, the then seat of Confederate government. With General Beauregard at Manassas Junction blocking the road, a battle was unavoidable. Aside from that, General Joe Johnston held Harper's Ferry, watched by General Patterson at Hagerstown. The need of the Baltimore & Ohio Railroad for purposes of supply and communication was imperative. Little did I suspect that its rescue was to fall to me, my first achievement.

Where was Cumberland relatively to Patterson at Hagerstown and Morris at Grafton? I consulted a map, gleaning nothing but the location of Cumberland on the Baltimore & Ohio Railroad, midway between Hagerstown and Grafton. The distance made support by either Morris or Patterson impossible; so that the occupancy of Cumberland looked like isolation. Over in Virginia lay Romney but a little removed from Cumberland. What if it were garrisoned by the enemy? That I was about to be put on trial was obvious—my first trial under conditions of self-dependency. A qualm of doubt and a shiver struck me. I knew so little of the regions to which I was going, and had so little of experience in military operations.

XXXI

The route to Cumberland—Reception in Indianapolis and Cincinnati —The arrival in Grafton—General Tom Morris—The situation at Cumberland—Colonel McGinnis—The arrival in Cumberland —The encampment.

THE route to Cumberland ran through Ohio to Grafton, where General Tom Morris had headquarters. Besides being an excellent officer, he was a personal friend whom I doubted not getting every particular of the status in Cumberland.

At Indianapolis the train rolled into the station with the city in attendance, though it was after midnight. There, too, the three companies of the place were set upon by friends and relatives in such numbers, and so loaded with delicacies from their kitchens, that schedule time was out of question. So a night was lost.

The reception at Cincinnati was even more memorable. To get to the Baltimore & Ohio Railroad we had to traverse the city. The day could not have been more favorable for display. Every bit of metal in the column, plate, buckle, bayonet, sparkled under touches of the clear sun. Fourth Street from pavement to house-top was a mass of excited humanity; yet the regiment dominated the spectacle — the men appeared so large in stature, and moved so in their unity like a machine, making withal so light of their arms and equipments. It was easy to imagine the street trembling under their unbroken tread. The cheers they received were but a fair return for their martial showing. Still I saw tears in many eyes. Women looking at the beaming faces in the ranks pitied the youthful strangers. The war was new, and everybody who had to do with it, even as a spectator of passing pageants, tender-hearted.

My train stopped in Grafton about noon. The soldiers everywhere present made it apparent that the town was in the grip of war. A man in uniform conducted me to General Morris. Orderlies were at his doors. Cavalrymen stood by their horses booted and spurred. Within, officers were at work, with clerks behind tables. The general met me cordially. He was making ready, he said, for a movement likely to end in an engagement with the enemy. The difficulties were increased by the inexperience of everybody.

"Where are you going?" he asked.

"I am under orders for Cumberland."

"And you report to whom?"

"I wish it were to you; as it is, I belong to General Patterson."

"Will you be at Cumberland alone?"

"Far as I know, yes."

He looked concerned, and said, "I wish you had company."

"What is the situation at Cumberland?"

"It is a Union city heavily sprinkled with mischievous secessionists. Romney is a day's march from it, and there is a body of Confederates in camp there from thirteen hundred to two thousand in number. I am afraid they will give you trouble."

"Is that report reliable?"

"I think so."

"Are there any obstructions of the road from Grafton to Cumberland?"

"Joe Johnston, you know, is at Harper's Ferry, so that beyond Cumberland the railroad is useless; but from this to Cumberland it is open unless at New Creek, where the bridge is in keeping of a company of loyal guards. As the force at Romney keeps very quiet, I can't see why they are there unless as an outpost to look after Johnston's line of retreat up Winchester valley."

"Then if I were to give Romney a shaking up, it would disturb Johnston some?"

Morris laughed, and said, "Make sure before you try that."

Then as I arose to take my leave, he said, further: "Going down, you had better keep a good lookout for bushwhackers. Make certain also of your engineer."

Fifty thousand cartridges had in the mean time been rushed aboard the train, of which forty rounds to the man were distributed. So that when I got beyond Grafton the atmosphere seemed to undergo a change. I was within the theatre of active war, and its possibilities, not to speak of its dangers, were about me. Of such also was the air I breathed.

Very naturally I did some thinking inspired by the news of a force at Romney. Instead of waiting for them to trouble me, why should not I take the initiative? The moral effect might reach clear to Harper's Ferry, particularly if I were successful, and that it would secure me immunity at Cumberland was certain. Then if I waited, Johnston was likely to reinforce the camp at Romney. And then if my attack were repulsed? My need was information of the country, and I tried the engineer. He proved to be intelligent, and when he clinched his assertion of loyalty by saying he was an Ohio man born and bred, he won my faith.

"It may be important for me to have guides familiar with the region between Cumberland and Romney,"

I said to him. "Can you name one likely to accept my employment?"

"Yes," he replied, "I know two. They live at Piedmont, the next town."

At Piedmont he brought them to me.

"What do you say to joining me as guides?" I asked them.

One of them laughed dryly, and said to the other, "They make it hot for us"; then, in a different tone, "We've no love for them, and we will go with you."

"What wages will you expect?"

"You'll feed us, won't you?"

"Yes, and more, too."

"Then not a cent."

"Can you go with me now?"

"Right off."

"Get aboard."

I took them in the engineer's cab with me, and they made a rough diagram of the lay of the land to Romney, showing two roads—one, the turnpike from Cumberland to Romney, twenty-three miles; the other, from Cumberland to New Creek by rail, and from the latter place across country, also twenty-three miles. The turnpike, they said, was constantly patrolled by horsemen, while the New Creek road was not watched, because nobody thought of danger from that direction. The objection to the New Creek route was that it was over mountains, and consequently hard on men afoot. There were also places along it where a company would laugh at a regiment. As for the strength of the force at Romney, they agreed that it was not less than twelve hundred nor more than fifteen hundred. They had seen the whole body on parade.

Upon this information, I resolved to attack Romney before going into quarters at Cumberland, and, thinking it best to enter the city in the daytime, bivouacked six or seven miles out on a branch of the Potomac.

That evening, in the light of a blazing camp-fire, Colonel McGinnis and I discussed a plan, and chose to take the New Creek road which, being unwatched, would give us a chance to surprise the enemy.

In the discussion we considered every objection to the movement. Forty-six miles, counting an immediate return as part of the march, would be unprecedented for infantry in one day; nevertheless, reducing the problem to one of physical endurance, we decided that the month of hard Zouave drilling just undergone at Evansville was to be treated as training sufficient for the task; besides which the men should travel light as possible. Once front to front with the rebels—in that day nobody spoke of them as Confederates—the *esprit* of the regiment could be relied upon, particularly if warm breakfasts in Romney were held out as an incentive.

I decided then to proceed to Cumberland first. That our presence in the city would be promptly reported to headquarters in Romney was quite certain; and the military there, reasoning that we would naturally require time to settle and get down to business before thinking about enterprises to their disturbance, would be all the more unsuspecting.

Keeping the companies on the train when arrived, I would ride as if looking for a camp-site; and then pretending that one near town in every way suitable could not be found, and that the place of bivouac the night before up the river was preferable, we would make a show of returning thither. Once under way, however, instead of stopping, we would continue on to New Creek. Starting from New Creek for Romney at four o'clock, I had no doubt of being able to march the twenty-three miles, nothing untoward occurring, by six o'clock in the morning — possibly sooner. In other words, I proceeded in the scheme of operation upon the presumption that all I did and said would be promptly carried to the man, whoever he was, my opponent in Romney.

The train rolled into Cumberland at daybreak. The city and all its vicinity lay in a shroud of mist. Evidently notice of our coming had not preceded us. As they moved slowly in, a small boy discovered the cars were loaded with soldiers. He ran giving the alarm. Presently some men came cautiously down the street; a little later women appeared; but there was no haste by anybody to greet us. At length I sent Adjutant Macauley for the mayor, and he responded in person. I told him who we were, and that I had been ordered by the military authorities to take charge of Cumberland and guard it. He expressed himself delighted by my arrival. He said he was a Union man, and that a majority of the people round about were in accord with him. He then courteously invited me to breakfast. In declining, I inquired if he knew of a ground conveniently near fit for a permanent encampment. There were several, he replied, and he would be glad to show them to me. I arranged then to ride with him and such of his friends as he might invite. The news respecting us spread rapidly after the mayor's departure, and soon the entire tenantry of the town flocked to see "the Hoosiers in the big gray breeches."

Colonel McGinnis and I made the rounds with the mayor and several of his friends, after which I expressed great regret that none of the places visited were as good for my purposes as the ground of our bivouac up the river the night previous. The search for one nearer town would be resumed in a day or two. For the present the men needed rest. Accordingly, at ten o'clock the train with the regiment, less two companies, pushed back up the railroad.

The two companies were left to pitch their tents and amuse the public.

XXXII

From New Creek to Romney—Capture of a rebel major—Surprise prevented—The broken suspender-buckle—The enemy retreats—The welcome of the negroes—The incident of the farm-house—Rebel supplies captured.

A STRONG detail was left at the bridge to guard the train; then about four o'clock in the afternoon, with eight companies, in all quite five hundred men, the march from New Creek to Romney began. Knapsacks, blankets, and haversacks were discarded and word given out that there was no hope of breakfast or dinner except we took the town. Silence was enjoined, or if a gun were fired, unless by my order, he who did it should be summarily drummed out of the service. With one of the guides, I took place at the head of the column on foot, like all the rest, thinking by my example to stimulate the weary and faint of heart.

Guessing at the time, I allowed a rest of five minutes at the end of every fifteen minutes. About midnight the stars went out, and the darkness became so deep that the files kept together chiefly by the grind of gravel under foot and the muffled rattle of canteens. What with the obscurity, and the frequent halts, and the difficult ascent of mountain crowding mountain in quick succession, progress was necessarily slow.

We came upon a straggling hamlet. In one house a light was burning, and, as luck would have it, a woman opened a door attracted by the commotion among the dogs; hearing us in passage, she screamed. In a minute the population was agog. Then—according to the story told me afterwards—a man led an unsaddled horse out of a back gate, and, by paths known to himself, rode hard as he could go to town.

On a few miles farther, another man rode unsuspectingly into us, and we captured him. He proved to be a rebel major. Dismounting him, and putting a soldier with a sore foot on his horse, I politely invited him to go with us, and he was pleased to accept. He was one of the worst scared men I ever saw.

Dawn was flinging its earliest glow into the sky, and, according to the guide, Romney not more than two miles away. Suddenly, while I was at the foot of the column seeing to something, there was a jam. What was the matter? Minutes were precious. I ran forward, and overtook a *contretemps* as ridiculous as it was provoking. The first company, closed upon the advance-guard, had come upon a noisy mountain stream, and the captain, noticing a log thrown to the opposite bank, was using it as a bridge, and when I reached him he was crossing his men one by one over it. The forenoon could have been easily exhausted in that way. Taking to the water at once, my example prevailed with the succeeding companies.

Hardly had the order of march been resumed when a party of horsemen, probably a vedette, appeared at the top of a low hill and fired upon my advance-guard, who engaged them pluckily and drove them off unassisted. Then I knew a surprise was no longer to be hoped; at the same time, by hurrying forward, the minutes of preparation to receive us would be materially lessened. At last our goal appeared, and this was what I beheld: The road ran down to a wooden bridge over the south branch of the Potomac; beyond the bridge it coursed sinuously up a long hill to the town on the summit. On the side of the hill, facing us and probably a mile away, stretched a line of men carefully ordered, their arms glittering in the sunlight. In the centre two field-pieces were conspicuous, as doubtless it was intended they should be.

Calling a halt, I hastened to the bridge to see if it was intact, and noticed on the farther side a two-story red brick house half curtained by orchard trees. It appeared deserted by man and beast; and for that reason partly, and partly because it so conveniently commanded the exit of the bridge, I regarded it something to beware of. Turning then to the aggregation on the hill-side, I estimated it carefully, taking my own command as a basis, at a thousand or twelve hundred. Of colors there were none to be seen, an absence due probably to the extreme youth of the Confederacy. The signs were that I was expected to attack by the road; but the hill being so steep that a change of front was impossible, if the assault were upon his left flank, the unwisdom of accommodating my enemy forced itself upon me. When I looked finally from the array to the town; some of the roofs showing on the height, the reserves there, if any there were, could not be seen. Indeed, I concluded the town abandoned by its inhabitants.

The advance-guard, when it came to me, was directed to rush the bridge, and observe the house from behind the embankment on the other side. Sure enough, upon their showing, a fire opened upon them. They returned it at a disadvantage on account of the trees; yet the interchange was lively and exciting. Then I led the first company across. A sergeant was struck, but saved serious injury by his suspender-buckle. Making use of a ditch by the roadside, my men speedily possessed themselves of the offending premises, but, sorry to say, not the occupants. They were too quick in getting away.

As in case of a repulse the bridge would be invaluable to us, a company was left in its charge. The house I ordered the captain to burn.

Then the command pushed on double-quick and with intervals taken, only, instead of following the road, it was turned to the right up a hill of meadow smoothness. At a short distance we came to a gorge with a rocky face on our side. Ordinary infantry, I am confident, could not have crossed without serious disorder. To my Zouaves it was scarcely an obstruction. At the farther side the ascent was gradual, and once on the top, as each man knew, the town was at our mercy.

There was no opposition, and, the summit gained, I closed intervals and changed direction left. Approaching the brow of the long hill which had been so lately occupied by the enemy in battle array, we were thunderstruck. Not a man was to be seen. The guns had been limbered up and had disappeared while we were crossing the gorge. Behind a line of skirmishers we advanced through the streets cautiously, but in time to see a mixed multitude of men, women, children, and soldiers in the distance flying for life under cover of a cloud of dust; and it was said they never stopped running until at Winchester.

We had won a town of pretensions all—never anything cheaper—for a broken suspender-buckle.

The bareback rider from the hamlet in the mountains had borne the news of our coming in such good time that the caution with which we advanced through the streets was unnecessary. If a white person remained in the place it was in a cellar or under a bed, where we did not care to look. Even the bank had been left to us; but as I set a guard over the building, the owners suffered no loss, unless it might have been in their breakfastless trip to Winchester.

But because the gentry had flown, it must not be supposed there was nobody at home. The colored people met us with the cheeriest welcome, and in time incredibly short there was not a hungry man in the regiment. Nor was it a common meal they set. It is but fair to the bread-winners of that day in Romney to admit the ample store of good things in pantry and smoke-house, and that the famous old Virginia flavor was in every dish the "aunties" were pleased to serve.

The camp adjoining town did not escape so lightly. Three wagons, with their teams, were impressed and loaded with equipments, guns, tents, and an excellent supply of medical stores. The provisions were condemned at sight and despoiled. With that exception, the find was pronounced lawful spoils of war.

At three o'clock, when inspection was had and the column formed for departure, the only curious things noticeable were packages, generally in clean white napkins, swinging from guns at shoulder. Some of them were opened with discovery of nothing more objectionable than edibles of one kind or another warm from the oven.

At the bridge, while the company left in charge of it were lunching, I observed that the brick house was standing untouched, and spoke to the captain.

"Didn't I tell you to burn that house?"

"Yes," he said, "but I couldn't."

"Why not?"

"Well, if you will hear him, I'll let this old man speak for me."

A gray-haired, farmer-looking person stepped up.

"The house is mine," he said, respectfully; "I raised a family in it, sir, and it is very dear to me. This morning, sir, some young men from the town came and took possession. I suppose they thought it would be a good place to fire on you. I couldn't resist them, sir. Then when the captain would have burned me out, I pleaded with him, and he agreed, sir, like a gentleman, to wait for you."

"Yes," said the captain, "I'll burn it now, if you say so."

I shook the old gentleman's hand, and told the bugler to blow "Forward."

Having repossessed ourselves of the train at the New Creek bridge, and loaded up our plunder, I left the teams, which were private property, to be returned to Romney; and at eleven o'clock at night we were in return for Cumberland.

Next day, in the afternoon, dress-parade was had as usual, nobody apparently the worse for the forty-six miles travelled, not to speak of the skirmish which was the incident of the march.

XXXIII

In camp at Cumberland—*Frank Leslie's Illustrated Weekly*—Congratulations from General Scott—Help refused—General Patterson—General McClellan—Corporal David Hay—The Fight of the Scouts—Colonel Biddle and the Pennsylvania Militia.

ACROSS a stone bridge over a little river, which was one of the ornaments of the old city of Cumberland, I found a plateau on a height, enough to accommodate the regiment in camp, and took possession of it. A more ideal site for the purpose cannot be imagined. Near it was a cleared field easily convertible into a drill-ground; and thus tricked out, we went to work as at Evansville.

The good results of the raid on Romney were not slow in showing themselves. The regiment took on the *esprit de corps* aimed at from the beginning; that it could march so far in a day, and, against odds, win a garrisoned town by the simple offer of fight, secured the confidence of the loyal people of Cumberland.

Then, when news of the raid went abroad beyond the localities first to feel its effect, not only was importance given to the affair; it received a welcome from the authorities and the public that astonished nobody so much as ourselves. Later in the war, to be sure, it had passed unnoticed. To illustrate—whereas, I had not thought of making a formal report, lest it should be misconstrued, and laughed at in military circles, an order from General Patterson to send him full particulars surprised me, and I hardly knew how to take it. The report sent was my earliest attempt in that line of literature, and a pretty poor one it was. Next the newspapers made much of the affair; and when an artist of *Frank Leslie's Illustrated Weekly* sought privileges in our camp,[1] I began to realize a distinction won. It was all very sweet, indeed; but the climax came in an autograph note of congratulations from General Scott, which I understood better when, a little later, intelligence reached us that General Johnston, upon hearing the tale of woe carried to Winchester by the frightened folk of Romney, had evacuated Harper's Ferry, believing himself seriously threatened from the west, while General Patterson was in close observation on the north. So, having given Romney the shaking up jocularly alluded to in my conversation with General Morris, at Grafton, much had come of it—namely, the release of the Baltimore & Ohio Railroad to the national authorities for supply and communication. This, doubtless, was what General Scott was thanking me for in his kindly note.

It must not be supposed now that I lapped myself in peaceful dreams because delightfully housed, so to speak, on the pine-covered height above Cumberland.

My first step was to establish a bureau of information. A gentleman in Cumberland undertook the delicate business. Through a secret correspondent he kept me posted as to affairs in Romney; among other things I heard promptly of the arrival there of cavalry, artillery, and infantry, four thousand in all, under a Colonel McD——d.

Judging that gentleman by myself, I fancied him sleeplessly anxious to repay my attentions by attentions in kind, particularly as he now had ample means with which to square the account.

[1] His drawings are in the *Illustrated Weekly* of that period.

I asked General Patterson for assistance; he could give me none. About that time General George B. McClellan relieved General Morris, and the same request preferred to him brought me the same reply. My condition then became one of isolation; and forced to take care of myself, I set to and studied the geography of the region.

The first need was a line of retreat, and I found one in a highway running northwardly into Pennsylvania.

Next there were but two roads of approach from Romney—one by the turnpike already mentioned; the other by way of Frostburg. With respect to the latter, the Mount Airy coal-miners were both numerous and loyal, and they readily agreed to keep watch over it for me.

Vastly more difficult was the problem presented in connection with the turnpike, for it included care of the roads, paths, and passes of the whole stretch of country between Cumberland and Romney. In that study I learned to appreciate the value of cavalry.

The conclusion may be inferred from what was done. Detachments were sent into the country to impress horses for the mount of a company; they came back with thirteen all told, and I had to content myself with them. They were pretty fair, but would have been condemned by a government inspector. After a dress-parade I called for volunteers, it being explained that they were to serve as scouts; to my surprise, the entire regiment stepped three paces front. Indeed, there was quite a controversy over the call. The command I gave to Corporal David Hay; and the duty was entered upon, it should be said, not one of the thirteen deterred by the superstition attaching to the number.

The presence of the superior force in Romney made formidable by cavalry and artillery, drew general attention to my position, and, the solicitude being unreasonably stimulated, all kinds of dreadful rumors were put in circulation about us. After little, the enemy moved out and burned the New Creek railway bridge; then, communication with Grafton being broken, it was announced that we were cut off, and there was fear in Indiana.

The situation did, indeed, become exciting; at the same time there was not a minute in which I was beyond helping myself. In saying this I am bound to give credit to the people of Cumberland. Without them it had not been possible for me to have held my position.

The rations gave out; my commissary bought of dealers in town all he required.

The ammunition threatened failure. Again the town came to my relief; and the world not having then advanced beyond the paper cartridge, Colonel McGinnis took a detail and made a fresh supply.

Then, too, a tobacco famine fell upon us. Not a man in camp, myself included, had wherewith to quiet the general wail. Banker Shriver heard of the condition, and came to our relief with an offer to advance a month's pay to every commissioned officer. The offer was gladly accepted. It is needless to say, I hope, that the good man was made whole to the last cent.

In the mean time I made ready against a possible necessity of getting away. There were a number of curios in my camp, relics of the late raid, and I did not relish the thought of making contributions of the kind in return, not even a handful of beans. Then shortly, what with impressed wagons and teams parked within the lines, the camp had a singular likeness to a county fair on its great day.

Once my scouts hastened in to report a column in

force from Romney moving over the mountains towards Frostburg by the only route to my rear. A little later a messenger from the miners at Mount Airy confirmed the news. It was wonderful how quickly the camp property was loaded into the wagons. When the scouts were all in we marched through the town. The consternation there was great. The flags on the housetops and along the streets disappeared, reminding me of delicate flowers hit hard by a biting frost. Cautioning the citizens whom I met to keep to their houses during my absence, especially after night, I took the road to Pennsylvania. The movement had every appearance of a retreat, and it was amusing to hear the men shouting at me, "Remember Buena Vista." After the train had been escorted beyond the intersecting road by which I surmised the enemy was coming, suddenly the column was faced about, and as the men caught my purpose they broke into cheers. Some days before I had chosen a ground in anticipation of the emergency upon me, and now returned to it, and made every disposition for battle. While waiting, horsemen from Mount Airy reported that the enemy, after advancing to a point about four miles away, had suddenly turned back towards Romney.

In the morning our tents again whitened the plateau on the heights above the city to the good cheer of the faithful; again their flowery flags re-illumined its housetops.

While in position out on the road waiting the pleasure of my opponent, Colonel McD——d, I was visited by an idea which, when in my tent again, I made haste to try. Among those to whom I had applied for assistance was Governor Curtin, of Pennsylvania. He, too, had failed to discover a possibility of helping me. Now I telegraphed him, renewing my request, and informing him that, if hard pushed, my intention was to retreat into his state; in which event it was more than likely the enemy would follow me, and prove the reputed wealth of his border counties in cattle and horses. Next day I was gladdened by notice from the governor of two regiments of his "State Reserves," with a battery of six guns, ordered to my support under Colonel Biddle. When, by the notice, they should have arrived, but had not, I rode out in search of them, and found a most ludicrous situation. The governor had instructed Colonel Biddle to go as far as the state line between Pennsylvania and Maryland, but not to cross it. This was provoking, for already I had mapped out a sortie against Romney. Still Captain Campbell of the battery gave me a hearty laugh. He had not taken kindly to the restraining order; he even thought it disgraceful, and when I came upon him his guns were all in battery, their muzzles extended over what he energetically denominated, "the damned state line." It was the extreme limit of his tether.

XXXIV

Between Romney and Cumberland—The thirteen scouts—Silverheels—Farley and Hay—Spoils of battle—Virginia losses—At the culvert—Hand-to-hand fight—Hallowell—The death of Hollenback—Search for the dead—Congratulations from Patterson, McClellan, and Colfax.

THE country between Romney and Cumberland is to be thought of in the time under consideration as very debatable. It swarmed with scouts of both sides; only those of the enemy roamed about in large parties, while in groups seldom of more than three mine lurked in the fastnesses. Occasionally shots were exchanged.

For two days I had gone without a word of the enemy. The intelligence office could get me nothing; neither could Corporal Hay. I began to suspect my opponent, Colonel McD——d, was again in motion, and that for better concealment of his plans he was curtaining the roads and passes with his cavalry. At all events, it was not safe for me to abide in such a state of ignorance.

In the morning of the third day, early, I called the corporal into my tent, and materially changed the directions under which he had been acting. This time he was to unite his thirteen men, take the turnpike, and keep it until he could bring me something reliable.

The brave man looked me in the face, and said, "Well, that means a fight."

And I answered, "If you can't do better, fight."

I went with him to where his comrades were in the saddle, and among them, and satisfied myself that they were all provided as well as could be. They had rifles with sword-bayonets—the latter fairly good for hand-to-hand encounter. They were young, enthusiastic, and by this time accustomed to scouting; as theretofore they had succeeded in driving everything before them, possibly their natural courage was too strongly tinctured with confidence.

Out of a vivid remembrance of what the little company actually did that day, as well as gratitude, I stop here to give their names, remarking that the original list had undergone a change. They were David B. Hay, E. N. Baker, Company A; Ed. Burkett, J. C. Hollenback, Company B; Tim Grover, James Hallowell, Company C; Thomas Brazier, Company D; George W. Wudbarger, Company E; Lewis Farley, Company F; Frank Harrison, Company H; P. M. Dunlap, Company I; Robert Dunlap and E. P. Thomas, Company K.

It was June 27th, too beautiful for anything but perfect peace.

I shook hands with each one of them, and, noticing Hay's horse, I spoke to him and asked if it was not new.

"Yes."

"Where did you get him?"

"I saw a man riding him over in the hills yonder and took a notion to him."

"He looks like running stock."

"So he is. In Romney they know him as Silverheels."

He had captured the horse in one of his many scouting scuffles up in the debatable zone.

Taking to the turnpike, the party disappeared; and what follows now is hearsay, but hearsay so well corroborated as to be entitled to implicit belief.

Hay kept the turnpike boldly, intending to make

prisoner of the first man he came upon, and squeeze him for news. A few miles out he rode up a hill, and from the top looked down into a village ambitiously christened Frankfort. He drew rein, shaking his hand to caution his followers. The one long street below was full of soldiers easily recognizable as infantry. Hitched to the fences he saw saddled horses which told him of cavalry thereabouts.

"We could have killed as many of them at one fire as we had rifles," he told me afterwards.

"Why didn't you?" I asked.

He shook his head. "The idiots! They had no lookouts, and shooting them would have been too much like murder."

Instead of firing, Hay and his party kept their place, and agreed upon an estimate of the number of the enemy; then they turned and rode a distance back to a divergent road leading up into wooded hills, and finally to the railroad. To save their horses they jogged slowly on, intending to try another but more obscure route to Romney. It was about eleven o'clock when, starting down a height somewhat steep, they overtook a body of rebel horsemen going in the same direction. There was no call of halt. Each scout stopped involuntarily. Then they unslung their rifles. Hay did the counting.

"There are only forty-one of them," he said, in a low voice. "What do you say, boys?"

"Go in, Dave."

"Are you ready?"

"All ready," they answered.

The Virginians were at serious disadvantage. The road under them was narrow, and furrowed by washouts; on their right the land dropped into a ravine; while the bank at their left sloped too steeply up for climbing except afoot. To 'bout face and charge, or even meet a charge, was impossible. In a word, they had no resource but to go on. All this Hay discerned.

"Come on," he shouted, at the top of his voice, forgetting to fire. "Come on. The best horse gets the first man."

The enemy heard the cry and drew reins. They saw Hay in the lead, Silver-heels plunging down, and behind a trail of men in big gray breeches, some brandishing short guns, some with sword-bayonets gleaming high in air, all yelling, all in motion, like bowlders let loose. Then they, too, set up a counter yell, and began crowding one another down the broken way fast as they could go.

Farley's hack put him next to Hay; the others had places in the charge according to the speed they could get out of their mounts. Not one hung back. At the foot of the hill, Hay reached the rear of the Virginians, and, firing first, hurled his rifle; then, pistol in hand, he lunged Silver-heels in. But presently the ground turned into an out-spreading level, and the advantages melting away, he found himself surrounded and a target for well-aimed sabres. He took one wound; then another; but for each of them he killed a man. When the revolver was empty, he flung it at the Confederate captain, and engaged him with his bayonet. A third wound; yet he kept his saddle. Half-blind with blood, and striking aimlessly, he had certainly been finished had not Farley rushed loyally to his aid. A fortunate shot struck the captain. Farley, dismounted by the collision, followed him to the ground. Then, before he could gain his feet, a man clinched him only to be knocked senseless by young Hallowell. Farley caught a horse and joined Hay again. About that time the Virginians, bareback, and in their flight, took to the railroad track. Over the ties, amid a thick dust of cinders, helter-skelter, each man for himself, they went headlong. Suddenly a burned culvert of depth and width yawned before them. Avoid it they could not; into it or over it they had to go. Eight men died there, and Hay would have been the ninth man but that he saw the obstruction and, as the only chance for life, took the leap. The horse fell dead on the farther side. When his comrades reached Hay, they found him sitting by Silver-heels, and crying, "He was not hurt, boys; his heart broke—that's all"; and that he always maintained.

The combat ended at the culvert; so, at least, Hay supposed; and the Zouaves employed themselves collecting the spoils. They first secured seventeen horses, with their equipments; then, going over the ground of combat, they counted eleven of the Virginians dead, three in the road at the foot of the fatal hill, and eight in the débris of the culvert.

Hay selected a successor to Silver-heels, after which, with much self-gratulation, light-hearted, and joking, the party set out for Cumberland. Soon, from loss of blood, the corporal grew so faint they had to stop and help him out of his saddle. They dressed his wounds again; still he had difficulty in riding. As a last resort, two of their number—Baker of Company A and Dunlap of Company I—were sent to a farm-house for a wagon. All this took valuable time. The sun rose up and stood above them at noon. Two o'clock, and they were yet helping Hay, and waiting for the wagon. Suddenly a fire opened upon them from a hill at their left. Hay had them put him on his horse; he could take care of himself, he said; and clinging painfully to the saddle, he managed to ford the Potomac and get to camp after night.

Though reduced now to ten men, most likely the whole of them had been saved could they have made up their minds to let the captured horses go. Years before Farley had lost one of his eyes; the sound one now served him well. He saw the Virginians were surrounding them. Behind him he beheld the glancing waters of Patterson's creek, and noted that the farther side of it, while scarcely higher than the ground they were then upon, was covered with large rocks washed white by passing floods. There were willows in clump also, and a general débris of logs and drift furnishing cover and concealment.

"Let the horses go," he called out; "let them go, and come in every one of you." And when they were all assembled, he sang out again: "It won't do to give in or stay here. Come, now, and let's rush for the big rocks yonder, and get the creek between the rebels and us."

They made the rush and reached the other shore of the creek. Farley looked them over. They were all there—ten of them—and in his words they were "sound as new fifty-cent pieces, and not whipped by a damned sight."

In the shelter of the logs and rocks, they counted over seventy Virginians afoot and running for the creek.

"Look out now, boys, and don't waste a cartridge. Remember how scarce they are." This was from Farley, and Hallowell replied, "Yes, and 'Remember Buena Vista.'"

As the enemy took the creek, splashing furiously, the rifles on the island all opened upon them, making the air hot and hissing. Some were hit; all who could recoiled, and, taking cover on their side, they began the exciting play of sharp-shooters, which was still in progress when the sun went down.

In the deepening of the twilight a party of horsemen were seen to join the Virginians. One of them, a tall man with a plumed, broad-brimmed hat, walked about in contempt of the bullets that sang about him. He took command, and under his inspiration the whole assembly of foemen arose, and, yelling, made another dash to cross the creek. Some of them were seen to fall in the water; but now there was a resolute, fearless leader and no recoil. They reached the island. No amount of courage was then available, so great was the odds in close quarters; yet over the bowlders, and through the tangle of logs and willows, a fight, hand to hand, went on, and there was heroism on both sides. Farley found himself confronting the tall leader, he of the broad-brimmed, plumed hat. The sword-bayonet in his hand was good, but the sabre of the other was better, and Hallowell saved Farley, but broke his rifle in the act. Nothing daunted, Hallowell stripped a dead man of his pistols in belt and resumed the combat. He brought the pistols into camp with him, and next morning I made him a present of them. Thomas killed two opponents with his rifle; while loading a third time, a bullet raked his temple and he fell senseless. A man in gray lifted a sabre to finish him, but was shot by Grover, and fell across the body of Thomas and died. In the darkness, when night was fallen, Thomas recovered consciousness; hearing no sound, he pushed the corpse off, secured his gun, and was in hiding when the enemy came to remove their dead and wounded. In searching the island, they discovered Hollenback shot through the body.

"Here's a Yankee," Thomas heard one of them shout.

"Come, my man, get out of this," another said; yet others cried, "Kill him, kill him!"

The poor fellow protested feebly; yet they made him rise and wade the creek. When they were gone with their prisoner, and all was still, Thomas escaped across the Potomac.

Meantime, Baker, and Dunlap of Company I, the two sent for the wagon, hearing the noise of the second engagement, turned their horses and galloped to camp. The regiment was at drill when they arrived. Two companies, under Major Robinson, started to the rescue, but though they travelled fast they were too late. The island was given over to darkness and quiet. They found traces of the fight in abundance—broken guns, accoutrements, and blood in red stains on the rocks—but that was all.

Next morning the major went back with the companies to search for Hollenback, and bury such dead as they might find. He returned with eight horses, and the body of the missing scout found on a farmer's porch warm and bleeding. The poor fellow had died of a bullet and bayonet thrust in his back. The major also brought me the story of the woman of the house.

"A little while ago," she said, "when they heard you coming, they set your man on a horse to take him off with them, for he wasn't dead. But he couldn't stand it, and fainted. They then stuck a bayonet through him."

"Did they bring anybody else here?" the major asked, seeing blood in spots in the porch.

"Oh yes," she said. "Me and my man came out while they were at work, and we counted twenty-three men laid out there side by side. Two or three of them were alive. I heard a man say that some of the dead ones had been brought out by the railroad. Among the lot there was a Mr. Ashby wounded." [1]

By "taps" the scouts, with the one exception, were all in camp. Thomas showed the furrow of the shot

[1] The Ashby referred to by the woman was reported to be a brother of the Ashby of "Black Horse Cavalry" renown. It was also reported that he afterwards died of the wounds received at Patterson's creek.

across his temple. Baker wore the cap of a Virginian—his own having been torn from his head. Dunlap, of Company K, had three bullet holes through his jacket and shirt. Hallowell displayed his pistols. Farley retained the handle of his bayonet shivered in the fray. Every one bore some proof of danger run, if only a bruised body or torn clothes. Withal, however, Corporal Hay was the hero. Three ghastly wounds entitled him to the honor.[1]

The second fight of that day took place, as it afterwards appeared, on Kelly's Island, at the mouth of Patterson's creek. Hollenback was buried in the cemetery of Cumberland. The loyal people of the city, men and women, participated in the funeral. The feeling on our side was prodigious; what it was on the other side may be imagined.

Such was the combat at Kelly's Island. I think it would have attracted attention at any period of the war; but coming as it did in the very beginning, the whole North accepted it as a test of personal prowess referable particularly to. the boast then so common, that in a fight one Southerner was the equal of five Yankees. Certainly the largesse of encomiums from headquarters and high places, and from the press, was liberal enough to satisfy any ambition.

General Patterson, upon receipt of my report of the affair, issued an order to be read to every command in his army.

"(General Orders No. 29.)

"HEADQUARTERS, DEPARTMENT OF PENNSYLVANIA,
"HAGERSTOWN, *June* 30, 1861.

"The commanding general has the satisfaction to announce to the troops a second victory over the insurgents

[1] Upon my recommendation, Governor Morton afterwards appointed Hay a second lieutenant.

by a small party of Indiana Volunteers, under Colonel Wallace, on the 26th instant. Thirteen mounted men attached to the regiment attacked forty-one insurgents, killing eight and chasing the rest two miles. On their return with seventeen captured horses, they were attacked by seventy-five of the enemy, and fell back to a strong position, which they held till dark, when they returned to camp, with the loss of one man killed and one wounded.

"The commanding general desires to bring to the attention of the officers and men of his command the courage and conduct with which this gallant little band of comparatively raw troops met the emergency, by turning on an enemy so largely superior in numbers and chastising him severely, and gathering the fruits of victory.

"By order of Major-General Patterson.

"J. F. PORTER, Assistant Adjutant-General."

The day after the fight, General McClellan telegraphed me for the particulars, and to my reply he sent the following:

"GRAFTON, VA., *June* 28, 1861.

"*To Colonel Lew Wallace:*

"I congratulate you upon the gallant conduct of your regiment. Thank them for me, and express to the party how highly I honor their heroic courage, worthy of their French namesakes. I more than ever regret that you are not under my command. I have urged General Scott to send up the Pennsylvania regiments. I begin to doubt if the Eleventh Indiana needs reinforcements.

"GEORGE B. MCCLELLAN, Major-General, U. S. Army."

Nor was that all. The gallantry at Kelly's Island had an echo in the marble chamber of the vice-president in the Capitol, and another in the White House. Mr. Colfax was pleased to write me:

"WASHINGTON CITY, *June* 28, 1861.

"MY DEAR SIR,—The whole city is ringing with the magnificent news from your scouting party, though it seems too splendid to be true. We had been all depressed by another slight reverse on the Potomac line to-day when in came the rumor of your despatch to General McClellan, said to be telegraphed verbatim to General Scott. Indianians, I need not tell you, feel prouder than ever of our volunteers, and I only hope it may be confirmed. The president told me day before yesterday that Indiana had won nearly all the glory so far, and taken about all the scalps. But this news eclipses everything. If it really be true, please present to the gallant boys the heartiest thanks of the Indianians here, especially of

"Yours and theirs very truly,

"SCHUYLER COLFAX.

"P. S.—The president, in his conversation with me, alluded especially to your splendid dash on Romney."

XXXV

Ordered to Martinsburg—Joe Johnston and Beauregard—Arrival of baggage-train—Meeting with Patterson — Mexican War reminiscences — Fitz-John Porter — Colonel Stone—The rivalry of the Massachusetts regiment—A competitive drill.

About eleven o'clock in the forenoon of July 7th, as nearly as I can remember, a special courier dismounted at the door of my tent and delivered a sealed despatch from General Patterson. Opening it, I took out an order directing me to march to Martinsburg as soon as possible.

"As soon as possible," was the postfix. As always upon the receipt of orders, my wits put themselves to work trying to discover the whys and wherefores governing in the quarters from which this one proceeded.

From the courier, and from general information as well, I knew an army was being massed at Martinsburg. I knew, also, that General Beauregard was in force at Manassas Junction, and that there was talk—much too loud, it seemed to me—of attacking him from Washington. I knew, too, that General Joe Johnston held Winchester with another army; and putting this and that together, the inference was plain that the concentration at Martinsburg had in some way to do with Johnston. A little study of the map, and it grew upon me that General Patterson was in position materially to assist the authorities in Washington when it should be decided to take the offensive against Beauregard. Thereupon the old itching to see a battle, a real big battle, with thousands engaged, surged back on me with even more than its original force. The keeping of Cumberland, personally useful in that it had called my resources into play, was but guerilla after all. A broader field, and relations with other commands, were within the longings now aroused; and I could but think what education there must be in the co-operation of a great army.

I made haste, yet it took the day to call in my scouts and, I may add, to allow farewells to friends in the city whose alarm ran high. If they were to be left without protection now, they thought it had been better had I not come. Fortunately for them, and my own peace of mind, Colonel Biddle, with his "Bucktails," crossed into Maryland to take my place. Governor Curtin had at last realized that the condition was war, in which state lines were to become myths more unsubstantial than flying gossamers.

My few sick were left in hospital, where, thanks to the good people, I knew they would be better cared for than on the march or in the field. With everything in wagon we took the road to Martinsburg.

The Potomac, when reached, had ceased to be a subject of remark to the regiment. Familiarity had done its work, and we took to the river and waded it in a matter-of-fact way.

Approaching Martinsburg, I noticed crowds of men in uniforms lining the road-sides, and as they received us with clapping of hands and loud laughter, I asked one of them what it meant.

"Oh," he returned, "we heard of your train, and we are out to see it. It's great, colonel, it's great!"

And it was great. Nothing like it of the kind had been seen. It came on composed of every conceivable wheeled vehicle, from one-horse chaises of Holmes's sort to "prairie-schooners," sixty-two in all. It rolled on slowly and solemnly, and with all manner of original noises.

"What do you carry in them?" one asked me.

"Regimental property, to be sure."

"Well, you must have struck a good quartermaster in Romney."

No person in authority presenting himself to direct me to a pace of encampment, I held on the main road till a roomy stubble-field invited me to come in, and I entered and took possession and discharged my teamsters, giving each one a quartermaster's certificate covering the use of his property. Thereupon we pitched our tents, and were installed as a part of an army indefinitely large.

General Patterson, to whose headquarters I immediately rode to report my arrival, was glad to see me, and had much to say that was complimentary. In course of the conversation I referred to the Mexican War, and asked him if he were not the officer who, in 1846, had ordered Colonel Drake, of the First Indiana, up to Monterey. He remembered the circumstance, and said he knew at the time that his action was without authority, and that he had misgivings about the treatment the regiment would get from General Taylor; still, he added, it was a venture with humanity at bottom, for such a want of wholesome food, such helplessness in suffering, such wholesale dying he had never thought to see in an American camp. While he was speaking I was struck with his likeness to General Taylor; only his countenance was not so densely stupid, while his uniform was in accord with his rank, and he wore blacked boots and a clean shirt.

The general introduced me to a number of his officers. One of them, Colonel Abercrombie, spoke of my father as a classmate at West Point. I listened to him with greater interest, knowing that it was he who won the recent skirmish at Falling Waters. For the same reason my pleasure was very sincere when told of my assignment to his brigade.

Colonel Fitz-John Porter, assistant adjutant-general, also honored me with a glance. I remember him as carefully attired, reserved in manner, quick in observation, graceful in person; in other words, looking the fine soldier. It struck me, too, that my Zouave jacket and breeches, by that time considerably worse of the wear, did not recommend me to him.

There, also, I met Colonel Stone, leader of a brigade. His open countenance, kindly voice, and hearty manner were singularly attractive. In his presence it had been impossible to forecast the misfortunes that befell him, stripped of command, and shut in a prison—for what, no man to this day has said. Nor did he know. Years after I met him in Egypt, the first general in the service of the Khedive. In Shepheard's Hotel one night he discussed his tribulations in America, and asserted, his eyes moist with tears, that he had no knowledge of a cause for them; neither did he know who his enemy was. He was even denied a court of inquiry. Indeed, his case is the one mystery of the war awaiting solution. Ever since that melancholy night I have had a conviction that General Stone was guiltless of any military crime—that he was simply the victim of some superior's spleen or jealousy.

Of all those met that day at General Patterson's headquarters, none impressed me as did George H. Thomas, then colonel commanding a brigade. He sat at a table the moment of my introduction, but arose and offered me his hand. His full, knightly figure and leonine face somehow told me of the soldierly soul of the man. The next time I met him was in the office of a station in Tennessee on the Louisville & Nashville Railroad. The promise of the early meeting in Martinsburg had been more than realized; he had developed into the best beloved of the Western army.

The division commanders under General Patterson—Major-Generals Cadwallader and Keim—I had not the good-fortune of seeing then or ever.

Returning to camp in the afternoon, I found the regiment in commotion. The men were sullen and angry. Some of them, it appeared, had climbed a fence across the road to watch another regiment at drill, but had been ordered down and off; the order had been seasoned with expletives, and sundry unqualified allusions to "damned Indiana grease-bags." A detachment had told itself off to resent the insult, and was then in the road waiting for the strangers to appear.

Here was an opportunity for a serious regimental feud, if not something worse, and I hastened to direct the officers of the day to stop the going out, and if any were out to bring them in. Thereupon I rode to see the offending body, which was yet at drill.

It was a Massachusetts regiment. One had only to glance at it to see how raw the organization was, and at the same time how beautifully it had been fitted out—thanks to the loving care of Governor Andrews. The uniforms were fresh; the tents immaculately white, and pitched with a precision certifying a master colonel, whoever he might be. The blue wagons in park, and the fatted mules about them, were all in keeping with their surroundings. Glancing at the band, however, one knew he had come upon the colonel's chief joy. Their horns in especial looked as if they had been made where brass was an original product, flowing like a river. Small wonder these petted sons of the old Bay State elevated their noses so airily at us.

I had not to be told that my neighbors, the officers in particular, held views of the West colored with uncomplimentary prejudices, and I thought it possible to revolutionize them at least so far as we were concerned. We had only to show them that we could teach them something, and I had an inspiration—they may have seen a company of Zouaves at drill, but not a full regiment.

Next day, in the afternoon, the band of my colleague from Massachusetts sounded the adjutant's call; mine did the same. His companies poured from their streets; so did mine. The idlers of the army assembled in force. Expecting nothing from us, they lent the inspiration of their presence to my neighbor, and were not ordered down and off. He broke into column; at the same time all my bugles sounded. As an excitant the rush of eight hundred vigorous men hither and thither in all the variations of manœuvre must be seen to be appreciated. First, the idlers came over to my fence. Next, a New York regiment in hearing hurried to us. Then the howling of our rivals in the opposite field rose into a gale often as their columns wheeled in marching so as to give us their backs, and I knew what that meant. My confidence increased.

Our field was bounded on the north by a rail fence; beyond the fence stretched a broad hollow; and beyond the hollow a low mountain arose covered to the top with a growth of scrubby pine-trees. Watching a time when the whole column of my unwilling friends over the way was marching from us, suddenly, every bugle sounding, I brought the Eleventh into line facing the mountain. Another blast, and away they went, making the rails fly—away down the hither face of the hollow, across the hollow, up the ascent then in their front reaching a quarter of a mile—up every step double-quick. At length the last man of them disappeared in the pines. Three minutes—five—ten—then the uninitiated on the fences were all hushed by the same wonder—how was I, on my horse in the field, to bring the regiment back? It was the supreme moment of my venture. I looked at my neighbor. The curiosity of his companies becoming ungovernable, he had brought them to a halt, faced my way. My bugler, taking the signal from me, blew "Retreat"; another, several hundred yards off in the hollow, repeated it; others up in the grove did the same. In good time the regiment, intervals kept and in fair line, and still in double time, burst into view descending the height. The waving of caps and the yelling with which they were greeted from the fences assured me, and I looked over at Massachusetts. They, too, were cheering in generous fashion. They had surrendered.

Across the hollow, over the fence, into the field, the well-doers came as they had gone; suddenly the bugle gave them "Lie down," and they dropped as one man in the stubble.

Fraternization of the men of the two regiments began at once. Next day my neighbors, the officers, did us the honor to call. Next day, also, a wagon passed into my lines bringing half a dozen boxes of tobacco, with the compliments of Daniel Butterfield, colonel of the Twelfth New York. After that, in a word, there were no lines in the army against the Eleventh Indiana.

XXXVI

General Scott in command—Johnston at Harper's Ferry—Beauregard at Bull Run—Diagram—General Patterson's operations—The movement on Manassas—The Eleventh Regiment's willingness to remain beyond term of enlistment—Its return to Indianapolis.

AT this time, it may be remembered, Lieutenant-General Scott was directing military affairs from Washington. When his acceptance of President Lincoln's call to command was announced the whole North felt relieved. Congratulations poured in upon him, but he had no time to answer them. The situation was too urgent. General Joe Johnston, with four thousand men, was in possession of Harper's Ferry, while General Beauregard menaced Washington from intrenchments along Bull Run. Drawing upon his vast experience, the veteran hurried to assemble protecting armies—one at Washington, another in Pennsylvania. Too infirm to mount a horse, he selected General Irvin McDowell to command the first and General Robert Patterson the second.

Busy days and sleepless nights were those for the old soldier, charged with the harassing labor of organization, and every moment in mortal concern for the colossal reputation behind him. Turning from the reports of quartermasters, commissaries, ordnance officers, and inspectors, which could not be passed, he gave his best thought to the map disclosing the positions of the armies relative to Washington; and just so often the diagram of an irregular triangle shaped itself under his dimming eyes.

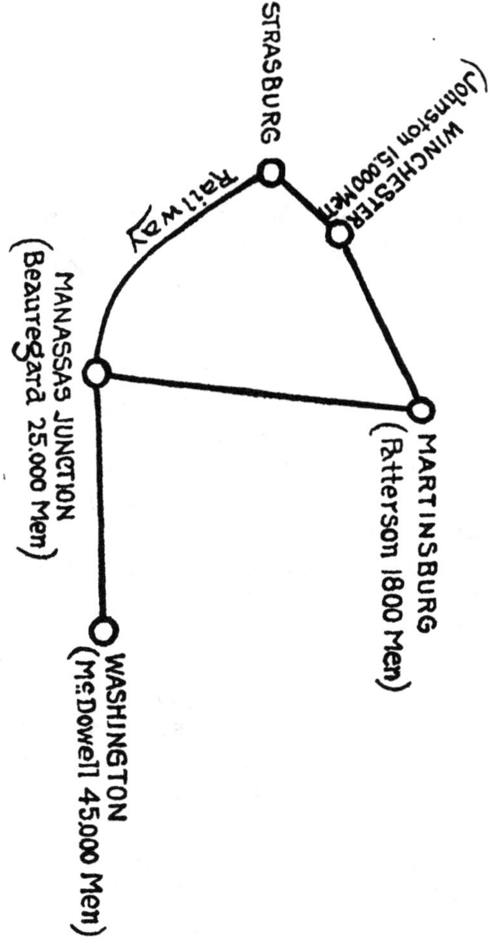

Washington was for the time the focus of all movement and all anxiety. When, finally, General Scott thought himself ready to give McDowell the word to advance against Beauregard, there was but one point about which he had misgivings; that is, he was certain of success if--and how long, if not nervously, the condition was pondered—*if* only Johnston could be held fast at Winchester.

Beginning with a perfect appreciation of the danger did Johnston appear on the field while the struggle was in progress, General Scott could not fail to see that either Johnston must be detained at Winchester or Patterson brought down to McDowell. I can imagine him weighing the chances. Often as he put his compasses on the map, the diagram fashioned itself before him; then he could not fail to see that Johnston at Winchester had the inner line against Patterson at Martinsburg, the railroad from Strasburg being such a factor. In short, the advantages were with Johnston. Still, Congress demanded a battle; so did the newspapers; so did the loyal people everywhere. Accordingly, the day being fixed, General Scott by telegraph sent General Patterson a final order, dated July 13th —"Make *demonstrations* so as to detain him (Johnston) in the *valley of Winchester*."[1] The end aimed at is stated together with the means of accomplishing it.

Now, a grave difference afterwards arose between General Scott and General Patterson touching the latter's operations under the order. I do not wish to be understood as the partisan of either; both have my profoundest respect; at the same time there ought to be no objection to a statement of the *demonstration* actually made by General Patterson in so far at least as it fell under my personal observation—I a participant. By going then to what General Johnston did, it is possible

[1] The italics are mine.

to discover the real secret of the loss to the Union arms of the battle of Manassas.

The order for General Patterson's movements bore date of July 13th. In the afternoon of the 14th I was notified that the army at Martinsburg would be put in motion the next day, and that I was to be ready to take my place in the column.

On the 15th the army started, Colonel Abercrombie, if I remember rightly, in advance. Where were we going? Everybody asked; nobody answered. The weather was intensely hot and dry, and the dust from the feet of the tramping thousands rose like an ochreous cloud. Noon, and still we marched, halting about three o'clock. Were we to go into camp? Colonel Abercrombie at length arrived and told me to dispose my regiment so as to make the men comfortable as might be, regardful of a probable alarm in the night. "We are at Bunker Hill," he said, "six miles from Winchester, and we will bivouac here." We had marched fifteen miles.

While coffee was making, I amused myself going from fire to fire listening to the comments of the men. They believed Winchester our destination, and that there, or on the road, we would have a big fight to tell about when back in Indiana. And I was of the same belief.

The situation was as novel to me as to them. Before retiring to my blanket, I wrote a letter to be taken to my dear wife, a farewell to her should the ultimate happen to me next day.[1] That there would be a battle I had not a doubt.

[1] Having some curiosity to see the letter after so long a time, I recently looked it up, and was not ashamed of the spirit in which it was written. Without being in the least gloomy, it shows a proper understanding of the possibilities confronting me, coupled with a willingness to face them. My wife, it should be said, has scrap-books always at my service. I sometimes think they contain everything I ever did or said.

It was a July sun, nothing diminished, that arose next day over the world, of which Bunker Hill, in Virginia, was now the centre. I was up to see it rise. The overhanging dust deepened in color to a brick red. Close behind, their muskets in stack, the men made coffee and lounged about waiting in momentary expectation of the familiar "Fall in"; but noon followed the morning, and evening the noon, and it was still quiet at Bunker Hill, in Virginia, only six miles from Winchester. In a fit of impatience, I grew presumptuous and rode to headquarters. Everything, they told me there, was hanging on the result of a reconnoissance in progress. Then my interest centred in the reconnoissance, it being, I was given to understand, strong enough in all the arms at least to get one look at the church spires of the town over against us. In the afternoon, towards sunset, it returned, reporting, as I was informed, that the road at some point near or far was obstructed by felled trees. Of all the officers in command brought back nothing was more certain than that he had not fired a gun; neither had he been fired at or seen an earthwork; had there been exchange of shotted courtesies we were near enough to have heard it.

Thus the 16th passed. I spent the night on the picket-line across the main road about four and a half miles from Winchester.

My field-officer lay with me under a tree. A calmer summer night could not have been. Our attention was forward in the direction of the enemy; and several times in the slow-going, long night we heard, or fancied we heard, in the universal stillness, trains in motion on the Manassas Gap railroad at Strasburg, eighteen miles beyond Winchester; we even thought we could distinguish between the sharp rattle of trains *coming* empty and the half-thunderous rumble of trains going laden. Was the enemy evacuating Winchester? Might he not be using his railroad, the complement of his interior line, to rush his army to the support of Beauregard at Manassas? In the oppressive silence we debated the question. Upon reporting in the morning, I suggested the possibility at brigade headquarters. The idea was met with a smile. *Now* it is known that the trains we fancied hearing in the calm night resonant afar were arriving to take Johnston's infantry and carry them at speed to Manassas, while his cavalry and artillery marched overland.

It should be said that my knowledge of the general military situation, what time I arrived at Martinsburg, including the status at Washington, Manassas, and Winchester, was from the source from which the enemy had his intelligence—the newspapers. That General Patterson supposed himself limited to mere *demonstration* I did not know; so, thinking he was out for a battle with General Johnston, the reader can judge my surprise when, at five o'clock in the morning of the 17th, the army was again deployed into a great column and set in motion towards Charlestown, where it went into bivouac sixteen or eighteen miles from Winchester. The movement had appearances of a retreat. Besides a heavy rear-guard, the main body was secured from surprise by flankers. Once there was a false alarm attended by a hurried closing up and forming for action.

Such being the end of the *demonstration* by General Patterson, in compliance with General Scott's order of the 13th, the effect may be tried in the light of subsequent history.

On the 16th—the day General Patterson spent in bivouac at Bunker Hill—General McDowell's army left Washington and marched to Centreville.

On the 17th the enemy at Centreville drew back to Bull Run, and General Scott telegraphed General Patterson: "McDowell's first day's work has driven the enemy behind Fairfax Court-House. Do not let the enemy amuse and delay you with a small force while he reinforces the junction with his main body." General Patterson replied, asking, "Shall I attack?" General Scott answered the same day: "I have certainly been expecting you to beat the enemy, or that you at least had occupied him by threats and demonstrations. . . . Has he not stolen a march, and sent reinforcements towards Manassas Junction?" [1] General Patterson replied: "The enemy has not stolen a march upon me. I have caused him to be reinforced." [2] Later in the day he added, "I have succeeded in accordance with the wishes of the general-in-chief in keeping General Johnston's force at Winchester." [3] The same day—the 17th—General Patterson, at four o'clock in the morning, roused his army from slumber, and retired with it from Bunker Hill to Charlestown. Most remarkable, however, while General Patterson was forwarding the last telegram quoted to General Scott, General Johnston, having made all ready, started — had advanced from Winchester to Manassas.[4]

On the 18th—General Patterson at Charlestown in absolute tranquillity sixteen miles from Winchester—General Tyler, against orders, was making the reconnoissance from Centreville that brought on the skirmish dignified by the Confederates into the battle of Bull Run, and General Johnson was en route with the larger part of his army.

On the 20th — General Patterson still in peaceful bivouac at Charlestown—General Johnston joined

[1] *Battles and Leaders of the Civil War*, vol. i., pp. 182-183.
[2] *Ibid.* [3] *Ibid.* [4] *Ibid.*

forces with Beauregard at Manassas. With eight thousand three hundred and forty men and twenty guns, he took position on the left of the Confederate army.[1]

On the 21st General McDowell, ignorant of General Johnston's presence on the field, attacked the left of Beauregard's position, and was repulsed by Johnston; and all through the terrible hours of that dark day General Patterson was quietly marching from Charlestown to Harper's Ferry, twelve miles farther from Winchester. One cannot help reverting to the assurance Scott gave McDowell, "that Johnston should not join Beauregard without having Patterson on his heels."[2]

I must be excused now from comment, leaving the facts recited to speak for themselves. Somebody blundered. That General Patterson did not follow at Johnston's heels had been excused on the ground that the term of enlistment of eighteen of his volunteer regiments was to expire within seven days, which would have been on the 24th.[3] The plea is not without force.

At Charlestown General Patterson issued an appeal to his command, representing the great necessity for its continuing with him ten days longer; in that time, he said, other troops would arrive. The question of staying was put to the regiments each in its quarters. Two consented—two only—the Second Wisconsin and the Eleventh Indiana. There were no other Western organizations in General Patterson's army.

Colonel Starkweather and I were so well pleased that, after the voting, we marched our men ceremonially to

[1] Beauregard, in *Battles and Leaders of the Civil War*, p. 202.

[2] General J. B. Fry, in *Battles and Leaders of the Civil War*, vol. i., p. 181.

[3] *Shenandoah Valley Campaign of* 1861. W. W. H. Davis.

the gate in front of the general's house and, halting there, notified him of the action taken. The old soldier came out and made a complimentary speech to us. While he was speaking, three of the regiments from his own state, Pennsylvania, marched past us going home. Their loud fanfaronade must have stung the speaker to the quick. I have never heard that the two consenting regiments were by name accredited for their patriotic stand.

The return home from Harper's Ferry was without incident. On July 29th the regiment arrived at Indianapolis, where it was handsomely received by the governor and the city. On August 2d the formal muster out took place, and the three months' service was at an end. Besides valuable experience acquired, we had availed ourselves of every opportunity to advance the cause.

XXXVII

The Eleventh Indiana—Its character—Tribute to General McGinnis.

WITH few exceptions the men of the Eleventh Indiana, in the three months' service, were in what may be called the efflorescent period of life; insomuch, in fact, that they had their regimental character largely from their buoyancy of youth. While appreciating the horrors which, by universal consent, make battles terrible, they yet had a pronounced anxiety to try them experimentally. They were of such varied occupations that it had been possible, I believe, to have overcome every difficulty ordinarily incident to soldiers in campaign. Indeed, I used to think that if transported in the remotest inhabitable part of the globe, where everything called for by civilization was in the raw, they could have taken care of themselves even to the making an acceptable state.

As respects the officers, their zeal was great as mine, while as drill-masters some of them were unexcelled. Foreseeing a demand upon my ranks to fill positions in other commands, I decided early not to try to keep any one who thought he could better himself by going elsewhere. The principle, however, did not apply to the officers, and, doing my best to retain them, I happily succeeded. They all proved themselves under the new enlistment worthy the most honorable mention; at the same time there was one for whom all the rest would have given way, and of him I must speak with particularity, if only to please myself.

Lieutenant-Colonel George F. McGinnis was a soldier

by nature. Added to the other indispensable qualities, he was master of the tactics then in usage. Stern and insistent where orders were concerned, he somehow managed to get the love of the men and hold it; wherefore the soubriquet, "Pap McGinnis." He had a horse, of course, but hated a saddle, taking to it only in battle. I can see him yet marching, a tall, ruddy, angular-looking person, swinging forward loose-gaited at the head of the column, his sabre tucked point foremost under his arm. At such times he had little to say. He gave step to the company next him, and the "pony" lads at the rear, troubled to keep up, showered him with blessings strangely mixed considering how every one of them would have died for him.

His promotions were rapid—from a private in the Eleventh to a captaincy; next lieutenant-colonel; then colonel; finally, in May, 1863, he was commissioned brigadier-general. As colonel he took part in the capture of Fort Heiman, opposite Fort Henry, and in the fall of Fort Donelson, and at Shiloh and the siege of Corinth. As chief of the First Brigade of the Third Division of the 13th Army Corps, he shared in all the honors of the Vicksburg campaign, including the battle of Port Hudson and Champion Hills. At the latter he was conspicuous, his brigade bearing the brunt and losing heavily, the casualties of the Eleventh Indiana alone amounting to one hundred and sixty-seven. Returning to Indianapolis, with two enlistments in the Mexican War and two in the civil war to his credit, the people of the county recognized the sterling qualities of the man by electing him auditor and then commissioner. He is still living. I meet him frequently, and always with feelings in which the fraternal surpasses the friendly.[1]

[1] He is at present [1901] postmaster of the city of Indianapolis.

XXXVIII

Eleventh regiment re-enlists for three years—Invited to join McClellan's command—Goes to St. Louis with Frémont—Headquarters—Inactivity—Cold reception—Transferred to Smith's division—Paducah.

THE ten days' overstay with General Patterson in Virginia threw the Eleventh Indiana behind in recruiting; nevertheless, it was mustered-in for three years on August 31, 1861. Then the question of lively interest to us all—where would we be sent?

General McClellan, attracted by our conduct while at Cumberland, had invited me to join him in the event of continuation in the service, and I confess to having been greatly flattered, for he was the genius then almost unanimously supposed to have been divinely appointed to save the republic. Everybody in the North spoke of him as the young Napoleon. By this time he was in Washington, called thither by Mr. Lincoln the day succeeding the disaster to McDowell at Manassas. Leaving my regiment to proceed to Indianapolis, I ran up to make the general's acquaintance and study the situation. He met me politely, and renewed the invitation. Two days, however, served to satisfy me that a Western regiment was out of place in an army exclusively Eastern, and I answered his overture, saying that unless he ordered otherwise I should stay in the West.

When, after the muster-in, I looked over the company rolls, to my surprise and pleasure comparatively few of the three months' men had gone to other commands. This left me all the better prepared for immediate orders, and on September 6th the regiment was in march to report to Major-General John C. Frémont, at St. Louis, Missouri.

The newspapers had kept me posted as to events in Missouri. With the story of Nathaniel Lyon I was familiar. Perhaps the remark may be allowed, that to my mind he has not received from his countrymen the meed he deserved. To the salvation of St. Louis, he added the victories of Dug Springs and Wilson's Creek, and then death in the midst of victory.

In the latter part of July, John Charles Frémont made his advent in St. Louis. There had been created for him a special command territorially so vast as to be of itself a temptation to a weak man. If his Western department had an eastern boundary, westwardly it was in a sense limitless. Lyon and Sigel—the latter another willing fighter—were still in the field; but he had thrown them measurably upon their own resources. Not a man or a gun went to their reinforcement. At Wilson's Creek they had fought twenty-three thousand Confederates, under General Price, with a patriot force not exceeding five thousand. True, Frémont garrisoned Cairo and partially fortified St. Louis; but the achievements seemed to have exhausted him for military performances, and he surrendered himself to politics. Ignoring a general government in Washington, he assumed dictatorial control of his department, took possession of public moneys, levied forced loans on what he apologetically called secession banks, and gathered about him a staff disproportionate in numbers, if not of his own choosing. Outside a coterie of devotees thronging the reception-room of his luxurious headquarters, everybody looked his way suspiciously, if not in dread. There were brave men in his *entourage* anxious to be doing, but they were without influence. He appeared busy; unfortunately, nobody could tell what about. President Lincoln—to Frémont unknown—was absorbed in conditions pertaining to Washington, especially in the organization of a sufficient army. His attention had not yet swung round to affairs west of the Mississippi, and he confided in Frémont, and at first smiled at the warnings of the press of the country sounded daily in his ears. Indeed, what with Frémont's Western department of vast and shadowy frontiers, and the unhindered will permitted that officer, no such opportunity to set up an independency of some kind had offered itself since Aaron Burr's days of mystery.[1]

Of much of this, particularly of General Frémont's management, I knew at the time but little. Rumors of the extravagance of some of his officers were in airing by the press, but I had not been called to investigate them. He himself was in alarm, excited by the operations of General Price, Ben McCulloch, and a devastating horde of Indians and Texans nearly as uncivilized, and his cries for troops were abroad in the land. I heard them, and, thinking they presaged immediate service in the field, requested Governor Morton to have me ordered to Missouri.

Upon arriving at St. Louis, about September 8th or 10th, my regiment was quartered in the shed barracks

[1] On August 31st, General Frémont proclaimed martial law throughout Missouri, and that all persons within certain defined lines taken with arms in their hands should be shot, and that the property, real and personal, of all persons in Missouri found guilty of taking an active part with the enemies of the government in the field, should be confiscated to the public use, and their slaves, if they had any, should be thereafter free men.—Lossing's *Civil War*, vol. ii., p. 64. This was usurpation, and Mr. Lincoln modified the order by revoking the parts pertaining to confiscation of property and the liberation of slaves. The time for emancipation had not come, and he reserved the act for his own hand.

said to have been erected by General Curtis. They were out in the purlieus and dirty and uncomfortable, yet they were accepted without grumble. Next day about nine o'clock I rode to town with a formal morning report in my pocket, intending, after delivering it to the adjutant-general, to pay my respects to the general commanding. Perhaps he might give me a hint as to when and where he would march me. Anyhow, a little politeness to the great man would do no harm. I might as well confess, too, that my curiosity to see him was quite lively. He was the great "Pathfinder," and had been a candidate for the presidency.

Finding headquarters was easy to the stranger. Everybody seemed to know where it was. I found it in a three-story house with a front, as I now recollect, flush with the street, and of elegance—the residence of a Colonel Brant. At the curbing a lot of horses were in care of orderlies. I was struck with the freshness of the saddle furniture, all strictly *réglementaire*. Dismounting, I looked for some one to come and take my bridle also; but no. Finally, I remounted, and rode along the street till I found a negro who was glad to serve me as orderly for a quarter. A sentinel at the door halted me to find out who I was. Admitted presently to a spacious room somewhat crowded with officers apparently in waiting, nobody received me or so much as noticed my presence. The opportunity to study the gentlemen in attendance was good. They were all in uniform, fine-looking, nice, very polite and sociable to one another, and without show of business; from which I inferred they were of the staff proper. All eyes, I observed, were watchful of a door connecting, it seemed, with another room, probably the adjutant-general's office. Pretty soon I caught myself attracted by the same door. An unarmed sentinel kept it, whereat I wondered. In the company there was one individual, slender-waisted, graceful-looking, young, and dressed in flaming scarlet from head to foot. He drew my attention; if I was going unnoticed, so was he. He spoke to no one; no one spoke to him. Lonesomeness is contagious. In that brief time I caught the feeling from him. Growing irritated at length, I summoned my courage, and singling out one officer whose countenance seemed a little chastened with charity for the meek and humble, I asked him if General Frémont was in. He looked me over—I was not in Zouave dress—and said "yes." Could I see him? He pointed to the sentinel, whom I approached, putting the same question and getting the same answer. "Could I see the general?" "Your name," he asked. I gave it to him, and he disappeared through the door, but returned soon to say:

"The general is too busy. Come again."

Not liking to be put off so summarily, I argued, "I am here to report the arrival of my regiment."

"Come again," he answered.

There was nothing else for me. Thinking if such were the awesome state outside headquarters, how overwhelming that pervading the inside must be, I started out, angry to my inmost being. At the door of exit I saw the young fellow in scarlet again. Curiosity getting the better of me, I pulled the sleeve of an officer near by, and asked, "Who is he?" The interrogated told me —"He? Oh, that is a Bulgarian! Hearing of our war, he came over with letters, and offered his services. Stanton (secretary of war), not knowing what to do with him, took him at his word, sent him out here to report to General Frémont, and he is now on the staff. He can't speak a word of English."

"How does he get along?" I asked.

"Heaven only knows," was the reply. A moment

after the official with whom I was speaking—he of the chastened countenance—added:

"He will do to stop a bullet." [1]

In the afternoon, about two o'clock, I gave the sentinel at the outer door another opportunity to salute me, but he did not; he let me pass, however, and that was the main point.

The anteroom was not so full of uniforms in the wear as in the morning, which I readily accounted for to myself: the patriots are at lunch, and, having nothing else to do, then philosophically tarry over the wine—or maybe they are discussing weighty military problems, for which, it must be admitted, the smoke of good cigars at table is more favorable than that other smoke out of the flaming mouths of battle. Happy fellows! I did not see the man in scarlet, though I looked for him; neither did I wait to see more of what I had already seen enough, but, going straight to the sentinel or orderly at the inner door, I asked him:

"Is the general in his office?"

"No, he is at lunch."

I persisted, "Is it worth while for me to stay?"

"I can't say," was the answer.

I went on, "I can see the adjutant-general?"

And the man replied: "Not now. He's at lunch."

Then I produced the morning report of my regiment, saying: "Sorry I can't see him. Here is a report. Please deliver it."

I turned away, and presently took to my saddle re-

[1] My sympathy for the Bulgarian, Charles Zagonyi, was so strong that I kept him in inquiry. At last accounts he was dead. In one of General Frémont's battles with Stonewall Jackson, in Virginia, he was sent on some business to a distant part of the field, and somehow got between the engaged lines. His scarlet suit made him a conspicuous target, and a sharp-shooter of one side or the other brought him down. I give the story as it came to me.

flecting. Well, Ben McCulloch, with his red men and white savages, can't be coming here in haste. This is a headquarters for politicians, not soldiers. And their chief—ah, once a candidate, always a candidate! It don't suit me. I will try and get away. Riding to the nearest telegraph station, I begged Governor Morton to have me, if possible, ordered to Cairo or Paducah. I think the next day was July 9th, and it was red-lettered by the receipt of an order directing me to put my regiment on a steamboat then at the wharf, and report to General Charles F. Smith, at Paducah, Kentucky. I stayed in St. Louis long enough then to ration my men for three days and hurried to boat.

XXXIX

Removal of regiment to Paducah—Map—Plans for opening the Mississippi River — Operations in central Tennessee — Note: Grant and the Philadelphians at City Point—Forts Henry and Donelson.

On the following page there is a map which I commend to the reader's attention. He will find it helpful, I think, to an understanding of the pages immediately following; aside from which, moreover, it includes a part of the country that must always have peculiar interest, if only because the grand operations which finished the Confederacy by cutting it in two had their commencement there.

I shall also presume to add to the map a legend or two explanatory of the positions occupied by the belligerents at the time of my arrival at Paducah, and how, in response to the exigencies of strategy, the positions came to be chosen.

The very first understanding between the North and South in connection with the war—tacit, of course—was that the South would content itself with holding its own, if it could; and therefore the defensive policy which marked its course from the beginning. Then the North, driven to act offensively, fixed its eyes upon two objectives: Richmond in the East, and in the West the opening of the Mississippi River to its mouth.

Now, the moral effect of the capture of the Confederate capital might have been greater upon the world outside than that which would follow the opening of the river;

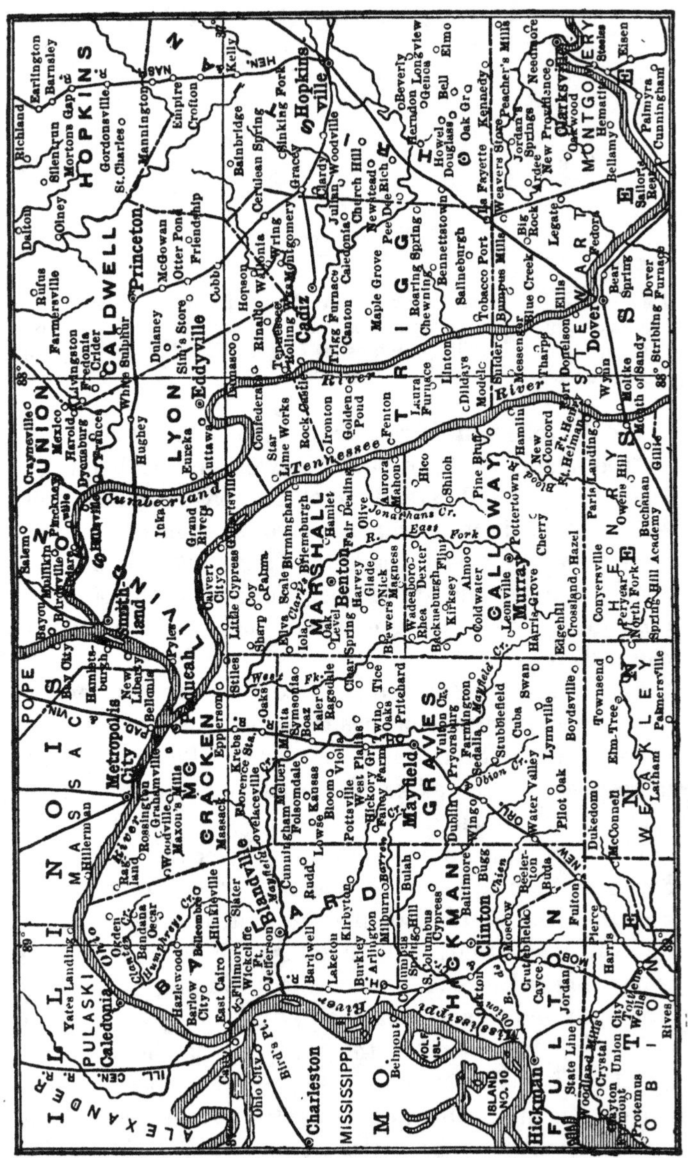

SCENE OF OPERATIONS IN WESTERN KENTUCKY AND ADJACENT TERRITORY

yet the latter was strategically the more important, and for two reasons: first, if the river were opened and patrolled by the Federals the Confederacy would be divided, and communication between the parcels made physically impossible; in the next place, the Confederacy would be at our mercy on account of the many lines of invasion offered by the river, leaving the Federals free to conquer in detail. So true was this that General Grant, at City Point, put pressure upon General Lee, in Richmond, barely enough to hold him and his army there until the river was reduced to possession, and Sherman, by marching to the sea, had demonstrated the emptiness and utter exhaustion of the South. Then Grant moved, crushing as he went.[1]

[1] At City Point, in 1864, I was General Grant's guest, by special invitation, and witnessed a scene of rare interest.

It was announced at supper that the general would receive a delegation of citizens from Philadelphia, coming with an unknown purpose.

"We must be there," said Bowers, the assistant adjutant-general; "and you must watch Grant when it comes time for him to reply. You see, if he's a little stumped, and wants a moment to think, he always gets it by striking matches, pretending he can't get one to burn. Sometimes he'll spoil a bowlful; but when he has his idea clear, the trouble is over. The match goes off all right, and, his cigar lit, he turns and speaks."

The meeting took place in the little box the general called his office. We were all there; so was the delegation. The spokesman took the floor and delivered a speech the substance of which may be given.

"General Grant, we represent the business men of Philadelphia, and have been charged to tell you frankly that the country is suffering, and that you must do something decisive immediately. In the South, and along the Mississippi, operations are going on by land and water, and everybody is active. Sherman is absorbing all the attention. He is thundering away in the heart of the rebellion. You alone are doing nothing. We have come to implore you to wake up."

Grant, at the end, turned to the mantel above the fireplace, on which there was a bowlful of matches and a box of cigars. Taking a fresh cigar, he struck match after match without avail; it looked

So it came about that, at the prompting of General Scott, President Lincoln requested Governor Yates, of Illinois, to occupy Cairo, at the junction of the Mississippi and Ohio rivers; and the governor made haste—in the latter part of April, if I remember rightly—to send two of his newly mustered regiments there under General Prentiss, thus forestalling the Confederates, and closing the Ohio River and also the Mississippi north of Cairo against them.

Then the Confederate authorities, alive to the importance of blockading the Mississippi south against the Federals, at length summarily brushed the film of Kentucky neutrality aside, and permitted General Polk to seize Columbus, next city below Cairo, fortify the bluff there, and assemble an army put variously at thirty or forty thousand in emphasis of menace. Hickman and Island No. 10, yet farther south were also fortified.

as if the supply would all go. Minutes passed; at last he struck fire. Then Bowers nudged me, and whispered:

"Listen—he's ready."

I give the reply substantially.

"Gentlemen," the general said, "I am glad to hear from you that the country has not lost its interest in the war. You urge me to move, and have been at pains to come and tell me that Sherman will shortly shut me out of public attention if I don't hurry and head him off. Well"—he stopped and whiffed a moment—"I will take you into my confidence, provided you do not take the newspapers into your confidence. Sherman is acting by order, and I am waiting on him. Just as soon as I hear that he is at some of the points designated on the sea-coast, then, the Mississippi River being secured for our boats, I will take Richmond. Were I to move now without advices from Sherman, Lee would evacuate Richmond, taking his army somewhere South, and I would have to follow him to keep him from jumping on Sherman. That would be very inconvenient to me, as it would compel me to haul supplies in wagons over unknown dirt roads to an unknown distance. I hope, gentlemen, you will report to your constituents how much obliged I am to General Lee for staying where he is; and be careful, please, to tell them that jealousy between General Sherman and me is impossible. Please smoke with me."

In May the gathering of Confederates at Columbus assumed such proportions that General Frémont increased the force at Cairo to five thousand men.

The Confederates then saw the possibility of invasion by way of the Tennessee River, and of turning their position at Columbus, and thought of occupying Paducah; but they were slow about it, and the Federals erected the military district of Cairo, and General Ulysses S. Grant, commanding, by a fortunate *coup* possessed himself of both Paducah and Smithland, and by doing so saved both the Tennessee and Cumberland rivers for future operations. This was in September; and without resting he strengthened his hold on Paducah, and placed Brigadier-General Charles F. Smith in charge.

In these latter moves there was much more than a hint of aggression, and to close the rivers against the Federals the Confederates again took thought, and built and armed Fort Henry, on the right bank of the Tennessee River, and Fort Donelson, on the left bank of the Cumberland. Opposite Fort Henry, on the Tennessee, they also threw up works, giving them the name Fort Heiman, which, being on a height, commanded the first-named fortification.

Such was the military situation when, on September 10th, at eleven o'clock in the forenoon, the steamer drew up at the wharf boat at Paducah and disembarked the Eleventh Indiana.

XL

Arrival in Paducah—General Charles F. Smith—His headquarters—Conversations—Promotion to rank of brigadier-general September 3, 1861.

It is wonderful what trifles serve to prepossess us favorably or unfavorably. At Paducah, for instance—a crowd of soldiers on the landing—a quartermaster with a wagon-train to haul our goods to camp—cheering in reply to cheering, and thunderous applause in recognition of the "Star-spangled Banner" by my band on the hurricane-deck as the boat touched the wharf—small tokens, yet they signified welcome, and appreciation, and comradeship, and a real soldier somewhere about in command of the place, all in such delightful contrast with that sodden reception at St. Louis.

Leaving the regiment to Colonel McGinnis, I rode to report to General Charles F. Smith, whom I was anxious to see. By reputation he was the best all-around officer in the regular army—a disciplinarian, stern, unsympathetic, an ogre to volunteers, but withal a magnificent soldier of the old school of Winfield Scott.

The house in which he quartered, at once his residence and office, stood in a spacious lot in style a Southern mansion centred in fruit trees and flowering shrubs. An orderly paced leisurely to and fro in front of the door, a sabre rattling after him over the gravelled walk. Seeing me dismount at the gate, he hastened out and took the reins—so unlike the one of his class doing duty in front of the great man's door in St. Louis.

"You want to see the general?"

"Yes—to report."

He hitched my horse and went before me.

"A moment," he said, at the door; and I waited while he went in.

"The general will see you," he said, coming back.

He led me through a hall, and into a room well furnished and warm, a fire burning cheerily in a grate. A broad table stood in the middle littered somewhat with books, writing material, a sword, sash, and gauntlet gloves—things noticed presently, for just then I had eyes for nothing but the man before me. He was very tall, erect, broad-shouldered, a symmetrical figure in a well-fitting uniform. He held his head high; long, white mustaches trailed below his chin shading his lower face; perfect health left its morning colors on his cheeks, and his blue eyes, bright with invitation, negatived the reputation he bore for sternness.

This description is elaborate, I know; and if one asks wherefore, the answer is ready—the man before me was by odds the handsomest, stateliest, most commanding I had ever seen, the one who has since remained in memory my ideal of a general officer. Probably better cannot be done than to add that his appearance has always helped me to a perfect understanding of the impression Washington is said to have left upon all who came near him.

"Colonel Wallace," said the orderly, going out therewith and closing the door.

The general did not move from his place before the fire, or even bend his head; much less did he come forward and shake hands; whereat I respected him the more, seeing then that he was a soldier without a tincture of the politician. To me, standing by the table uncapped, he said, simply, "You have just arrived?"

I answered respectfully.

"You found a quartermaster at the landing with wagons?"

"Yes—and I am obliged to you."

"Well, come round this evening."

The interview was closed, and I retired. After supper I waited upon him, and, the visit being purely social, he put his stateliness aside, and amused himself—and me as well, for I could see his object—with questions aimed at what I knew of soldiering and the service I had seen. When I arose to leave, he went with me to the door, and said: "Our situation here is somewhat precarious, and will be until the fort I have in process of construction is finished. Come again, to-morrow afternoon, and we will go over the map together."

I went away pleased, thinking he would not have asked me to return so soon, and for such an object, had he not seen in me wherewith to be pleased on his part.

Next afternoon the general spread a large map over the table, and pointed out how easily General Polk could make a dash from Columbus, and harry us at Paducah, and why he should do it. I asked if he knew General Polk's strength. "Yes," he said; "report gives him about ten thousand men, with additions coming in rapidly."

"Well," I asked, "say he takes Paducah, what can he do with it?"

Then, with his finger, he pointed out the Tennessee and Cumberland rivers, saying, "These are lines leading into the heart of the seceding states, and, with Paducah fortified, you see how tight he locks them against us."

"Yes," I said, "but what is to prevent Grant from crossing the river from Cairo and cutting him off?"

Smith laughed, and replied: "To attempt that Grant must have a force sufficient to give Polk battle, and"—he grew serious—"Frémont is too intent upon schemes of his own to think of strengthening us. I wonder he let your regiment come here."

Then for a time he smoked silently, half bent over the map, and I, impressed by his remark about the Tennessee and Cumberland rivers, followed them in their tortuous courses, vaguely suspecting the use to which they would be put.

The evening passed pleasantly. He led the conversation throughout, speaking of the war, and so constantly that it became apparent he thought of nothing else. I knew he must be rich in reminiscences, that he must know the old officers, Scott, Harney, Twiggs, and tried to divert him to them, but without success. He alluded several times mystically to some grand operation then in the forward perspective, and which, when undertaken, would be worth a long, ordinary life to every one engaged in it. What it was he did not then disclose, but I could see how the very thought of it stirred him to enthusiasm. "Opportunities — opportunities — opportunities," he kept repeating, with the eagerness of a young man.

My return to camp was with a feeling of content founded upon the flattering notice taken of me by my new chief, at which, it is true, I wondered. Then the great something ahead—though dealt to me in allusion, it warmed my fancy as it had his blood. What was it? What could it be? Anyhow, I was warned to get ready.

The day following, leaving the regiment to settle itself in camp, I rode to see what the army of which I had become a part was like. It was of all arms, about five thousand strong, mostly Illinoisans, new, of course, but of excellent material. One regiment in particular attracted me — the Eighth Missouri, Morgan L. Smith, colonel; and of him and his more anon.

Then again drilling, drilling. The days were filled with it. Meantime, the fort grew and put on an air of strength, and in further defence we constructed a long stretch of palisading. Occasionally, too, as if to keep us reminded of what time was bringing, our vedettes were driven in, and the pickets put to trial by the enemy, and to every alarm we turned out, not being able to distinguish the true from the false. In it all there was an excitement which I confess I enjoyed.

One day an official communication astonished me. It was from the adjutant-general at Washington. I tore the envelope open, wondering why he addressed me directly. Now, I had not thought of being brigadier-general; neither had any one notified me of an effort to that end in my behalf; yet here was formal notice of a commission carrying that grade on the road for me. I put the paper in my pocket, and poked about all day, saying nothing about it to anybody.

To accept the appointment was to leave the regiment, now an object of immense pride. In the next place, I knew nothing of the duties of a brigadier, my brigade association having been too limited to help me pick up information about them from observation; and, being caught unawares, it made me shiver to think of the responsibilities of the place, especially of its responsibilities in battle, that supreme trial in the preparation for which I was at that period all engrossed. What should I do? I felt the urgencies of ambition; but love of the regiment pulled against them, while my ignorance sapped my confidence. At length I concluded to consult General Smith; what he said, that I would do.

In the evening I found him sitting before the fire a picture of comfort. There was no litter on the table this time—only a decanter, with glasses, all on a silver platter, and a pitcher of water. Without rising, he said: "Bring up a chair. It's chilly outside." And then, when I was seated: "What is it? Anything I can do for you?"

I gave him the communication from the adjutant-general, and he read it gravely, and, rising, said, "Well, sir, what of it?"

Then I, too, stood up, and answered with his directness, "Will you tell me if I ought to accept that appointment?"

"Why not?"

"Because I don't know anything about the duties of a brigadier-general.

He was surprised, and after regarding me sharply for a moment, as if to settle a doubt, he said: "This is extraordinary. Here have I been spending a long life to get an appointment like this one about which you are hesitating; and yet that isn't it—that you should confess your ignorance—good God! Who ever heard of the like?"

He went to the table, filled two glasses from the decanter, and offered me one of them.

"Had you come here not doubting your sufficiency," he said, "I should have decided you meant a parade of your good-fortune; as it is, I say accept—accept by all means—and I will give you the benefit of what I know about the duties of the place, be it much or little. We can always make something of a man who is willing to admit that he don't know it all."

Then from the mantel he brought a book which I recognized as the *United States Army Regulations*, and when we were seated he gave me a free-and-easy lecture of which I still remember some of the points.

"I divide the duties of a brigadier-general into two

classes," he began—"those owing to his immediate superiors, and those owing to his command; and of the first, first . . . Obedience being the soul of military organization, I hold it the beginning and end of duty. It is the rein in hand by which the superior does his driving. . . . The difference between a captain and a general with respect to duties is that the general is a captain with multiplied and extended relations. . . . The chief duties of a general to his command may be classified —the enforcement of discipline—tactical instruction—care of the health of his men—and they are all important because tending to efficiency, the measure of which is the exact measure of his own efficiency. . . . Government furnishes everything actually needful to the good condition of the army; and of us—you and me, for instance—it merely asks in return that we know how to get those things, and to help us to the knowledge it has furnished a system of formal requisitions which fools call 'red tape.' But I"—he stopped and held up the well-known volume in blue—"I pronounce it the perfection of wisdom, since by it alone the government is enabled to keep accounts, prevent waste, and assert the principle of personal responsibility. Here is that system—in this book, more indispensable to every officer than his sword, for even in battle he can make out with a riding-whip. As the preacher knows his Bible, as the lawyer knows his statutes, every general should know the regulations and articles of war. Here they are within these lids"—and I noticed he fondled them caressingly—"here he will find every duty relative to the care of his command defined and prescribed. . . . It is not possible for a general always to see with his own eyes, or be in two places at the same time; hence the device of a staff—that is, an *alter ego* for every duty. . . . Staff-officers should be men of aptitude and experience, not figure-heads or mere pretty men. . . . In battle a general's duties, in so far as they are reducible to rule, are—first, to fight; second, to fight to the best advantage. . . . Genius is determinable by the manner of obedience. A fort is to be taken; genius consists in finding a way to take it with the least appreciable loss. A campaign is to be planned; genius proves itself by devising the best plan; at the same time, strange as it seems, he the most capable in planning may be the most incapable in execution, making two different qualities. The great genius is he who possesses both the qualities. . . . Battle is the ultimate to which the whole life's labor of an officer should be directed. He may live to the age of retirement without seeing a battle; still he must always be getting ready for it exactly as if he knew the hour of the day it is to break upon him. And then, whether it come late or early, he must be willing to fight—he *must* fight."

I went back to camp from the lecture a much wiser man, and a very grateful one; and when the commission came it was accepted. Its date is September 3, 1861.

XLI

Taking leave of the regiment—The staff—Tearing down the rebel flag—General Smith's attitude—Grant's visit at Paducah—Damaging newspaper stories.

UPON qualifying under my new commission, life seemed to deepen in tone—that is, it seemed to take on a seriousness theretofore unknown to me, due probably to a consciousness of introduction to a field of action higher and broader than any I had been used to thinking about. Not that I was elated or that my vanity underwent any increase having a richer morsel to feed upon; it is the truth, honestly confessed, I was too anxious for either of those effects—anxious lest I should fail the honor to which I had so unexpectedly risen. Yet I sent to Chicago for shoulder-straps and new saddle-housings; and when they came, and the eagle of the colonel gave place on my shoulder to the star of a brigadier, I mounted them with what doubtless appeared to others the most unaffected cheerfulness.

In looking back now I find a peculiar pleasure in recalling that in the midst of my own good-fortune, calling it such, I did not forget to exert myself in securing the appointment of Lieutenant-Colonel McGinnis to the vacant colonelcy; and when he was commissioned—thanks to Governor Morton's appreciation of the soldierly qualities of the man—I had a comfortable feeling that the regiment was in hands as safe as my own, if not safer.

The parting with the regiment took place at a dress-parade and without ceremony. Calling Colonel McGinnis to my right, I presented him as my successor so well known that eulogy was unnecessary. With good wishes for every one standing under the colors, the sincerity of which might not be doubted, for it was with the utmost difficulty I kept in voice, I rode away amid cheering, and established headquarters in a house near by secured for me by my quartermaster.

General Smith assigned me a brigade composed of the Eleventh Indiana, Colonel George F. McGinnis; the Eighth Missouri, Colonel Morgan L. Smith; the Twenty-third Indiana, Colonel W. C. Sanderson; Battery A, of Chicago, Captain James Smith, and Company I, Fourth United States Dragoons, Lieutenant Powell.

The possession of a command required me to select a staff, and in doing this I was regardful of the sage advice of General Smith already given. Captain Fred Kneffler became my assistant adjutant-general; Captain Joseph P. Pope, commissary; Captain Charles W. Lyman, quartermaster; Thomas W. Fry, surgeon; Lieutenants James R. Ross and Addison Ware, aides-de-camp, and the Rev. John D. Rogers, chaplain. My obligations to these officers, I pause to say, continue with all their original force notwithstanding most of them are asleep in their long homes. Association with them taught me the exquisite propriety of the use of the term *family* in definition of the relation between the chief and members of his staff—a relation of which confidence is the primary element.

General Smith, to whom I carried the staff-list, notified me, confidentially, that important movements involving his whole division would be shortly set afoot, notwithstanding the approach of winter. "You know the initiative is on us," he said, cheerfully, adding, "and every moment of time should be put to good use."

Accepting the hint, I bent all my energies to making ready.

That men before whom such action was in near prospect should know one another smacked, I thought, of sound philosophy, and with that in view I brought the several camps into a more neighborly group. Then I inspected every command, trying it at drill, the infantry in especial.

Sanderson, of the Twenty-third Indiana, had some obsolete ideas acquired by him in the war with Mexico, of which he had been a reputable officer. To shake him free of them, I opened a school of instruction for him and his subordinates. The results were quick and gratifying.

Smith, of the Eighth Missouri, proved himself really uncommon. The faculty of disciplining raw soldiers had been in him at birth. A deficiency in college and drawing-room graces in no wise detracted from his efficiency as a soldier.[1] To my surprise, not knowing him, I found his regiment wonderfully up in the tactics, Zouave and ordinary.[2] The confidence that existed between him

[1] After the battle of Shiloh, Morgan L. Smith, upon my recommendation, was made brigadier-general. Subsequently he arose to a full major-generalship, the promotions being in each instance for good conduct in action.

[2] It became the rule with me to omit nothing in my power likely to beget, with officers and men over whom I reached control, that certain feeling impossible of definition except by the French *camaraderie*, which, to my understanding, means something akin to brotherhood more than mere companionship. At all events, the word had never a better illustration than by the relation that sprang up between the Eighth Missouri and the Eleventh Indiana, a fiery actuation of youth which age has not been able entirely to cool. As a consequence, a singular confusion of lines, to speak after the manner of soldiers, marked their intercourse, not alone while they were of the same brigade and division, but afterwards as well. In 1864 the Eleventh Indiana was holding Helena, Arkansas. A transport, carrying the Eighth Missouri en route to New Orleans, stopped there

and his men could not be credited to any persuasive arts on his part; he was in speech the roughest commander I ever met. His officers were able, and they rendered him united support.

As for Company A, Chicago Light Artillery, I doubt if another aggregation like it ever answered at reveille in any army. The reference is not merely to courage and general proficiency, though in those respects the company equalled the best, but to accomplishments picked up in course of city life and peculiarly theirs; insomuch that it had been possible for them to have responded with *éclat* to almost any social demand, for on their roster there were musicians, singers, *raconteurs*, comedians, journalists, and artists of every kind. The night after publication of their assignment to my brigade, they sent me an invitation to come and see them in camp, itself an elaborate wonder. At the gate they received me with a function which was such a medley of fun and frolic that my dignity came to grief at once. That they followed with minstrelsy and a collation. Of their fighting I will speak hereafter. The world does not know how heroically they behaved at Donelson. After this I fell to thinking of the hundred and more royal good-fellows as one man, and that the spirit of Taillefer, the last of the Minnesingers, had taken possession of him.

The work that fell to me was hard and monotonous,

to deliver government stores. To keep the Eighth on board, the steamer was anchored several hundred feet out in the boiling current. No sooner did she begin swinging to her cable than every man of the regiment who could swim, fully a third of the whole number, plunged into the water, without undressing, and swam ashore. The captain, in great distress, went to the colonel; he could not wait an hour. "Never mind," said the colonel, laughing. "The boys have gone to see the old folks. They'll be down when their visit is out. Go on." It was a month before the Eleventh, into whose arms they landed, would let them all go.

relieved, however, by the very perceptible progress of my brigade. Indeed, affairs were going well with me when an accident occurred that upset my little cup of content—an incident of dismal future consequence.

I happened one day to be with General Smith at his house. Captain Newsham, his assistant adjutant-general, came into the room and reported a mob at Mr. W——k's across the street. The general told him to go and disperse it. Presently an orderly appeared, and said it was the Eleventh Indiana, with others of the Second Brigade, taking a secession flag from W——k's house. General Smith grew excited.

"How's this?" he asked, sharply.

I assured him I knew nothing about the affair, but would see about it and report.

I reached the scene in time to find Captain Kneffler, my adjutant-general, at fisticuffs with Newsham. With some trouble I separated them. Newsham was pursued with clubs and stones. After rescuing him again, I returned to W——k's just as the stars and stripes supplanted the stars and bars on his house. From a post of the front gate, I ordered everybody off to his quarters. They went cheering; whereupon I returned to General Smith and reported. His excitement had increased in the mean time. In all his years of service such a thing, he said, had not happened to him. He would make an example of the officers engaged in it. I ventured to suggest the number whom he would have to arrest—nearly the whole brigade—and, dwelling upon W——k's imprudence, and the natural indignation of the men, I finally got the old soldier calmed down.

"Here—sit down here, and write a general order to be read to the division. They are not soldiers yet—only politicians. You know them better than I do. Write."

And I wrote.

Next afternoon the general order was published to the division over the general's name. The order is still extant. No one has ever suspected the authorship.

This affair, apparently so trifling, worked me an injury of long standing. Unfortunately, it furnished the newspapers a welcome theme. Accrediting me with the outbreak, they complimented my patriotism, and denounced General Smith. Nobody but a traitor, they proclaimed, would have found fault with the substitution of the flags. From Paducah the story passed to headquarters at Cairo, thence to headquarters at St. Louis, in both of which the military offence was seen and discussed as of my incitement and I incontinently set down for a political demagogue.

Seeing the trend of the affair, I carried it to General Smith. He laughed at me.

"Why," he said, "don't you see? If I can stand to be accused of disloyalty, what have you to grumble at?" In another interview he grew angry.

"Disloyal—I? The —— scoundrels!"

Suddenly he stopped.

"What an ass I am making of myself! A few days more, and I'll have a chance to show if I am a traitor. It's their day now; it will be mine then."

He stubbornly refused to allow me to card the papers in his behalf or my own.

Another circumstance of bad result to me is to be mentioned.

In the latter part of October, 1861, General Ulysses S. Grant visited Paducah accompanied by his staff. Not having rooms in his house for the entertainment of the entire party, General Smith requested me to take some of them; and, with his usual courtesy, he allowed me to choose whom I preferred. General Grant and

Major John A. Rawlins, his adjutant-general, were assigned to me.

It is to be remembered now that in October, 1861, General Grant was comparatively unknown. He had already rendered valuable service to the Cause in the seizure of Paducah and Smithland, but the time had not yet arrived when the prescience and promptitude shown therein admitted estimation. He had not even fought the battle of Belmont. So when, with General Smith and Major Rawlins, he alighted from a hack in front of my house, I received him as I would any other undistinguished officer of his rank.

The afternoon was dark and chilly. A good fire burned in the parlor. My servant took the belongings of the strangers, hats and overcoats; after which General Grant drew his chair towards the grate, and said, spreading his hands before the blaze and looking around:

"Well, this is cheerful!"

I recollect, also, the firelight illuminating his face and shining through his beard cut short, deepening its natural reddish tinge. Two other things *apropos* his appearance, and distinctly recalled: one, a uniform coat off-color and the worse for tarnished brass buttons; another, that there was nothing about him suggestive of greatness, nothing heroic.

I opened a box of cigars, and he smoked incessantly and talked freely, but without an allusion to the war, much less the military situation.

After dinner, which was chiefly of commissary stores, General Smith called and took my guest walking. In the two hours they were gone, I suppose they discussed the business to which the honor of the visit was due.

The evening passed delightfully. That the audience became interested may be imagined from the fact that

Grant and Smith did the talking, in course of which they plied each other and us with reminiscences of Mexico and the war of 1846. As a narrator Grant was the better of the two.[1] Not until near morning did the session adjourn.

Next day General Grant inspected the camps and returned to Cairo.

The week was hardly out before newspapers began reaching Paducah laden with lurid accounts of the meeting at my house. It was an orgie, a beastly drunken revel led by both Grant and Smith—so the story ran. There were liquors and cigars on the night in question, and some singing, but no intoxication or anything like a revel. Nevertheless, a charge against General Grant of habitual drunkenness arose about that time, and spread through the country, greatly to his mortification and detriment, and some of his friends, thinking the slander had its origin the night he was my guest in Paducah, were disposed to hold me responsible for the publicity of the affair. In self-defence, I finally traced the offensive articles to a regimental chaplain, and induced him to resign. The general himself, I think, acquitted me of blame, but certain members of his staff, subsequently my enemies, were not so generous.

The matter of the flag was not so easily settled, except with General Smith, and will have another appearance later on.

[1] General Grant could not make a speech; in amends for that, however, he was really a fine talker, and particularly excellent in description.

XLII

The advance to Viola—Burning of the town—*Conestoga* and Lieutenant-Commander Phelps—The fugitive slave—The reconnoissance at Panther Island—Fort Henry—Colonel Lloyd Tilghman.

THE railroad from Paducah to Union City, with a branch thence to Columbus, was in fair condition, and, if it did not make General Smith nervous, put him at least upon guard. I think he had a feeling that if he were Bishop Polk, and master of an advantage like that road, with rolling stock—the Confederates had been careful to secure every locomotive and car—he would not sleep until Paducah was repossessed. He had only to imitate Joe Johnston's march from Winchester to Manassas—that is, despatch his artillery and supplies by rail, and the infantry and cavalry "overland." Grant at Cairo, having to mobilize and cross the Mississippi, was not nearly so deterrent as Patterson at Bunker Hill.

The surprise of a chief of General Smith's experience was difficult, if not impossible. The ordinary resorts of picket and vedettes were not enough for him. He kept a correspondent in Columbus, and in the country between Paducah and Mayfield maintained an outlying detachment of mixed arms varying in strength from one to two thousand men.

This duty was an experience in partisan warfare not without value. When it was intrusted to me I was flattered. The work was hard. Mud, rain, frost, occasional snow, swamps, bad roads, tangled woods, and sunken creeks unbridged were the concomitants, and my orders were not to allow myself to be drawn into a serious engagement. A town of four or five houses and a saw-mill, called Viola, I converted into a centre of operation. Once the enemy marched into Mayfield four or five times my force. By a passing countryman I sent the officer a challenge to come out and try conclusions. Instead of accepting the bluff, he took the road to Columbus. Perhaps he, too, was under orders not to fight. Once he beat up my pickets. Forming behind Mayfield Creek, I offered him battle, but he again declined. The courier with my report to General Smith gave out fighting in progress. In a time incredibly short I was reinforced by hundreds of stragglers who had somehow smuggled themselves out of the camp at Paducah. I went to sleep one night in Viola. Upon rising in the morning mine was the only house standing. The others, saw-mill and all, were ashes. I tried earnestly to discover the perpetrators. In expeditions like the one in which I was engaged, the commanding officer is all-powerful. The near completion of our forts brought the duty to an end, and I received the thanks of my superior and was immensely pleased.

A few days after General Grant's visit to Paducah, I was sent with a flying column down through the same debatable region to reconnoitre and break up a Confederate camp located, as General Smith had heard, a few miles out of Columbus. The camp was found and burned. Afterwards, to my astonishment, I heard that my movement, in combination with another crossed to the left bank of the river from Cairo, had been a feint to occupy General Polk's attention while General Grant fought the battle of Belmont.[1] That, it turned out, was the business which had brought the district com-

[1] The battle of Belmont took place October 6th.

mander to Paducah. As a secret it had been well kept.

In January—the 10th, I think—General Smith conducted his whole command on a march memorable to every man who participated in it.[1] Through Graves County into Calloway County far down towards Fort Henry he led us. The country had become an ocean of mud, and there was rain and melting snow, and from the beginning to end no dry place to set a foot could be discovered. Hard—very hard—a genuine foretaster. General Smith could have had comfortable houses often as night overtook us; but such was not his habit when on the road. I remember finding him one fluvial midnight in a dog-tent half filled with straw. In such manner he silenced the croakers.

After that Calloway *voyage*—the term is not unreasonable—I took to drilling my brigade in marching, and with the best results; in view of which it has been ever since a wonder to me that a practice of such importance is so persistently neglected, specially where the commands are large and mixed. To "get there" is one thing; to "get there" to the best advantage is another.

There came to me then—it was in the latter part of January—an experience so altogether novel and full of excitement that in my best thought I class it as of

[1] By the unknowing this movement has been criticised. It looked like a purposeless feint against Fort Henry. It was really a movement in combination. While General McClernand, with a column on transports, descended the Mississippi and, landing on the Kentucky shore, threatened Columbus from the rear, two other columns were marching as if to support him—Paine's from Bird's Point, in Missouri, Smith's from Paducah; at the same time a third pushed up to Smithland. This stir, deepened by the simultaneous apparition of gun-boats on the waters in unexpected places, must have been confusing to the enemy. It was the promised grand campaign in preliminaries.

my choicest memories. Lieutenant-Commander Phelps, of the navy, called at my house one day and said that with his boat, the *Conestoga*, he was going up the Tennessee River to take a look at Fort Henry. The authorities, military and naval, meaning Halleck, Grant, and Flag-Officer Foote, were desirous of all the information obtainable about that stronghold; though the particulars wanted were—had new works been added to the old, and had the armament been strengthened? Satisfaction on these points would call for a close inspection. The lieutenant-commander closed his explanation by inviting me to go with him. He would be glad to show me what a willing host can do on shipboard.

The courtesy was one to be instantly accepted. The experience would be novel. I could see somewhat of sailor life under unusual conditions. Besides being an officer of ability and dash, Phelps was a gentlemen refined, well-read, and a delightful companion. I hurried an orderly to General Smith with an explanatory note, and, receiving the permission I sought, gladly accepted the invitation.[1]

Being a landsman of the ultra-lubber variety, I shall not try to describe the *Conestoga*. Indeed, I remember not more of her than that she was flat-bottomed, very broad, and black all over; that her upper deck was in the style of a sea-goer, with bulwarks up to my shoulder; that there was a great gun at her bow, and that the pilot-house and commander's quarters were on the upper deck. I remember, also, the exceeding whiteness of the planking of that deck, the stealthy silence of the

[1] There were twelve gun-boats constructed for river service. Of these, seven were protected with plates two and a half inches thick; the rest were tin-clads—that is, sheathed in armor merely bullet-proof. Andrew H. Foote, the flag-officer, commanded the flotilla.

ship's going, and the cheerfulness with which everybody on board went about his duty.

So, too, at meal-times, the table-cloths and napkins did such honor to the laundry, and the table-ware was so above suspicion, and the courses brought on were of such wholesome variety and masterly preparation that I could not help rating my host for the advantages of his service compared with ours of the land.

The river was in good boating condition, and very beautiful despite the touches of winter apparent in the trees.

At the coming of night we invariably dropped anchor in the middle of the stream. We held no communication with the shore. Hamlets and farm-houses were frequent; but the people seemed to keep watch against us, and at sight of our smoke in the distance vanished, how and where Heaven knew. The gun-boatmen enjoyed the terror they inspired.

At length we reached a stretch of water long extended, and as the anchor went down, Phelps said: "Here we stop for the night. To-morrow about nine o'clock I will give you a look at the fort." As he spoke, the boat, obedient to the current under her, dropped slowly back, and directly hung nose up-stream.

The sun had then an hour and a half in which to make its descent; and already evening, its silence more noticeable because of the cessation of the engines and the smothered cough of the escape-pipe, was settling over the land and river. Suddenly the baying of a hound was heard. It came from the left shore, and, startled, we looked that way; nor we alone. Every man on the deck stopped in his employment and looked.

At our left, beyond a margin of water seventy-five or eighty yards in width, and very still and smooth-flowing, the shore was thinly fringed with half-grown willows, fast being denuded of leaves; beyond the willows stretched a cornfield bounded on its farther side by a fence and a woods. Every eye was fixed on the woods. Another deep-mouthed note of the hound—and another—and another—and then a chorus of yelps fast and furious.

"There's a pack of them," said Phelps; "and the fox is not far off."

Then there arose a nearer burst in louder concert.

"A fox, did you say, sir? It's a man, sir. Look—he's jumping the fence."

And following the sailor's pointing, sure enough a negro ran out of the woods and fairly threw himself over the rails.

I had brought a field-glass with me, and, finding it helpful to my interest in the outing, was wearing it at the instant. To take it out and hand it to Phelps was instantaneous.

"There," he said, quickly; "I see it now. They are hunting the man with blood-hounds. He sees the ship and is heading this way."

He took the glass down and his face was flushed.

"The small boat! Out with it—quick!"

Men never sprang with more alacrity to obey an order.

Now I had heard of hunting slaves with blood-hounds, but never thought of actually seeing such a chase. Sympathy for the fugitive, quickened by impulsive, wrath against his pursuer, whoever he might be, shook me through; and when the dogs doing the baying burst out of the woods, half a dozen of them, and, taking the fence at a bound, came crashing through the frost-burned corn-stalks, I confess to being ready to kill. Then, a minute later, when three men on horseback rode out of the woods hallooing and flourishing whips, they, not the dogs, drew the rush of my murderous feeling. Meantime, the negro appeared half across the field. He was hatless and coatless, and the tatters of his shirt fluttered like ribbons behind him, and in his awful terror he shrieked, "Help! help!" and now and then he stretched a hand towards the ship, possibly to the flag then in sight. Meantime, also, the small boat was down and flying to the rescue. I have seen many races in my life, but never one of such compounded interest as that one—never one that so sickened me.

Phelps, watching as well as he could through the glass, unsteady on account of his excitement, dropped it presently, and ordered a rifle brought him, adding to me, "He'll not make it." And across the water he sent an order to his boatmen: "Faster — faster, lads" — this though he knew they were rowing for dear life.

Three rifles were brought loaded. Phelps took one and I one.

"Shoot at the pack," he said.

"Never while those devils on horseback are courting a shot."

They were then halted at the fence. He fired, and missed; so did I. The dogs gave him no heed; the men scurried back into the woods. I shoot well ordinarily; but in this instance the bearing hand was too shaky, and often as the affair has recurred to me I have been thankful for my failure.

The negro came on yelling "help" at every step; the dogs behind were gaining fast, and their baying had in it a triumphant strain. The boatmen, too, were making their oars bend like green withes. On the deck everybody was holding his breath. It was crisis time.

"Take to the willows," Phelps shouted. Like myself he had forgotten he had a gun. And whether he heard or not, the "man and brother" gained a tree, and rose clinging to a branch just as the hounds snapped at his heels. A trifle later the boat ran in under him, and the sailors landed and drove the hounds off with their oars.

"Bring the man aboard," Phelps shouted, and turned away relieved.

"It was a close call," I said.

"Life is filled with close calls," he returned. "It may be our turn to-morrow."

I never saw a more piteous human being than the negro at last on deck, carried thither, and laid down helpless. His bare, black skin glistened through his torn clothes. His face looked as if some one had thrown handfuls of ashes in it, and he lay speechless, and gasping for breath.

"Take him to the doctor," said Phelps, adding: "The affair is over. To your quarters, men."

Presently silence reclaimed the ship.

When the fugitive came round, he told an old story of slavery. A longing for freedom — an attempt to escape — discovery and pursuit. He was not sent back — or rather nobody ever appeared to demand him.

Next morning the vessel was under way early. We breakfasted as usual, after which I accompanied Phelps in his rounds of the quarters. There was no excitement and but few words; yet even I could see the readiness for action. The inspection ended by our bringing up at the bow. The big gun there stood out uncovered, looking for all the world like a long, black, lathe-turned log. At hand lay a red flannel bag which I recognized at once as the regulation charge of powder, and by it a shell suggestive of a nail keg standing on end. The men serving the monster fell into position and saluted. Two sailors I observed leaning over the bulwark, one on either side of the bow, gazing into the water. They did not look up.

"We are going slow," I said to my host.

"Yes," he replied, "we are in the torpedo zone as reported."

I looked at the two sailors at the bow, and understood why they were fishing with their eyes so intently in the water. I, also, mentally approved the going slow.

Afterwhile some one called out, "Yonder—who are they?"

"Where?"

"On the left bank, pretty well up."

Phelps whipped out a long binocular hanging strapped to his shoulder, and, making it ready, followed the shore slowly.

"Soldiers, mounted and going full speed," he said. "If the enemy is not already notified of our coming, he will be."

"Vedettes," I suggested.

"Very likely."

"What island is that ahead?"

"Panther Island."

He went to the man at the wheel, and presently we were entering the western channel of the island. I could not help admiring the good sense of the manœuvre. Upon rounding the insular obstruction, the *Conestoga* would be in sight and in easy range from the fort; instead, then, of offering the vessel broadside on to the multiplied chances of a hit, should fire be opened upon her, our bow, built strong for fighting, would be the target; at the same time we would be in position to reply immediately.

Phelps then rejoined me. The moment, I freely admit, was warm with interest.

"If they open on you," I asked, "will you fight?"

"No, my business is to look, and if I should shroud the ship in smoke my occupation would be gone."

We cleared the channel and moved out boldly into the main stream. Nobody spoke; everybody strained his eyes seeing what he could of the stronghold at the end of at least two miles of unbroken waterway.

I saw, among the things now in memory, first a flagstaff; what the flag on the staff was could only be conjectured, there not being breeze enough to blow it out; then a fortification built squat on low ground. Three bastions offered fronts to us, and in embrasures I counted three heavy guns commanding all down the river. One bastion extended its outward angle into the river. I saw roofs of sheds, barracks for the garrison, and other guns defending on the land side where all was clearing. What interested me most, however, was the sight of the three great guns manned and trained on us. We had not surprised the enemy. Would he fire? The *Conestoga*, I have said, was a tin-clad. One shell exploded in her hulk might send us all to the bottom.

The boat slowed, then came to a stand-still. The view was fair. Heaven's best light was in our favor. While we were looking, a man, evidently an officer, stepped out on the parapet by the big gun of the lower bastion of the fort, and entertained himself returning our bravado like for like.[1]

"I am satisfied," Phelps at length said. "There is one large gun newly mounted—the third one from the water-battery."

Putting up his glass, he turned to the wheel-house

[1] I saw General Lloyd Tilghman after the surrender of the fort, and recognized him as the officer who came out on the parapet, glass in hand, to see the *Conestoga*. It was not a thought in my mind then that within a month I would be his successor in command.

and waved his hand, and the boat began dropping back —back—and almost before I knew it we were behind the screen of Panther Island. And so ended the last observation of Fort Henry before the grand expedition assembled and moved against it.

XLIII

The brigade organized—The advance upon Fort Henry—Fort Heiman — The *Conestoga* — John, the horse — The Chicago Battery — Pete Wood's Minnesingers — The occupation of Fort Henry —The mail-bag.

One evening General Smith sent an orderly for me. It was in the last week of January, and cold. A fire burned in his grate. He spread a large map on the table and descanted on the grand movement he had been promising me. I remember his saying, his eyes glistening with pleasure, "It [the movement] will begin here"—he laid a finger on Fort Henry—"and end here" — in the same way designating Corinth. "At Corinth there may be a battle, though not necessarily; if we hurry, there will not. The transports are assembling at Cairo. Meantime, you are to go to Smithland and inspect the regiments there, and organize them into a brigade and make them ready to take the field at an hour's notice. A boat is now waiting for you. Here is the order."

During this speech he was the picture of cheerfulness. I fear I was not, for he asked, sharply, "What's the matter now?" And I answered, "I would prefer my old brigade to a new one."

He laughed at me. "Go 'long! You are not relieved. Only be back in time."

There were five or six regiments at Smithland, and a battery or two. To organize a brigade, find the senior colonel, put him in command,[1] and do the inspection took me three days. On the fourth I was in Paducah again, report in hand.

Then General Smith took us; and the drilling was incessant, varied by reviews and inspections. In these latter he always appeared mounted, and in the full regalia of a brigadier-general.

On Sunday, February 1st, I think, a number of empty steamboats arrived and tied up at Paducah. Then, the same day, there was riding in hot haste from camp to camp; tents went down, and the streets filled with troops in orderly march to the river. The excitement was tremendous, for now no one was so dull as not to know the meaning of the sudden break-up. Before night the second division of the Army of the Tennessee was snugly afloat.

Next day seven gun-boats, four of them armored, black, creeping, menacing, ugly objects to look at, passed the city upward-bound. Among them I recognized the *Conestoga*. Behind followed a long line of transports in convoy, each loaded to the guards with the first division from Cairo, Brigadier-General John A. McClernand commanding. Then arose a hurricane of cheers long continued, and the rivalry of bands playing, flags streaming. Next, one by one our boats swung into the brave procession. We waved adieus to Paducah, and for the time forgot it in the new interest born of the mighty business on which we were embarked. The getting ready for this movement had been immensely laborious, including, as it did, the collection of supplies and ordnance stores, and their shipment, to say nothing of the ordering of the army, so nicely antici-

[1] It is my recollection now that Colonel Chetlain, of Illinois, held the oldest commission, and was placed in command. He was a very excellent officer and accomplished gentleman.

paßed that it stood in columns instantly upon landing—such were the elements of the first test of capacity imposed upon General Grant. There is no law more absolutely just than that by which in military operations the credit or discredit, according to results, is inseparable from the responsibility.

The going was mostly at night. Stopping in good time the day following, about five miles below Fort Henry, McClernand's division landed on the right bank; ours drew to the left bank; and, under cover of the gunboats, the debarking of both took place, after which they went into bivouac.

The details of the operation had not been confided to me. In some particulars, however, I was well informed. Thus, I had already viewed the fort from the *Conestoga*. It had been permitted me, also, to see on General Smith's table in Paducah a sketch of an unfinished fortification crowning a height on the western side of the river, Heiman by name, borrowed from its commander, a German colonel of a regiment of Irishmen in the Confederate service. Two hundred feet at least above the level of the Tennessee, it dominated the whole site of the main works, its *vis-á-vis*, Henry. So, when we landed I saw what was expected of General Smith, and from that hint worked out the general scheme to which we were now committed past withdrawal. Foote was to attempt reduction of Fort Henry; McClernand, moving upon the right bank, was to assist Foote, and catch the garrison did it try to escape by land; Smith's part of the programme was the capture of Fort Heiman. And what should these endeavors be but simultaneous? What a spectacle, could one see it!

The second night, while we lay in bivouac, there fell a rain, which, besides flooding us and the country roundabout, started the river, already high, to rising.

In the evening of the 5th an officer brought a note to General Smith, who told me when the man was gone, "Everybody is to pull up to-morrow at eleven o'clock." He looked then at the sky and at the coffee-colored water creeping over the low places of the land, and added, grimly, "It will be a hard road—but we'll get there."

In a mood of royal expectancy, I called the servant who took care of John, my horse, the noblest of his kind.[1] "Groom him now, and feed him well. He will have heavy work to do for me to-morrow." And I sat till night fell watching that what I ordered was done.

General Paine, if my recollection serves me, commanded General Smith's First Brigade; anyhow, by

[1] I loved this horse passionately. For five years he was my faithful, intelligent servant and friend; and in all that time there was never an hour in which I would not have gone hungry and thirsty if, by so doing, it had been possible to have saved him. He was in my mind when, long afterwards, in *The Wooing of Malkatoon*, I wrote these lines:

> But Othman waved them off: "Bring me my horse.
> But yesterday from noon to set of sun
> He kept the shadow of the flying hawk
> A plaything 'neath his music-making feet.
> I will not comrade else."
> Tent born and bred,
> The steed was brought, its hoofs like agate bowls,
> Its breast a vast and rounded hemisphere,
> With lungs to gulf a north wind at a draught.
> Under its forelock, copious and soft
> As tresses of a woman loosely combed,
> He set a kiss, and in its nostrils breathed
> An exhalation, saying, to be heard
> By all around, "Antar, now art thou brute
> No longer. I have given thee a soul,
> Even my own."
> And as he said, it was,
> And not miraculously, as the fool
> Declares; for midst the other harmonies
> By Allah wrought, the hero and his horse
> Have always been as one.

ten o'clock in the forenoon next day the second division stood to arms.

At eleven o'clock the advance-guard, preceded by a detail of horse, took a road—there was but one—the division following, my brigade in the lead. The general trend was parallel with the river at our left. Occasionally a gun-boat abreast of us, suspicious of the shore ahead, would send a tentative shell into the woods; whereat the toilers in the columns cheered. Suddenly —somewhere between twelve and one o'clock—we were startled by the report of a heavy gun up the river. I could see nothing of the river up or down; yet I knew that the leading boat, the flag-ship probably, had turned the corner of Panther Island, and found itself in instant engagement with the fort. I could fancy them, then, the four in armor, one by one rounding the island, giving space to the left as they made the turn, in line directly, and moving forward, bow on, firing—firing, for that matter, while the manœuvre was in progress.

In a short time the ships passed us. I could tell that by the firing. Then they increased their speed. Presently they were between us and the fort—that we knew because the shells of the latter, over-elevated, sailed roaring and screaming into the tree-tops, darkening the air with fragments of limbs. Indeed, the margin separating us from the line of hostile fire was at times preciously narrow, but the effect was to energize everybody in the march. Did a sheet of backwater spread itself across the road, or a bog intrude, or a tree, no matter—there was a cheer, and a rush, and the obstacle lay behind. I can shut my eyes now, and, thinking back through the years as through a mist, hear Pete Wood's Minnesingers[1] halloo their guns through a swamp with-

[1] Battery A, Chicago.

out the loss of an inch of interval. Much I doubt if there ever was a march distinguished like that one; for what with the cannonading of the fleet and that of the fort, the interchange became an almost unintermittent thunder which the ponderous missiles in flight converted into an infernalism indescribably awful. And to make the situation more peculiar, we could see nothing of the fight on the river — to us hastening through the woods, it was all smoke, sound, and fury. The most we could assure ourselves was that somebody was getting hurt.

An hour and a half thus—hell on the water, herculean effort on our part. Once we stopped to improvise a bridge by which to pass our guns. At last we were approaching Heiman. In a turn of the road the height had been seen. General Smith was riding with me.

"Halt?" he said, pulling rein and listening. "The firing has stopped."

So it had.

I suggested pushing on with a regiment. He peremptorily refused.

On a little farther a horseman from the front rode to him and reported Heiman evacuated.

"How do you know?"

And the soldier answered, "I have been in."

"The devil!"

Then the general turned to me.

"It is just as well. Move on and take possession."

Thinking how curiously downright hard fighting was always escaping me, or I it, I rode over an earthwork on the height, and by chance drew rein before the door of a tent circular in form, sixteen feet in diameter, with three feet of wall, above which all was the Sibley tent doubled.[1] I

[1] This tent, in fair condition, is now hanging from a peg in the

dismounted and passed in. By the centre-pole stood a table with papers on it in careless heaps, a glance at which told me that Colonel Heiman had headquarters here. I put a gentleman of my staff in charge of the papers, and went on into a marquee adjoining where an agreeable surprise awaited me. Dinner was ready. I looked into a kettle yet boiling and discovered a block of fresh pork "done to a turn." By the kettle a pot simmered, spraying the air with the aroma of coffee. A pone of corn-bread freshly baked adorned a bench near by, and under the lid of a mess-box rudely constructed a little rummaging disclosed salt, pepper, vinegar, and white sugar in lump. General Smith, upon invitation, came and shared my good-fortune. The absence of Colonel Heiman was never more sincerely regretted. Out of a small contribution foraged from General Smith's right pistol-holster we drank the excellent German's health.

Before sitting down to the meal, I took a survey of the post we had so easily won. Though unfinished, a stiff fight could have been made from it. From a parapet on the east side I looked at Fort Henry, across the swelling flood of the Tennessee within easy cannon range. The stars and stripes flew out lazily from the stump of a flag-staff. The salient angle of the water-bastion seemed submerged. Smoke in clouds rolled away from the ruins of what had been the barracks, and men in blue swarmed through the works. A few hundred yards off lay the four black gun-boats which had done the chore of conquest, apparently none the worse for the fierce affray. Up the river, vanishing round a bend,

attic of my home in Crawfordsville. It has sheltered me many times since its capture in fishing and hunting excursions.

I may also remark that I indulge in this description with the less compunction, having on two subsequent occasions been made the victim of somewhat similar despoilment.

Phelps, with the tin-clads, was hastening under press of steam to materialize the victory, by opening the greater waterway into the heart of the offending Confederacy.

After dinner a soldier brought in a bag, tied, not locked.

"Mail," he said; "just found."

I had him cut the string and empty the contents upon a table. They were letters unopened; the carrier had doubtless delivered them, then fled. I gave them to an officer for examination. Along towards evening he reported:

"There is nothing here of military importance. But" —his voice softened—"look at these. My mother might have written them to me. There are the same prayers in them for their side which we hear for our side—prayers, too, to the same God. I would like to know what you think of them."

And I replied, after having gone through them: "I acknowledge myself wiser for a new lesson. The people of the South believe they have a Cause; and certainly every one of them who is in the field soldiering for that Cause must be respected; he may be misguided, but he must be honest."

From that hour I have not ceased to act upon that principle.

XLIV

Lieutenant-Commander Phelps and the *Conestoga*—Grant's council of war—McClernand—The attack on Donelson decided—Left behind—Major Ross makes a suggestion—In readiness to join Grant—The night-watch.

GENERAL SMITH was called to Fort Henry the afternoon of its fall; whereupon the command at Heiman devolved on me.

There had been some mysterious things about the disappearance of my predecessor in possession,[1] so, in ordinary caution, I had my cavalry out testing the roads for miles, while scouting-parties of infantry poked into the woods and thickets of the vicinity. Then, discovering nothing to make me uneasy, I sat down to wait for the next lesson in grand strategy. Where would it take us? Up the river? Or across to Dover, the little old shire town of Stewart County, Tennessee, to-day better known in history as Fort Donelson?

One has to be a long time in army life before he learns the high art of graceful waiting. The river filled the wide gorge between Heiman and Henry brimful, an angry, seething, yellow lake safe only for steamboats. Morning and evening guns called to us from the other side, and were answered regularly. Though the weather continued warm, even springlike, the air hung thick with moisture, admonishing me that winter could not

[1] Not until after the collapse at Fort Donelson did I learn that Colonel Heiman had gone over to that stronghold, and taken a very creditable part in its defence.

be far away, and that the campaign must go on whether the flowers bloomed or Boreas blew, it was mine to see to the efficiency of my men. Inspections were the orders of the day, in quarters, close and more business than ceremonial, and I signed requisitions on the quartermaster freely for blankets, shoes, and overcoats.

The second duty of a general is to his command—such has been the teaching of my veteran friend and instructor at Paducah, and now I was trying to do honor to the recollection. And in truth I found great peace of mind in seeing the "boys" look comfortable and ready as possible for the worst change the season had in store.

As I was still of the Second Division, General Smith's officers came over occasionally to see me, bringing news of which every hint of remotest relation to the next step forward was especially welcome.

Flag-Officer Foote, they told me, had gone back with his heavy iron-clads to Cairo. What for? *Repairs*, they said, winking. Then, according to habit, I put this and that together, with conclusion that the gallant old conventicler, having done the Confederacy all the mischief in sight on the Tennessee River, would appear next in the Cumberland, signifying Donelson, of course.

A few days later I heard from my friend, Lieutenant-Commander Phelps. He had returned from his sweeping reconnoissance up the Tennessee to Florence at the foot of the Shoals. He told of bridges destroyed, of supplies in store burned, of transports beached and sunk, of a Union sentiment yet alive, and of lovers of the old flag in numbers to take care of themselves if only they had arms. I wrote him my congratulations, and regrets at not having been with him.

I heard also of reinforcements in energetic rush to

our assistance. Encouraging, certainly, and of effect to awaken interest and inquiry into what the enemy was doing. Of him, however, but little could be had. General Johnston had been jolted hard by the fall of Fort Henry, and in acknowledgment of the blow had withdrawn his headquarters from Bowling Green, Kentucky, to Nashville. Indeed, it was not difficult for me to fancy, tyro as I was, that the very length of his line of defence, stretching from Columbus to Cumberland Gap round by Nashville and Bowling Green, was crowding the nights of the trained soldier with anxieties lest it turn to gossamer breakable at a breath of strenuous war. That he should be speeding reinforcements to Donelson could be guessed. If he failed in defence of that place, if it went the way of Fort Henry, Nashville was lost to him; then, the Tennessee open to Florence, where should the fox find its next hole? [1]

Fort Henry was surrendered on February 6th. On the 10th, if I mistake not, an orderly crossed the river with a note for me, sealed, informal, but very interesting. There would be, it said, a meeting of general officers at headquarters next day. Time—two o'clock, afternoon. My presence was desired.

This, I saw, meant a council of war. How often had I read of such affairs in books of war! Now I was to see one and have a voice in it.

I took a skiff, and set out for headquarters in the

[1] Even with Donelson safe, it is doubtful if General Johnston could have remained at Nashville; for with the Tennessee open both places were practically turned. In fact, I can think of no military problem more interesting to a student than the consequences of the withdrawal by the Confederate leader at this time of all his forces to a point south of the Tennessee. That he worried with the problem there can be no doubt; and I have often thought him deterred from such a course by the idea of risking the life of his Cause upon one battle, an Armageddon, say at Chattanooga or Corinth.

forenoon to give myself a look at Fort Henry. The devastation astonished me all the more when I recalled the short time in which it had been accomplished. Theretofore shot and shell, though in ammunition-boxes, had seemed mere harmless toys; now the awful force latent in them was demonstrated. When in the water-bastion, by the disabled columbiad which Tilghman had served to the last with his own hands, I could not refuse him my admiration.

General Grant had his headquarters, as I now recollect, on the steamboat *Tigress*. Getting to and from it was easy. Not an armed sentinel could be seen on the landing or on the vessel. Of military state there was none—that had gone out, it pleased me to remark, with the illustrious "Pathfinder."

I found my own way into the ladies' cabin. A section of the dinner-table and a few chairs completed the furnishment. General Grant was there, of course. Rawlins, his adjutant-general, sat at the table. I can also recall the presence of Generals Charles F. Smith and John A. McClernand. There were two or three others whom I cannot name.

It struck me that the company were in icy binding; probably because, like myself, they were mostly new to the business. Our uniforms and swords, worn in compliance with etiquette, may have had to do with the frigidity of the occasion. General Smith came to me and asked how we were getting along at Heiman; aside from that there was not the slightest pretence of sociability, no introductions, no bowing, no hand-shaking, no conversation.

After little, General Grant stepped to the table and said, ever so quietly: "The question for consideration, gentlemen, is whether we shall march against Fort Donelson or wait for reinforcements. I should like to have your views." He looked first at General Smith—we were all standing—and Smith replied, "There is every reason why we should move without the loss of a day." General McClernand, taking the sign next, drew out a paper and read it. He, too, was in favor of going at once. It had been better for him, probably, had he rested with a word to that effect;[1] as it was, he entered into details of performance; we should do this going and that when we were come. The proceeding smacked of a political caucus, and I thought both Grant and Smith grew restive before the paper was finished; then, as if in haste to preclude argument instantly that the reading ended, Grant turned to me, nodding, and I said, "Let us go, by all means; the sooner the better." Fast as called on, then, the others responded yes. I noticed Rawlins making note of the expressions as they were given. Finally, General Grant wound the meeting up by saying: "Very well, gentlemen, we will set out immediately. Orders will be sent you. Get your commands ready."

This, to my knowledge, was the only council of war General Grant ever called. That the opinions submitted had any influence with him is hardly supposable. There is evidence that he had already determined upon the movement.

At Heiman, to which I returned upon the closing of the council, notice was given me in the night of the 12th that the advance against Fort Donelson would begin in the morning. This, of course, did not surprise me, but when the same messenger put into my hand

[1] The unpleasantness between Grant and McClernand became notorious; and I have sometimes thought that on the part of the former it had origin in the reading of that paper. The assumptions in connection with the matter, were noticeable, and could hardly fail to be offensive to a superior officer.

an order designating me to be left behind, my disappointment may be imagined; nor could I wring soothing out of the circumstance that command of the two posts, Henry and Heiman, was intrusted to me, except that as base of the operation in hand it had to be held in safety. Thinking to facilitate communication with the front, I recrossed the river at daylight, and established headquarters in a steamboat there, taking two companies of infantry over with me.

February 12th is remembered as a day of summer. River, land, and sky fairly shimmered with warmth. Overcoats were encumbrances. Yet the balm and beauty only aggravated the chagrin I could not help feeling at being left behind. After posting the companies to the best advantage, the object being to take care of the public property, I called my staff together, and from camp-stools on the hurricane-deck of the boat we watched the happier fellows of the divisions, McClernand's and Smith's, form, drop into column, and march away, flags flying, drums beating. By noon the last detachment of them had disappeared.

In full belief that our brigade was at least the equal of the best in the outgoing columns, the group around me on the deck shared my feeling, and were melancholy enough—Kneffler, Lyman, Pope, Ross, and Ware, all so young, enthusiastic, and full of life and ambition. One of them still lingers—a gray old reminder like myself.

These began talking about the prospects of taking Donelson, when a presentation by Ross, who was an officer of unusual capacity and information, interested me.

"There are not force of men enough," he said; "and unless he gets reinforcements, I look for Grant to come back."

One of the party challenged the remark.

"Well," Ross returned, "let us see. First, he is

going against fortifications, and should have three to one at least, though I would feel that much better had he five. He is going, too, without siege-guns. The roads, you know, are so bad that the guns of that class are still on the boat yonder. In the next place, if we divide the reported strength of the enemy by two, there are eighteen thousand men, if not twenty thousand, behind the works, which are said to be scientifically built—that is, so many to our fifteen thousand."

"Oh, we have more than that, certainly."

Ross drew out a pocket memoradum-book.

"Let us see again," he said, computing as he read. "McClernand's division, the first, is of three brigades, of which the first, Oglesby's, has five regiments of infantry, five companies cavalry, and two batteries; the second, W. H. L. Wallace's, is of four regiments infantry, one of cavalry, and two batteries; the third, Morrison's, is of two regiments infantry only. Going then to the second division, Smith's, it has three brigades, of which the first, MacArthur's, has three regiments of infantry; the third—there is no second—Cook's, has five regiments of infantry and three batteries; the fourth, Lauman's, is of four regiments of infantry and a company of sharp-shooters.[1] Now, giving six hundred men as the average of the infantry regiments, eighty to a cavalry company, and one hundred and fifty to a battery, there is in round numbers a total of fifteen thousand men. Then, turning to me, Ross asked, "Now what do you think of it?"

"Where did you get all that?" I inquired.

"As to our own division, Smith's, we are all posted. Then as to the other—well, I spent yesterday afternoon in McClernand's camps."

[1] [There was a Fifth Brigade, Colonel Morgan L. Smith commanding, composed of the Eleventh Indiana and Eighth Missouri.]

"Very well, I'll answer you. Let us go to the cabin."

They followed me below, and stood a round while I prepared a note for sending.

"It is my opinion," I then said, "that before twelve hours we will be ordered to Donelson. If there is a soldier in command there, he will meet General Grant on the road going, and fight him in the open. At all events, the general will find it difficult to surround eighteen thousand men — saying there are no more— eighteen thousand behind works with fifteen thousand. I think he will make that discovery this afternoon. The order may come to-night, and be urgent. Anyhow, we'll get ready." Lyman was quartermaster, so I turned to him. "Here, go and have four boats steamed up ready at a moment's notice to cross to Heiman and bring the brigade over. I want but one trip. You understand?" Then I spoke to Ross. "Here is a note, and, as you are responsible for this excitement, take and deliver it. It reads"—and they all gathered closer to me—

"HEADQUARTERS, SECOND BRIGADE, SECOND DIVISION,
"ARMY OF TENNESSEE, *February* 12, 1862.

"COLONEL MORGAN L. SMITH,—I think it very likely we will be wanted over at Donelson to-morrow, and the need of us may be urgent. Be ready to go in haste. Get the regiments out, and have arms stacked in the company streets. Wood should keep his horses harnessed while standing at their picket ropes. Issue three days' rations of coffee and bread. Boats will come to bring you all at one trip. The cavalry will be left in charge of the post and property. Yours,

"LEW WALLACE, Brigadier-General Commanding."

The afternoon and evening, and on far into the night, I spent on the deck of the boat listening. Its captain, intensely Union, passed the time with me.

"We ought to be hearing from *them* now," he said once; "the wind is whisking round."

"Whisking? Which way?" I asked.

"To the north."

"God forbid!" I said. "Our people have gone over there without tents, most of them without overcoats." A shiver shook me.

Within half an hour, sure enough, clouds shut out the stars, and a wind of strength, with snow on its wings, blew directly from the north. Still I kept the deck, so strong the fascination of the work in progress. Occasionally we heard, or fancied we heard, the report of guns in the distance.

"There!" and the captain sprang to his feet. "That's one! They're at it!"

And it did seem so.

XLV

Encamped at Dover—Ordered to Donelson—Mrs. Crisp's house—Grant's headquarters—Report to Grant—Assigned to centre position in the line of battle—Separated from the Eleventh Regiment—Lunch with Grant—Thayer.

My disappointment was indescribably keen when the night of the 12th and all the 13th passed uneventfully to us. Nothing from the front, only rumors of the most unreliable "grape-vine" variety. Nevertheless, I availed myself of the do-nothing condition to look out a little for myself. Why not? That is, I seized two wagons of four mules each. In the first I put the Heiman tent, a stout dry-goods box containing a mattress, a pillow-case, and three genuine blankets. But as they did not fill the body of one of the roomy vehicles, I completed the load of both with cartridge-boxes. Lyman superintended, and I may anticipate by saying here that no luckier forethought ever befell a veteran, much less a first campaigner—a remark which may be safely left to the outcome.

The night of the 14th I went to bed, lamp burning, boots on. About one o'clock a sergeant of the guard awoke me to announce a courier from the front, and directly the courier put into my hand a sealed envelope which I opened and eagerly read, first glancing at the signature — John A. Rawlins, Assistant Adjutant-General. It was the expected order, and, minus the usual caption, read very nearly: "You will report here immediately, bringing your brigade. Leave guards at Forts Heiman and Henry—a strong one at the latter."

Very seldom in my life have there been instances in which my signature has been given more willingly than to the receipt for that bit of paper.

Within five minutes everybody of military connection with me was up and booted and spurred. The boat resounded with the stamping of horses going ashore.

In ten minutes three steamboats were casting off and swinging into the river bound for Fort Heiman; Ross having already taken one with him, the transportation required for the ferriage of the troops was ample.

By three o'clock hundreds of little fires along the shadow-browned shore were pouring streams of sparks on the fitful wind. The brigade, shorn of its cavalry, had arrived and disembarked, and was making coffee; and one had only to listen to know how glad the men were, especially Pete Wood's children of the guns, the Minnesingers. They jollied rag-time cantatas in the teeth of the biting wind—sang while easing the brassy tubes of their much petted guns down the narrow gang-planks. Ah, I thought, if an enemy ever starts covetously for those guns; what a merry time he will have getting them!

With a pang of regret very distinctly remembered, I left the Twenty-third Indiana to garrison Fort Henry. The order was received with a tremendous howl which I pretended not to hear. Then, day beginning to break, the marching commands fell into column—the Eighth Missouri, then Battery A, then the Eleventh Indiana—to whom, one not more than another, the twelve miles to Donelson would be little more than a wholesome constitutional to a vigorous man.

As I was taking to horse, the captain of the boat came up with a half-bushel basket in hand.

"Here," he said to me, "is my contribution to the Cause--sandwiches, chicken and ham, bread, coffee in bottles, boiled eggs, a layer of pies, and a jorum or two."

"For me or the hospital?" I asked.

"For you and yours—and down in the bottom, good luck, good luck!"

He deserved the grateful hand-shake he got. Then I called Johnson, my servant, and put the basket in his charge, and him in the first wagon with the other property.

"Don't take your eyes off those things till I call for them. Hear, eh?"

I turned to business then with the assured sense of all right peculiar to men who know whence their next meal is coming.

Once in motion by the Telegraph road, chosen because of its better reputation, the men afoot pushed on with the genuine free step habitual to the trained Zouave, indifferent to mud and glazing pool. Ears and noses flamed like patches of red flannel, and occasionally eyes blinked to the flying frost-flakes; but the spirit was irrepressible. They sang striding on, and cheered; and more than once, looking back, I was conscious of a wish, hazy and undefined, to see that aggregation deployed in front of something impossible, with an order to charge—this never dreaming how soon the wish was to pass into actual trial.

At a point nearly half-way to Donelson, I changed from the Telegraph road into the Dover road; after which, favored by the wind, the pulsing sound of cannon became more frequent and distinct. After while we fell in with a patrol of horsemen whose offer of guidance I accepted. The chief regaled me with news, saying, among other things, that the army was in position, McClernand on the right, Smith on the left; that there had been heavy fighting the day before, McClernand having undertaken to effect a lodgment in the enemy's outwork; that he had been repulsed with loss;[1] that the enemy was being heavily reinforced from up the river; that we would be right welcome—he knew it, because everybody was beginning to think Grant had a worse Johnny's nest to deal with than he had first supposed. By cross-examination, however, I drew one large crumb of comfort from the gentleman; in effect, that a big reinforcement was then just below Dover, with Foote and his conquering gun-boats.

Near eleven o'clock we came to a house which our patrolman said belonged to a Mrs. Crisp; he also vouchsafed the information that just then General Grant was using it for headquarters; whereupon I became interested in the abode—enough at least, to note that it was a poor, little, unpainted, clap-boarded affair of the "white trash" variety, of logs, and a story and a half, with a lean-to on the side of our approach, half-room and half-porch. Smoke poured from the chimney, giving a guarantee of comfort within. Nor did I fail to observe the array of orderlies in the environment, and the herd of picketed horses, and the coming and going of officers and other orderlies, the whole signifying business in a flush verging on heat.

My bugler, at a word, sounded "Halt." Other buglers down the column near and far repeated the call; and, in dismounting, it delighted me that the Eighth, instead of breaking ranks and throwing themselves down as the tired and undisciplined always do, closed files and grimly stood at order arms. I needed no messenger from McGinnis to tell me the Eleventh was doing the

[1] This was the very gallant but unsuccessful assault by Colonel Morrison upon the middle redoubt of the Confederate intrenchments.

same. Of course, the eyes of the unoccupied were ours, and the impression was all one-sided.

I made way to the porch, and through a crowd into the cabin. The aides, Lagow and Hillyer, were standing before an old-style country fireplace, large and with logs blazing in a bed of coals. They were sworded for duty, and touched their caps. General Grant stood by a table moved out into the middle of the room, dictating something to Captain Rawlins, who was seated, back to me, writing. Colonel Webster looked on near by listening. Now and then the report of cannon, no longer in the distance, beat in with startling force.

I took off my cap and stood waiting. The general noticed me with a nod, but went on with Rawlins. When through, he came to me and said, pleasantly, but without offering a hand, "Good-morning, general, I did not expect you before two o'clock."

"I knew you would send for me," I replied, "and made ready in advance."

He gave me a quick glance, and smiled.

"What did you leave at Heiman?" he next asked.

"My cavalry."

"And at Henry, what?"

"The Twenty-third Indiana."

He turned to Rawlins. "Note that."

For the life of me, I could not tell whether he approved or disapproved. Then he continued, "You bring with you, I understand, the Eleventh Indiana and the Eighth Missouri?"

"Yes, and Battery A, Chicago," I answered.

"That is right. We are a little short in artillery." He looked at Rawlins again. "Is the order for General Wallace ready?"

"Not yet," the captain replied.

"It makes no difference. General Wallace will no doubt accept it verbally."

"Certainly."

He fixed his gray eyes on me, and asked, "Who is your next officer?"

"Colonel Morgan L. Smith."

"Very well. Tell Colonel Smith to march the Eighth and the Eleventh and report with them to General Charles F. Smith."

This, be it said, was a shock. There was separation in the words. The gray eyes were on me.

"And the battery?" I asked, steadily as I could.

"That you will keep."

And thereupon, not being able to see a brigadier's command in a battery, though composed of Minnesingers, I knew there was something behind.

"Give me attention now," the general said, almost without pause. "There are some regiments coming up from the river. They should be here by one o'clock." He took a paper from the table. "Here's a list of them." He read, and then said: "They will form the Third Division of the Army of the Tennessee, and you are assigned to command it. You had better take the list."

I took it from him.

"You will notice," he continued, "that the ranking colonels are there given, Thayer, of the First Nebraska, and Cruft, of the Thirty-first Indiana. They will command brigades. If I am mistaken, and somebody else is senior, you will make the correction when not so pressed for time. Just as soon as the organizing is finished, you will take position in the centre of the line, with McClernand on your right and Smith on your left. Your part will be to hold the centre, and resist all attempts of the enemy to break through. You must not assume the aggressive. Those are your orders. It is about noon, isn't it?" he asked Webster.

And Webster answered, "A little after, I think."

"Very well." And again turning to me, and unbending somewhat, the general said: "You will lunch with me. Bring the gentlemen of your staff."

"Smith will need a guide," I said.

"Certainly. Something for you, Lagow."

The captain stepped forward with alacrity; and, taking his hat from the table, the general followed me out on the porch, where, after I had communicated with Colonel Smith and collected my staff-officers, he stood till the last file of the column passed before him. And the passing was as if on parade. There was no cheering. Most likely, he was unrecognized.

Then, as we went back into the house, General Grant said, quietly: "The brigade, you know, belongs to Smith's division. I understand why you don't like to part with it."

I had tried not to flinch, but he had seen through me.

The lunch was had in the room adjoining that doing duty as office—a bedroom. I took it. A plain board laid on two chairs served as table. Some biscuit, hard as ice, beans boiled with flitches of salt pork, hot coffee, and pickled cucumbers, acid enough to parboil the throat, constituted the fare. There were no apologies; then *sans cérémonie*—and I saw no one stand back.

It is true the dishes partaken of at that lunch were neither numerous nor rich; to make it memorable, however, it had what I had never heard before—armies in battle for orchestra, and intermittent cannonading for music.

By-and-by the troops were reported approaching from the river, which meant the division intended for me. I hurried out and took position by the road-side with my staff, all mounted.

Then there went by me the Thirty-first Indiana, Colonel Cruft; the Twenty-fifth Kentucky, Colonel Shackelford; eight companies of the Forty-fourth Indiana, Colonel Reed; and the Seventeenth Kentucky, Colonel McHenry. These were assigned as of the first brigade; and calling Cruft out of the column, I gave the command of it to him.[1]

Next in the passage were the First Nebraska, Colonel Thayer; the Seventy-sixth Ohio, Colonel Woods; and the Sixty-eighth Ohio, Colonel Steedman. These were assigned to Colonel John M. Thayer, who, by some misunderstanding, entitled himself "Commanding Third Brigade," instead of the second. In that capacity he made his report after the battle.[2]

The provisional promotions of Cruft and Thayer brought their lieutenant-colonels, Osborne and McCord, to command their regiments.

I found myself then at the head of a division of seven regiments, the total of which we roughly estimated at six thousand men. With a report to that effect, I returned to General Grant, and asked him, as I knew nothing of the country, to give me a guide to my position in the line of investment.

Riding from the back porch of the Crisp house to the head of the column, I put it in motion, thinking, while listening to the guns in lively give and take ahead of me, "Now—now, *certainly*, I will see a great battle."

[1] This assignment was a very pleasant tribute to an acquaintanceship begun while Colonel Cruft was a student of Wabash College He arose soon after to be brigadier-general.

[2] The day following, while in action, the Forty-sixth Illinois, Colonel Davis, the Fifty-seventh Illinois, Colonel Baldwin, the Fifty-eighth Illinois, Colonel Lynch, and the Twentieth Ohio, Colonel Whittlesey, reported to me, and, on account of lack of time for other disposition of them, they were given temporarily to Thayer.

XLVI

Take position—Cold weather—Heiman's tent—The captain's basket —Foote's defeat—The disabled gun-boats.

THE centre of the line of investment, General McClernand on my right, General Smith on my left—such was the position I was to take.

"You will hold the position to prevent escape of the Confederates, without assuming the aggressive"—such was the order for my government.

When I requested a guide to show me the position, General Grant did me the honor to send his adjutant-general with me. It was about two o'clock when the column moved, taking what Captain Rawlins called the Wynne's Ferry road to Dover. For quite a distance a thick wood screened us from view of the enemy, but pretty soon we began descending into an open swale; then, looking over my left shoulder, I caught sight of the fort on a height probably a mile distant.

The Thirty-first Indiana was in lead of the division, and instantly that its colors appeared in the open of the low ground, the site of the fortification whitened with clouds of smoke, of which the roll and volumed outswell reminded me of the breaking of spinnaker-sails on racing-yachts. Then, in a jiffy, the bellow of the guns were upon us, followed by puffs of pallid smoke and sharp explosions in the air overhead, which I knew to be shells intended for us. And then, too, I knew myself under fire, but did not at the moment think of it gravely, so intent was I watching how the men took it.

The space to be crossed before reaching cover was three or four hundred yards; seeing which some one suggested double-quicking; instead of that I sent word to Colonel Cruft to set all his drums and fifes going, my argument being that the double-quick would soon degenerate into a run, while inspiring contempt of shells in the beginning was better than demoralizing the men with fear of them. The music began, and the stiffening up was magical. I myself became perfectly conscious of the effect.

Wood, from his place between the brigades, sent one of his officers for permission to go into battery and return the fire, but I forbade it.

The noise of the guns, and their reverberations peculiarly lively at that point, were much alike; but in the diapason my ear quickly separated one report; while always succeeded by a singularly shrill whistling of the missile in passage, the sound resembled that of clapboards clashed against clapboards, or of lumber dropped upon lumber in the unloading of cars. I heard the *voice* often through the siege in the night as well as the day, a rasping dissonance not without a comical touch.[1]

There had been probably a hundred and twenty-five or thirty shells and shot fired at the regiments during that deliberate passage; yet, when we were in position, I rode back to the rear and could not hear of a man hurt. I was careful to have the fact well published.

Captain Rawlins at length stopped, and said: "We have come far enough. Halt here."

"This, then, is the centre of the line?" I asked.

"Practically," he answered.

I looked around. We were on a road, with the ground in declension on the right, but level in front and on our

[1] When, after the surrender, a one-pounder piece was discovered among the guns captured, the mystery was fully explained.

left. A thick wood shut the position in, hiding it from the fort.

"How far away is McClernand?" I inquired of the captain.

"About half a mile."

"And Smith?"

"A little farther—possibly a quarter of a mile."

My surprise was great. I had been thinking of a connected line throughout.

Then I asked: "Suppose I want to communicate with them? I see no road."

"Your messenger must take to the woods."

My astonishment grew apace. "What? Why hasn't the enemy come in here and cut you in two?"

"Because"—and Rawlins laughed—"there's but one soldier among them; and he is third in rank."

"What's his name?"

"Buckner."

"Simon Bolivar? I know him personally. Who are the others?"

"One is Floyd, the other Pillow."

Just then the report of a gun passed sullenly through the woods, and a shell exploded a short distance up the road.

"That is from the fort?" I asked.

"Yes."

"Well, I have the direction. How far off is it?"

"About half a mile."

"And to get by me Mr. Floyd must come through the woods on the left or down this road?"

"Yes."

"I see now why I was sent for; and I thank you for coming with me, captain, and for information. With your permission, I'll get ready."

The captain turned his horse about and rode away,

saying, "I will see you in the morning, if not sooner."

As a first step, I had the regiments of both brigades broken into column of companies and arms stacked. Then I picketed my front. Small fires were allowed well down the slope at the right, the smoke not to rise above the tree-tops, lest it should attract the attention of the enemy. Officers were warned to keep their men close by, ready to fall in at a word. Then my wagons were brought forward and the tent pitched. The teamsters and Johnson, my servant, were put in charge of it. They were not permitted to build a fire. The snow was all of a couple inches deep on the level; on the south side of the logs it had collected in cadaverous drifts. Frost in specks of glancing sheen still streaked the air. We walked about and beat our bodies to keep up circulation, teeth chattering meanwhile like castanets. Shade of Thor, how cold it was! Yet there was nothing to do but wait and be ready.

At three o'clock, or thereabouts, we were permitted an unexpected diversion. The boom of a gun heavier than any we had yet heard, and farther off, rolled through the woods from down the river.

"A gun-boat," said Kneffler.

Another boom like the first, only nearer. Then an answer, but muffled as by a house on a hill in intervention.

"That was from one of the river batteries," I said.

Two—three guns in the distance—four! Then the batteries—there was no mistaking them—replied in quick succession.

"Foote is on the rampage. It's a battle." And as I spoke my blood ran quicker and warmer.

The wind blew from the north, and the condition of the atmosphere did not lend itself generously to the conveyance of sound; still the roar of the double eruption, now from battery, now from boat, magnified itself. Then the interchange became an increasing thunder, and we knew the sturdy flag-officer was closing in on his enemy. At times we even fancied hearing shot in impact against armor-plate, whereat we, in safety, mere auditors, felt the flesh crawl upon our bones, and thought how hot it must be down there.

Now nearly everybody, the Confederates, of course, and of ours all in the least possessed of map-knowledge of the locality, understood Foote's object in attacking was not merely to silence the batteries, but get his gun-boats above the fort. Then, the river in his possession as far up as Nashville, the garrison must either fight out of the limbo they were in or surrender. So, if the besieged and the besiegers alike stood at attention, as it were, while the struggle was on; if in the hour and more I did not hear a shot fired along our front; if even the sharp-shooters were quiescent, nothing could be more natural. I remember the little of stir on the part of the men of my division about me in the time, and that when any of them had anything to say it was in a low voice—as if even a whisper were out of order.

The sun made ready to drop behind the western wall, and the wrack continuing, it crept into our bones, slowly blending with the frost already there, that Foote was having a harder time here than at Fort Henry. A dropping-off in his fire was noticed; we hated to admit it, but all at once it quit altogether. We looked at one another like sick men.

"Whipped!" said Kneffler, with a prefix sometimes excusable to the ear but never to the eye.

And it was so.

Then, as there was no telling what the enemy, encouraged by his victory, might attempt in the night, I busied myself making ready for him. The picket reserves were strengthened and deployments provided for. Low fires near the arms in stack were allowed.

The big Heiman tent proved a welcome refuge, and, with my staff, I heaped blessings on the captain of the steamboat. While we were sounding the depths of his basket, I remembered, with a wrench of spirit, that my horse had gone since early morning without a drop of water or a bite of food. I reproached myself bitterly. It had been so easy to have dropped a bag of oats in one of the wagons! A teamster came to my help with a capful of shelled corn. Then, in place of water, the noble brute was given a long tether that he might make the most of the snow. Hard, truly!

And from pitying the horse my sympathy went out to the men. By that affinity which always lies coiled up in a great common cause, though strangers, they were brethren. I got up often in the night and looked out at them around the insufficient fires, dark groups wrapped in blankets. Once I joined a party of them. They recognized the uniform, and, by giving way, silently invited me to come in and warm.

"It's cold, boys," I said, rubbing my hands over the struggling blaze.

"Yes," one of them answered, half jocularly, "my father has his pigs all tucked away in good, sweet straw."

"I came out to comfort you," I rejoined.

"Have you a feather-bed apiece for us?"

They laughed.

"No, but seeing there is no place to lay the beds unless in the snow, I have something better. Is it any lighter, do you think, on the fellows over there in the trenches? If you are cold, how much warmer are they?"

I had evoked the right principle.

"That's so. If they had stayed at home and behaved themselves, we wouldn't be here."

There was an expletive with the speech which is left out.[1]

[1] Foote, in attacking, moved in two lines; the first, composed of the *St. Louis* (flag-ship), *Pittsburg*, and *Louisville*, all armored; the second, of the *Conestoga*, *Tyler*, and *Lexington*, all unarmored. The *Carondelet* seems to have served as a free-lance in the fight. Of the other part, there were two batteries, upper and lower, armed with twenty heavy guns, to which the boats could return compliments with but twelve. The batteries had the further advantage of being on a hill-side, at a height enabling them to reach the decks of the vessels, their most vulnerable points. Yet Foote advanced to within four hundred yards of his enemy. Once he drove the gunners out of the upper battery. At the end of more than an hour of incessant battle, the *Louisville* was disabled, and drifted down the river. The *St. Louis* was soon after in the same condition; and a little later the *Pittsburg* and *Carondelet* fell into desperate straits and the fight was over. The calamity happened just when the gun-boats were about to pass the fort into the river above it.

XLVII

John, the horse—McClernand falls back in disorder—A precarious position—Major Brayman—A panic—Rawlins—The rout turned —Colonel W. H. L. Wallace—Wood's battery.

THE morning of the 15th crawled up the eastern sky as a turtle in its first appearance after hibernation crawls up a steep bank. Just before it shook out its first faint signs of life, I went out to look after my horse John. Poor fellow! The blanket I had loaned him helped comfort him; but he had lapped up all the snow in the circle of his tether, and *that,* not to speak of the appeal in his eyes, told me how he suffered for water. I had about made up my mind to take chances and have an orderly lead him back to the first running stream, when an unusual sound off to the right front of my position attracted me. I listened. The sound broke at a jump into what was easily recognizable as a burst of musketry. What was it? Who was making it over there? I stepped to the tent, pulled the flaps of the door aside, and said: "Wake, gentlemen, and come out. There's something for you."

They came in haste.

"Listen!" I said.

By that time the sound had swelled into a—well, I could think of nothing so much like it as fire-crackers in barrels wasting their Christmas music in simultaneous explosion.

"What do you think of it?" I asked.

One of them thought it McClernand assaulting the works.

"No," I replied, "the fort is here more to our front."

Then Ross said, "The Johnnies are out pitching into McClernand."

In a little while guns joined in.

"There! That settles it," I said. "Get out your horses. It looks as if we were to have it in boat-loads to-day."

Meantime, the blanketed groups about the fires were astir and listening.

John was brought me, and I rode to Cruft and Thayer. Both were directed to have their men breakfast and stand by their arms. Cruft was told to call in his extra guard details.

At my tent again, I borrowed a capful of corn for John, and, while he was eating, the ever-handy basket surrendered its contents, and we were content to take our coffee out of the bottles cold.

By the time we were through the noise over at the right had swollen in volume, until it bore likeness to a distant train of empty cars rushing over a creaking bridge.

Then the absence of the cavalry, in idleness on the height of Heiman, struck me regretfully. Here was a rare chance to make them useful. In twenty minutes they could have informed me of what was happening to the first division. As it was, my orders were to be respected—that is, there was nothing for me but to keep my place, letting come what might.

The situation was very trying. Questions thronged in on me, all the output of imagination, but not less confusing on that account.

What, for instance, if the enemy had received reinforcements from Nashville in the night, making him once more superior to us in numbers? What if the demonstration at the moment going on over in McClernand's zone of investment were but a feint, leaving me or General Smith on my left the real object of impending attack?

I tried, next, to anticipate what might come round to me. To get at my position there were but two directions from which an assault could come; they were by the road in my front and through the woods at my left. This simplified the situation amazingly, and left me to decide the tactics proper in both eventualities, which was "a short horse soon curried."

These things anticipated and determined on, I fancied myself ready—something, to my mind, as needful to a commander as having his command ready—indeed, I am not sure but it is of first importance.

The noise kept grinding on without lull or intermission. An hour—two hours—would it never end? The suspense became torturous. At last a horseman galloped up from the rear. He gave me the name of Brayman, major and assistant adjutant-general.

"I am from General McClernand," he said, "sent to ask assistance of you. The general told me to tell you the whole rebel force in the fort massed against him in the night. Our ammunition is giving out. We are losing ground. No one can tell what will be the result if we don't get immediate help."

A dilemma this, and a serious one. I explained my orders to Major Brayman, and then despatched Lieutenant Ware at speed to the Crisp house for permission to help McClernand. This was about eight o'clock.

In good time Ware returned, and reported General Grant on board the gun-boat *St. Louis*, in conference with Flag-Officer Foote. Nobody at headquarters felt authorized to act on my request. Major Brayman left me. The battle, meantime, roared on.

Afterwhile a second messenger came from General McClernand, Colonel ———, a gray-haired man in uniform. His news could hardly be worse, and he spoke with tears in his eyes.

"Our right flank is turned," he said. "The regiments are being crowded back on the centre. We are using ammunition taken from the dead and wounded. The whole army is in danger."

My impulse had been to send help at the first asking; that impulse was now seconded by judgment. Disaster to the first division meant exactly what Colonel ——— had said. If that division were rolled back on me, a panic might ensue. In the absence of the commanding general, the responsibility was mine. A regiment was not enough to meet the demand. The colonel had come attended by a younger man whose name has slipped me, and I said, "Tell General McClernand that I will send him my first brigade with Colonel Cruft. I will retain this gentleman to serve as guide."

Thereupon I hastened to Colonel Cruft, and, after explanation, ordered him to take his command rapidly as possible and report to General McClernand.[1] Cruft

[1] As an indication of the character of the man, General McClernand's report of his part in the capture of Fort Donelson is a very remarkable paper.

For example, he says in that report: "The Seventeenth Kentucky, Thirty-first Indiana, and Twenty-fifth Kentucky, commanded by Colonel Charles Cruft, coming up between nine and ten o'clock, A.M., was hailed by members of my staff with encouraging words, and formed as a reserve in the rear of the Twenty-ninth, Eighth and Thirtieth (Illinois). The Forty-fourth Indiana, Colonel H. B. Reed, followed about an hour after, and formed in the rear of the Thirty-first." From this it would appear that the importunities of McClernand's first messenger and the tears of his second meant merely that their chief was not in need, except of a reserve.

In return for one-half of my command sent him, to say nothing

acted promptly, and moved off through the woods under direction of the guide.

This left me only Thayer's brigade and the Minnesingers, whom I joined. Afterwhile Captain Rawlins came out to me, and I gave him an account of the messengers from General McClernand, and of what I had done with Cruft.

While we talked, stragglers from the fight appeared coming on the run up a half-defined road that dropped with the decline of the ridge we were on and led off to the right. We scarcely noticed the fugitives, so much more were we drawn by the noise behind them. *That* grew in volume, being a compound of shouts and yells, mixed with the rattle of wheels and the rataplan and throbbing rumble of hoofs in undertone.

"What can that be?" Rawlins asked.

"It beats me. But I'll find out," I said.

I called to an orderly, "Ride and see what all that flurry means." And as a suspicion of the truth broke through my wonder, I further bade him: "Don't spare your horse. Quick!"

Then, as Rawlins and I sat waiting, an officer mounted and bareheaded and wild-eyed, rode madly up the

of the responsibility assumed by me in face of orders, General McClernand also says in the same report: "The reinforcement was generously brought forward by Colonel Cruft upon his own responsibility, in the absence of General Wallace, his division commander, in compliance with my request, borne by Major Brayman, assistant adjutant-general of my division." This is not only a repudiation of my sympathy for him in his distress, but is a charge that in a crisis I was absent from my division. Fortunately, Colonel Cruft is a witness in my behalf. In his report of the fight, he says: ". . . At eight-thirty, A.M., General Wallace's order was received to put the brigade in rapid motion to the extreme right of our line, for the purpose of reinforcing General McClernand's division." See *Rebellion Records*, series 1, vol. vii., p. 243.

road and past us, crying in shrill repetition, "We're cut to pieces!"

Now I had never seen a case of panic so perfectly defined, and it was curious, even impressive. Rawlins, however, was not disposed to view the spectacle philosophically. Jerking a revolver from his holster, he would have shot the frantic wretch had I not caught his hand. He remonstrated with me viciously, but the orderly came back at full speed and with an ominous look on his face.

"What is it?" I asked.

And he said: "The road back there is jammed with wagons, and men afoot and on horseback, all coming towards us. On the plains we would call it a *stampede.*"

We looked at each other—Rawlins and I—and there was no need of further question. *The first division was in full retreat.*

"What are you going to do?" he asked.

"There's but one thing I can do."

"What is that?"

"Get this brigade out of the way. If those fellows strike my people, they will communicate the panic."

"Where will you go?"

"To take that way," pointing to the rear, "is to retreat, and carry the panic to General Smith; so I'll go right up this road towards the enemy."

"Good-bye," Rawlins said. "I would go with you, but this thing must be reported."

He rode slowly off, thinking, doubtless, that he might alarm the men whom he must pass if he hurried.

Then, at my word, the drummers beat the long roll. The men took arms. "By the right flank, file left!" And out of column of companies they went so neatly that I asked Thayer where the regiments were from, and he said, "From Buell's army." And, my confidence rising, I said: "Good! Now, right shoulder, shift, and double-quick."

I gave an instant to the coming mob, and, believing from the sound that there would be time to get the last of my regiments clear of it and contagion, I called to my staff and hastened forward.

Cruft, I discovered, had, in his haste, left his pickets to my care, and I sent an officer to assemble them into column. I also discovered that the road by which we were moving veered somewhat to the right of the fort. Then, the woods still covering us, I came upon numbers of men—how many I may not venture to say—in squads, companies, and fractional regiments under lead of officers. Some of them bore regimental colors. They were not in the least panicky—not even in a hurry.

Once I asked, "Where are you from?"

"From the front, where else do you think?" And there was a roar of laughter.

Of another party, a good-sized battalion, I inquired, "What's your regiment, men?"

"Oglesby's. Have you seen him? He's hit."

Still another answered the same inquiry, "McArthur's."

"Where are you going?"

"We're looking for ammunition. Got any?"

And that was the general cry, "Cartridges, cartridges!"

I saw, finally, an officer riding slowly towards me, one leg thrown over the horn of his saddle and four or five hundred men with a flag behind him. I galloped to meet him.

"Good-morning," I said. "May I ask who you are?"

"My name is Wallace," he returned, stopping.

"Oh, you are Colonel W. H. L. Wallace! Well, my name is Wallace."

"Lew Wallace, of the Eleventh Indiana?"

"The same."

We shook hands, he saying: "Our names, and the number of our regiments—mine is the Eleventh Illinois—have been the cause of great profanity in the post-office."

"Mixture of letters, I suppose?"

"Yes."

I noted him hurriedly, a man above medium height, florid in face, wearing a stubby, reddish beard, with eyes of a bluish cast and a countenance grave and attractive.

"I take it, colonel, you are getting out of a tight place."

"Yes, we got out of ammunition."

"That's bad," I said; "but I can help you. Down the road by a big tent, which is mine, and at your service, you will find two wagons. They, too, are mine, and loaded with ammunition. Help yourself, and tell McClernand to do the same."

"Thank you. I will do it."

His men were halted; facing them, he called out in a cheery voice, "Forward."

"A moment, colonel," I said. "Are the enemy following you?"

"Yes."

"How far are they behind?"

Just then the head of my column hove in view. The colonel saw it.

"Are those yours?"

"Yes."

"Well"—his face took on an expression of calculation—"you will about have time to form a line of battle here."

"Is that so? Then please give my men room to come—and good-bye, colonel. I'll see you again."

We shook hands and separated.[1]

A word from one so cool and thoughtful as Colonel W. H. L. Wallace was enough. The moment called for action. I saw it with a great jump of the heart, though the necessities of the situation gripped my senses hard. I looked over the ground right and left, and saw the surface open and smooth, then in front, and discovered myself on the brow of a descent, down which the road narrowed as it dipped between walls of brush and low trees of second growth. As a position, the advantages were all mine. And now to get in my line! The Minnesingers in the road, a regiment right of it, another left.

"Ride," I said to Ross, "and tell Pete Wood to come. Tell him he has the right of way, and to stop at nothing."

Ross scarcely took breath before he was gone.

Thayer came up, and I gave him the situation.

"File the First Nebraska to the right, the next regiment to the left. The two will support the battery between them here. Make a second line of your four regiments, and hold it in reserve behind the First Nebraska."

Thayer was quick, yet I helped him. And while we worked, I heard the rattling of wheels and whips cracking like pistols, and, looking back, beheld Pete Wood coming. I have lived long, and seen many things thrilling, but never anything to approach that battery. It drove forward full speed, the horses running low, the riders standing in their stirrups plying their whips, guns

[1] I am sorry to say I never met him again. His light went out at Shiloh, and it was that of a man gallant as one may ever hope to encounter. And here I may as well answer a question often asked. I do not know of any relationship between Colonel W. H. L. Wallace and myself. I do know, however, that I should be very proud did such exist. Had he lived, high rank was just ahead of him. He possessed all the elements of a great soldier.

and caissons bouncing over root and rut like playthings, the men clinging to their seats like monkeys. No shouting—only Wood in front with his sword waving "Forward." I fancied the trees trembled as the wheels rolled by them; I know the ground shook earthquake-like. Well done, Battery A! Well done, my Minnesingers! You treated me there and then to the most splendid and inspiring spectacle in the repertoire of war. I have not forgotten it—I can never forget it.

And yet not too soon!

For while I watched the amazing advent, down the road in front rifles began to crackle and bullets to sing in the air. I beckoned Wood, and probably shouted, "Hurry, hurry!"

The firing seemed right on us, not fifty paces away. I noticed it extending rapidly, despite the undergrowth, in front of the First Nebraska, and formed a theory respecting the attack. Instead of advancing in line of battle, the enemy had marched up the cramped road in files of four, and, meeting us unexpectedly, were trying to deploy. It was a tactical mistake with a terrible penalty in payment. All we had to do was to ply them with fire. Thayer had then got the First Nebraska and the Fifty-eighth Illinois in line, the former next the road on the right. I gave him a sign. He spoke to McCord, of the First Nebraska. I saw their muskets rise and fall steadily as if on a parade-ground. A volley—and smoke—and after that constant fire at will fast as skilled men could load.

Then Wood arrived, and without slackening speed wheeled his first section into battery right across the road. I heard him shout: "Grape now. Double-shot them, boys!" He could not see the foemen, I knew. But why look for them? Was not their fire sufficient? Almost before the wheels were stationary his guns opened; a moment more and I lost sight of guns and men in a deepening cloud of smoke. The gallant fellows were doing the right thing. A section on the right of the first one, and on the left a section. Now, indeed, they will be more than men who, only fifty paces off, can deploy into line in face of the First Nebraska and my Minnesingers!

Having time then to give attention to the support on the left of the battery, to my astonishment I found next the guns a company of the Thirty-second Illinois. It did not belong to my command, and how it came there I do not know. It was ready to fight; that was enough. I let the captain (Davidson) alone. The Fifty-eighth I broke half to the rear. As yet its colonel, not having been attacked, had reserved his fire.

This was the moment of the arrival of the Forty-sixth Illinois, Colonel Davis; the Fifty-seventh Illinois, Colonel Baldwin; the Fifty-eighth Illinois, Colonel Lynch; and the Twentieth Ohio, Colonel Whittlesey. The Fifty-eighth Illinois I posted on the left of the Fifty-eighth Ohio; and the pressure being too great to ask about seniority, the other new-comers were thrown into column of regiments, and marched across the road as an additional reserve to Colonel Thayer. The truth is, I did not know anything of the strength of the enemy, or where the brunt of his attack would fall; particularly as firing was audible at a distance on my right, and cannon were beginning to help the assailants in my front. In such a situation I fancied it impossible to have reserves in excess.

The fight was now set, and we were on the defensive. For three-quarters of an hour it went on, confined, strangely enough, to the space covered by the First Nebraska and Battery A. Occasionally Woods, of the Seventy-sixth Ohio, from his position on the right of the First Nebraska, threw in a volley left oblique. The Confederate artillery, having to fire up-hill, was of no service. Their shot and shells flew over the trees. I would not be understood as speaking lightly of the Confederates. The struggle on their part was to get into line, and in that they were persistent to obstinacy. Twice they quit, then returned to the trial. A third time repelled, they went back to stay. From a height Colonel Cruft saw them retreat pell-mell into their works. General Buckner, however, softens the description. He speaks of the repulse as a "withdrawal without panic, but in some confusion."

When the affair was over our loss struck me most strangely, it was comparatively so trifling—Battery A, three wounded; the First Nebraska, three killed, seven wounded. This was due partly to our advantage of position, and in part to the desultory and up-hill work of the enemy. As to the Confederate loss, I saw dead men in the brush and in the road enough to sicken me. Several of the desperately wounded we picked up and cared for as if they were our own, though the greater number of those unfortunates had been carried off by their comrades.

I lost no time in sending pickets to cover my front; then, quiet restored, congratulations were in order.

Cruft not having reported, a scouting-party found him intact on a height over on the right, which I ordered him to hold. After making connections with him by a line of skirmishers, the division, grown to pretentious proportions, was more carefully established in its position. There we waited. At intervals shells from the fort sailed over our heads and on into the woods; and it was observable that the men received them with jeers and jokes. Nothing *veteranizes* soldiers like a successful fight.

The success, it may as well be admitted, more than gratified me. With a brigade thrust between it and its over-confident pursuers, I had been instrumental in relieving the first division from an imminent peril. And when, next day, Captain Hillyer, aide-de-camp, sent me a note, saying, "*I speak advisedly.* God bless you! You did save the day on the right!" I had no doubt my conduct was fully appreciated at headquarters.[1]

[1] General McClernand, in his official report, acknowledged that his whole command fell back from the left of their position in the morning four hundred yards, and that I formed a portion of my fresh troops in front of his second line. He then proceeds to rob Lieutenant Wood and Battery A of credit by giving the repulse of the enemy to Captain Taylor, of his division. He even claims the Confederate dead found in the road after the repulse. Nowhere in his report is there a shadow of acknowledgment to me or my division, not even for the ammunition with which his men supplied themselves out of my wagons. All he plausibly can he appropriates to himself.

XLVIII

Before Donelson—General McClernand—The road recovered—The Eleventh regiment reappears — Troops on the hill-side — Cruft and Ross.

I HAD long since learned that proud men in the throes of ill-fortune dislike to have the idle and curious make spectacles of them; especially do they hate condolence; wherefore I refrained from going to take a look at the first division reorganizing in my rear. It seemed to me a good time to attend to my own business.

However, as the town clocks in cities of the country endowed with such luxuries were getting ready to strike three, an officer rode up from the rear, and hearing him ask for me, I went to him.

"Are you General Wallace?" he asked.

"I am—at your service."

"Well," he said, "I am—"

Just then a round shot from the fort, aimed lower than usual, passed, it really seemed, not more than a yard above us. We both "ducked" to it, and when I raised my head almost from my horse's neck the stranger was doing himself the same service. We looked at each other, and it was impossible not to laugh.

"I don't know," he said, jocularly, "in what school you were taught to bow, but that one was well done."

"Yes," I retorted, "mine was nearly as low as yours."

To which he added, "They were both behind time"; meaning that they were given after the ball had passed.

Then he took up his fractured remark.

"I was about to say I am General McClernand."

Now I had known General John A. McClernand by reputation as a Democratic politician. His speeches in Congress had been frequent and creditable. My predilections were all on his side, and I ran him over with interest. His face was agreeable, though weather-beaten and unshaven. The snow light gave his eyes a severe squint. His head was covered with one of the abominable regulation wool hats hooked up at one side. Besides being thin and slightly under average height, he was at further disadvantage by sitting too far back in his saddle, and stooping. We shook hands, and he was giving me the details of his battle of the morning, when General Grant joined us, mounted, and attended by a single orderly. I noticed papers in General Grant's right hand which had the appearance of telegrams, and that he seemed irritated and bothered trying to keep some active feeling down. Of course McClernand and I saluted, and gave him instant attention.

From the hollow in front of my position a dropping fire kept ascending.

"Pickets?" General Grant asked.

"My pickets," I replied.

"They will get over that afterwhile," he remarked; then, seriously: "Foote must go to Cairo, taking his iron-clads, some of which are seriously damaged. We will have to await his return; meantime, our line must be retired out of range from the fort."

He stopped. The idea was detestable to him—bitterly so, and, seeing it, I asked to make a suggestion.

He turned to me with a questioning look.

"We have nobody on the right now," I said, "and the road to Clarksville is open. If we retire the line at all, it will be giving the enemy an opportunity to get away to-night with all he has."

Grant's face, already congested with cold, reddened perceptibly, and his lower jaw set upon the other. Without a word, he looked at McClernand, who began to explain. Grant interrupted him.

"Gentlemen," he said, "that road must be recovered before night." Gripping the papers in his hand—I heard them crinkle—he continued: "I will go to Smith now. At the sound of your fire, he will support you with an attack on his side."

Thereupon he turned his horse and rode off at an ordinary trot, while following him with my eyes, wondering at the simplicity of the words in a matter involving so much, I saw Colonel Morgan L. Smith coming up the road beyond him at the head of some troops, and guessed who they were.

General McClernand then spoke. "The road ought to be recovered — Grant is right about that. But, Wallace, you know I am not ready to undertake it."

The significance of the remark was plain. The road in question ran through the position his division had occupied in the morning; and feeling now that General Grant had really been addressing him, General McClernand was asking me to take the proposed task off his hands. I thought rapidly—of my division, by Cruft's return intact, and reinforced—of the Eleventh Indiana and the Eighth Missouri so opportunely arrived—of Colonel Morgan L. Smith — of the order holding me strictly to the defensive now released.

"Did you send to General Charles F. Smith for assistance?" I asked McClernand.

"Yes."

"Well, I see some troops coming, ordered probably to report to you; if they are, and you will direct the officer commanding to report to me, I will try recovery of the road."

At McClernand's request one of my aides—Ross, I think—rode at speed to meet Colonel Morgan L. Smith. Returning, he said, "It is Colonel Smith from General Charles F. Smith, ordered to report to General McClernand."

"Go back, then," said McClernand, "and tell the colonel that I request him to report to General Wallace."

Whereupon I said: "It is getting late, and what is done must be before night. If you will excuse me, I will go at it."

"Certainly," McClernand replied, adding, "I have two or three regiments in order under Colonel Ross, of my division, whom you may find useful."

"All right; send them on."

And as General McClernand left me, I sent to Colonel Smith directing him to halt his regiments behind the battery; with my staff, I then set out to see as much as possible of the ground to be recovered, and decide how best to arrange the attack. My horse objected to the dead men still lying in the road; but getting past them, the hill dipped down into a hollow of width and depth. At the left there was a field; all else appeared thinly covered with scattered trees. The pickets in the hollow were maintaining a lively fusillade, so I turned into the field. I could then see the road ran off diagonally to the right. A bluff rose in front of me partially denuded, and on top of it Confederate soldiers were visible walking about and blanketed. Off to the left the bluff flattened as it went. In that direction I also saw a flag not the stars and stripes, and guessed that the fort lay in studied contraction under it. I saw, too, a little branch winding through the hollow, and thought of my poor horse, then two days without water. The men keeping the thither height caught sight of my party, and interrupted me in the study of their position.

Their bullets fell all around us. One cut a lock out of the mane of a horse of one of my orderlies. But I had what we came for, and got away, nobody hurt.

Upon my rejoining them at the battery, the old regiments (Eighth and Eleventh) cheered me; whereat the fort opened, firing harmlessly at the sound. The Eleventh, from their stacked arms, crowded around John—"Old Balley," they called him—and filling a capful of crumbled crackers, some of them fed him what he would eat. They would have given him drink from their canteens had there been a vessel at hand to hold the water.

While that went on, I got my orders off. Cruft was told, by messenger, to take his brigade down into the hollow, and form line at the foot of the hill held by the Confederates, his left resting on the Wynne's Ferry road. When in position he was to notify me.

Smith was informed of what I have called the bluff, and told that it was to be his point of attack—that he was to conduct the main attack, supported by Cruft on his right and by Ross on the left, and that he was to make the ascent in column of regiments.

Thayer I directed to keep his present position, holding his brigade in reserve with the battery.

By-and-by Colonel Ross—he of Illinois—came up, bringing the Seventeenth and Forty-ninth Illinois regiments that had behaved with distinction in Colonel Morrison's misassault of the 14th. To him I explained that his position would be on the left of the main attack as a support.

I also gave notice to Smith and Ross that I would personally put them in position.

When these preliminaries were disposed of, I looked at the sun and judged that there were at least two hours left me for the operation.

While waiting to hear from Cruft, I chaffed with the old regiments. Of the Eighth Missouri I wanted to know at what hotel they had put up for the night.

"At the Lindell, of course," one of them responded.

"How were the accommodations?"

"Cold, but cheap."

This excited a great laugh.

Halting in front of the Eleventh, I said: "You fellows have been swearing for a long time that I would never get you into a fight. It's here now. What have you to say?"

A spokesman answered: "We're ready. *Let her rip!*"

Very un-Napoleonic, but very American.

Then heavy firing arose out of the hollow, and soon afterwards a man galloped up the hill to tell me that Colonel Cruft was in position, his left on the road.

"It is time to move," I said to Smith.

"Wait until I light a fresh cigar."

That done, and Colonel Ross told to follow, we set off down the road. Hardly had Smith, with whom I was riding, got half-way across the hollow, going straight for the bluff, when a fire ran along the top of it and bullets zipped angrily through the trees, showering us with leaves and twigs. To reply would have required a halt. At the foot of the ascent I left my Missouri friend, saying, "Try the Zouave on them, colonel, and remember to deploy McGinnis when you are nearly up."

Colonel Ross, to whom I rode next, had deployed his command. Going with him until clear of Smith's ground, I asked, "You understand your part, colonel?"

"Yes," he said, "it is to take care of the left of the main attack."

It took me but a moment to get to Cruft, who was exchanging a ragged fire with the enemy above him.

"Colonel Smith is next you on the left," I said to him.

"Keep a little behind his line, and when you have cleared the hill, swing left towards the fort, pivoting on him."

I hurried then to the open field spoken of; and by the time I reached it, selected a stand-point for general oversight, and adjusted my field-glass, the advance had become general where Ross and Cruft were ascending slowly, inch by inch, the musketry had risen in measure, and the trees stood half veiled in a smoke momentarily deepening.

Presently my glass settled on Colonel Morgan L. Smith and the climb in his front, which I judged of three hundred short steps. In the patches of snow on the bluffy breast I also noticed some clumps of shrubs and a few trees, and here and there what appeared to be outcropping of rock. The disadvantages were obvious; yet, counting them as odds in the scale of chances, they were not enough to shake my confidence in the outcome, for there were advantages to be taken into the account—among them the Zouave training of both the regiments, meaning that they were nimble on their hands and knees far beyond the ordinary infantrymen, that they could load on their backs and fire with precision on their bellies, and were instinctively observant of order in the midst of disorder. Indeed, *purpose* with them answered all the ends of alignment elbow to elbow.

While making these observations my attention was drawn off by musketry blent with the pounding of artillery in the distance over at the left. It was General Charles F. Smith's supporting attack as promised by General Grant. Then it came to me suddenly that the crisis of the great adventure was on the army, and that as it went the victory would go. A feverish anxiety struck me. My tongue and throat grew dry and parched. I have the feeling now even as I write, such power have incidents at times to stamp themselves on memory.

Returning then to Colonel Smith, I saw skirmishers spring out and cover the front of his column. To my astonishment I also saw the man himself on horseback behind his foremost regiment, bent on riding up the hill—a perilous feat under the most favorable circumstances.[1]

I would like to describe the ascension of the height by the regiments under Smith, but cannot, for, take it all in all, it was the most extraordinary feat of arms I ever beheld. In the way of suggestion merely, the firing from the top was marked by lulls and furious outbursts. In the outbursts the assailants fell to their hands and knees, and took to crawling, while in the lulls—occasioned by smoke settling so thickly in front of the defenders that they were bothered in taking aim—yards of space were gained by rushes. And these were the spectacles impossible of description. To get an idea of them the reader must think of nearly two thousand vigorous men simultaneously squirming or dashing up the breast of a steep hill slippery with frost, in appearance so many black gnomes burrowing in a cloud of flying leaves and dirty snow. As they climbed on the alignment with which they started became loose and looser until half-way up it seemed utterly lost. There was no firing, of course, except by the skirmishers, and no cheering, not a voice save of officers in exhortation. Occasionally we heard Smith or McGinnis, but

[1] I asked Colonel Smith afterwards what he meant by riding. He gave me a characteristic reply. "I thought the sight of me would encourage the boys." In further illustration of the man under fire, a bullet cut his cigar off close to his lips. "Here," he shouted, "one of you fellows bring me a match." The match was brought, and, lighting a fresh cigar, he spurred on and up.

most frequently the enemy flinging taunts on the laborers below. "Hi, hi, there, you damned Yanks! Why don't you come up? What are you waiting for?"

They were nearing the top, probably a third of the distance remaining, when the Eleventh, in loose array as it was, rushed by the left flank out of column. They stumbled, and slipped, and fell down, but presently brought up, and faced front, having uncovered the Eighth. To get into line with the latter cost but a moment. About the same time I saw the skirmishers drop and roll out of sight, leaving the line of fire unobstructed. A furious outbreak from the enemy and both regiments sank down, and on their· bellies half buried in snow delivered their first ragged volley. The next I saw of them they were advancing on their hands and knees. That they would win was no longer a question.

I gave a glance in Cruft's direction and another to Ross. Both were well up in their sections of attack. Just then some one near by broke into a laugh, and called out, "Look there!"

"Where?" I asked, not relishing the diversion.

A party of surgeon's assistants, six or eight in number, seeing us in the field, and thinking it a safe place, started to come across. A shower of bullets overtook them, and when my eyes reached them they were snuggling in the snow behind the kits they carried. And when I remembered how thin the kits were, nothing but oil-cloth, and not more resistant of a minié-ball than tissue-paper, I excused the laugh by joining in it.

Another look towards Cruft, another to Ross, then a brief study of Smith's forlorn hope, by that time nearly to its goal, and I took action.

Regaining the road, I hastened into the hollow, and

when about half-way across it noticed a slackening of the enemy's fire; then, hardly a minute elapsing, it ceased entirely. The meaning was unmistakable. We had won! Calling Kneffler, I told him to go to General McClernand and tell him we were on the hill, and that he would oblige me if his artillery did not fire in our direction.

In these moves my horse had answered me readily but with his head down—a thing that had not happened before. The other horses of the company were worse off. There was need for me up on the height, but we stopped by the little brook and broke through the ice. While the poor brutes were drinking greedily, Colonel Webster came to me.

"General Grant sends me," he said, "to tell you to retire your command out of range of the fort and throw up light intrenchments. He thinks it best to wait for reinforcements."

I gave a thought to the position just recovered, with loss unknown, and asked the colonel, "Does the general know that we have retaken the road lost in the morning?"

"I think not," he replied.

"Oh, well! Give him my compliments, colonel, and tell him *I have received the order.*"

Webster gave me a sharp look and left me. I had resolved to disobey the direction, and he saw it, and justified me without saying so—as did General Grant subsequently.

XLIX

The height won—The dead on the field—Johnson, the servant—Stores stolen—The sleep on the field—Major Ross—The flag of truce—The entrance to Fort Donelson—General Buckner and staff—Captain Walker—The formal surrender—Union advantages.

The sun was just going down when, with my staff, I rode on to the height just won. To my eager search for what of war and combat it had to offer there was at first nothing which one may not find in any neglected woods pasture; only the air was heavy with the sulphurous smell of powder burned and burning, and through the thin assemblage of trees there went an advancing line of men stretching right and left out of sight. My first point was to catch that line.

The enemy had not waited the coming up of the Yanks. His main body had retired towards his works, and the three commands, Cruft's, Ross's, and Smith's, with just enough resistance before them to keep their blood up, were pushing forward at a pace calling for energetic action if they were to be brought to a halt. That done, however, the three were closed on the centre; then, skirmishers being thrown to the front, we advanced slowly and cautiously.

It was not long until we came on the aftermath of General McClernand's morning struggle. Dead men, not all of them ours, were lying in their beds of blood-stained snow exactly as they had fallen. And the wounded were there also. These, fast as come upon, were given drink and covered with blankets, but left to be picked up later on; and there was no distinction shown between the blue and the gray. The wonder was to find any of them alive.

While following the line I saw a man sitting against a stump in a position natural as life. Besides the Confederate homespun of which his clothes were made, he sported a coon-skin cap with the tail of the animal for plume. His eyes were wide open and there was a broad grin on his face. I would have sworn the look and grin were at me, and, stopping, I spoke to an orderly.

"Find out what that fellow means by grinning that way. If he answers decently, help him."

The orderly dismounted and shook the man, then said, "Why he's dead, sir."

"That can't be. See where he's hit."

The cap when taken off brought away with it a mass that sickened us. A small bullet—from a revolver, probably—had gone through the inner corner of his eye leaving no visible wound, but the whole back of the head was blown off and the skull entirely emptied.

On a little farther we rode over the body of a Confederate lying on his back spread-eagle fashion. A gun clutched in his hand arrested me.

"Get that gun," I said, and one of my men jumped down for it.

It is in my study now, a handsomely mounted, muzzle-loading, old-style squirrel rifle. Sometimes I take it out to try at a mark, when, as a souvenir, it strikes me with one drawback—touching it is to revive the memory of its owner looking up at the sky from his sheet of crimson snow; and that he brought the piece to the field with him intending to kill Yankees as he was in the habit of killing long-tailed rodents does not always suffice to allay the shiver it excites.

It is to be remembered that, in common with my whole command, I was profoundly ignorant of the topography of the locality. That we were moving in the direction of the fort I knew rather as a surmise than a fact. The skirmishers kept up their fire; otherwise the silence impressed me as suspicious. Once I heard the report of a great gun in the distance, and shortly a shell of half-bushel proportions went with a locomotive's scream through the tree-tops; whereupon we knew ourselves in the line of fire from the gun-boats in the river. Disagreeable—yes, vastly so—but there was no help for it. Right after—indeed, as if the unearthly scream of the big shell had been an accepted signal—the holders of the fort awoke, and set their guns to work—how many I had no means of judging.

Through the woods then there sped a peculiar short-stop whistling; nor was there need of one of greater experience in battle to tell us that we were objects of search by cannister and possibly grape-shot. Fragments of the limbs above us rattled down, and occasionally—the thing of greatest impression upon me—a sharp resound, like the cracking of green timber in a zero night, rang through the woods; and that we also instinctively knew to be bullets of iron embedding themselves in some near-by tree-trunks.

Now, as I have no wish to take credit not strictly my due, the effect of this visitation startled me—the more so as it came in the nature of a surprise. I asked myself, however, "Where are we going?" And as the answer did not come readily, I made haste to order another halt.

It happened that my position at the moment was behind Cruft's brigade in what I took to be the road to Charlotte, also the object of anxious solicitude. Making way through the halted line, the situation revealed itself. There, not farther than three hundred yards, a low embankment stretched off on both sides, and behind it, in the background, rose an elaborate earthen pile which a drooping flag on a tall, white staff told me was Fort Donelson proper. Some field-pieces behind the low intrenchment were doing the firing, supported by men lying in the ditch. The heads of these bobbed up and down; and every time one of them bobbed up it was to let loose a streak of brilliant flame, with a keen report and a rising curl of smoke as close attendants. In front of the outwork far extending were our skirmishers behind stumps and logs, and in every depression affording cover, and they, too, were shooting. The interval of separation between the enemies ranged from eighty yards to a hundred and fifty.

The scene was stirring; but it must not be thought it held me long—far from it. While I looked, a sense of responsibility touched me with a distinct shock. What next?

Two things were possible; to continue on or go back out of range. The first meant an assault, and I doubted my authority to go so far. It seemed a step within the province of the commander. Perhaps he was not ready to order it. To be successful, moreover, there was need of support; otherwise the whole garrison could be concentrated against me. So, resolving the skirmishers as they were into a grand guard, Colonel Morgan L. Smith in charge, I retired the line five or six hundred yards.

There was nothing for us then but another night in bivouac without fires, and nothing to eat but crackers; literally suffering from the pinch of hunger added to misery from the pinch of cold. Yet I did not hear a murmur. This, I think, because there was not a soldier there so ignorant as not to know the necessity of keeping a tight grip upon our position.

With the advent of darkness the gun practice ceased, and later even the pickets quit annoying one another. Then silence, and a February night, with stars of pitiless serenity, and a wind not to be better described than as a marrow-searcher.

About one o'clock, having gone the rounds with Colonel Smith, I thought to make avail of the general calm by a visit to my tent, and a pull at the basket which, when last inspected, seemed good for a breakfast and a lunch at least. Besides that, having advised Cruft, Smith, and Ross (he of Illinois) of my intention to storm the outworks of the enemy at break of day, provided no order to the contrary reached me from General Grant, it would be convenient to stop and see how Thayer was getting along, and move him over during the night ready for the morning's work.

I set Thayer in course of preparation, leaving Ware, of my staff, to guide him to a position on the right of Colonel Cruft; then, with Ross and two orderlies, I pursued on. The tent stood solitary. Even the wagons were gone. I had expected a fire — and Johnson in charge. Drawing the door-flaps aside, I called the man. No answer. We went in. The box that had contained my bedding was empty. Blankets, pillows, mattress, all were gone. Match in hand, we looked with the eagerness of hunger, but uselessly. The basket was keeping the rest of the property company. What had happened? If General McClernand's soldiers still in the vicinity had looted the tent, they could not have made way with my servant. We called him unavailingly. Thereupon we tried him, and found him guilty. I will not repeat the language with which we burdened the pronunciation of our judgment. There being nothing else to do, we remounted and returned to the command. After that I fear we too frequently classified Ben Butler's intelligent contraband with princes, and applied the old moral.

The situation upon our return had in no respect changed. The same general hush prevailed. Behind their stacked muskets the thousands walked about, stamped, danced, threshed their bodies with their numbed hands, and kept the struggle with Jack Frost heroically going. If they were tired, hungry, cold, sleepy, so were we. Everybody watched the sky in the east, and had some Gheber of the kind sung by Tom Moore arisen and preached to us as became a fire-worshipper, there is no telling how many converts he might have made.

By-and-by Colonel Ross, of my staff, pulled my sleeve and whispered: "I have found a log back here big enough to break the wind. By crawling in behind it, and spooning, we may get a nap. I have scraped the snow away and spread a blanket on the ground."

"Where did you get the blanket?"

"Took it from my horse. Serve yours the same way, and we'll have cover."

I accepted the offer and the suggestion, and lying down with Ross behind the log actually slept. Waking, at length, my bedfellow was gone. He had slipped out and left me to what slumber I could snatch. Nor that only—he left me the blankets and his overcoat as well. I rubbed my eyes and, half awake, thought of the gulf of difference between a white gentleman and an ungrateful negro. To be sure, I was not long in overtaking my generous friend and restoring his property.

It was near day when Colonel Thayer's eight regiments began to arrive and take position one by one on Cruft's right in prolongation of the line. As this formative operation was in view of the enemy, I wondered at his silence. It looked as if the fight were out of him.

At length, the formation completed, we stood ready to rush the intrenchments. Only, why didn't the order come? At all events, the Confederate flag was yet flying over the fort faintly visible "in the dawn's early light."

"There—what's that?" said one of my party, in a surprised tone.

"Where?"

"There—coming over the breastwork."

Two men rode over the parapet. One of them carried a white flag on a pole, lance-fashion. Not caring to have my arrangement spied upon, I told Captain Kneffler to go ask what the flag wanted.

Kneffler, making haste, met the men before they reached the pickets. After a talk with them, he hurried back and reported.

"The bearer of the flag," he said, "is Major Rogers, of Mississippi.[1] He brings a request from General Buckner that you refrain from further hostilities, as he and General Grant have been in correspondence about a surrender, and they have reached an understanding. The major has a despatch for General Grant which he wants permission to deliver in person."

This was great news indeed—news to justify a display of excitement. The report, however, not being altogether satisfactory, I went out to sound the messenger further.

The introductions were stiffly ceremonious, in course of which it came out that the officer accompanying the flag-bearer was General———.[2]

[1] This is the name of the officer as given in my official report.

[2] Bushrod Johnson, according to present recollection.

"Do I understand, gentlemen, that the surrender is perfected?"

"I do not know if a formality will be required," the general replied. "With that exception it is a surrender."

"Are you ready to give possession?"

"Yes. The troops are drawn up in their quarters, arms stacked."

At this I felt a quick thrill, which, if the reader pleases, may be set down to a recognition of an opportunity and an irresistible impulse to get there first.

"Then it is now business?"

The general bowed.

I lost no time. To Ross I said, "Go with the major here to headquarters. Let him deliver his despatch to General Grant. Tell the general, also, that I am in possession of the fort and all belonging to it." Then to Kneffler: "Do you ride to the brigade commanders, and tell them to move the whole line forward, and take possession of persons and property. Tell them to see to it personally that their men are kept in close check—that I want the business done as delicately as possible. Not a word of taunt—no cheering."

The general looked at me gratefully; whereupon I asked him if he knew where General Buckner was quartered, and he replied, "I left him in the old tavern."

"Well, if you say so, I will ride to the tavern with you. General Buckner and I are personal friends. I have the highest respect for him, and it may be I can do him a good turn."

My new acquaintance borrowed the flag from his associate, telling him, "You won't need it." Then to me, "Our people are in a bad humor; but I will be glad to have you go with me."

In passing over the breastwork, I saw men lying in

the ditch dead and half buried in the snow, horrible objects to sight and thought. Here and there inside the intrenchment the garrison stood drawn up in regimental lines behind their muskets in stack. I noticed those we came upon closely. Many were wrapped in blankets of which no two were of the same hue, though butternut and gray were the prevailing colors of their wear. They were mostly a thin-visaged set, angular, tall, light-haired, whip-corded. One had only to look into their faces to know what extremes of hard usage they had been put to, and how much society in general owed to soap and water, combs and towels. I thought they really appeared two or three trifles worse than their enemies outside. They eyed me sullenly, and several times it crossed my mind that I was doing an imprudent thing.

We came to the tavern at length, a one-story affair seen more frequently in that day than in this. I found myself next in a shallow hall, and, stopping there, requested my friend to be good enough to give my name to General Buckner. He passed through a door at the farther end of the hall, and, returning presently, told me to walk in. He did not follow me.

General Buckner sat at the head of a table with officers, eight or ten in number, at the sides. He arose upon my entry, and met me in the centre of the room, grave, dignified, silent; the grip he gave me, however, was an assurance of welcome quite as good as words.

Turning then to the table, he said, waving his hand: "It is unnecessary to introduce you. You know them all."

I glanced at the gentlemen there, and one by one they came forward and gave me their hands. I had met every one of them two years before when General Buckner's guest at the encampment of the Kentucky State

Guard in Louisville. Their hand-shake was cordial, but they were not in talkative mood. I understood their feeling, and respected it. Two of them had won my regard especially—Major Casseday, Buckner's adjutant-general, and young Tom Clay.[1] The latter was last to come forward. He put his hand in mine, and, turning his face from me, cried like a child—and I could see nothing unmanly in his tears.

The general then inquired if I had been to breakfast, and having answered no, he said, "I'm afraid you are a little late, but we will see." He called a patronymic sounding of the cotton-field, whereat a negro thrust his head through the door.

"Another breakfast here," said the general. "What have you?"

"Nothin' 'cept cawn-bread, sir."

"No bacon?"

"You'se done had it all down to de rine."

"Coffee?"

"Oh, a little water 'll resto' de coffee."

"Bring it then."

I had interrupted the party in the midst of their morning meal, and we ate—and there was no apology for the commissariat. But none the less I decided in my own mind that the surrender had not been any too soon.

The talk became general—about the war, more particularly incidents of the battle. It amused me to observe how honest they were in the belief that we had fifty thousand men with more in hourly arrival. As the idea helped soften the pangs of defeat, I did not disabuse them of it.

Once I said something to General Buckner about the

[1] He was the grandson of Henry Clay, the grand old man of his day and generation.

old flag—I think it was in an expression of wonder that his congress gave it up for a new one.

He brought his hand down on the table. "The old flag! I followed it when most of your thousands out yonder were in swaddling clothes—in Mexico—on the frontier—and I love it yet."

The speech was not meant for retort.

He asked me, afterwhile, "What will General Grant do with us?"

This question was of graver moment then than ever again, and I answered to the best of my light: "I can't say. But I know General Grant, and I know President Lincoln better than General Grant, and I am free to say that it is not in the nature of either of them to treat you, or these gentlemen, or the soldiers you have surrendered, other than as prisoners of war."

"Well," he said, "I thought as much. The only favor I have to ask is that I may not be separated from my friends here."

"May I say as much to General Grant when he comes in?"

"Yes—certainly."

In the midst of this conversation there happened an incident in every sense strange. We heard a knock at the door of entrance, and to the acknowledgment "Come in," an officer entered clad in blue, with gold lace on his cap and sleeves. Advancing towards the table, he observed me and stopped in evident embarrassment. Then bowing—none of us could tell to whom—he took off his cap, bowed again, and said, "I beg to be excused, gentlemen." With that he walked out. General Buckner looked at me, and asked, "Do you know him?"

"Never saw the man before," I replied.

"He's of your navy—so much is certain," the general said; adding to one of his men at the table, "You had better follow him, captain, and see that no harm comes to him."

The captain hastened out.

Now the sequel gives the incident its character, making it so extraordinary that I choose to insert it as of the text rather than a note.

About two years after the surrender at Donelson a uniformed gentleman came to see me at my headquarters in Baltimore. He introduced himself with a card.

"I am Lieutenant Dove, of the United States navy," he proceeded to say. "You may remember an officer of the navy entering the dining-room of the old tavern in Dover the morning of the surrender of Fort Donelson."

"Yes, I remember. We were at breakfast."

"I am that officer, and ever since that morning I have been in suspension?"

"What for?" I asked.

"At sight of the flag lowering on the fort, Captain Walker, of the *Carondelet*, ordered me to land and secure the surrender to the navy—that is, to him. I reached headquarters, and was about to make the demand when I saw you, and, inferring your rank from your shoulder-straps, I judged myself too late, and retired, not wishing to have a scene. In that you have my offence."

"I see. I was in your way."

"You were there before me. But you can now do me the greatest possible favor."

"What can I do for you?"

"State the facts—that you saw me enter the room that morning—that you were there before me. Such a statement filed with the department will bring me release from suspension. Restoration to duty must follow."

Of course I gave the poor fellow the statement he asked, and it had the effect anticipated. Probably no better example of the keenness of professional rivalry ever offered itself.

Returning to my narrative—my division advanced promptly as ordered, and took general possession of town, fort, prisoners, and property. An hour and a half elapsed, and I was still with General Buckner, when General Grant was announced as in the public room of the tavern. Joining him there, I presented General Buckner's request not to be separated from his staff-officers. General Grant very promptly replied that what was to be done with the prisoners, and where they were to be taken, were questions to be decided by the president; yet he thought General Buckner's wish reasonable and natural; by which I understood he would use his influence to have it gratified, and I so informed General Buckner.

Somewhere towards noon it came out that a programme of entry by the army into the fallen fort had been arranged, in which, by way of special honor, the right of the procession had been accorded General Charles F. Smith and his division.

I never saw the order, and cannot say what mention of the third division it contained, if any. Place in the procession, however, could not have been given it as at the time of the grand entry it was too busy—that is, such of them as were not in the cordon around the prisoners, and guarding the property taken, were doing their best to restore "the inner man" by feeding it with things warm and solid. As for myself, had the question of precedence in honor been referred to me, it should have been settled exactly as it was settled; for nothing of gallantry in the whole war surpassed General Charles F. Smith's charge upon the enemy's works in support of the recovery of McClernand's lost position on the right.

Thirteen thousand prisoners taken, possession of the Cumberland River acquired, making Nashville untenable by General Albert Sidney Johnston, and the military prestige of the South shattered beyond repair, were the results, material and moral, of the fall of Fort Donelson.

L

The return to Fort Henry—A new command of twelve regiments—Captain Hillyer—The report—Coldness at Grant's headquarters—The Third Division—The sword from Crawfordsville.

FORT DONELSON fell to us in the morning of February 16, 1862. That same day, in the afternoon, an order came to me as follows: "To secure the glorious victory acquired by our arms, and to perpetuate it, the general commanding deems it highly important that the utmost vigilance should be observed to guard all points captured. It is ordered, therefore, that General L. Wallace return to Fort Henry, Tennessee, with two brigades of his command, and Willard's and Bulliss's batteries. Curtis's Horse is attached to the command of General Wallace."

I was as glad to get back to Fort Henry as I had been at being ordered to Fort Donelson. This, not merely because of general need of rest and recuperation, but also to escape the confusion and disorder that struck the new conquest almost irrepressibly. To the undisciplined the demoralization of a victory is but a little less than that of a defeat.

In forming my column of return, Colonel Morgan L. Smith, with the Eighth Missouri and the Eleventh Indiana, had fallen in. I had doubts of the propriety of the thing, but they were as anxious to stay with me as I was to have them, and, to say truth, it was not in my heart to order them out. Next day, however, while the regiments were making themselves at home in the dismantled fortress on the Tennessee, there came a peremptory order to send both them back to General Charles F. Smith, *their rightful owner*. The intimation was of a new kind of larceny, and that I had been guilty of it. Return took place promptly, with an apology.

In comfortable quarters on the steamboat once more, I wrote and forwarded a report of the part my division had borne in the capture of Fort Donelson. Then there happened a circumstance trifling in itself, but of great influence on my subsequent life in the army. Indeed, I still think it the origin of a trouble that was to go with me through life.

One morning within the week after the report had been sent to headquarters, Captain W. S. Hillyer, aide to General Grant, appeared on my boat, having ridden over from Donelson. After some general conversation, he drew a document from his pocket, saying:

"Here is your report of the Donelson affair. On reading it, I saw you had omitted mention of a point of importance which I doubt not you will see the propriety of inserting."

As the captain was the identical person who had sent me the note declaring I had saved the day on the right at Donelson, I very naturally saw a friend in him, and took the report, remarking: "Certainly, captain. What is it?"

"You omitted to mention that you had seen Captain Lagow (associate aide) and myself delivering orders during the fight."

It is to be said now, in justice to my insight, sharpened by years of practice in the courts, that I saw the importance of complying with the request, since the two aides had the ear of the commanding general night and day. To be perfectly frank, I not only saw the importance of obliging Captain Hillyer, but became anxious to oblige him. Unhappily, I had not seen him or Captain Lagow at any time during the fight, much less delivering orders.

The dilemma can be instantly seen. Either I must tell an official lie or make two powerful enemies at headquarters.

"Captain," I said, "leave the report with me, and come back an hour hence."

Thereupon I called in the officers of my staff, and asked each one of them if he had seen the captains or either of them at any time during the action. They all answered no.

Then, in my anxiety, I did an unprecedented thing. I called in my orderlies, and put the same question to them. They, too, answered no.

When Captain Hillyer returned my mind was made up.

"Here is the report," I said. "It is not changed. The fact is I did not see you or Lagow during the battle, as you seem to think. Sorry not to be able to oblige you. Please return the paper to the files. Now, won't you stay and take dinner with me?"

He declined and disappeared.

Not long then until, on going to headquarters, I was forced to take notice of a winter that had fallen upon the occupants there—a kind of interior winter peculiar in that it reserved its frost and ice for me. Still, General Grant's demeanor continued friendly, and, relying upon it, I gave myself no concern, except to do promptly and as best I could all required of me in the way of duty. Afterwhile, however, the winter reached him—but of that when its turn comes.

In proof of General Grant's friendliness to me shortly after the capture of Fort Donelson, there are evidences which it would be pleasant to have noted and read.

LEW WALLACE,
Major-General United States Volunteers (1862)

Thus, in his official report of that success, there is the following mention, which I copy verbatim: "To division commanders, however, Generals McClernand, Smith, and Wallace, I must do the justice to say that each of them were with their commands in the midst of danger, and were always ready to execute all orders, no matter what the exposure to themselves." [1]

A few days after affairs at Donelson had quieted down a reorganization of the army took place. This by a carefully considered order dated February 21st, from which I take the liberty of quoting a paragraph:

> "Third Division, Brigadier-General L. Wallace commanding:
>
> "First Brigade: Eighth Missouri, Eleventh, Twenty-fourth, and Fifty-second Indiana Infantry, and Bulliss's battery.
>
> "Second Brigade: First Nebraska and Fifty-eighth, Sixty-eighth, and Seventy-eighth Ohio Infantry, and four companies of Curtis's Horse.
>
> "Third Brigade: Twentieth, Fifty-sixth, and Seventy-sixth Ohio and Twenty-third Indiana Infantry, and the remainder of Curtis's Horse." [2]

From a brigade of three regiments infantry to a division of twelve regiments! Yet, as I am making confession, it might as well be thorough—my greatest personal satisfaction was due to discovery of the fact that in the confusion and feverish excitement of real battle I could think. I do not expect this discovery at first to make the impression on the reader it did on me; but if he will

[1] *Rebellion Records*, series 1, vol. vii., p. 160. The grammatical error in the extract must be that of somebody else than General Grant. Papers of his own writing are remarkably free from such faults.

[2] This paragraph of the order is also given verbatim.—*Rebellion Records*, series 1, vol. vii., pp., 469–650.

reflect a moment, the fulness of my meaning will probably dawn upon him.

The above is only an extract. The order from which it is taken, No. 6 of the series of Fort Donelson General Orders, is worthy remembrance as creative of the Army of the Tennessee, an organization unexcelled, if importance of service to the Cause and the gallantry and devotion of its members are considered. That is to say, General Order No. 6 divided the army assembled at Fort Donelson into divisions as follows:

First Division, Brigadier-General John A. McClernand commanding.

Second Division, Brigadier-General Charles F. Smith commanding.

Third Division, Brigadier-General Lewis Wallace commanding.

Fourth Division, Brigadier-General Stephen A. Hurlbut commanding.

Another division, Brigadier-General William T. Sherman's, came later, and then it assumed designation as the First, exactly why I do not know.

A few days afterwards the newspapers announced that McClernand, Charles F. Smith, and I were to be promoted major-generals. In so far as the news concerned me, I gave it no attention; in fact, I did not believe it. To be sure, Donelson had been an affair of complication and trial, and it had given me a degree of confidence in myself; still, I remembered the shrinking and shivering with which the promotion to the brigadiership had been attended. I remembered, also, that "Major-General" was the highest rank in the American army as the law then stood, lifting its attainment to a height beyond my ambition.

I was still at Fort Henry when an expressman entered my headquarters one day, and on my table laid a box done up in heavy ducking and tagged to me. The man delivered a sealed envelope also addressed to me, and, opening it, I found a key and a letter. The letter was from a committee at home, informing me that at a public meeting of my fellow-citizens in Crawfordsville, it had been resolved to present me a sword. The inscription on the scabbard, they said, would furnish a full explanation. There, on opening the case, in a bed of silk-plush and covered with chamois, lay the sword, handle and scabbard all a-glitter. One had only to look at it to know it was intended for occasions of highest ceremony. I sought the inscription before drawing the blade, and it read, "Presented to Brigadier-General Lew Wallace by his fellow-citizens of Montgomery County in recognition of his gallantry at Fort Donelson." The beautiful gift was, of course, gratefully accepted. It is now in the panelled recess over the mantel in my study, along with other relics of my military service — swords, pistols, stirrups, bridle-bits, spurs, and flags.

LEW WALLACE

LI

New opportunities for Grant—General Albert S. Johnston—Grant made a major-general but removed by Halleck—The advance—Smith in command—Arrival at Savannah, Tennessee—Smith's accident and death—Movement to Crump's Landing.

THAT General Grant caught instant sight of the golden opportunities now open to him, and that he as instantly set out to make the most of them, cannot be denied. From Donelson he hurried to Nashville, intending at least to help in securing that city, leaving General Smith, with his division, to occupy temporarily the fortified places on the Cumberland; at the same time steamboats began arriving at Fort Henry in numbers to leave no doubt of a campaign in quick design up the Tennessee. All this was educational to me, and I watched it with intensest interest.

By-and-by it appeared that, on the fall of Donelson, General Albert Sidney Johnston, having nothing else to do, made speed to get out of Nashville with all that remained to him. He was next heard of at Murfreesboro. Then Generals Buell and Grant met in the abandoned city; and as the former took possession, the latter dropped back to Fort Henry, bringing Smith with him.

At Fort Henry, General Grant found he had been made major-general, and that his command, under the name of District of West Tennessee, had been extended to take in territory from Cairo to the State of Mississippi, the region between the Mississippi River and the Cumberland included. Then, it having been given out confidentially that his "headquarters were to be in the field," we knew whither we were bound, and made ready for departure.

About March 1st, in the midst of the bustle of preparation, a bruit sped through the camp of such amazing import that everybody stopped everybody else to ask:

"Have you heard the news?"

"What?"

"Grant's removed."

"Oh, that can't be!"

"But *they* say it's so."

"What's he removed for?"

"Nobody knows."

"Who did it?"

"Nobody knows that, either."

And because nobody did know, the circumstance took on an increase of mystery, and drew sympathizers in crowds to the landing in front of the general's steamboat. This continued until it became of notoriety that General Charles F. Smith had been chosen successor in command. The quieting down which then ensued was not from any failure of sympathy for General Grant; it was due rather to a restoration of confidence in the management and outcome of the enterprise about to be undertaken.[1]

[1] We now know that General Grant was suspended from command by General Halleck, and that to get backing for the step he telegraphed General McClellan, under date of March 3, 1862: "I have had no communication with General Grant for more than a week. He left his command without any authority, and went to Nashville. . . . It is hard to censure a successful general immediately after a victory, but I think he richly deserves it. I can get no returns, no reports, no information of any kind from him. Satisfied with his victory, he sits down and enjoys it without regard to the future. I am worn out and tired with his neglect and in-

The day of departure at length came round. I can give but a faint idea of the spectacle of the embarkation. One must think of thirty thousand uniformed men in array on the river-bank, drums going, arms glistening, and nearly seventy steamboats with smoking funnels at anchor ready to haul in and take their assignments aboard. He must think, too, of the excitement that prevailed, of the cheering, and braying of bands, and the waving of flags; for this, it is to be remembered, was a victorious army that knew its strength and rejoiced in it.

The divisions marched aboard according to their numbers; and it happened that General Sherman led the movement. He had come up from Paducah with a division drawn in great part from General Nelson, of Buell's army; yet there was no jealousy of him—it was too early in the war for jealousy. And when the procession was formed and all in motion, the Tennessee River, always beautiful, was never more so.

I can see the boats now crowded below and above with their precious humanity; I can see them now in graceful onward sweep, some in dangerous tilt, churn-

efficiency. C. F. Smith is almost the only officer equal to the emergency." —*Rebellion Records*, series 1, vol. vii., pp. 279, 280.

To which McClellan replied: "Do not hesitate to arrest him (Grant) at once if good of the service requires it, and place C. F. Smith in command. You are at liberty to regard this as a positive order, if it will smooth the way."—*Ibid.*, 680.

Then, under date of March 4th, General Halleck further reported to General McClellan: "A rumor has just reached me that since the taking of Fort Donelson General Grant has resumed his former bad habits. . . . I do not deem it advisable to arrest him at present, but have placed General Smith in command of the expedition up the Tennessee. I think Smith will restore order and discipline." —*Ibid.*, 682.

General Halleck took all these bitter things back (*Ibid.*, 683), and restored General Grant to command—that is, it took him about ten days to hear from the army and the American people.

ing the sparkling flood with their huge wheels, and loading the scurrying winds and pearl-blue sky with clouds of sulphurous smoke, yet gay with flower-like colors of streaming flags. I can hear the hoarse coughing of the pipes, the cheering, the music, and the boisterous echoes hurtled back upon us from rocky bluff and wooded shore. And in thought of it all I would grow young again, but for the other thought always waylaying the first—I cannot hope ever to see the like again, much less to be a part of it.

My quarters were on the *John J. Roe,* a lumbering boat of huge proportions, and crowded; and while the day lingered I kept to the pilot-house anxious lest something of the heroic going should slip me. The unarmored *Tyler* and *Lexington* had preceded us by two or three days, and explored the banks and bends; so there was little danger from the enemy. My feeling all the time was that there should be somebody somewhere on the shores to enjoy the wonderful spectacle we were offering—somebody to look at us if not signal a friendly welcome. But no. The houses and cabins here and there were in their accustomed places, and the landings were as of yore, and the dingy towns reminded us of society and trade and peace; but as a rule desertion was over them all; and if now and then a hat was waved or a handkerchief shaken out in cheer, something in the environment always showed itself to whisper of the war as a recognized condition.

We arrived finally at Savannah, on the right bank of the river, the shire town of Hardin County, Tennessee. There were steamboats in multitude tied to the shores, some empty, others still loaded. On a bluff arose the mansion of a gentleman named Cherry, and over it floated a Union flag. A skiff put out, and, meeting me, directed that all the vessels of my division find berths on the side opposite the town, and tie up there, keeping the men aboard. The house with the flag on it General Smith occupied as headquarters.

In the evening, just after sundown, General Smith came over in a yawl, and walked into my cabin unannounced and unattended. He interrupted my expressions of surprise.

"I am on business," he said. "Are you alone?"

We soon had the cabin.

"Now, have you a map?"

I brought him one, and, unfolding it, he continued: "Down in Paducah, you may remember, I once told you of Corinth as a place of strategic importance. Well, I think we are going there now just as quick as we can dispose of a couple of preliminaries. There are not more than ten thousand Confederates keeping it. Give me your attention."

"I am following you," I said.

"One of the preliminaries is to cut the railroad connecting Corinth and Columbus on the north; the other is to cut the railroad from Corinth to Decatur and Chattanooga on the east. This last I have given to Sherman; the first is to be yours, and for that you are to go on up to Crump's Landing, four miles above Savannah, from which there is a road, said to be good, leading to Purdy."

Bending over the map, he traced the road with his finger.

"You understand? Very well. Now, how to do the thing. I might have sent you an order, and left you to your own devices, but knowing it a business new to you, I have come over to try and help you with suggestions."

He heard my thanks, and must have seen a voucher for their sincerity in my face, for he continued at length, and carefully. The substance of the instruction was that I should use my cavalry to do the work of disablement, sending it ahead for the purpose. To support the cavalry, and give it something to rally on in case of trouble, I was to keep at convenient distance with my infantry. At the end he told me of General Cheatham, at Pittsburg Landing, six miles by land above Crump's, with a force reported in excess of my division.

"But here," I remember him saying, "see this creek—Snake Creek. It is out of its banks, and Cheatham on the other side with but one bridge by which he can possibly get at you—and that"—he looked at me with a twinkle in his eye—"is called Wallace's Bridge.[1] You must keep it well watched.

I accompanied him, when he had finished the lesson, down to the guard of my boat. There he gave me his hand with a friendly good-night, and stooped to get into the yawl drawn up to receive him. It was then dark. In a moment he lost balance and fell forward, raking the sharp edge of a seat, and skinning one of his shins from the ankle to the knee—a frightful hurt. One of the boatmen raised him up. I urged him to stay the night with me, my surgeon being at hand. Clinching his teeth against the pain, he half groaned:

"No—too much business."

And as they rowed him away out of the darkness he sent me "Good-night." I was never to see him again. Returning to the Cherry house, he took to his bed and, lingering, died.

I must be permitted a farewell to General Charles F. Smith. He made no pretensions to civil attainments of any kind; it is my belief, however, that a reputation

[1] Whence the name, and how derived, I have never learned. It borrowed nothing from me.

like Thomas's, and an esteem indistinguishable from glory, like Sherman's, had been his could he have lived to the end of the war. And descending to particulars, could he have marched against Corinth immediately after the assemblage of the army at Savannah, the order for which I know he felt sure of receiving, there had been no battle of Shiloh with its lights and shades, nor would Pittsburg Landing have a place in history except as the base of a successful military operation.

I went to him a stranger without recommendation, an unknown volunteer, and he waived such prejudices as he may have had against officers of my class, and admitted me to his confidence. Why, I cannot conjecture, unless for a reason like that of the master-workman who sees a possibility of achievement in a piece of undressed wood or in a primitive block of stone. Then, when I think of his last kindness to me, coming in person to show me how to make the most of an opportunity given, is it strange if I become instantly conscious of a place of tears in my heart? And that whatever else forty years may have taken from me physically, or in the way of preception, I am grateful that they have left me able still to see an ideal friend in my ideal soldier, and venerate the hero even as I loved the man.

The scheme of my commander was clear to me. It was to let drive with all force against Corinth before General Albert Sidney Johnston could collect an army strong enough for resistance;[1] and at hampering General Johnston, and isolating the town, my enterprise and that of General Sherman's were aimed. In other words, I saw he meant me to hurry. So he had scarcely reached the opposite side of the river before the chiefs

[1] If he had not orders to this effect, I am satisfied he expected them.

of my brigade were in receipt of directions and their boats under way.

It is not my intention to enter into the details of what happened to me and my command in doing this bit of work. Suffice it that I secured possession of Crump's Landing in the night, after a trifling skirmish, and, moving the division out from it, succeeded—thanks to Major Charles S. Hayes and his battalion of the Fifth Ohio Cavalry, not to speak of the instructions received from General Smith—in seriously crippling the Mobile & Ohio Railroad north of Corinth.[1] General Cheatham, instead of interfering with me, retired from Pittsburg Landing after destroying Wallace's Bridge over Snake Creek down by the river. General Sherman proved less fortunate in his undertaking.

At Crump's Landing I received an order directing me to take post there.

[1] *Rebellion Records*, series 1, vol. x., pp. 8, 9, 10, 11.

LII

The topography of the Snake Creek region—Bell and Carpenter—A choice of roads—The bridges—Johnston's advance—The messenger to Grant—Grant in Savannah, Tennessee.

THE ground back of Crump's Landing—or Crump's, as we soon came to speak of it—was high, open, easily drained, and defensible. After establishing the brigades in camps, I had my own tent pitched on a point overlooking the landing, the road to it, and a wide range of the river up and down.[1] I was then in condition to study the situation, and all that it required of me.

The need most pressing was knowledge of the country. Fortunately, there were Union people willing to give me that, so, with their assistance, I made a diagram, an unartistic breast-pocket affair, very serviceable, however, and so frequently consulted at the time that it is easily reproduced now. I venture to recommend it to such as care to follow me in what is to come.

Now, if one looks at the diagram, it must become obvious that at Crump's my relations with the main army were dependent upon the two bridges over Snake Creek, Wallace's, down near the river, and the other up several miles above Wallace's. These I had inspected very early by Major Hayes, of the cavalry, and he reported both of them dismantled and impassable. The creek itself he described as a sheet of dead backwater, its shores a bog of unknown depth. In short, communica-

[1] A tablet has been erected to show the site of the tents at the Landing.

tion with the main army then on the south side of Snake Creek was closed, except by boat on the river.

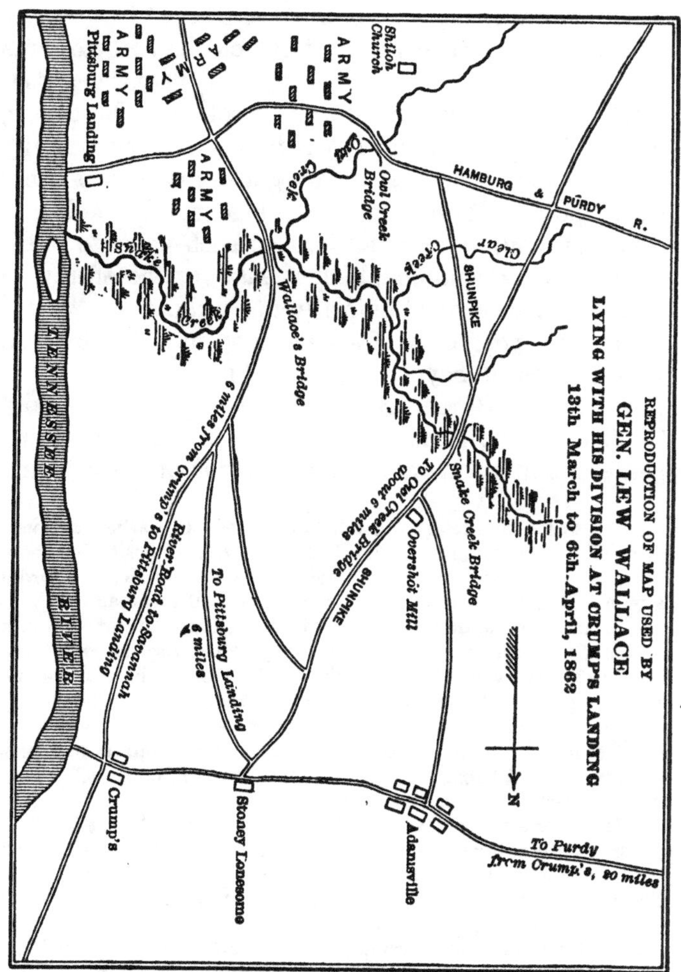

It occurred to me then, suppose Crump's attacked by a superior force, I could not join the main army, the natural thing to do; neither could it support me by land. Practically, this was isolation; and once more I found myself thrown upon my own resources. All that could be required of one commanding an independent army in face of an enemy was required of me.

A troop of cavalry was sent out on the road towards Purdy, west of Crump's, to ascertain if there was a Confederate force anywhere in that direction. The troops, mere sabre-goers, were waylaid in a narrow pass by bushwhackers armed with shot-guns, and driven back; whereupon I argued that the bridge on the Mobile & Ohio Railroad, which I had been at such pains to break up, was in use again, making it easy for the enemy to direct an attack on Crump's from Purdy.

The bare possibility of such a happening required me to keep posted beyond my own lines. So I selected three scouts, Horace Bell,[1] a citizen of Indiana, and Carpenter[2] and Sanders, enlisted men. Bell and Carpenter I sent to operate in the direction of Corinth, and

[1] Bell was a character. Just before the war his father had been in a jail at Portsmouth, a suburb of Louisville, opposite Jeffersonville, charged with aiding in the escape of a slave. Horace, hardly a man at the time, crossed the Ohio River, and in broad daylight, axe in hand, broke down the door, took the old man out, and in a skiff under pistol-fire brought him safely to the Indiana side. His hatred of slavery and slave-holding had deepened into a passion. It was reported while in my employment that he was a double spy —for me and for the enemy. He certainly had *entrée* at Corinth. I taxed him with the charge one day, but he laughed, and said: "Don't be afraid. God helping me, I can't forget where home is." That he dealt fairly with me I have always believed.

[2] Carpenter's method was also peculiar. Hiding during the day, he fared forth at night, and filled his budget of news from the kitchens of the houses in the vicinity, having first ingratiated himself with the colored servants. The gossip with which he spiced his reports was often amusing even when not important. In telling me of soldiers thus heard of he would say, with earnestness, "Now divide that by two, for you see, with darkeys the gun is always *one* and the man carrying it *two*."

Sanders out towards Purdy; and thereafter nothing in force, not even a squad of bush-rangers, moved between Corinth and Pittsburg Landing or between Purdy and Crump's that I did not hear of it in good time.

Then I took another step. General Grant had been released from the suspension devised for him by General Halleck, and, coming up to Savannah, relieved General Smith, fixing his headquarters in the Cherry house instead of with the army at Pittsburg Landing—a circumstance which convinced me that the idea of making haste to Corinth had been abandoned. This disquieted me. I regretted the opportunity going, if not gone.

No less discomforting was the news brought me by Bell of what was doing in Corinth. General Albert Sidney Johnston, he said, was massing a great army there. Generals Hardee, Polk, and Breckinridge, with their commands, were already on the ground, while General Bragg, of Buena Vista renown, had a heavy contingent hurrying up from Florida. Trains on all the roads were in hum, shuttle-like, night and day. In short, the general appearances were that while we were in check waiting—for what, I could not see—the enemy was getting nearer a good ready every day, and might be looked for to beat us up. And then, what if he should conclude to let drive at me? This idea sat up with me, so to speak, spoiling my rest, until at length I resolved to get out of my isolation and its discomfort by remaking a road so that the main army could get to me—or, the emergency governing, I to it.

But which road—there being two, one to Pittsburg Landing, the other to the camp of the First Division (Sherman's) already known as "the right of the army"—should I take in hand? It seemed logical that the going or the coming would be to or from the front rather than to Pittsburg Landing, the base. And why not say right here; it never entered my head that a force from Corinth meaning battle, and large enough, could close in upon our divisions south of Snake Creek without full knowledge of it at headquarters.

So, having to choose one of the two roads mentioned, I consulted my *vade mecum*—with permission, it shall be hereafter called *map*—and noticed the thoroughfare from Stoney Lonesome southward, and that it forked a little way out, one branch going to Pittsburg Landing by Wallace's Bridge, while the other, known as the Shunpike, led off towards the right of the army. The first branch ran northeastwardly, the second southeastwardly, and whether one wanted to get to Pittsburg Landing or to the right of the army, he would have to ride about six miles—that is, both the thither terminals were approximately equidistant. Such being the case, I decided to restore the Shunpike and its connections, and intrusted the work to Major Hayes, of the Fifth Ohio Cavalry. More specifically, his orders were by corduroying and rebridging to put the road clear to the right of the army in condition to send or bring a battery over it on the run. Then as Major Hayes and his working parties needed caring for, I moved the Second Brigade (Thayer's) out to Stoney Lonesome, and, to keep the road secure after its reconstruction, I sent the Third Brigade (Colonel Wood's) into camp at Adamsville; Stoney Lonesome being two and a half miles from Crump's, and Adamsville five miles.

Under the restoration of the Shunpike, moreover, lay a bit of strategy which I nursed hopefully. That is, if the enemy succeeded in driving my brigades back to Crump's, the exposure of his flank and rear must be fatal to him, provided the body sent to my assistance by the newly bridged route came promptly and in sufficient strength. This one look at the map will demonstrate. Indeed, I had a feeling that with the road repaired my command would not be molested.

Somewhere in the last week of March, Major Hayes reported the work done; and to be certain of it, I rode with him and one of his companies from Stoney Lonesome to Pittsburg Landing, and back again. The sloughs along the way I found well corduroyed, while the bridges over Snake Creek and the two lesser streams beyond it were really substantial enough to have answered every purpose, commercial as well as military. Hayes's men had even made the bridge over Owl Creek passable. I remember this the more distinctly because of a very decided opinion that Owl Creek, and the bridge over it, and their keeping, all within easy cannon-shot of General Sherman's right brigade, were within his zone of care, not mine. Nor is it yet out of my recollection that while at Pittsburg Landing that day, in company with Colonel A. H. Markland, the very successful postal-agent for the army, I called on General Grant, who happened to be up from Savannah, and reported the opening of the Shunpike and the disposition of my brigades. Returning to Crump's, I slept soundly, for in accounting with my sense of responsibility there was an immense relief in the consciousness that my command was no longer isolated. It gave me confidence also to know everything ready as could be did the enemy make up his mind to engage in a tilt with me at Crump's.

At Crump's also, in the same last week of March, the commission of major-general reached me; but so absorbed was I in the conditions, and in struggling to get ready for the trial so manifestly right at hand, that after qualifying I dropped the precious sheepskin into my mess-chest, thinking, however:

"It's the last round. I can't get higher."

For under the law as it then existed "major-general" was the ultimate of high rank, corps being still unknown in our military organization. As I was in my thirty-fifth year, the youngest of the grade in the service, I now often look back wondering where I got the confidence that possessed me; and sometimes there steals into the reflection a vague suspicion that the thing called courage, if a quality at all, is chiefly compounded of inexperience and ignorance. Nevertheless, the promotion had its initiative in General Grant's recommendation, not in any striving of mine, and in that view it was doubtless easy to convince myself that he must have seen some probabilities of promise in the raw material. At all events, I was very sincerely grateful to him.

An incident occurred about the same time which, though inconsequential, gave me great satisfaction. A courier from Adamsville brought notice of a threatened attack upon the Third Brigade in station there. Smith's brigade set out from Crump's in a time incredibly short, and Thayer's, warned to be ready, fell into column as the First sped by it. The distance was double-quicked with but three short rests, and before midnight the whole division was in place for battle. With the rising of the sun the enemy disappeared, leaving us to return at leisure. The promptness, the zeal, the endurance, and anxiety of the men were inspiring, and thereafter the great coming event seemed slow. I could have trodden on its heels to hurry it.

It turned out, however, that the event needed no urging.

April, milder than in the North, ushered itself in. There were showers, with spells of sunshine, and the river at the foot of my bluff began to show signs of recession. About as the sun set, Thursday, the 4th,

Bell, the scout, came into my tent, evidently the worse of a hard ride, and said, abruptly, "I bring you news, sir."

"Well, what?"

"I picked up some prisoners coming in, and turned them over to the provost."

"Oh! Is that all?"

"No," he answered. "The whole rebel army is on the way up from Corinth."

"How is that?" I asked, rising.

"It's so, sir. They set out this morning early. By this time they are all on the road."

"The whole of them, you say, batteries and all?"

"Batteries and all."

I felt a sensation to the roots of my hair.

"How strong are they?"

"By my calculation, sir, fifty thousand, at least. They are in four corps—Hardee's, Bragg's, Polk's, and Breckinridge's—Hardee has the advance, Breckinridge brings up the rear."

The tent grew confining. I walked out, he after me.

"Where is General Johnston?"

"He is with them, chief man."

"Whom do you think they have in eye?"

"They are pointed towards Pittsburg Landing."

"And not here?"

"No—Pittsburg Landing. I rode part of the way with some friends in Hardee's corps."

"And they may be looked for—when?"

"One of the bridges of the main road is down, and in places the corduroy is afloat. They can't, with all they have to carry, make the distance before to-morrow in the night."

I went into a cross-examination, and, though Bell met me squarely, I somehow could not bring myself to give him perfect credence. General Johnston, by his account, was ready sooner than I thought. In the midst of my questions, my other scout, Carpenter, rode up to the tent. Dusk was then settling down, spreading its film over the section of the world we were occupying. The man seemed excited.

"Good-evening, Carpenter. What do you bring?" I asked.

He glanced at Bell, and answered, "I suppose you have heard all I have to tell—and more, too."

"Out with it."

"Well, Johnston's cut loose and is making for Pittsburg."

"How do you know?"

"A company of cavalry camped in front of old Mrs. ——— last night, and the officers took supper at the house, and gave it out that the army was to break camp to-day. I laid low to see, and if one man passed my hiding-place since morning thousands were with him—men afoot, men on horses, men on gun-carriages even."

I looked at Bell, and Bell looked back at me, and he said, "Yes, you see, sir."

Then telling them to go to their quarters, I went into my tent, and commenced a note to General Grant setting forth the substance of what the two scouts had brought me. While writing, I heard angry voices outside, and, going to the door, saw Bell and Carpenter face to face, pistols in hand. They were desperate men, and unflinching. I got to them, nevertheless, in time to separate them. What they quarrelled about I never learned.

The note to General Grant I finished by candle-light, and then called for Simpson, the orderly.[1]

[1] I mention Simpson in my report of the battle of Shiloh, and, later, had him commissioned second lieutenant regular army.

"Here," I said, giving him the sealed despatch, "I want this put into General Grant's hand. His boat has not gone down to Savannah yet, and he may stay the night at Pittsburg Landing. Anyhow, get your horse, and take it."

"And if the general should be gone when I get there?"

"Then give it to the postmaster at the Landing [1] to deliver to General Grant first thing in the morning. Tell the postmaster the despatch is from me, reporting news of the enemy, and that it must be delivered without fail."

Simpson was a regular of Company I, Fourth United States Dragoons, and in his third enlistment. There was no better horseman nor braver man. He was my favorite orderly.

"What road shall I take?" he asked.

Then it occurred to me.

"Try Wallace's Bridge. The river is going down; maybe the bridge is passable. Try it anyhow. We may need to know."

As he went out, I inquired if he wanted company. He replied, "No, sir."

Near two o'clock in the morning Simpson returned and reported. He had crossed Wallace's Bridge, he said, but with some trouble getting to it. Somebody had relaid the plank. The backwater covering the approaches was still belly-deep to his horse. Infantry could go through it, but not artillery.

"What about the despatch?"

"General Grant had gone down to Savannah when I got to the Landing, and I woke up the postmaster, and gave the despatch to him, with the directions you gave me. I put it into his own hand, sir."

[1] This official was an army postmaster then recently established in the log-house at the Landing.

This affair has recurred to me often. Sometimes I think the report should have been forwarded by an officer of my staff specially; and I would have taken that course with it—for I thought of doing so at the time—only I feared being considered pretentious. The lesson had from General McClernand in the council of war at Fort Henry was yet in my mind; it was that few things are so offensive as over-officiousness in a subordinate. Besides that, what right had I to suppose General Grant was not on the watch, with more facilities at his command than belonged to me? What an implication, moreover, that he did not know his enemy was coming upon him? Still, were the thing to be done over, I am free to say I should communicate the news to headquarters promptly either in person or by an officer. As it is, whatever my belief may be, founded upon the statement of my orderly, I do not *know*, and therefore cannot say, General Grant ever got the despatch. In view of subsequent events, it is but justice to allow him the benefit of the doubt.

As for myself, I believed Bell, corroborated as he was by Carpenter, and lost no time in communicating the intelligence to my brigade commanders. And more—I directed Major Hayes next day to have the Shunpike patrolled as far as Owl Creek, letting me know instantly as possible of interruption. He was further ordered to have report sent to me at Crump's every hour, day and night. And he did so faithfully, I think, up to Sunday, April 6th.

LIII

The ride to Stoney Lonesome—Whitelaw Reid—"Agate"—The first order from Grant—The second—The third—The Shunpike—Wallace's Bridge—The countermarch—A night in the rain—*En route* for Pittsburg Landing—Brown and Thayer.

April 6, 1862!

The gray light was still in the eastern sky, trembling between vanishing night and opening day, when a sentinel put his head in my tent door and woke me.

"I hear guns up the river," he said.

I had only to put on my boots and slip into my coat. In a few seconds I was out listening. Sure enough, there were outbreaks of musketry, with cannonading at short intervals. My staff-officers joined me, and there was no disagreement.

"It's a battle."

A steamboat, an adjunct to my headquarters, lay tied up at the landing. Thinking the ominous sounds might be better heard on the water, in company with Whitelaw Reid,[1] who was sharing my tent as guest, I went down to the boat. A number of officers and visiting citizens were on the hurricane-deck exercising their ears. There, too, the opinion was unanimous—

"It's a battle."

It was then six o'clock. I did not hesitate longer. To my aide, Captain Ross, I gave directions to ride to Colonel Thayer, at Stoney Lonesome, and tell him to

[1] Mr. Reid was military correspondent of the Cincinnati *Gazette*, and wrote under the pen-name of "Agate."

form his regiments on their color lines, and hold them for speedy movement; that the First Brigade (Smith's) and the Third (Wood's) would join him at his camp. From Thayer, Ross was to go on to Adamsville, and tell Colonel Wood to bring his brigade back to Stoney Lonesome, as the concentration of the division would be immediate. Colonel Morgan L. Smith was then notified to take his command to the rendezvous. All camp equipage was to be brought to Crump's, where a sufficient guard would be detached to take care of it.

Now, whatever the merits or demerits of the foregoing scheme of action, the reader should not be allowed to suppose it impromptu; on the contrary, it had simmered in my mind the three days and nights since my scouts reported General Johnston's advance. Would it fit the conditions I had imagined? That was all I wanted to know.

My last preparatory order brought John to the Landing. I went ashore to see him. The good horse might have to suffer again; but, fortunately for him as well as myself, the season of snow and boreal winds had passed.

By this time I had taken on enough old-soldier habit not to get excited too much for breakfast, and we took it on the boat, "Agate" with us. While at table we heard the cheering with which the First Brigade set out for Stoney Lonesome.

At seven o'clock we were again on the hurricane-deck looking down the river for the appearance of General Grant's steamer, my interest heightened by expectation, for I felt confident that the general would stop long enough to order me to march to the battle. As the river had fallen sufficiently to leave the lower road practicable, though difficult, would the order be for Pittsburg Landing or the right of the army? With the division concentrated at Stoney Lonesome, I was ready for either.

About half after eight o'clock the *Tigress* came up and veered over to the side of my boat. General Grant stood on the second deck by the railing. A number of persons other than his staff-officers, strangers to me, were present with him. Lashings were applied, and, when all was silent, he spoke to me on the hurricane-deck. The conversation is given almost word for word.

He asked, "Have you heard the firing?"

And I answered, "Yes, sir, since daybreak."

"What do you think of it?"

"It's undoubtedly a general engagement."

This was the moment for the order. I leaned forward to catch it, and had instead:

"Well, hold yourself in readiness to march upon orders received."

I was disappointed, and returned: "But, general, I ordered a concentration about six o'clock. The division must be at Stoney Lonesome. I am ready now."

He hesitated, evidently turning an uncertainty over in his mind, and then said: "Very well. Hold the division ready *to march in any direction.*"

A stir and some undertalk among those about me followed the last speech, but I stopped it with my hand. The lashings were unloosed. A small bell on the *Tigress* tinkled; she moved off, gathering power, and I lingered in my place until she disappeared around the upper bend at racing speed.

"Gentlemen," I said, "we will get our horses and do our waiting at Stoney Lonesome."

Before leaving the boat I inquired for Mr. Reid. He had gone, nobody knew whither. But having great faith in the self-caring abilities of newspaper men, I felt more curiosity about him than anxiety.[1]

Setting out for the rendezvous at Stoney Lonesome, my last act was to have a horse tied to an elm-tree.[2] An orderly in charge had orders to allow no one to mount the horse unless he bore an order for me from General Grant; then the orderly was to guide the messenger to Stoney Lonesome. This, as may be seen, was to help hurry the order forward.

The scene at Stoney Lonesome was alive with interest. The Third Brigade had not arrived; yet the First and Second were an army of themselves. The men stood in dense groups about their stacked arms. The musketry ruffled the air distinctly, while the guns were subjects of exclamation—"There! Hear that! Now they're at it! Just listen!"

Officers crowded around me, and to allay their very natural anxiety I detailed the interview with General Grant. We all agreed that the coming of an order depended upon the fortunes of the fight; meantime it was for us to wait patiently as possible.

Ten o'clock, and no order.

I sent Lieutenant Ware to hurry Colonel Wood down from Adamsville.

Ten o'clock and thirty minutes.

Still the pounding of the guns and the ruffling of musketry in the south, but no order.

Eleven o'clock.

The impatience of the mettlesome spirits around me was continually bubbling over. I sent Captain Ross to Crump's. A courier might be there delayed.

[1] Mr. Reid, it afterwards appeared, feeling the need of getting to the field early, had gone quietly aboard the *Tigress*.

[2] The elm has been reduced to souvenirs. Even the stump is gone. The average relic-hunter is insatiable, and not always discriminating.

Eleven o'clock and twenty minutes.

Up the road, coming from Crump's, I saw Captain Ross with a stranger on the horse that had been left at the Landing. They were riding fast.

Eleven o'clock and thirty minutes.

The stranger with Ross drew rein and dismounted. He gave the name of Captain Baxter, with the affix *Chief-Quartermaster*, meaning on General Grant's staff.

"I have an order for you," he said to me. "Here it is."

At this, those surrounding closed in, while Captain Baxter put a piece of paper in my hand. I read what was on it twice over. Now memory does not fail me. I see that paper yet, a half-sheet of common foolscap, ruled. I see the tobacco stains on it, and the further defacement of boot-heels. I see a hurried scrawl in pencil, not ink, without address or date—unenveloped and unsigned. Here it is, almost, if not quite, verbatim:

"You will leave a sufficient force at Crump's Landing to guard the public property there; with the rest of the division march and form junction with the right of the army. Form line of battle at right angle with the river, and be governed by circumstances."

Now nothing could have been less complex; a child could have understood the scrawl; yet, after the second reading, I did what years of practice in the courts made easy—I analyzed it, finding four things wanted of me:

1. A guard to be left at Crump's.
2. A junction with the right of the army.
3. Formation of a line of battle after the junction, its front at right angles with the river.
4. Fight, if the battle was yet on—that being the circumstance which was to govern me.

But there was a preliminary. With the half-sheet of foolscap in my hand, I asked Captain Baxter:

"Whose order is this?"

"General Grant's," he replied.

"Why is it not signed by somebody?"

And he explained:

"General Grant gave me that order on the field verbally. Fearing to make a mistake in the delivery, I put the order in writing, as you see it, coming down the river. For that purpose I picked the paper from the floor in the ladies' cabin; and, not having ink, I used a pencil."

To which I returned: "Very well, captain, I accept the order, and you may so report to General Grant. Now, how is the battle going?"

"We are repulsing the enemy," he said.

Thereupon some of the younger officers launched out disconsolately, and, though holding my tongue, I shared their chagrin.

Colonel Thayer, standing by my side, held out his hand for the paper, and I gave it to him; passing generally around then, it finally reached Adjutant-General Kneffler, who carelessly thrust it under his sword-belt and forgot and lost it.

Captain Baxter left me presently to retake his boat.

There remained then but two points for consideration: Where was the right of the army? and, of the two roads heretofore mentioned, which should I move by?

As to the first point: The right must be where the morning found it, unless it had been moved forward. Captain Baxter settled that when he said the enemy was being repulsed.

With respect to the road to be taken, the lower or river road, that by way of Wallace's Bridge and Pittsburg Landing called for a march of eight and three-quarter miles—that is, six to Pittsburg Landing and two and three-quarters to Sherman's camp from the Landing. So, to save the two and three-quarter miles, and because it was nearer the right and in better condition, I decided to go by the Shunpike.

Saturday morning I had ordered three days' cooked rations; now I gave till twelve o'clock for dinner, cautioning commandants that they must be on the road at noon. And at noon exactly the march began, the cavalry leading; the Twenty-fourth Indiana advance-guard, Thayer's brigade, with the Ninth Indiana battery, following; then Smith's First Brigade, with Thurber's Missouri battery sandwiched among the regiments. Such was the order of march, the Third Brigade not having reported.

The going was swift and without incident. Past the old overshot mill, past Snake Creek, past Clear Creek, and no enemy—not a shot. Once I allowed a rest of three minutes, but before the time was up the men arose of themselves and fell in, shouting: "Forward! Forward!" For now we were nearing the fight, and with every step it made itself more distinctly present. God help us, there was never music with motive to action, and such inspiration in it, as that of battle!

The last file of the rear-guard had put Clear Creek behind it, and the guard itself was stepping long and fast. One o'clock and thirty minutes by the watch. We were doing splendidly. Then I was overtaken by a young man with a lieutenant's shoulder-straps. I noticed his horse breathing quick and splattered with mud from nostrils to fetlocks. He was a blondish person in cavalry uniform, minus a cap. A streak of blood frilled his forehead. Riding to my side, he saluted and said, "General Wallace?"

"Yes," I replied, without drawing rein.

"General Grant sends his compliments. He would like you to hurry up."

Without stopping, without a question, I returned, "My compliments to General Grant, and tell him I am making good time, and will be up shortly."

The courier left me, going by the rear, though I did not notice it at the time.

This message was of an import to have drawn attention and led to inquiry but for the fatal answer of Captain Baxter—"We are repulsing the enemy." Indeed, I had been under the influence of that answer since the departure from Stoney Lonesome. If the enemy is being repulsed, I had asked myself, what need is there for me; and Baxter had silenced the question. It must be for a flanking operation or pursuit. The firing had moved obliquely to our left, and I settled discussion of the circumstance, thinking of Baxter, and arguing, "The enemy has been driven from the right to which we are going, but he is still making it warm over on the left nearer the river." This at the time—not yet two o'clock—was satisfactory to the gentlemen who heard it as well as to myself.

A few minutes after two o'clock—in the excitement I did not look at my watch—another interruption came along. Captain Rowley, of General Grant's staff, rode up from the rear. He was greatly excited.

"I've had a devil of a time in finding you," he began.

I checked my horse.

"What's the matter?"

"I've been sent to hurry you up."

"That's the second message of the kind. I don't understand it."

"Where are you going, anyhow?"

"To join Sherman."

"Sherman!"

"Yes."

He plucked my sleeve. "Come with me aside here."

At the edge of the road, out of hearing, the captain broke out: "Great God! Don't you know Sherman has been driven back? Why, the whole army is within half a mile of the river, and it's a question if we are not all going to be driven into it."

Now, I would be very disingenuous not to admit myself more than shocked by this intelligence, heightened in effect, as it was, by Captain Rowley's energetic style of expression. We say in common phrase, "Oh, he's *rattled!*" And I know the word is slang; nevertheless, I dare to use it because it so nearly describes the condition into which I was flung mentally. Beaten—that army! Incredible! The idea struck me dumb — too dumb for question.

Fortunately for me, the eclipse of my faculties did not last long, and I was able presently to comprehend that, with my division, *I was actually in rear of the whole Confederate army!*

It gives me a world of satisfaction now, late as the hour is, to remember that, in the worst stage of the shock I struggled with after Rowley's announcement, my only thought was how best to serve the comrades in awful peril down by Pittsburg Landing.

With me, subject to my word whether forward or back, were four thousand men who had come to the honorable estate of soldiers at Donelson. Why not wait for Colonel Wood and his two thousand of the Third Brigade, and then go on? *That* was my impulse. The advantage of an attack in the rear would be mine; and, though more might not have been in my power, I could at least have distracted the enemy and compelled him to notice me. Detachment from his engaged lines — saying he had no sufficient reserve —

would have served Grant and his fighting remnants by giving them a breathing-spell in which to reorganize and take new positions. Indeed, such a course might have been their salvation, and I would have tried it had I been left to myself. *Unfortunately,* in that moment of suspense I received from General Grant his *third order* to me since morning.

Turning to Captain Rowley, I asked him, peremptorily:

"Does General Grant send me orders?"

"Yes," said the captain, "he wants you at Pittsburg Landing—and he wants you there like hell."

That decided me. The words were rough, but the captain's excitement was great, and I passed them the more willingly since they shifted the responsibility of action from me to General Grant.

"Do you know of a cross-road from this one into the river-road?" I asked Rowley.

"I know of none," he said.

"Not forward, but back?" I persisted.

"I know of none," he repeated. "I went first to Crump's Landing; they told me there that you were at Stoney Lonesome, and I overtook you from that place."

Seeing Rowley could be of no service as a guide, I despatched Simpson and Fletcher, orderlies, to return along the line of march and bring me a resident of the country—forcibly, if he refused to come peaceably.

Addressing myself to the captain, I then said: "To obey General Grant, I must first back the column out of this. Tell him I accept his order, and that he may look for me at Pittsburg Landing, which I will reach soon as possible by way of Wallace's Bridge. Tell him I will get there, if I have to fight my way in."

Rowley left me at that, going to the rear.

It will be observed, doubtless, that in all this interview nothing was said to Captain Rowley explanatory of how I came to be on the road by which he overtook me. Had I thought myself on a wrong road, it strikes me as a fair inference that I would have been swift in calling for Baxter's memorandum.[1]

As soon, then, as the order could be carried to the front and rear of the column, a countermarch by brigades took place,[2] Hayes, with his cavalry, being left to take care of the rear. Great was the wonder on the part of the men, and it was by no means silently indulged; for every one of them had by that time worked himself into fighting tension, and to be pulled away just when on the edge of the battle was past understanding.

Returning, we met the orderlies bringing a guide, from whom I learned of a cross-road from the Shunpike we were traversing into the lower, or river, road to Pittsburg Landing, not on my map. As the guide reported it available though difficult, I turned into it, head of column right. While making the change of direction, the Third Brigade came up and took its place, completing the division. Colonel Whittlesey, claiming seniority of commission, was then given the brigade.

The progress was toilsome and intolerably slow. To help the push forward, I sent my entire staff down the column. While in advance of the advance-guard, wait-

[1] This manœuvre has been severely criticised; and, referably to time, it is indefensible. A *right-about* of the column would have expedited the march. My object, however, was to get certain regiments whose fighting qualities commanded my confidence to the front; for that I chose the countermarch, and next day the forethought was amply justified.

[2] *Apropos* of my failure to get to the field Sunday, the first day of the battle, various statements have appeared in the earlier histories of the war. Some say I lost my way; others that I took the wrong road; others that the march was circuitous owing to a guide. Some deal with me in a friendly spirit; others maliciously. I give the facts, and beg to be judged by them.

ing, Colonel McPherson (afterwards major-general) and Major Rawlins, assistant adjutant-general, met me, having, like their two predecessors, been despatched to hurry me forward. This meeting occurred on the right of the cross-road a short distance from its merger in the river-road.

The account of the battle these new couriers brought me was even more sickening than Captain Rowley's. Rawlins, of an earnest, devoted nature, was terribly excited. McPherson was more quiet and thoughtful. Neither of them asked explanation of me; and supposing, as they were of General Grant's staff, that they knew my march to join the right of the army was by order, I volunteered no explanation. In fact, I did not once think of wrong or mistake. Rawlins soon expressed dissatisfaction with the progress making. I assured him the division was doing its best. He next insisted that the batteries should be abandoned—they were hampering the infantry. That advice I also rejected. His next proposal was to send the regiments forward as fast as each one arrived. That I also refused. There should be no piecemeal in the business. To make an impression the division must go as a unit — so I argued. To McPherson he privately suggested arresting me. McPherson did not encourage the idea. Dismounting and taking seat upon a log, I announced that there should be no forward movement until the column was closed up. General Grant, I said, wanted the division, not a part of it; the necessities were plain. The two then left me, returning the way they came, by Wallace's Bridge.

All went well marching on the high ground of the cross-road; but when we descended into the places softened by the receding backwater from Snake Creek, it was out of one hole into another, all bad enough for infantrymen afoot, but very trying to artillery horses.

The great strain came, however, when at last we passed into the lowlands of the creek; there an extended opening through the woods signified a roadway out of sight under a sheet of yellow liquid broken occasionally by tussocks of black mud. At the edge of the bog I took a look, and would have stopped for soundings, only the guns of the fight in progress on the other side resounded high and clear, and there was awful appeal in their near roar. The plunge had to be taken; we must get on. I watched the advance-guard as it came up. I suppose they felt as I did, and in they went. Uniforms and personal comfort were as nothing.

By-and-by the First Brigade essayed the crossing. Colonel Smith led them. I spoke to him. "Soon as you reach firm ground on the other side," I said, "deploy, and, if an enemy interposes, don't stop to fire, but rush him with the bayonet." [1]

In a few minutes, under the trample, the sheet covering the roadway turned into thick mortar of the color of dirty chocolate. Seeing this, I sent for the lieutenants in command of the batteries—Brown, of the Ninth Indiana, and Thurber, of the First Missouri.

"Look at it. Can you get through?" I asked them, thinking of their guns and caissons.

Both gave me the same answer—"We'll try, sir."

I watched them as long as they were in sight. The teams rolled from side to side, staggering and stumbling. Sometimes a horse would go down head under, and, rising, beat the air frantically. The axles of the ponderous carriages left wakes behind them like mud-scows. Then, often as a stall occurred, a regiment, overtaking

[1] Berg's sharp-shooters were the only strangers Smith discovered, and they disappeared before he could communicate with them.

the unfortunates, would stop to help them out. Swinging the dripping prolongs on their shoulders, they would lean forward and, with a "Heave, O!" and an "Altogether, now!" drag horses and guns together out of the depths.

The going was slow. A fire of impatience burned the soul within me, and I kept my eyes on the sun, which seemed to go down with the leap of a diver, and still the old bridge (Wallace's) rocked under the tread of companies in hurried passage.

Now I had no doubt of finding somebody on the farther side of the creek waiting for me. Rowley, Rawlins, and McPherson had been so eager to have the division up that, having reported my coming, I was sure that one or the other of them would meet me, or at least have a guide ready to take me to some chosen position. They knew I knew nothing of the situation at the Landing.

The battle, it should be borne in mind, seemed now to pause, and its fury underwent a noticeable lull. What did it mean? My anxiety reached its limit; the things I wanted to know the most but sharpened it. Where was our line? Where the enemy? There must be some vantage of position; was I left to find it as best I could? Certainly no reader can be so dull as not to see how vital these points were, and his astonishment will be in proportion when I tell him that not a soul was present to receive me, nor did anybody come. Once more I was cast upon my own resources.

To add to the difficulties of my position, night fell, with the heavens above us a floor of utter darkness. Mist from the great swamp enveloped us, and soon it began to rain, and nowhere could a camp-fire be seen. Fortunately the fall of night put an end to the battle, and I knew both hosts, or the survivors of them, were seeking rest, each in the place it occupied when the light went out.

I must not omit that, while the twilight yet lingered and the advance-guard was drawing near the bridge, groups of fugitives from the fight met us, flying they knew not where—unarmed, hatless, wild-eyed, covered with mud, many of them dripping with the chocolate water of the creek, and all shouting:

"We're cut to pieces! Go back while you can!"

With levelled bayonets they were turned out of the way. Their warning cries were answered with curses. Fear is a special artist, and for his painting he keeps colors of his own.

So in files of four, and feeling for the road, the brigades staggered on. Finally they came to high ground, and when, riding in advance, I thought there was solid earth enough to accommodate the divisions, I ordered halt, and facing to the right, effected an alignment. Pickets were sent out at once.

Where was the enemy? Where our own army?

Then the clouds overhead thickened and burst, and it was rain, rain, by the bucketful, but no lightning.

The river was not far off—not more than half a mile, if the bridge we had just crossed had been correctly placed on the map. Half a mile for a great army to lie down in! Heavens, how narrow the margin! Yet there was neither picket nor sentinel to cry us halt!

My orderlies dispersed themselves to the left and rear. Now and then they brought stragglers to me, and I examined them.

"Where is General Grant?"

They did not know.

"Where are Sherman and McClernand? Where the army?"

They did not know.

"Where is the enemy?"

No two of them pointed in the same direction.

Then I rode out myself, along the road by which we had come. Presently I nearly rode a man down.

"For God's sake, don't run over me!" he cried.

"Who are you?" I asked.

"Union," he replied.

"Your name and regiment?"

"I am Sergeant Kaufman, Company I, Fourth Dragoons."

His company had been of my brigade in Paducah, and I knew him. Having been exchanging shots with the enemy when night fell, he gave me the information of which just then I stood in greatest need—that my division was on the eastern slope of Tilghman's Creek, a wet-weather brook emptying into Snake Creek; that the enemy held the opposite slope; and that the intervening hollow was about four hundred yards in width. The sergeant guided me down into the hollow beyond our pickets.

"There," he whispered—"see the top line of the trees against the sky?"

"Yes."

"Well, *they* had a battery here"—pointing with his hand—"when the sun went down, and we all quit."

Taking the course, I returned and posted the ten guns of Brown and Thurber so that they might open a concentrated fire on the position indicated as soon as there was light enough to see across the hollow.

I dismounted then, and, to escape the beating of the rain, covered my head with my cape and crouched close under the sheltered side of a tree. Of the thousands who had faithfully followed me through the long, hard march, no one had the best bed, yet there were all apparently asleep. Only through the sloughing of the wind and the splash of water one voice from the front kept crying:

"Help! Help!"

And the words were long-drawn, so shrilled by agony and despair I could not shut out a vision of the sufferer, his face upturned and bleaching in the wash of the pitiless storm. To get to him was impossible; so for hours the call continued, keeping me reminded that I was on the field of battle not yet ended.

All in all, I never knew a bivouac so fearfully attended. Still I carry with me a distinct remembrance of a satisfaction that did much to counterbalance the insufficient cover of the friendly tree. I knew where the enemy was, and to what point of the compass my front should be established. I fancied, moreover, that a happy chance had dropped my command into a relative position hardly possible of betterment. So, after sending word to Smith, Thayer, and Whittlesey to rouse early and form facing the west and parallel with the road by which we had come, I amused myself thinking of the surprise I had in store for the enemy on the opposite hill, and went to sleep.

LIV

The Army of the Tennessee—Map—No general-in-chief—Grant still at Savannah — No knowledge of Johnston's advance — No intrenchments—No line of battle—Grant in limbo—General Sherman's statement—Colonel E. C. Dawes—Grant—Jacob Ammen—McClernand.

It would be very imperfect work did I now fail to tell about the struggle towards which, under such peculiar crcumstances, I spent so many precious hours marching.

We have seen the composition of the Army of the Tennessee, and how five of the divisions—McClernand's, Prentiss's, W. H. L. Wallace's, Hurlbut's, and Sherman's—assembled at Pittsburg Landing, and how mine came to be left at Crump's.

To facilitate understanding of the ground and the relation of the divisions each with the other in their encampments, an informal map following Thom's survey is appended. I think one has only to glance at it to see that, with the exception of Sherman's and Prentiss's, the sites of the several camps must have been chosen without the slightest reference to a possible attack.

From the front to the river, say from Sherman's right on Owl Creek, the space occupied was nearly three miles in depth; while from Owl Creek on the right to Lick Creek on the left a line of battle two miles in length could have been conveniently accommodated. Indeed, it is difficult to imagine a location more susceptible of defence, and great credit is due General Charles F. Smith for sagacity in selecting it.

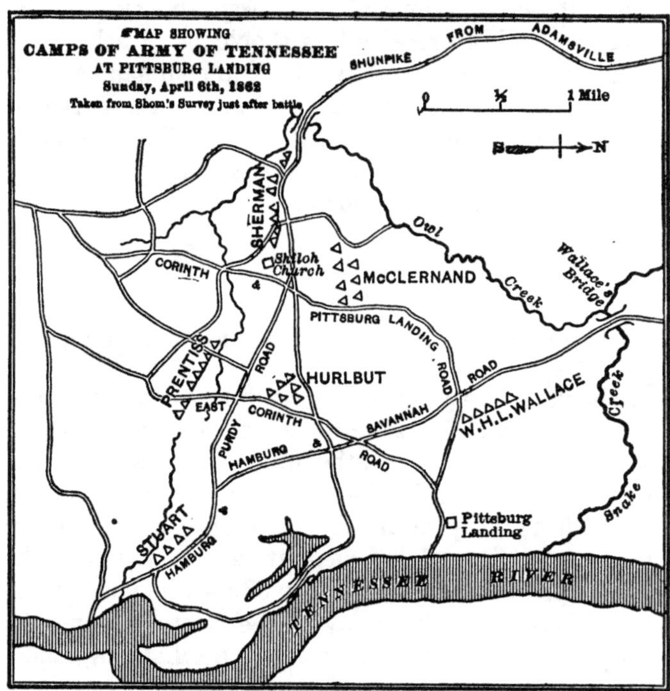

That this ground, so well chosen, was not successfully defended Sunday, April 6th, admits, in my judgment, of explanations in no wise impeaching the courage of the rank and file of the army.

In the first place, each of the five divisions had a commander of ability on the ground; that, however, cannot be said of the commanders. *Their* superior was in headquarters at Savannah, ten miles below Pittsburg Landing, on the opposite bank of the Tennessee River.[1]

[1] General Don Carlos Buell was gravely censured by a commission because at the opening of the battle of Perrysville he was in camp four miles to the rear of the fighting-line without signal-corps connection.

Secondly, though with knowledge of an enterprising enemy at Corinth, none of the most ordinary preparations was made to receive him should he attack.

Thirdly, not one of the five division commanders had knowledge of the approach of the Confederate army and its deployment for battle until its first line was upon them. Nor was General Grant better informed.

Lastly, the army was surprised.

I

There was no General-in-Chief with the Army

I should be very much pained did any one construe the statement about the absence of General Grant at the beginning of the battle into an aspersion of the great soldier. That his headquarters were at Savannah April 6th he never regarded as a subject of accusation. He supposed it well known that he was there at the time by order and in furtherance of a scheme of General Halleck's to have the Army of the Tennessee and the Army of Ohio assembled at Pittsburg Landing; then, the junction effected, he (Halleck) was to hasten down from St. Louis, take the field in person, and at the head of the combined forces move on Corinth; whereupon, applying the turning process to Columbus, Island No. 10, New Madrid, and Memphis, those strongholds were to fall, and the Mississippi, with a little more of like persuasion, to drop back into our possession. The design was truly Napoleonic; but exactly why General Grant should be required to await the advent of General Buell (marching from Nashville across the country) at Savannah, rather than with his army at Pittsburg Landing, is trying to common-sense. The irreverent among us went so far as to suspect General Halleck of jealousy. There are some men not to be contented with a dividend of glory; they must have it all.

At first glance this disposition of General Grant by General Halleck, switching him off and leaving him, as it were, on a side-track, does not seem so harmful; but let us see.

Wires for telegraphing had not been stretched between Savannah and Pittsburg Landing; neither had the Army of the Tennessee been as yet provided with a detachment of the signal corps. In other words, there was no communication to be had except by steamboat. The condition wrought was that of an army in presence of an enemy without a commanding general.

That General Grant, thus in limbo, wrestled with his superior's order by frequently visiting Pittsburg Landing in his boat, always returning to Savannah for the night, proves him sensible of the awkward disposition made of him, and that he felt it was not the close personal touch with his army required of a general engaged in a serious field operation. In the vital matter of observation of the enemy, for instance, he found himself driven by sheer dependency to choose from his division commanders one with whom he could correspond confidentially.

Of the five division commanders one only was of West Point extraction. Very naturally, I think, General Grant chose him for his correspondent;[1] and Major-General McClernand was never heard to complain, much less protest, because Brigadier-General Sherman was so honorably signalized.[2] The distinction carried

[1] *Personal Memoirs.*

[2] General Halleck wrote General McClellan, February 19, 1862: "It was decided in the Mexican War that regulars ranked volunteers without regard to date." How far General Grant approved this atrocious utterance may not be said. He had been in civil life

with it extraordinary responsibilities. He was to be eyes and ears for his chief at Savannah—a sleepless sentinel on a high tower, and the enemy always in sight below him. We will see presently how he discharged his trust. We will also see what befalls an army engaging in battle without a commander, there being anything like equality on the part of the foe. Fighting without unity is only heroism of a mob a little qualified.

II

No Preparation to Receive Attack

Generally the first thing a commanding officer thinks about when in position and conscious of a possibility of assault by his enemy is defences; and if he has a staff, he calls for his chief of engineers, and has him devise something. At Shiloh, Colonel McPherson is said to have made a survey with intrenchments in view, then advised against them, giving for argument that a line of works would have to be in rear of the advanced line of encampments.[1] But that General Grant tells the incident it would be incredible. The approval of McPherson's advice I regard as a fatal misstep. That there were no intrenchments of any kind was the argument that determined General Johnston to sally from his fortifications at Corinth and take the offensive.[2]

General Grant's apology for the failure to intrench is ingenuous. He says he had no idea the enemy would leave strong intrenchments to take the initiative when

long enough, I think, to have learned that nothing could so certainly demoralize an army constituted, officers and men, of volunteers as such an idea put in practice.

[1] *Personal Memoirs*, by General Grant, vol. i., p. 332.

[2] *Life of General Albert Sidney Johnston*, by William Preston Johnston, p. 567.

he knew he would be attacked where he was if he remained.[1]

General Sherman, in his *Memoirs*, treats the neglect very differently. "We did not fortify our camps against attack," he says, "because we had no orders to do so, and because such a course would have made our men timid." There is not a veteran living who does not know that if General Sherman had thought of breastworks or rifle-pits in front or in rear of his brigades, he could have had them on his own order. Then as to making the men timid the pretext is shocking to common understanding.[2]

This, though the most serious oversight in preparation, was not the only one by any means. The advance line of battle was incomplete. It had dangerous lapses in its formation. Thus, the left regiment (Fifty-third Ohio) of Hildebrand's brigade, Sherman's division, was separated from the regiment next it on the right by an interval of two hundred yards, while the troops nearest it at the left were one-half mile distant. That is, there was a half-mile wholly unoccupied between the left of Sherman's division and the right of Prentiss's.[3]

And yet, I am sorry to say, there were other inattentions equally conspicuous. A battle being imminent, it is usual to clear the fighting force of impediments—such as subtlers and their tents, the sick, women, teamsters and their wagons, and non-combatants generally. So,

[1] *Personal Memoirs*, by General Grant, vol. i., p. 333.

[2] The "Hornet's Nest" is in point here. It was an abandoned road washed out by rains to a depth of twenty or thirty inches, and screened by a thicket. Our men laid down in the hollow, and for two or three hours held the position against the choicest chivalry of the South led by General Johnston in person.

[3] *My First Day Under Fire*, by Lieutenant-Colonel E. C. Dawes. *Sketches of War History*, vol. iv., published by Ohio Commandery, Loyal Legion.

too, hospitals are erected at convenient sites in the rear, and marked by yellow flags; they are also provided with stretchers and details to serve them. Finally, but by no means least in importance, each division is followed by extra supplies of ammunition in wagons, moving as it moves. It remains to be said that the battle of Shiloh was fought without one of these preparations in advance, except in the case of General McClernand, whose bitter experience at Donelson taught him to keep boxes of cartridges always at call.

III

There was a Surprise

I do not flatter myself that my opinion will settle the vexed question of a surprise of the Army of the Tennessee on Sunday morning; still I do think it in my power to set others, notably the historian, in the way of getting at the truth.

As a result of my studies of the *War Records* and reliable contemporaneous history, I say that in my judgment the Army of the Tennessee, Sunday morning, April 6th, did not know the Confederates were in its front in force intending battle until the firing at the commencement of the struggle gave general notice of the startling fact. I say further, and deliberately, and conscious of the meaning of my words, McClernand and Prentiss were no better off; neither were Hurlbut nor W. H. L. Wallace, the other division commanders; and most astonishing, General Grant and his *fidus Achates*, General Sherman, were in the same state of ignorance. Now, can I make these affirmations good, the surprise follows as a matter of course. The reader has a right, I think, to the evidence governing me.

The Army

In the nature of things the masses of the soldiery could not have known more of the enemy about to engage them than their general officers; so I will commence with the officers.

Sherman

In course of a reconnoissance from Pittsburg Landing, made by General Sherman early as March 16th, he learned from the country people along the road "that trains were bringing large masses of men from every direction to Corinth." [1] This was enough, certainly, to have put and kept him on inquiry, and suggested resort to some of the usual methods of getting intelligence of the enemy, touching which Napoleon has said, "It is a fact that when we are not in a desert, but in a peopled country, if the general is not well instructed it is because he is ignorant of his trade." [2]

From March 16th to April 2d, General Sherman, indifferent or in lordly contempt, seems to have allowed General Johnston to travel his road to readiness in peace. There is literally nothing of record to show so much as an effort by him to penetrate his opponent's headquarters or the camps surrounding them in swelling clusters. Yet was he the chosen of General Grant!

From March 16th to April 2d—seventeen days. In that short time, as if to prove the energetic genius of General Albert Sidney Johnston, the Confederates grew into an army—then into a great army—and then, on April 3d, in four corps under the preferred officers of the old regular army establishment, the samė genius set out from Corinth for Pittsburg Landing—set out to

[1] *Memoirs* (Sherman's).

[2] Napier's *Peninsular War*, vol. i., p. 242.

beat his enemies in detail, Grant first, then Buell—to surprise Grant's legions asleep in their tents.

And now surely the curiosity of the reader must be piqued to see how the Southern general succeeded. Whatever befalls, it cannot be said that the enterprise was unheroic.

On April 4th, at noon, a picket of seven men and a lieutenant in General Sherman's immediate front mysteriously disappeared. The cavalry (Major Ricker's) and detachments from the brigades of Colonels Buckland and Hildebrand—all of General Sherman's division—took the road to find, if possible, what had become of the picket. Hearing musketry and three cannon-shots, the general himself, his staff attending, rode out to the picket-line a mile and a half in advance of Shiloh church. Buckland and Ricker, returning, told him they had encountered infantry, artillery, and cavalry. Buckland, in a written account, says: "As I rode up to Sherman at the head of my column, with about fifteen prisoners close behind me, the general asked me what I had been doing. His manner indicated that he was not pleased." [1] Ricker, writing of the same occurrence, is more explicit. "When we got back to the picket-lines," he says, "we found General Sherman there with infantry and artillery in line of battle, caused by the heavy firing of the enemy on us. General Sherman asked me what was up. I told him I had met and fought the advance-guard of Beauregard's army—that he was advancing on us. General Sherman said it could not be possible. Beauregard was not such a fool as to leave his base of operations and attack us in ours—mere reconnoissance in force." [2]

[1] The *Memoirs* (Sherman's) *in the Light of the Record*, Boynton, p. 29.

[2] The original of this paper is in the hands of Major Ricker's son

General Sherman forwarded a statement of Colonel Buckland's to General Grant at Savannah. We will presently see the impression made upon that officer.

Colonel Appler, of the Fifty-third Ohio, above mentioned, was in an extremely nervous state, Saturday the 5th. A picket-line of men in butternut clothes were reported to him as having been seen, the colonel ordered the regiment formed, and sent his quartermaster to General Sherman with the story. The quartermaster came back, and said: "Colonel Appler, General Sherman says, 'Take your damned regiment to Ohio. There is no enemy nearer than Corinth.'" At 7 P.M., Colonel Hildebrand sent word to Appler that General Sherman had been to his tent and told him (Hildebrand) that the force in front of our army had been definitely ascertained to be two regiments of cavalry, two regiments of infantry, and one battery of artillery.[1]

In August following, General Sherman, testifying as a witness in the trial of Colonel Worthington, said of the Buckland-Ricker discovery: "We knew then that we had the elements of an army in our front, but we did not know its strength or destination."

General Sherman dated his official report April 10th, and he says in it: "On Saturday the enemy's cavalry was again very bold; *yet I did not believe he designed anything but a strong demonstration.*" [2]

We have the doughty gentleman's opinion down as late as seven o'clock Saturday evening; and, as he bluffly refused to credit General Johnston's army in his front at

who, in a letter to me, says the general's manner and speech were so offensive that his father turned away and abruptly left him.

[1] Lieutenant-Colonel E. C. Dawes, *Sketches of War History* (published by Ohio Commandery Loyal Legion), vol. iv.

[2] *War Records*, series 1, vol. x., p. 248.

that late hour, it becomes a point of redoubled interest to learn, if possible, exactly when his eyes were opened to the actual situation. Fortunately, we are able to slake our curiosity. In the same official report he says:

"About 8 A.M. I saw the glistening bayonets of heavy masses of infantry to our left front in the woods beyond the small stream alluded to, and became satisfied *for the first time* that the enemy designed a determined attack on our whole camp." [1]

Eight o'clock Sunday morning! It was, indeed, the eleventh hour; but in that hour the man awoke from his deadly scepticism and bravely asserted the skill and other high military qualities that afterwards made him the Second Soldier of the Republic.

Grant

General Grant's apology for not intrenching might be quoted again, but I will pass it, there being so much else to prove him as densely ignorant of the enemy, their strength and whereabouts, as his confidential correspondent—indeed, that in this important matter he was dominated by that officer.

Buckland's account of the affair of the outposts on the 4th instant, received through General Sherman, General Grant telegraphed to headquarters in St. Louis, dated April 5th, saying, with other things of less pertinency:

"They [the enemy] had with them three pieces of artillery, and cavalry and infantry. How much cannot of course be estimated. *I have scarcely an idea of an attack*

[1] *War Records*, series 1, vol. x., p. 248.

(*general one*) *being made upon us*, but will be prepared should such a thing take place." [1]

We have seen the extent of the preparations.

One looking for evidence on the point under consideration will be rewarded for his trouble by digging a little in Badeau's *Life of Grant*. Thus, a telegram from General Grant to General Halleck is there quoted, dated April 5th

"*The main force of the enemy is at Corinth*, with troops at different points east. . . . *The number of the enemy at Corinth, and in supporting distance from it, cannot be far from eighty thousand men.*"

This, it is to be observed, General Grant believed only the day before the battle. It sounds and seems incredible!

I might rest with that telegram; but there is more to the purpose.

Colonel Jacob Ammen commanded the Tenth Brigade, Nelson's division, Army of the Ohio. He reached Savannah with his command before noon of April 5th. From the diary of his keeping I make an extract:

"About 3 P.M. General Grant and General Nelson came to my tent. General Grant declined to dismount, as he had an engagement. In answer to my remark that our troops were not fatigued, and could go on to Pittsburg Landing, Tennessee, if necessary, General Grant said: 'You cannot march through the swamps; make the troops comfortable; I will send boats for you Monday or Tuesday, or some time early in the week. *There will be no fight at Pittsburg Landing; we will have to go to Corinth, where the rebels are fortified.* If they come to attack us,

[1] *War Records*, series 1, vol. x., p. 89.

we can whip them, as I have more than twice as many troops as I had at Fort Donelson.'"[1]

So did this speech impress Colonel Ammen that he says, in the same paragraph of his diary:

"As the division is to remain here some days, I issued orders to the Tenth Brigade for review and inspection to take place Sunday, April 6th, 9 A.M."[2]

On the 6th, leaving his teams and artillery at Savannah, Nelson marched his division through the swamps to Pittsburg Landing. Why not on Saturday?

Finally, General Grant's stop by my steamboat at Crump's will be remembered. Nor will his order to me be forgotten: "You will hold your division ready to march in any direction" — such was its purport. And my telling him that I was then ready brought no change in the direction. More's the pity! For I had in round numbers seventy-five hundred effectives at that moment in my division, and nearly all of them had been seasoned in the dry-kiln of battle at Donelson. Now, if General Grant knew then, or had reason to believe that General Albert Sidney Johnston had leaped lion-like upon the shoulders of his army and was bearing it to the ground, would he not have ordered me to the field at once? At eleven-thirty o'clock, when his order to march did at last reach me, it was too late for victory; everything, himself included, was in slow retrocession to the river, driven by the enemy he supposed at Corinth.

McClernand

The camp of the First Division (McClernand's) lay about three-quarters of a mile rather to the left rear

[1] *War Records*, series 1, vol. x., p. 330. [2] *Ibid.*, p. 114.

of General Sherman's—so very near, in fact, that one would think the "gentleman from Illinois" should have been told about the affair of the outposts on the 4th—this, if only to have given him an opportunity to draw his own conclusions. But no. There is a paragraph in his official report, filed shortly after the battle, which convicts him of the ignorance of his associate commanders. I give it entire.

"Early in the morning of Sunday, the 6th of April, hearing sharp firing at short intervals on my left and front, in the direction of Sherman's and Prentiss's divisions, I sent a messenger to General Sherman's headquarters *to inquire into the cause of it.* Soon after my messenger returned with General Sherman's request that I send a battalion of my cavalry to join one of his, for the purpose of discovering the strength and design of the enemy."

The inference here partakes of certainty. Would General McClernand have addressed such an inquiry to General Sherman had he been at any time taken into confidence and told of the enemy present in force?

McClernand's inquiry, however, must have been forwarded before eight o'clock, for with Sherman the strength and design of the enemy had yet to be discovered.

Hurlbut and W. H. L. Wallace

Hurlbut's camp was near a mile and a quarter in rear of Prentiss's, and W. H. L. Wallace's fully two miles and a half behind Sherman's. Neither Hurlbut nor Wallace had occasion to be on the lookout for attack, and, not being called on for picket duty, neither of them concerned himself with what might take place in the region extending forward of Prentiss and Sherman. So, on Sunday morning, most of General Hurlbut's troops were at breakfast when the firing began,[1] and it was then Prentiss communicated what he calls "the fact of the attack in force." [2] This notice, sent at daybreak, must have been received in the time a horseman could gallop to the headquarters of the officers named.

Now Hurlbut and W. H. L. Wallace were soldiers of equipoise and sterling courage. If they had previously heard of the activity of the enemy out in front, the news was doubtless tempered by Sherman's idea of a reconnoissance; still, the announcement of an attack in force must have astonished them. We may be sure they got their divisions in readiness. We may be sure, also, they felt the absence of General Grant. Each chief of a division left to his own judgment, what if there should come a clash of judgment? What if Prentiss and Sherman should happen to make the same request of Hurlbut or Wallace, or both of them at the same time? What a multiplication of the perils of mistake!

Prentiss

We come now to Prentiss—General Ben, as his soldiers loved to speak of him. What knowledge had he of the danger piling up in his front? At what hour Sunday morning were his eyes opened upon the reality?

He says, in his official report,[3] that on Saturday evening he supported his outposts with ten companies of infantry under Colonel Moore, of the Twenty-first Missouri, who returned to him about seven o'clock with advices of "activity in the front." This news Prentiss disposes of as "an evident reconnoissance of cavalry." In plain speech, like Grant, Sherman, McClernand,

[1] Colonel Veatch, in *War Records*, series 1, vol. x., p. 220.
[2] *Ibid.*, p. 278. [3] *Ibid.*, p. 277.

Hurlbut, and W. H. L. Wallace, General Prentiss late Saturday evening had no idea of a general attack impending. Nevertheless, he materially strengthened the guard stationed out on the Corinth road.

Now we cannot get the time of Prentiss's awakening as exactly as we have Sherman's, but we come, as it were, in a hair's-breadth of it. He says, in the same report, that his advanced pickets were driven in at daybreak; whereupon Moore promptly engaged the enemy. Then, he adds, a little after daybreak he ordered his entire command into line. Then, a little later, Moore having come back severely wounded, and with all his men, the enemy close at their heels, Prentiss, unable longer to refuse the evidence of his own eyes, notified Hurlbut and W. H. L. Wallace of what he calls *the attack in force*. Then, shortly after six o'clock, he says, the entire line was under fire.

I think, now, time were poorly spent arguing that, when the commanders are taken unawares their army is not.

That General Grant and his lieutenant, Sherman, were caught so flagrantly may astonish their admirers; it should not, however, for in the Shiloh period they were both at school, learning to apply military principles acquired by them at the academy long before; one of them, it may be further said, graduated after Vicksburg, the other on the road to Atlanta.

LV

General Albert Sidney Johnston—Lee—Departments of Virginia and Tennessee—General Johnston's plan of attack—Confederate testimony as to the surprise of Grant—Colonel Jordan—William P. Johnston—Whitelaw Reid—The events of Sunday morning.

Having exposed, as it were out of their own mouths, the deplorable ignorance of the division commanders of the Army of the Tennessee, and of the commanding general who should have been with his men, but, through no fault fairly attributable to himself, was not — in ignorance, I mean, of the enemy and his movements from Corinth to Shiloh — let us turn to that enemy and hear from him. If surprise there was, perhaps he will tell us whether it was complete, and, what must be of lasting interest, how it was accomplished.

I make no apology for calling the Confederates into court. They are of the same stock with us, neither better nor worse. That they were brave should make us the more ready to believe them, speaking or writing; and who shall say they were not brave?

When the Confederacy was launched, almost the first thing authorized by law was the appointment of five military officers with the rank of *general*. Strange to say, measuring the fame of the men now, Albert Sidney Johnston became the senior of Robert E. Lee—on the roster he was No. 1 and Lee No. 3. Such was the estimate of the men at the time of their appointment. If, subsequently, Johnston fell short of Lee, it was due to a reason which I have never seen taken into the account. The defence of the State of Virginia was geographically the limit of Lee's duty, and he was favored with means. On the other side, consider that which fell to Johnston. His department was "the northern frontier west of the Alleghanies, and a portion of that mountain-barrier."[1] Consider its vastness, the lack of men and material, the difficulty of defence because of the many openings for invasion, some of them navigable waterways leading far up and down into the heart of the country. Viewed thus, Lee's task was difficult, while Johnston's was impossible; and I think the latter saw and to himself acknowledged the impossibility straightway after the fall of Donelson. Or, if he had a reliance at all, it was in the incapacity of such as might be his opponents-in-chief — General Halleck, for instance, who had no genius except as a marplot, in which he was incomparable.

While at Bowling Green, and on down until his light went out at Shiloh, all the time of his exercise of command, General Johnston somehow contrived to keep informed of his enemy. So, after his retreat from Bowling Green to Nashville, and from Nashville, and while at Corinth, where he arrived on March 24th, he kept track of General Buell, march by march, by what agency we know not.

Genius has an insight of its own, the badge by which it is made known. General Johnston could not fail to see through the design of the joinder of the armies of Grant and Buell. There is no doubt in my mind that he hurried to Corinth thinking General Halleck was making him a present of an opportunity as good as

[1] *Life of General Albert Sidney Johnston*, p. 292.

if to order. Then his counter-plan—Grant first, Buell next—a matter of detail. In ten days he had forty thousand men to operate with.[1] Think of the care and consuming energy that work of assemblage and organization required of him!

At length General Johnston heard of General Buell's approach to Savannah. The hour to strike was come. Then, knowing the situation at Pittsburg Landing perfectly — that the army there had no general-in-chief, that the camps were unintrenched, that guard duty was without system and grossly neglected, that nothing was known of his preparation or of his coming—he issued *Special Order* No. 8—a document wonderfully well drawn by General Beauregard—and gave his corps commanders the night in which to study and familiarize themselves with the order of march and battle. Such was *Special Order* No. 8.

To attack in the morning of the 5th (Saturday) — that being the original purpose—one day was allowed to make the march and a night to get into position, Mitchie's house serving for direction and point of assemblage. But the roads were found almost impassable. Some of the commands failed the rendezvous.

Thus Hardee, of the Third Corps, was at Mitchie's in the morning of the 5th instead of the evening of the 4th.

Bragg, of the Second Corps, bivouacked the night of the 4th in rear of Hardee.

Polk, with two of his divisions of the First Corps, following Hardee at an interval of half an hour, halted near Mitchie's in the morning of the 5th.

[1] The figures are given from the despatch General Johnston wired President Davis under date of April 3d (*Life of General Albert Sidney Johnston*, p. 554).

Breckinridge, with the reserve corps, effected the junction at five o'clock Saturday afternoon.

And so, by reason of the failures, it befell that Sunday, April 6th, became the great day instead of Saturday, the 5th.

Not until five o'clock Saturday afternoon did the entire Confederate army stand deployed in three lines—Hardee's first, Bragg's eight hundred yards in rear of Hardee, Polk's in column of brigades not far from Mitchie's, Breckinridge on Polk's right. Meantime, that no unfriendly eye might see what was going on in the neighborhood of Mitchie's, troops of cavalry well supported held the roads and paths in the extended fronts of Prentiss and Sherman. At sundown of the 5th they were a compact curtain hanging against the whole western sky opposite Shiloh Church; nor might anybody push through it except at peril.

I think it pardonable now to try and imagine General Johnston's feelings when the last report, "All ready," was brought him. Men are alike, only some have more iron in their natures than others. How often, what time it shone, he had consulted the sun!—for such is the out-door man's mode of telling how much or little time he may have. He could not help seeing there was then—five o'clock afternoon—an insufficiency of daylight for the work before him. Night battles are seldom satisfactory. The foe whom he was going against, moreover, were not of the kind to be finished at a volley—they were Americans. He made haste and called his corp commanders into council.

Colonel Jordan, General Beauregard's chief of staff, has left us an account of this meeting, "held," he says, "in the open air, at an intersection of roads, and within less than two miles of Shiloh Church," which, with the soldiers engaged on the Union side, always means General Sherman's headquarters. There were two speakers, so to say, Beauregard and Johnston.

Beauregard advised that the expedition be abandoned and the whole force returned to Corinth. That certainly was extraordinary, but not so much so as the reasons advanced for the opinion. To them I now ask particular attention.

"It was scarcely possible," General Beauregard is reported to have said, "that they [the Confederates] would be able to take the Federals unaware, after such delay and the noisy demonstrations which had been made meanwhile. He urged the enemy would be now found intrenched and ready for the attack; that success depended upon the power to assail them unexpectedly, for they were superior in numbers and in large part had been under fire."

Colonel Jordan concludes his report of General Beauregard's remarks by a significant remark of his own: "And this unquestionably was the view of almost all present."

So, in issuing from their own elaborate intrenchments at Corinth, the Confederate commanders made no doubt of taking the Army of the Tennessee unawares. At the last moment, however, General Beauregard, because he was a trained soldier himself, could not believe the trained soldiers on the other side kept no sufficient lookout or had not intrenchments of some kind.

The large part of the council was with Beauregard. This, it seems to me, but increases the interest in Johnston's reply. We can imagine the group turned to him. Unfortunately, the reporter gives us a poor, meagre, colorless version of what he said; which was "that he recognized the weight of the objections to an attack under the circumstances involved by the unfortunate loss of time on the road. But, nevertheless, he hoped the enemy was not looking for offensive operations, and that he would yet be able to surprise them; and that, having put his army in motion for battle, he would venture the hazard."

And now, by Confederate authority, was the Army of the Tennessee surprised?

In the first place, I have conversed with many Confederates, officers and men, participants in the battle, and cannot recall one of them who did not, and with great and most pleasurable emphasis, claim a surprise.[1]

This, however, is good only as far as it goes. Something published is necessary, and if it should be of record, admitting investigation, so much the better. So we will resort to the old-fashioned exhibit process.

I will begin with General Basil Duke, well and most favorably known in the military circles of both the great sections whose differences made Shiloh a possibility. General Duke is still living, a very brilliant gentleman of Louisville, Kentucky, where he is regarded as the soul of genuine honor. He says:

"If General Grant was ignorant of Johnston's forward and aggressive movement until the blow fell, it argues that his subordinates, nearer the front, were also ignorant

[1] Not long since, advised that this writing was close at hand, and wanting particularly from gentlemen of the Confederate side some authority upon Shiloh the authenticity of which they most freely indorse, I invited a number of them, all of high rank and well known and respected, to dine with me at the Louisville hotel. The affair passed most agreeably, and I came away next day with *The Life of General Albert Sidney Johnston*, by William Preston Johnston (D. Appleton & Company, New York), which they said was the completest and the fairest rendering of Southern accounts of the battle. The indorsement was a compliment to the book, and I have accordingly followed it in the foregoing sketch.

of it, for any information procured by them would have instantly been forwarded to him. If General Grant knew Johnston was advancing and meant to give battle, how came he to be at Savannah on Saturday night, and not on the front, where, before and after this battle, he was accustomed to be, and where General Sherman, who, in this respect, practised what he preached, says that a commander-in-chief should ever be when battle is imminent? Above all, it is inconceivable and inexplicable, if the Federal commander realized the danger and actually expected attack, why a strong, continuous line of pickets was not thrown out, some hundreds of yards at least, beyond the ordinary camp guards, and extended along the entire front of the army, not merely in front of Prentiss's division, a precaution that officer seems to have taken without suggestion from or conference with any other; and it is difficult to understand why a part of each division on the front was not made to bivouac on their arms during the nights of the 4th and 5th, and held ready to support the pickets. Two corps of Johnston's army reached Mickey's [Michie's] on the 4th; the entire army was assembled there on the evening of the 5th, with strong picket lines well advanced. For two days, then, before the battle, the forest immediately in front of the Federal position, and less than four miles distant from Sherman's encampment, was thronged with Confederate battalions.

"The Confederate order of attack was arranged on the afternoon of the 5th, and, speaking from a recollection of what I witnessed myself, I would say that the Confederate outpost vedettes and the most advanced Federal sentinels were not more than a mile apart. Everything that transpired along the front and in the camp which we were able to observe was matter of constant and curious remark during those two days. If any recognition of our presence was obtained, it could be discovered by no sign, noted by no movement of preparation in that seemingly careless host. A general feeling of amazement pervaded the Confederate ranks at the apathy or ignorance of their adversary; and much of the impetuous confidence which characterized them on the morning of the battle was due to the indications which convinced them that they had surprised their foe."

"General Sherman is credited with having said recently that the stories so frequent at the time of the battle, of men having been shot or bayoneted in their tents on the morning of the 6th, were utterly without foundation. He is mistaken. Very many such instances occurred. It was quite a common thing to see dead men, half clad, lying in tents perforated with bullets, and, in some cases, stretched at the entrance or entangled in the tent-cords as if killed just as they were rushing out. If the Federal army at Shiloh was not so completely surprised as so large a body of men can ever be, then its commanders have a more serious charge to meet. If they were not taken unawares, how can they possibly explain the disadvantage at which they suffered themselves to be taken? What possible excuse can they offer for their careless array and evident want of preparation for immediate battle?"

"No courage, however, can overcome the ill effects of surprise or lack of tactical preparation. It was impossible that the hastily arrayed and ragged Federal line, although the ground on which it was posted was well adapted for defence, could long withstand an assault so skilfully ordered and energetically directed." [1]

The author of *The Life of General Albert Sidney Johnston* has, in the text of his work, the following:

"Whether Grant and Sherman used all requisite vigilance or not, they believed that the Confederate army was at Corinth, twenty miles away, and only a brigade at Mickey's [Michie's] when that army was unfolding for

[1] *History Fifty-third Ohio Regiment*, p. 56.

an assault upon them. Whether they were 'surprised' or not, the attack upon them was *unexpected*, and their own words show that a thunderbolt from a clear sky could not have astonished them more than the boom of artillery on Sunday morning." [1]

Replying to Badeau's denial of a surprise in his *Life of Grant*, the same author says:

"The readiness for attack consisted in what? Some colonels strengthened their pickets, one general sent a regiment on reconnoissance, and another had his horse saddled before breakfast." [2]

The author is supported by Confederate military authority of the highest rank — General Bragg, for instance:

"Contrary to the view of such as urged an abandonment of the attack, the enemy was found utterly unprepared, many being surprised and captured in their tents, and others, though on the outside, in costumes better fitted to the bedchamber than to the battle-field." [3]

Here also is General Preston:

"General Johnston then went to the camp assailed, which was carried between seven and eight o'clock. The enemy were evidently surprised. The breakfasts were on the mess-tables; the baggage unpacked; the knapsacks, arms, stores, colors, and ammunition abandoned. I took one stand of colors from the colonel's tent, which was sent by me next morning, through Colonel Gilmer, to General Beauregard." [4]

Colonel Jordan, already mentioned as of General Beauregard's staff, has left a statement:

[1] *Life of General Albert Sidney Johnston*, p. 576.
[2] *Ibid.*, p. 577. [3] *Ibid.*, p. 590. [4] *Ibid.*, p. 590.

"Officers and men were killed or wounded in their beds, and large numbers had not time to clutch up arms or accoutrements." [1]

Now, inasmuch as I know the unreasoning obstinacy of prejudice, I think it best to conclude this chapter with a little seasoning of the Confederate testimony. So I select a few paragraphs from a report furnished his paper, the Cincinnati *Gazette*, by the late Republican candidate for the vice-presidency, Whitelaw Reid, formerly a reporter and correspondent, one of the ablest, most fearless, and reliable of his day. It may be recalled that on Sunday morning Mr. Reid stepped from my boat at Crump's onto General Grant's, and accompanied him and his staff to Pittsburg Landing. As he remained on the field through the two days of battle, I think he may be regarded an eye-witness of the tale he tells, which is, in part, as follows:

"Almost at dawn Prentiss's pickets were driven in; a very little later, Hildebrand's [in Sherman's division] were; and the enemy were in the camps almost as soon as were the pickets themselves.

"Here began scenes which, let us hope, will have no parallel in our remaining annals of the war. Some, particularly among our officers, were not yet out of bed; others were dressing, others washing, others cooking, a few eating their breakfasts. Many guns were unloaded, accoutrements lying pell-mell, ammunition was ill supplied —in short, the camps were virtually surprised—disgracefully, it might be added—unless some one can hereafter give some yet undiscovered reason to the contrary, and were taken at almost every possible disadvantage. . . .

"Into the just-aroused camps thronged the rebel regiments, firing sharp volleys as they came, and springing

[1] *Life of General Albert Sidney Johnston*, p. 590.

towards our laggards with the bayonet. Some were shot down as they were running, without weapons, hatless, coatless, towards the river. The searching bullets found other poor unfortunates in their tents, and there, all unheeding now, they still slumbered, while the unseen foe rushed on."

END OF VOL. I.

www.ingramcontent.com/pod-product-compliance
Lightning Source LLC
LaVergne TN
LVHW010524100826
845148LV00001B/82

* 9 7 8 1 4 2 5 5 7 3 6 8 3 *